LADY MARY WORTLEY MONTAGU

ROMANCE WRITINGS

Lady Mary Wortley Montagu

ROMANCE WRITINGS

EDITED BY
ISOBEL GRUNDY

CLARENDON PRESS · OXFORD
1996

Oxford University Press, Walton Street, Oxford OX2 6DP

Oxford New York
Athens Auckland Bangkok Bombay
Calcutta Cape Town Dar es Salaam Delhi
Florence Hong Kong Istanbul Karachi
Kuala Lumpur Madras Madrid Melbourne
Mexico City Nairobi Paris Singapore
Taipei Tokyo Toronto
and associated companies in
Berlin Ibadan

Oxford is a trade mark of Oxford University Press

Published in the United States
by Oxford University Press Inc. New York

British Library Cataloguing in Publication Data
Data available

Library of Congress Cataloguing-in-Publication Data
Montagu, Mary Wortley, Lady, 1689–1762.
Romantic Writings / Lady Mary Wortley Montagu.
1. Man–woman relationships—Fiction. 2. Autobiographical fiction,
English. 3. Love stories, English. 4. Women—Fiction. I. Grundy,
Isobel. II. Title.
PR3604.A6 1996 823'.5—dc20 95–25046
ISBN 0–19–818319–4

1 3 5 7 9 10 8 6 4 2

Typeset by Alliance Phototypesetters
Printed in Great Britain
on acid-free paper by
Biddles Ltd,
Guildford and King's Lynn

ACKNOWLEDGEMENTS

My greatest debt is to those who own and care for MSS: to the Right Honourable the Earl of Harrowby and the Harrowby MSS Trust for generous permission to publish 'Indamora to Lindamira', the 'Court Tales', and 'Princess Docile'; to the Scottish Record Office for 'The Sultan's Tale'; to Sheffield City Archives for the 'Italian Memoir'; and to archivists like Jane Waley and Michael Bosson.

I owe heartfelt thanks, too, to research assistants and those who have helped me with linguistic matters: to Lisa Dempsey, Linda Sinclair, Christina Sommerfeldt, Michael Londry and Margaret McCutcheon; also to Vivienne Bosley, Joan Brumlik, and Nicole Mallet, who gave advice; to Doreen Nystrom and Patrizia Bettelli, whose respective knowledge of French and Italian, and whose shared interest in the issues involved in translation, was invaluable; to Betsy Sargent, the first 'outside' reader of 'Princess Docile'; to Alice Cherubini and Michaela Offredi for help on the ground; and to Violetta Papetti, in association with whom I began my work on the 'Italian Memoir'.

My sense of gratitude for the researches and the friendship of the late Robert Halsband increases with the years. The present custodians of the Halsband MSS in Butler Library, Columbia University Library, have been most helpful. So have the many friends who have provided encouragement, consolation, and odd scraps of information. Among those friends I am lucky to be able to count relations, and students, and members of the international community of those who are interested in early women's writing.

CONTENTS

ABBREVIATIONS

INTRODUCTION

IN Lady Mary Wortley Montagu's lifetime it was hard to distinguish response to her writing (even admiration) from response to her as a person. 'Lady Mary . . . shines like a comet', wrote Joseph Spence in 1741; 'she is all irregular, and always wandering . . . born with fine parts enough for twenty men'.[1] Spence, a scholarly, professional man, was able to muster literary as well as personal admiration, and to translate this into action: he was instrumental in the appearance of Montagu's poems in Dodsley's immensely successful *Collection* and so—for the moment—in the literary mainstream.[2] Meanwhile their more famous publicizer, Horace Walpole, whose relation to social norms was more tortuous than that of Spence, first judged them 'too Womanish', and later noted that they 'don't please, though so excessively good'.[3]

Her prose writing (always excepting her letters) never approached even this ambivalent degree of endorsement or recognition. Her diary, whose existence she disclosed to her daughter only in the last days of her life, was lovingly and well-meaningly burned. Her 'History of my own Time' was (so she said) no sooner written than destroyed by herself.[4] The works collected here (apart from one juvenile piece) have never been printed before, and probably date from after her meetings with Spence and Walpole in 1740–1. Even if she had ever met with an opportunity to show them off, they would surely have proved far too irregular and womanish to please.

It is tempting to read her fictional Sultan's statement as her own: 'tho' I don't remember that any of my ancestors condescended to relate a Story themselves, I don't see why I should not set the example of it' (below, p. 17). Through the mouth of a patriarch who differs from her in race, sex, rank, religion, and country, she articulates her remoteness from the dominant tradition of fiction-writing, and her internal conflict between class pride and literary ambition, both of which she found equally necessary to her sense of self. Such

[1] *Letters from the Grand Tour*, ed. Slava Klima (1975), 356–7.
[2] Spence's transcript is Cornell MS E6004; *A Collection of Poems: By Several Hands*, published in Jan. 1748, included fifteen of Montagu's poems in vol. iii; the 2nd edn., published in December, transferred them to vol. i.
[3] *Correspondence*, ed. W. S. Lewis *et al.* (1937 ff.), xiii. 234, xix. 450.
[4] *E&P* 18; *CL* iii. 18–19.

conflicts and such bizarre juxtapositions are the very soul of her fiction.

The writings collected here span the first half of the eighteenth century. Lady Mary began by 'step[ping] forward beyond the lists', as Samuel Johnson was to put it,[1] with a challenge to the established producers of fiction on their own ground. She did it in the genre of short fiction which Margaret Anne Doody calls 'the medium which allows the greatest degree of questioning, a medium which permits the author (often through another narrator) to move out of the assumed structure of things, to hold definitions of reality to question.'[2] When, at the age of 14, in 1703 or 1704, she copied her epistolary 'Indamora to Lindamira' neatly into a handsome folio album, she invited readers to compare it with (implicitly, to judge it superior to) its original, the successful *Adventures of Lindamira, a Lady of Quality* (1702), which was 'Revis'd and Corrected' (probably, that is, written) by Thomas Brown.[3] About a year later she transferred her novel with some revision to a new, leather-bound collection presented as if for print. The title-page reads 'The Entire Works of Clarinda, London'; the preface briefly and graciously apologizes for her sex, lack of education, and age.

'Indamora to Lindamira: Her Life Writ in 5 Letters' is the only one of Lady Mary's surviving fictions whose audience can be fairly well identified today. Those who compared 'The 2 Lives' were Lady Mary Pierrepont's circle of friends: teenage girls of the nobility and the rising middle class. 'Indamora's' readers must have included those named in the albums in which it is inscribed: Mary's sister Lady Frances, later Lady Mar; Sarah Chiswell or Cheswell, whose father had been employed by Lady Mary's father and whose brother-in-law (the immediate head of her family) was rector of the church containing the Pierrepont tombs; and Jane Smith, daughter of a politician, who later made her own living as a holder of posts in the royal household.[4] To these may have been added Lady Henrietta

---

[1] *Rambler* 93 (ed. W. J. Bate and Albrecht B. Strauss, 1969, ii. 133–4).

[2] 'A Regency Walking Dress and Other Disguises: Jane Austen and the Big Novel', *Persuasions*, 16 (1994), 75.

[3] At this stage Lady Mary's novel was titled 'The Adventur's [*sic*] of Indamora' (in H MS 250, a vellum folio volume, containing mostly poems, from which a number of pages have been cut out). *Lindamira* was reprinted in 1713, 1734, and 1949.

[4] Lady Mary (1689–1762) and Lady Frances (1690–1761) were daughters of Evelyn Pierrepont, Earl and later Duke of Kingston, and of Lady Mary (Feilding); Sarah (d. late in 1725) was daughter of Charles Cheswell, agent to the Duke; her sister Anne married

Cavendish Holles (heiress of Welbeck Abbey and nearest neighbour to the Pierrepont girls), and others with whom Lady Mary was only a few years later exchanging literary comment, books, and unpublished manuscripts, like Mary Banks (whose attorney father was rising from the middle ranks into the gentry) and Frances Hewet, a married woman of a generation older from the same area and circle.[1]

At this date Lady Mary (an earl's daughter) wrote for a readership from both middle and upper ranks, in a popular genre, on a favourite theme: a young woman's progress towards marriage. Her model, *Lindamira*, centres on its heroine's courtship, though it surrounds this with extraneous matter: sub-plots, satirical portraits, and travel-book material. Lady Mary's story omits all but the central courtship. Her Indamora declines taking her fate into her own hands: asserting that one should never disobey a father 'in so important an Affair' as marriage, she is enabled to escape the consequences of her submissiveness when her sister proves willing to rebel. (Her father's tyranny is laid at the door of that handy scapegoat, a stepmother.) As her story unfolds, Indamora finds herself almost continuously in a state of amazement: at young men's falling in love with her and at the hero's every action, from appearing unexpectedly in her presence to duelling, suffering shipwreck, and coming back from his supposed watery grave once she has married another. She asserts herself only in renunciation: in preferring not to disobey her father, and in invoking her honour to repudiate any claim on her by her lost love. Otherwise her actions are ambivalent and limited: witnessing her sister's disobedient match, wishing for the removal of an unwanted suitor (which precipitates the duel), weeping (an act full of semiotic significance), letting herself be persuaded to marry out of pity, and fulfilling her year of mourning when death relieves her of her husband (just as her sister's marriage and then the duel have ridded her of previous pursuers).

Humphrey Perkins, Rector of Holme Pierrepont; Jane Smith (d. 1730), daughter of John Smith, Speaker of the House of Commons, became Maid of Honour to Queen Anne shortly after 1704, and to Princess Caroline in 1715.

[1] Lady Henrietta (1694–1755), later Countess of Oxford, was daughter of the 1st Duke of Newcastle; Mary Banks (d. 1726), daughter of Mary (Hancock) and Sheffield attorney Joseph Banks, who married Sir Francis Whichcote in 1717, arranged Lady Mary's access to MSS by her friend Mary (Molesworth) Monck (H MS 77, fos. 114–20); Thomas, husband of Frances (Bettenson) Hewet (1668–1756), had a nearby estate and made himself useful to both Lady Mary's and Lady Henrietta's fathers (Portland MSS Pw2, 107, 108, 200, Nottingham University).

The two versions of this tale reflect Lady Mary's adolescent development. Her command of romance diction and conventions became more certain. In her revised text it is Indamora's husband, not her uncle by marriage, whose business takes her to Holland: perhaps a clue to the author's sense of increasing proximity to the adult, business-managing generation. She was a meticulous artist: her revision includes small alterations of word-choice, word-order, or structure, in almost every sentence, and a wholly new set of personal names. The later version moves Indamora's responses closer to her always impeccable behaviour. In the early version she not only 'thought [the hero] very Aggreable' when they first met, but says he had 'so much wit—that—I—was mightyly pleas'd with his Conversation' and 'went home thinking of Nothing but' him. The revision locates his agreeableness in fact rather than in Indamora's feelings, and reduces the rest to her going home 'more thoughtfull then Usuall' (below, p. 4). Similar smoothings occur elsewhere: the older Lady Mary uses somewhat less downright terms to describe the hated stepmother, and downplays the immense wealth which Indamora is left possessing. She retains, however, uncritical acceptance of high-flown fictional style and romance ideology.

Without acting for herself, without stepping out of line, Indamora reaches the safe haven of marriage and the prospect of endless bliss. The vigour she lacks in action she amply displays in narrative: the story's single-minded concentration and breathless speed give it an intensity which is absent from its model. It takes the prospective actualities of its author's experience (parental authority and marriage choice) and sets them against a fictional backdrop of travel, sensational incident, and danger. While the hero repeatedly faces the threat of violent death, the heroine faces being appropriated against her will. She makes something stylish and colourful out of negotiating the prosaic transition from daughter to wife; she displays ideal virtue, and wins her ideal reward.

This was to be the last appearance of virtue rewarded in any invented narrative by Lady Mary. A decade elapsed before her next known foray into fiction and first into print: *Spectator* essay no. 573, which appeared in 1714.[1] Once more taking a male-authored text as her starting point, she now challenges not only its pre-eminence but also its ideology. Her depiction of an unrepentantly assertive and

---

[1] *E&P* 69–74.

predatory widow answers Addison's picture of women as parasites on men by depicting a succession of male would-be exploiters hoist with their own petard. Montagu rewards her widow with money to spend and liberty to spend it: pleasures not socially sanctioned for female aspiration, and achieved here by other means than female virtue.

Narrative remained one of Montagu's favourite forms—in letters, poems, and essays—at every stage of her writing career. The works gathered here, however, are her more substantial pieces of prose fiction. All except 'Indamora' were apparently written in her European 'exile' which began in 1739. All (excluding the non-fictional 'Italian Memoir') relate more closely to French than to English traditions of fiction. Written with no prospect of an audience, they are the product of a leisured and largely solitary life; none is datable with any precision. None is titled: all titles in the volume except 'Indamora' have been supplied by the editor.

All of these tales exist in draft form only. 'The Sultan's Tale' is incomplete, and may have been a unit in a larger composite whole like the series (perhaps complete, perhaps not) of the 'Court Tales'. 'The Sultan's Tale' begins and ends in mid-sentence; from the preamble it belongs in a series, and the Sultan tells it as a story about women's failures in chastity, to counter some tale told by the Sultana Queen (or perhaps by the Vizier) which must have celebrated women for some particular excellence. Though words are missing both at the beginning and at the end, the story seems complete in itself; apparently someone detached the gathering which contains it from a larger unit which may have contained the series.

The oriental setting probably owes less to Lady Mary's own taste of Turkish life (now many years in the past) than to the oriental fictional tradition going back to Madeleine de Scudéry and Hortense de Villedieu. By using an oriental frame for a (presumed) collection, Montagu relates this piece to the 'Arabian Nights' tradition: to translated or adapted works of Antoine Galland, François Petis de la Croix, and such imitators as Thomas Simon Gueulette, all of whom were among the authors she owned.[1] In *Histoire de la Sultane de Perse et des visirs* (1708), by Petis de la Croix (owned by Lady Mary), a frame story of lascivious second wife and dutiful son (like Phaedra and Hippolytus) introduces propaganda tales told by the sultana to

---

[1] Wh MS 135.

prejudice her husband against his son, and told by the viziers to blacken women in general and the sultana in particular. Montagu seems to allude to this framework, though her mood is quite different, and reflects the redesigning of the oriental tale for satire—an increasingly popular technique among French writers, notably Voltaire. Even her mixture of oriental with Graeco-Roman was not unprecedented.[1]

This tale, like her others, confirms the impression that her library gives of her familiarity with the French tradition. Even in 1739 (before her European sojourn began) she owned almost as many books in French as in English.[2] A high proportion of these were fiction. In 1710 she had voiced appreciation of Delarivier Manley but thought her outshone by Anne Marguerite Petit Du Noyer. In French literature she found a fiction that was predominantly the creation of women (and noblewomen at that), and also a strong element of what we should now describe as feminism. Pierre Bayle's *Dictionnaire* of 1697 proclaimed that the best French novels had for some time been written by women (a judgement heatedly reversed in the *Encyclopédie*'s *roman* entry in 1765).[3] Lady Mary's taste for Scudéry is well known; less so is her knowledge of Scudéry's successors, both female and male. In the jumble of opinions which she recorded in her commonplace-book in the late 1750s are many comments on French authors—Clément Marot, Boileau, Lafayette, La Rochefoucauld, Fontenelle, Dacier—as well as on French historical figures. 'M[adame] de Villedieu is a better writer than Crebillon &c', she notes, with the same gender partiality that informs her comparisons of Elizabeth Singer Rowe and of Laetitia Pilkington with Pope.[4]

Besides Galland, Petis de la Croix, and Gueulette (four titles by this last), Lady Mary's library included Claude Prosper de Crébillon's *L'Écumoire* (subtitled *histoire japonaise*), and Voltaire's

---

[1] Raymonde Robert, *Le Conte de fées littéraire en France de la fin du xviie à la fin du xviiie siècles* (1981), 10; David S. Reynolds, *Faith in Fiction: The Emergence of Religious Literature in America* (1981), 9–14.

[2] See Isobel Grundy, 'Books and the Woman: An Eighteenth-Century Owner and her Libraries', *English Studies in Canada*, 20 (1994), 9 ff.

[3] *CL* i. 15–16; Joan DeJean, *Tender Geographies: Women and the Origins of the Novel in France* (1991), 5–9, 162 ff.; Nicole Mallet, 'Guerre du sexe, gloire du texte: Les Voix et les voies de la contestation féminine au xviie siècle', in Marguerite Andersen and Christine Klein-Lataud (eds.), *Paroles rebelles* (1992), 55–111. In her cryptic 'Heroism not fit for our Sex in England', Lady Mary was contrasting her native country, socially, with Venice; but she may have alluded also to a French literary tradition (*CL* iii. 223).

[4] CB, fos. 8–12 (9, 11), 22; copy of Pilkington's *Memoirs* at Sandon Hall.

Candide (one of the two latest-dated books she owned, bearing her accolade, 'delicieux'). Voltaire's archetypal naïf hero, born in print in 1759, was probably too late to influence her, though his adventures make an instructive comparison with those of her naïve heroine, Princess Docile. But the French tradition which nurtured *Candide* offered Montagu not only a distinctive female voice in fiction, not only sultanas and viziers, but also a host of usable models. It taught her a *précieux* tone which is 'gallant, natural . . . highly provocative, extraordinary, bizarre, and implausible'; a seriousness blended from the *risqué* and the fantastic; and a mix of genres, periods, and settings used to call in question European religious and sexual norms.[1]

Her Sultan doubly distances his tale by invoking interaction between mortals and the (to him) alien gods and goddesses of Olympus. Considering that it turns on women's deficiency in chastity as exposed by a magical test, and ends with a public humiliation of those who resort to cheating at the test, it is a surprisingly good-humoured, non-punitive story. Flora and Diana combine to identify the unchaste among Queen Emma's attendants, and the tale closes on a metamorphosis as Diana throws off her mortal disguise. But Venus may be felt to have won on points: she has outwitted the virtuous immortals by a simple mechanical invention, and the guilty mortal lovers, her clients, are never punished or even reproved. The frame story shares this good humour, in contrast with, for instance, Delarivier Manley's *Almyna* (1706), whose heroine loses her life in consequence of trying to convince a sultan that women have souls. Montagu's Sultan has even his modest attempt to reprove women subverted by his carnivalesque tale.

It is impossible not to suspect in 'The Sultan's Tale' (about a female ruler consulting with a trusty confidante on the problem of her attendants' sexual morals) some reference to Augusta, Princess of Wales. Lady Mary's daughter, Lady Bute, was patronized by the Princess, though she never held a post among the 'maids of honour (not of maids the strictest)', as Elizabeth Montagu called them.[2] Elizabeth Chudleigh (who *may* be the Iphigenia of this story) continued, long after she had become notorious, in the service of the

---

[1] Robert, *Le Conte de fées*, 4; Jack Zipes (ed.), *Beauties, Beasts and Enchantment: Classic French Fairy Tales* (1989), 7, 9, 10.

[2] *Letters*, ed. Matthew Montagu (1813), iii. 158. For Chudleigh see Betty Rizzo, *Companions without Vows: Relationships among Eighteenth-Century Women* (1994), 61–82.

Princess, whose virtue remained unquestioned (until the rumours began, around 1755, of her misconduct with Lady Bute's husband). Some details of 'The Sultan's Tale' (like the fact that the fictional confidante has a sister) rule out a direct parallel, but the possibility of some allusion remains.

This tale apparently shorn of its companion tales is followed here by a pair of tales set in the French court of, it seems, the early 1690s, which may have been part of a longer sequence. I have called them 'Mademoiselle de Condé' and 'Louisa'. The former has a lacuna of unknown length in the manuscript; fittingly, in view of the dark tone of most of Montagu's fiction, it is the development of potentially happy (though ultimately doomed) love which is missing. These tales are set at the court of Louis XIV; the central male character in both, and link between the two, is closer to a villain than a hero. Montagu calls him the 'Duke d'Enguien' (generally spelled d'Enghien): the title borne by the eldest sons of the princes de Condé, a cadet branch of the royal Bourbons. She makes her Duke the picture of a romance hero—handsome, magnetic, irresistible—and in doing so detaches him from any historical individual. Even if the Condé heir whose dates fit her story had been known as d'Enghien (which, in fact, he was not), the actual man would contradict the fiction, since like all his line he was short in stature, ugly, and even deformed. It seems likely that this tampering with fact was intentional. The imaginary character who uses his power and charm as destroyer of women is a type of the dominant male; he has no historical existence, any more than the Sultan who tells stories about Diana and Venus.

'Mademoiselle de Condé' might well have been called 'Mademoiselle de Condé and Monsieur de Fontenelle'. Both the unfortunate lovers deserve their title billing: the aspiring author (who actually existed, but was not actually guilty of such temerity in love) as well as the rank-blind princess. Montagu's Duke d'Enguien, brother to the princess, is equally merciless in his punishment both of Fontenelle's presumption and of her stooping. The penalty paid by Fontenelle is to be left in ignorance (deceived, banished, believing that her love was nothing but cynical pretence), while hers is the knowledge of good and evil (knowing the worth of the lover she has lost and knowing how he now, mistakenly, despises her). But the story needs to be titled from Mademoiselle de Condé alone, to point the parallel with Louisa, the Duke's next victim. Having ruined his sister's life by breaking up her love affair with a commoner, he ruins the commoner Louisa's life by causing her to fall in love with him; in each case it is the woman's sense of honour, her absolute requirement of the highest moral standards from herself, that precipitates her destruction.

Montagu prefaces 'Mademoiselle de Condé' with a dedicatory letter to [La Grande] Mademoiselle which, from the paper and handwriting, must have headed this pair (or perhaps this series) of short 'novels'. Having provided 'Mademoiselle de Condé' with closure, she added a link between its close and 'Louisa's' opening. She entertained the idea of closing this second tale with the Duke's death, which would surely have terminated the series. Having decided to let her anti-hero live, she may possibly have intended to let the series continue.

Evil and horror escalate during the course of the two extant tales. D'Enguien's intervention in his sister's life is calculatedly cruel; the ease with which he perverts the loyalty of her maid reveals something of his power's extent; and the gratuitous pain of M. de St André's humble and hopeless love opens an extra glimpse at the end of the story down vistas of further suffering. But all this finds some counterweight in the two lovers' unworldly idealism and their brief happiness. In 'Louisa' evil holds all the cards. Madame de Maintenon's charitable seminary is a front for procuring nubile girls for royal dukes; Louisa succeeds to her friend Mme de Nerville as only the latest in the Duke's string of sexual victims; she is barred from finding any pleasure in love almost from the beginning by a guilty conscience; she is absolutely isolated. The Duke's wife and sister as well as her own trusted mentor collude in attempting her honour, and, when they fail at that, in destroying her liberty and happiness. Her open-eyed, high-minded sacrifice of herself in marriage does nothing to lighten the Duke's persecution: nothing but her death will do. It is not much of a consolation that she possesses the single loyal maidservant in Montagu's fiction after 'Indamora'.

Modern readers may think of these stories as closer kin to Pierre Choderlos de Laclos's *Les Liaisons dangereuses* than to any of their predecessors. But the dedication to Mademoiselle de Montpensier helps to place them. The texts most closely connected with Montpensier were in Lady Mary's library:[1] the *Nouvelles françaises*

---

[1] Wh MS 135.

in which she was moving spirit or co-author with Jean Regnault de Segrais; her memoirs, which remained unpublished till 1726, almost thirty years after her death; and Lafayette's novel about her. In all these works female heroism (which is not identified with the preservation of chastity, but may express itself through that means as well as through intellect, beauty, and strength of mind) is crucial; it shines out in a guilty and power-crazed world, but it is generally defeated.

Montagu's French court tales raise the further issue of dialogue with the English fictional tradition. Whether or not 'Mademoiselle de Condé' reflects any influence of the similar love of a great lady for her social inferior in John Webster's *The Duchess of Malfi*, 'Louisa' surely reflects Delarivier Manley's seduction fictions on one hand and Richardson's *Pamela* on the other. Montagu orchestrates her 'warm' scenes in the manner of Manley, dwelling on the details of the heroine's bodily response to pressure from outside and desire from within; but she assembles the emotional and moral context in the manner of Richardson, making it Louisa's first priority to preserve her self-esteem, which she can ensure only by continuing her resistance through progressive deprivation and isolation. In both these tales Montagu writes as if she had heeded Richardson's and Johnson's call for fiction to depict goodness in action: but her working model of female goodness is one of honour and heroism, not of submissiveness and conformity.

Whereas on the one hand Scudéry's and Lafayette's heroines had achieved public recognition of their moral triumph by abjuring desire, and on the other the scandalous heroines of Villedieu and Eliza Haywood make no special claim to moral high ground, Montagu's Mademoiselle de Condé and Louisa (despite their disparity in rank) are identical in being both paragons of honour and altruism *and* acute and passionate in sexual feeling. The princess has the temerity to pursue her illicit love; the orphan flees in defence of her virginity. These French heroines show their goodness in opposite ways—by loving in defiance of social constraints, and by resisting illicit love. But neither hesitates to feel and express passion; and the transgression of one and resistance of the other cause them to set their unaided selves uncompromisingly against the norms and prescriptions of their society. Montagu has no truck with the plot (so widespread in the English fiction of this date) which shapes the protagonist to social demands and expectations. Unlike Henry Fielding or the

Richardson of *Pamela* (though like Sarah Fielding) she eschews the kind of transformative happy ending by which society escapes ultimate condemnation.

Written in solitude and ennui, 'Mademoiselle de Condé' and 'Louisa' must date either from 1742–6, or more likely from 1746–56, the decade in which Montagu also worked on the short-lived history of her own times. The same period may have produced 'La Princesse Docile'; but her crabbed handwriting in the latter suggests alternatively a still later date, in the years immediately following 1756. It is not certain therefore whether 'Docile' or the 'Italian Memoir' is the earlier text.

In a collection of romance writings, the 'Memoir' is an anomaly.[1] It earns its inclusion here because it needs to be printed and available to students of Montagu, and because it shares with 'Docile' on the one hand its Gothic and excessive elements (here presented as actual fact) and on the other its autobiographical character (literal here; occluded and allegorical in 'Docile').

Lady Mary's 'Italian Memoir' tells one version of her decade in the province of Brescia; her surviving letters, mostly to her daughter, Lady Bute, tell a different version. Publicly, she expresses her content with the retirement which gives her leisure to distil the wisdom of a lifetime; only gradually as the years go by does the idea of exile sometimes find its way into the letters. Privately, her retrospective account, compiled with the intention of suing Count Ugolino Palazzi for fraud and theft of money, relates a survivor's story of long-continued and reluctantly recognized persecution: a whole series of depredations both overt and covert, escalating to veiled threats of violence. The prevailing mood contradicts that of the letters; but whereas the letters foreground the author's feelings, the 'Memoir' presents a factual narrative which is curiously drained of affect.

Amid professions of extravagant devotion which Lady Mary presents as if she took them at face value, all the Palazzis evidently assume that an elderly foreign woman (all alone and presumed to be wealthy) can have no right to any cash, jewels, or land to which the head of a noble family in the prime of life does not have a better claim. To tell such a tale poses problems for the victim-narrator, who finds herself deprived of her customary self-presentation as capable and

---

[1] See Isobel Grundy, 'Lady Mary Wortley Montagu's "Italian Memoir" ', *Age of Johnson* (ed. Paul J. Korshin), 6 (1994), 321–46.

decisive: deprived both of the moral high ground and the heroic energy of her fictional heroines. Not only must she relate how she was persuaded or browbeaten into buying houses and lands which she did not really want (and which proved, too late, to be not legally saleable); she must also admit how repeatedly she allowed matters to slide, on the grounds that small sums of money, small instances of deceit and treachery, were not worth bothering about. Assuming a stoic indifference to material things comes to appear not merely affectation but idiocy.

While Palazzi rages, sobs, or threatens suicide, the protagonist represses any emotional reaction except a contemptuous pity which seems not commensurate with his advantage over her. The repression of feeling runs parallel to a refusal of action. Again and again Lady Mary buries herself in her books, her walks, her garden, averting her eyes from her pressing problems. Incident is piled on incident (some suggesting a Gothic novel and some a comic opera) without precipitating any significant progress in what one might call the plot. It is an endless repetition of petty clues that makes Lady Mary belatedly recognize that she is being detained against her will; in the same manner, a whole sequence of tampering with the records of these events produces her eventual moment of heroic defiance. Even her escape to Padua and Venice does not deter Palazzi from following her, inserting himself into her domestic arrangements, and enacting a statement to the public about the normality of their relations, designed to pre-empt the story which she might, and which here she does, tell.

Her version is (in the absence of her diary or her history of her own times) ostensibly her most extended surviving autobiographical narrative. Its idiosyncratic Italian marks it as close to her own words. (The only Italian sentences she is certainly known to have composed are two in a letter to Francesco Algarotti in 1757.[1]) Yet, written in a scribal hand for a hypothetical court of law to deliberate, expressing a subjectivity tightly reined in, it has the air of an official document rather than an item of *belles-lettres*. It is generically unique.

Haunting parallels persist, however, with 'Princess Docile', the most substantial piece of prose fiction to survive from Montagu's writing lifetime. Docile is in some respects a self-portrait (though

---

[1] *CL* iii. 117–18. An apparent abstract, in Italian, from some of her letters to Lady Bute may be someone else's translation (H MS 81, fos. 299–302; Montagu, *Selected Letters*, ed. Grundy, forthcoming).

Montagu's many admirers may be loath to acknowledge the Princess's traits in her creator) as well as an astute comment on the female predicament in general. The Princess has from nature her beauty and her intense desire to love and be loved; she is magically gifted with perfect docility (meaning both submissiveness and facility in learning). The result is an improbable paragon whose good qualities make her consistently the pawn of less altruistic people. She repeatedly lays herself open to those who betray her by false professions of love, traduce her with slander, and bully and cheat her out of her kingdom and all her possessions including herself.

Her absurdly idealistic education (in both its phases, religious and philosophical) has parallels in what Lady Mary recalled of her own: the pious and superstitious governess and the unspecified influences which taught her contempt for social conventions like those of rank and wealth.[1] Some circumstances of Lady Mary's marriage (the loss of a suitor for whom she felt passionately,[2] the flurried elopement to marry a man she deeply respected but probably did not love, the humiliation of bringing nothing with her to him) may be hinted at in Docile's. The Princess's husband, Sombre, with his honour, jealousy, and inflexibility, his passion for Docile and his persistence in believing the worst of her, unavoidably suggests Edward Wortley Montagu. It is tempting to pursue further parallels with actuality, wondering what Fortunate/Goodhope owes to Lady Mary's acquaintance with self-made politicians like James Craggs the younger, or what the Kingdom of Good Children owes to the Republic of Venice.[3]

But the element of autobiography is limited in at least two important ways. First, Montagu also draws on traits and opinions of her own for male characters who are as remote from any ideal as is Prince Sombre, projecting aspects of herself even onto such unlikely personages as Fortunate and the Knight of Malta (below, pp. 156, 183). Secondly, autobiography and the fictional tradition go hand in hand. Her childhood reading in Scudéry had offered her the paradigm (which continued to inform later Frenchwomen's writings) of

---

[1] *CL* iii. 25–6, 36.

[2] *CL* i. 127.

[3] Irrelevant to the fiction, but irresistible to the imagination, is the coincidence of name with Fortunatus, formerly Massoud, Lady Mary's putative black grandson, who was unfortunate in his life and in his death at 25 (Jonathan Curling, *Edward Wortley Montagu, 1713–1776: The Man in the Iron Wig* (1954), 205, 233–7, and *passim*).

marriage as necessarily oppressive, converting men into tyrants and women into slaves.[1]

Just as the 'Court Tales' suggest *Les Liaisons dangereuses*, so 'Docile' suggests *Candide*; but the relation of Montagu's to Voltaire's satire is probably again that of sister-, not daughter-text. Produced after attentive reading of the new English novelists of social realism (Richardson and both Fieldings), 'Docile' takes one sideswipe at *Pamela* (below, p. 111) and comments obliquely on *Clarissa* by making its pattern heroine interested in literary and scientific learning, and susceptible (more than once) to sexual desire. It does clearly comment on the newly emerged conventions of the English novel, but chiefly by the negative means of ostentatious concern with different themes and purposes. Instead of entering into sustained dialogue with English novelists, it follows 'The Sultan's Tale' and 'Court Tales' in dialogue with the tradition of philosophic fiction, primarily French. The naïve heroine serves as a device for examining religious doctrine, power politics, gender relations, sexual practices, and the relevance of literature and scientific learning to life. She has the excessive sensibility and excessive suffering found in heroines of Lafayette and Anne Ferrand in the late seventeenth century and Mlle de Lubert in the mid-eighteenth;[2] but the dangers of sensibility are the crux of only one episode in the story. Docile moves on from one milieu and one issue to another in picaresque style, while different satiric targets succeed each other with the pace and drive of Menippean satire. Like Swift, Voltaire, and other writers in this tradition, Montagu here flits from genre to genre, and touches none that she does not parody.

'Docile' is mock-romance, mock-picaresque, mock-fairy-tale (like the second generation of *contes*, which mock the happy endings of the first): Montagu's beneficent fairy exercises patronage on the basis of chance acquaintance, and benefaction on the basis of error; her visitor from another planet contributes nothing to the earth and gains nothing from it; the mystery surrounding Fortunate's birth is

---

[1] *Le Grand Cyrus*, book x (Ian Maclean, *Woman Triumphant: Feminism in French Literature 1610–1652* (1977), 117; DeJean, *Tender Geographies*, 142 ff.).

[2] DeJean, *Tender Geographies*, 260 n. 38. Thomas DiPiero calls the Princess of Cleves 'a quixotic innocent in a corrupted court where everyone reads better than she does' (*Dangerous Truths and Criminal Passions: The Evolution of the French Novel, 1569–1791* (1992), 132). Lady Mary owned Lubert's fairy stories *La Princesse Lionnette et le Prince Coquerico* and *La Princesse Sensible et le Prince Typhon* (both 1743); her own in that genre might have been titled 'La Princesse Docile et le Prince Sombre'.

never solved. Montagu denies any didactic utility to works like *Télémaque* and *Pamela*, without claiming it for her own; her *philosophe*, though both learned and high-principled, is as much out of touch with the real world as the hermit whose idea of the good life is to stand fleabitten in the desert while his raised arm gradually decays. She paints the horrific effects of artificial sensibility without allowing Madame Good Sense to make emotional contact with Docile at all. Prospective life-partners successively on offer for her are a rigid, old-fashioned, honourable misogynist, a delightful, even generous hedonist who however sees love-objects as virtually interchangeable, an entirely conscienceless self-made man who subordinates all others to his own interests, and a frippery aesthete.

Of topics dear to the emerging English novel, conduct-book virtues like chastity and obedience to authority are not advocated here, and the much-canvassed issue of whether a woman—or anyone—can truly love a second time is no issue at all. Docile's propensity to obey is presented as a handicap (resoundingly so at the end of the first section), but with this propensity goes a readiness to set her own moral imperatives above obedience, as when she gives away the royal jewels. Her chastity, similarly, is an aspect of her honour or her morality: as a supposed widow eager to marry her new lover she allows her period of mourning to be whittled away, though not so much as he anticipates. When she first falls in love (with a man she hardly knows), the narrator effectively debunks the established concept of female virtue by defining it as 'that she should fail to recognize her own sentiments, and that she should struggle against them in proportion as she began to understand them'. But unlike heroines of didactic novels, Docile never learns to feel guilty and inadequate until she is taught this lesson by Sombre. Whereas such novels tend to ask how heroines can be better fitted to the world, 'Docile' tables an indignant question as to the causes of the world's moral inadequacy to its protagonist, both as woman and as human being.

'Docile' may be read not merely as, like *Candide*, combating philosophical optimism, but as breathing despair. *Rasselas*, after all, was read this way, and the young people in *Rasselas* are at least allowed to soften their disillusioning acceptance of the world with continuing daydreams, including the feminist dream. Montagu, like Voltaire, provides the closure which Johnson refuses. The opposed conclusions of on the one hand Candide contentedly cultivating his garden, and on the other Docile denigrated and self-mortifying, reflect the

life-experience of their authors and perhaps the opportunities open
to them as male and female. But to raise the question of feminism is
to identify the element in 'Docile' which saves it from being merely
depressing. Feminist criticism, though sometimes all too ready to
combat one set of prescriptions by setting in place another, can provide both welcome and analysis for such resistance, such anger in a
fictional text. The anger and resistance conveyed by authorial tone
in 'Docile' enable it to clarify many of the issues which give *David
Simple* its similarly crushing finale; they also supply an element lacking in the constrictive outcomes of *The Female Quixote* or even
Millenium Hall. It is the author's mediating vision which makes this
story exciting, never plaintive: a vision lacking either the placidity of
a sage or the punitive expectations of a prophet, but wry, witty,
worldly, and womanly.

Montagu's feminism constantly queries received opinion
(through the authorial voice, and through repeated and varied role-
reversals) as it tracks its hapless heroine through a world of male
power. Its judgements on this world are sharp and clear: too much
obedience, too little thought, too much honour, too little pleasure,
too much exploitation of others for gain, too little love (either maternal, homosocial, or erotic). It constructs no utopias (unless we count
the Kingdom of Good Children). Utopia-building involves tight
control, at least in imagination, over every aspect of social activity.
Montagu's fictional societies are all courts, and those who impose or
attempt to impose control are almost always uncompromisingly presented as tyrannical. (King Goodchild is again a partial exception,
paradoxical since the values he imposes are libertarian; he might be
seen as a tyrant by the priests who are forbidden to learn to read.)
Lady Mary's aristocratic Old Whiggism is less ready to prescribe social remedies than is the new bourgeois liberalism.[1]

In her commonplace-book Lady Mary jotted, 'romances should
be wrote for the use of old women'.[2] In 'Docile' she set about
remedying this lack through analysis and mockery of the hetero-
sexual plot: through a novel without a (mortal) hero. Every one of the
men in Docile's life has some qualities which Lady Mary warmly
respected—Sombre's integrity, Fortunate's executive abilities and
high culture, and the capacity for pleasure variously displayed by

---

[1] *CL* iii. 277; see Ruth Perry, 'Bluestockings in Utopia', in Beth Fowkes Tobin (ed.),
History, Gender and Eighteenth-Century Literature (1994), 159–78.

[2] CB, fo. 8.

King Goodchild and the Knight of Malta—but none of them has the respect for a woman that might conceivably make a good relationship. Gender politics are neatly and succinctly related to mainstream politics through the Prince of Venus. He is Docile's counterpart in virtue and integrity, the masculine ideal although—or because—feminized in his charms and his modesty; and he calls to mind the naked American Indians facing European arms (below, p. 134).

Lady Mary pitied her cousin Sarah Fielding for the financial need which drove her to publish; modern readers may be inclined to regret the material comfort which preserved Montagu from any such need. Perhaps nothing but the pressure of imminent publication would have made her mould an extended work into final form. 'Docile', confidently as it moves from fairy-tale opening to abrupt and brutal conclusion, has extruded an incomplete fragment from an unrealized different version. This fragment, though it may well pre-date the present main text of 'Docile', is perhaps best regarded as a potential, not actual, separate work.

In the main text Docile's life-choices appear each in the guise of some man or other. In Fragment II she explores a choice which has no male representative, and which in life was supposed at least by Lady Mary's English contemporaries to be closed to women: the choice of science. Perhaps Montagu discarded this draft because Docile's assertive manner in it undermines her consistency. The Knight of Malta, too, appears differently in this debate, which turns on learning, not love. Gender roles are emphatically and repeatedly reversed, the female debater being serious in her science and her philosophy, while the male has only a dilettante interest planted by a woman who wanted to 'form his mind' (below, p. 190). He constantly gets issues confused; he argues for applied science only, and for limiting one's interests to the sphere of home. He has in the past found that mental activity impairs his sexual function, as so many men argued that it would do for women. Yet many of his ideas—about the vanity of (male) intellectual pundits and the debt humanity owes to improvers in domestic arts like cookery—are Lady Mary's own.

Lady Mary seems to have entertained a private agenda in Fragment II: that of contesting or reshaping the gender relations depicted in Francesco Algarotti's *Newtonianismo per le dame*, published in 1739, in which a courtly male scientist playfully mingles his instruction to a noblewoman with condescending gallantry. This suggests that she may have worked on 'Docile', in some form or other, over a period of many years; but answering Algarotti could have been a project either of the early 1740s, after her erotic disillusionment with him, or the early 1750s when she spent time at Salo, which like Sirmione (setting for the dialogues in *Newtonianismo*) was an idyllic landscape on the banks of Lake Garda, or the later 1750s, when she rebuilt her friendship with him. Fragment II contains the germ of a story as destabilizing to moral and ideological categories as 'The Sultan's Tale', or else a paradoxical essay akin to 'Sur la Maxime de Mr de Rochefoucault'.[1] But at this stage of Montagu's life it seems that the carnivalesque work remained either unwritten or unpreserved, while the completed 'Docile' is one of wholly consistent ironic disillusion.

Feminist scholarship is seeking to move on from rediscovery of lost texts from the past, to adequate contextualizing criticism of such texts. The unread stories presented here are typical of what Nancy K. Miller calls the 'under-read' or '*sous-lu*' in their very resistance to categorization. Two of them are linguistically marginal as well, since they are likely to be read mostly in translation. The history of the novel (which they might have changed) moved on without them. The house of English fiction at mid-century (whether of the Richardson–Henry Fielding canon or the Haywood–Lennox–Collier–Sarah Fielding canon) cannot accommodate them without major alterations. 'When I print,' their author wrote, 'I submit to be answer'd and criticis'd.'[2] I hope she will now find not only readers but also enthusiastic and discriminating critics.

---

[1] *E&P* 157–64.   [2] *CL* iii. 95.

TEXTUAL NOTE

APART from supplying capitals for proper names and to begin sentences, I have followed the spelling and capitalization of the MSS (all but the 'Italian Memoir' wholly or largely in Montagu's hand). Minimal alterations have been made to punctuation to enable easier reading; for the same purpose very long paragraphs, and those containing dialogue, have been split up. Like many of her contemporaries, Montagu punctuated very lightly and separated sentences by commas at least as often as by full stops. She makes no use of inverted commas; I have compromised on the eighteenth-century practice of using these to begin and end a piece of direct speech, but not to re-surround parenthetical phrases like (*said she*). Montagu's occasional portmanteau words (like 'inspite' and 'assoon') have been divided, and standard abbreviations, such as '&' for 'and' and 'wth' for 'with', have been expanded. Her usage in these matters is not consistent. One special case is 'D.', which she writes in 'Court Tales' with both 'of' and 'de' or 'd' '; I have expanded to 'Duke'. I have used [ ] for editorial additions, and < > for words which are present in MS, but hard to read. Obvious slips (e.g. may for make) have been corrected. Any substantive revision in MS has been noted; practice for 'Indamora', a special case, is described in its Textual Note. Montagu's minor changes like 'is' to 'was' or singular to plural, or the insertion of omitted words above the line, have been left unrecorded. In French, she used none but acute accents (or made acute and grave with identical strokes); where she uses either accent I have chosen the correct one. (Her slapdash handling of accents and of homophone endings like '-er' and '-ait' is not unlike that of contemporary francophones such as Françoise de Graffigny.)

My practice regarding punctuation, abbreviations, etc. takes into account the expectations which eighteenth-century authors held about the passage of their work from MS to print. Of the MSS here reproduced, Montagu gave most careful attention to copying 'Indamora' and 'The Sultan's Tale'. But she would have relied on a printer to polish or supply punctuation. Printers produced authorized versions.[1]

---

[1] Cf. Thomas E. Kinsella, 'The Conventions of Authenticity: Boswell's Revisions of Dialogue in the *Life of Johnson*', *Age of Johnson*, 6 (1994), 248–52. Boswell's general reliance

Despite Montagu's own dictum that texts are 'often corrupted and always injured by translations', her foreign-language writings (the 'Italian Memoir' and 'Princess Docile') are printed in translation, with the originals supplied in appendices. Textual notes to these works are attached to Montagu's original text if they need its reading to make sense; their position is flagged in the translation with 'See Appendix, p. ooo'.

on his printer reached a peak over quotation marks, about which his own practice was wildly inconsistent.

Indamora to Lindamira[1]
Her Life Writ in 5 Letters

To the Reader
I have read somewhere a book thus intitled
The Adventures
of
Lindamira a Lady of Quality
Written by her own hand to a Freind in the country.[2]
In one of Lindamira's Letters She Desires her freind Indamora to
requite her with the Hystory of her Life—I have writt it on my
own Invention.
I Desire the Reader wou'd Compare
The 2 Lives.

Textual note. Copy-text is Lady Mary's album, now H MS 251,
filled in her mid- or late teens (see Isobel Grundy, ' "The
Entire Works of Clarinda": Unpublished Juvenile Verse by
Lady Mary Wortley Montagu', *YES* 7 (1977), 91–107). I have
modified her punctuation and capitalization more frequently
here (where she marked most new lines with capitals) than in
later texts. From her earlier version, 'The Adventur's of
Indamora' (in H MS 250, whose contents were 'writ at the age
of 14'), come the address to the reader, which is absent from
H MS 251, and the textual variants recorded in notes.

Lady Mary made minor revisions to almost every sentence
of her novel: she changed all the names, and often did the same
with tenses, conjunctions, and prepositions. She added or

---

[1] Both were popular romance names. Lindamira has an inset story in Lady Mary Wroth,
The Countesse of Montgomeries Urania (1621); Lindamire is the heroine of *Le Favory* (1665),
by Marie-Catherine Desjardins, Mme Villedieu. Dryden's heroine in *Aureng-Zebe* (pub. 1675)
is Indamora; so is Louise de Quérouailles, Duchess of Portsmouth, in a fictionalized bio-
graphy, *Amours of the Sultan of Barbary* (1689). Later, in 1714, Steele wrote of Lindamira in
*Tatler*s 9 and 22, and Pope and Arbuthnot gave both names to Siamese twins in *Memoirs of
Martinus Scriblerus*.

[2] [?Thomas Brown], *The Adventures of Lindamira, A Lady of Quality: Written by her Own
Hand, to her Friend in the Country* (London: Richard Wellington, 1702; 2nd edn. 1713; 3rd, as
The Lover's Secretary, 1734; repr. ed. Benjamin Boyce, 1949). John Richetti calls it the finest
pre-Richardsonian amatory fiction (*Popular Fiction before Richardson: Narrative Patterns,
1700–1739* (1969), 169).

deleted adjectives and descriptive phrases, and reordered sentences, often retaining all the original elements. On the whole she pruned more than she expanded, moved further from common life into romance, and made Indamora more circumspect. I have footnoted only the following: names (at first mention), significant details added or dropped, and significant changes in meaning or style.

Indamora to Lindamira was first published by the Juvenilia Press, Edmonton, Alberta, 1994, with illustrations by Juliet McMaster, and notes by Susan Hillabold which I have, by permission, drawn on here.

Letter first[1]

Your obliging Account of your Life my Dearest Lindamira, makes it imposible for mee to refuse your request of concealing no passage of mine from [you], and I'me too asur'd of your Freindship to beleive you will ever discover any thing that I have a mind to keep secret. Without Ceremony[2] I'le begin (in your immitation) at my 16 year. T'was long before that, I had the misfortune of loseing a vertuous and tender mother.[3] As Young as I was then so near a loss very sensibly greiv'd mee. My Only sister Felicia[4] (who you know is a year younger then I) was not of so malencholy Temper and was les trouble'd.

My Father, Diphilus,[5] was very kind to us and remaining un-marie'd till I was 16 wee flatter'd our Selves hee wou'd never give us a mother-in-law,[6] and was exstreamly surpriz'd to see him marie'd to Eurinoe,[7] a Lady about 30, rich, a widow and of a very imperious temper,[8] and She had a son of my Age. I disemble'd my dislike of her as well as I cou'd, but my sister was not so capable of Disguising her

---

[1] In H MS 250 this letter begins, 'My Dearest Dear Lindamira'; the salutations, gradually dwindling to 'Dear Lindamira', are not woven into the prose as in the later version.

[2] makes it . . . Without Ceremony] Causes mee to Comply with Your Desire of hearing my Adventures. But my Dear you must not exspect to see so much Wit in my Letters as I find in yours—but Sans Ceremony (H MS 250).

[3] H MS 250 adds 'who died before I was 10 year old'.

[4] In H MS 250 Berenice.

[5] From Greek, meaning 'loving twice'; changed from 'Araxis' (H MS 250).

[6] Stepmother. H MS 250 continues: 'but wee had not long them aggreable Hopes, for to our Great Surprizal . . .'

[7] Meaning 'of broad knowledge' or 'know-all'; changed from 'Albinia' (H MS 250).

[8] H MS 250 adds 'She no sooner Came into our House then the Order of every thing was Chang'd to my Great Discontent.'

Sentiment and she openly show'd her Disattisfaction, which Indiscretion soon made my mother-in-law her profest Enemy.[1] To mee she show'd a little more Complaisance, designing Mee for her son, and my father wholly govern'd by her Consented to what she pleas'd. The young man was not ill made nor senseless and I can give no reason for my Aversion to him, who finding I was resolv'd against him wou'd have perswaded his mother not to Constrain my inclination and was generous enough to say hee wou'd refuse my hand if I deny'd him my heart. She was resolv'd upon it and said she wou'd have an absolute Authority over mee.[2] Philocles[3] tormented mee no longer with his detested pasion and which was only (I beleive) disemble'd in Complaisance to Eurinoe's commands; hee adres'd himself to my sister who was not like mee insensible of his merrits.[4] They exchang'd hearts and vows and I was a witness of their Contract. My mother-in-law persecuted both her Son and Mee, as to my sister wee knew t'wou'd bee in vain to Ask her Consent.[5] She made my father make use of his Authority Over mee and I was forc'd seemingly to comply.

Philocles and Felicia resolv'd to fly from a Tyranny they cou'd no longer Endure. Hee had his estate out of his mother's power and they was resolv'd on a private [marriage]. I wou'd have Diswade'd my sister from it for I think nothing ought to make one Disobey a Father[6] in so important an Affair, but her Lover's Arguments had more Power over her then mine and t'was in vain to Oppose it. At last I consented and one evening on pretence of walking (wee liveing in the country)[7] she met Philocles at a little Inn[8] where hee had provided a parson. They was Married before mee and some trusty Servant, Horses was Ready and hee carried her to a house of his 12 mile from Ours.

---

[1] H MS 250 adds 'and resolv'd to doe her all the ill offices in her Power.'

[2] She was . . . over mee.] She told him he was a fool and I shou'd doe as she Pleas'd (H MS 250).

[3] Meaning 'lover of glory', cf. below, p. 127; changed from 'Lycias' (H MS 250).

[4] H MS 250 adds 'in fine, 3 months after'. A contract was at this date a legally binding ceremony.

[5] H MS 250 adds 'But she hateing Berenice and being an Imperious Woman scorn'd her will shou'd be Crost.'

[6] Indamora is enabled to avoid this marriage without disobeying.

[7] Lady Mary was to report rather glumly from Wiltshire in 1710, 'The Diversion is walking . . . but then you may walk 2 mile without meeting a living creature but a few straggling cows' (*CL* i. 42).

[8] H MS 250 adds 'half a mile from my Father's house'. The marriage is presumably by special licence, as Lady Mary's was to be.

Diphilus and Eurinoe soon knew of their flight and sure there was never fury more Violent then my Mother-in-law's. My father greiv'd so much I repented My haveing aided their design, hee grew so Malencholy Eurinoe fear'd some Languishing Distemper wou'd seize him and advis'd him to goe to London where (she said) She hop'd the deversions of the town wou'd cure his Greife.

Wee went and oh what a sensible Joy was it to mee to See that great Town which I had heard so Much of but never till now saw. Wee took a house which had a pritty Garden Looking into St. James park. My Mother-in-law went every day abroad and was in all the belle Assemblies but never suffer'd mee to stir out hardly to Church, which you may beleive my dear Lindamira was not at All Agreable to one of my Age, I grew very malencholy and My father gave mee leave sometimes to walk in the Mall to devert mee, with my Woman Florimel.[1] One evening I saw a Gentlemen [*sic*] very well drest of a very good mein come out Of a Chair[2] when I enter'd it, hee bow'd respectfully and gaz'd So earnestly at mee that I blush't and made hast away. Hee Enquir'd[3] my name and then approach'd mee, and said hee had the honnour to bee very well acquainted with Eurinoe but did not know she had so great a beauty in her House. Hee perform'd this Little complement with an admirable good grace[4] and entertain'd mee that night very agreably and with a great deal of wit and [I] went home more thoughtfull then Usuall.[5]

That same Night Lothario,[6] unfortunately, saw Something in my face that hee lik'd. I need not give You his Carecter and my Dear Lindimira can't bee Ignorant of his person whose Equipage[7] has made So much noise in the world. Hee made preposalls of marryage to my father who bid mee look upon him as one design'd for my husband. I was not soe foolish (tho' I knew very little of the Town) not to put a great Difference between him and Cleonidas (the gentleman

---

[1] In H MS 250 'Celena'. The Mall, in St James's Park, was close to home.

[2] A sedan chair. In H MS 250 Indamora uses not a chair but 'the Coach'.

[3] Hee Enquir'd] He sent his Servant to My footman to Enquire (H MS 250).

[4] H MS 250 adds 'and I must own to my Dear Lindamira I thought him very Aggreable.'

[5] great deal . . . Usuall] so much wit—that—I—was mightyly pleas'd with his Conversation. He Led me to my Coach and I went home thinking of Nothing but Myrtillo, that was his Name (H MS 250).

[6] Name from the seducer in Nicholas Rowe's 'she-tragedy' *The Fair Penitent*, produced 1703; changed from 'Erastus, a Beau, or to give you his Truer Carecter a Fop' (H MS 250).

[7] i.e. his carriage, horses, liveries, etc. This sentence is absent from H MS 250, and the fop's proposal is related more briefly.

that Entertain'd mee at the Park). I melted in tears at Diphilus Feet but it was in vain, hee left mee and went out with My mother-in-law, and (Good God) how was I surpriz'd at the sight of Cleonidas, who came in half an hour after, but how was my Amazment encreas'd when hee made a Warm declaration of love. I was unuse'd to such Discourses, blush't and look'd I beleive very Silly, he beg'd leave to ask mee of my Father and I told him it was from Diphilus that hee must exspect his Answer. His preposalls Were more advantageous then[1] those of Lothario but my Mother-in-law govern'd and she thought it too [good?] a match and she prevail'd with my Father to give him a Positive Denyall and they proceeded so far as to forbid him the house.[2] All this was Infinitely Displeaseing to mee but my Discontent was very much Encreas'd, when Eurinoe told mee my wedding cloaths was bought[3] and I must bee Lothario's as soon as the[y] was made for every Thing else was concluded. I durst not reply but went into my Chamber where I wept till I was weary and then read Grand Cyrus[4] and was amaz'd to hear Florimel tell mee when I left off that t'was past twelve. The moon shone bright, t'was a calm Night[5] and she easily perswaded mee to take a turn in the Garden. I went leaning on her, but how Surpriz'd was I to see Cleonidas Come from behind a marble Mercury.[6] I was running into the House when hee got hold of my hand and said, 'Cruel Indamora, Doe you joyn with Diphilus to make mee wretched?' I chid him for his boldness. 'What wou'd you have mee doe (cry'd hee), this was My only way to see you.' In short hee said a thousand tender Pasionate things to mee, hee beg'd [me] to fly from the Tyranny of My Mother-in-law and take refuge in his Arms, but it was What I wou'd never consent to. 'Will you then bee Lothario's,' Said hee, looking on mee

[1] His . . . then] He left me in an amazment I cannot Describe. He came next Morning with more advantagious proposalls then (H MS 250).

[2] Denyall . . . house] Denyall and he us'd Arguments and Intreatys to no Purpose. He was for a month every Day with Araxis, but was at last forbid the house (was there ever any thing so rude to a man of his Quality) (H MS 250).

[3] wedding . . . bought] the writeings were Drawn and my wedding Cloaths makeing (H MS 250).

[4] Madeleine de Scudéry, *Artamène, ou le grand Cyrus* (1649–53). In 1739 MWM owned a copy of this romance, which includes an analysis by 'Sapho' of women's inadequate education and the way that marriage turns men into tyrants. In H MS 250 Indamora chose Gauthier de La Calprenède's *Cléopâtre*, which Montagu later owned (Wh MS 510).

[5] t'was a calm Night] and made a 2d Day. There was no wind, all the House was a bed (H MS 250).

[6] Presumably Mercury in his capacity as messenger of the gods rather than as patron of thieving; a Venus in H MS 250.

tenderly. 'Noe' reply'd I,[1] 'but I wou'd bee rid of him without being
Criminal.' Hee said hee wou'd Try to doe what I desir'd. It begun to
bee light and wee Separated after a hundred Adeius and [I] return'd
to my Room With Florimel,[2] but I forget how I tire my Dear
Lindamira, Whose most faithfull Servant is—

Indamora

Letter the Second

Next morning (my dear Lindamira) I faintly chid Florimel, who
knew by my undisembling eyes I was not so angry as I pretended.
Diphilus and Eurinoe Din'd abroad that Day and I spent my time in
thinking of Cleonidas, who was not indifferent to mee. In the
Evening my Father and Mother came home, hee seem'd much discontented and lock'd himself in his Closet, she rail'd at Cleonidas
with so much fury It was imposible to understand the cause of her
Complaint, and she Was too animated to speak plain. She was so us'd
to doe things Without reason that I took no Notice of her Noise but
went into My Chamber to avoid it. I had not been there a Quarter of
an hour When Florimel brought mee a Note which was deliver'd her
by a Strange Porter who stay'd not to bee ask'd Questions, and oh
Heavens! how was I surpriz'd to see Words to this effect.

Pity my tortures charming Indamora, when I say I must leave you (and perhaps for ever). Lothario is Dead, and I have obey'd your Commands in free-
ing you from that troublesome Lover—Can I[3] leave England without
seeing you—Noe! for heaven's Sake madame,[4] if ever one thought of mee
aproach'd your breast contrive some way to give mee Liberty to sigh a last
Adeiu and Asure you spite of time and absence th'idea of the Charming
Indamora shall ever fill the breast of your Faithfull C.

Never was Greife more Violent then mine—I wept, and Florimel
thought I shou'd never have done weeping. I answer'd his Note (for
in the post script there was a derection) thus.

---

[1] 'Noe,' reply'd I] I asur'd him I . . . wou'd never marry his rival. This sattisfy'd him a
little, but All his Eloquence cou'd not make me promise to be his (H MS 250).

[2] after a . . . Florimel] with Griefe on both sides—I went to bed thinking on him (H MS
250).

[3] Can I] what Can I say—I am Distracted to think I must (H MS 250).

[4] Noe! . . . madame] I Cannot bear the Thought, no my Charmer I'le stay I'le Dye but I
will once more see you—(H MS 250).

Sir,

I never Immagin'd what I innocently said without design Shou'd have such terrible effects, nor bee the cause of an Action which ruines your self and sensibly afflicts mee,—You ask to see mee, and I ought to refuse you but—come and use the same means you did Last night to see

Your Servant Indamora.

The rest of that day was spent in very malencholy thoughts and I must own I found more tenderness in my heart for Cleonidas then I immagin'd I had.[1] The Apointed hour came (12) when Diphilus and Eurinoe was in bed, I went into the Garden with Florimel and found the poor unhappy Lover there exspecting mee. Hee told mee hee had Challeng'd Lothario, Who was Brave enough to meet but haveing No Skill in fenceing quickly fell.[2] He entertain'd mee in the moveingst Terms and oft swore Etternal fidelity. Light Appear'd (or if you please Aurora)[3] and wee must separate. He bid mee adeiu so pasionately and with all the marks of greife, Love and Dispair that then it was my Dear Lindamira I was no longer mistress of my Actions.[4] I burst into a flood of tears.

'Is it posible (cry'd hee) the beauteous Indamora can take any part in my Sorrows?' 'Ask nothing,' reply'd I, 'but—goe.' We bid a thousand adeius and with a sigh I constrain'd My self to turn from him and went leaning on my Woman into the house more dead then alive.[5] That morning hee went part of his wa[y] to France. I heard oft from him. 3 weeks after this cruel Accident My Father dy'd and not Long Eurinoe surviv'd him.[6] She beg'd my pardon for all the Uneasynesses her ill humour had caus'd mee, she gave mee all her Jewells, but her estate to her Son who she was reconcil'd to before she dy'd and saw both him and my sister. Hee invited [me] to Stay with him at Lauretta, I did goe and there had the honour of your Acquaintance. I never pass'd 3 weeks pleasanter, I heard oft from Cleonidas and enjoy'd the Companny of my ever dear Lindamira Who will allways possess the Largest share in the Freindship of

Indamora.

---

[1] very malencholy . . . I had.] wishing for Night (H MS 250).

[2] Who was . . . fell] and Kill'd him (H MS 250).

[3] Light . . . Aurora)] Aurora Appear'd (H MS 250).

[4] I was . . . Actions] that in spite of my self (H MS 250).

[5] We bid . . . alive] Adeiu then, (said he kissing my hand) 10 thousand Adeius—hee left me unable to answer Him but by sighs and tears—he went—Celena led me to my Chamber where I was no sooner A bed then a 100 Different Thoughts perplex'd my mind (H MS 250).

[6] and not . . . him] which exstreamly troubled me and 4 months after Albinia (H MS 250).

Letter the third

Somewhile after my Dear Lindamira Left Lauretta, my sister was brought to bed of a Girl and she oblig'd mee to stay 2 months longer and all that While I heard nothing from Cleonidas which exstreamly Trouble'd mee. Felicia forc't mee to tell her the cause of My Malencholy, she was soe kind to pity mee and Philocles was one of the most earnest in petitioning his pardon, but in Vain, for Lothario was Near Relation to the King's favourite. I grew Acquainted with a lady call'd Amestris, she was near 30, Aimable enough. Phylomont her husband was in France. Her Conversation was mighty agreable,[1] she was pleas'd to Show a great deal of kindness for mee,[2] and I told her my Tenderness for Cleonidas. She comforted mee and told me how Manny traverses[3] had hinder'd her happiness. 'Yet see (said she) I have been long arriv'd at the end of my wishes, beleive [me] Indamora (continue'd this Lady) heaven makes Vertuous Lovers it's peculiar care.'—

One Evening when she came to see mee I perceiv'd an unusuall Chagrine in her eyes. I press'd to know the cause and she show'd mee a letter from her husband which desir'd her to leave England the first Opertunity, and she asur'd mee she was only sorry to leave mee, but if I wou'd consent to goe with her [her] Soul wou'd bee Entirely fill'd with joy. She made mee very civil preposalls, and I consider'd this the only way to see my Cleonidas. It was with a great deal of difficulty[4] that my Brother and Sister consented to this journey. At last I left Lauretta tho' not without Sheding an infinite Number of tears, but No sooner had I lost sight of my Dear Native Shore then all my courage Left mee. Then dear Lindamira I thought of you[5] and all them Freinds I Left, I concluded I Shou'd never see them more and wept as if all my fears was come to pass, and Amestris Laugh't at my weakness. Wee landed happyly, and without anny Accident arriv'd at Paris.[6]

---

[1] In H MS 250 Amestris and Phylomont are Dalinda (who additionally 'had a good Wit and had read much') and Palamede.

[2] H MS 250 adds 'I had a great Freindship for her and wee was oft Together'; Dalinda speaks of 'the Amours of Palamede and her self' and 'their Loves'.

[3] Obstacles.

[4] great . . . difficulty] world of Trouble (H MS 250).

[5] all my . . . of you] I burst into a fit of Violent Weeping. Then Dear Lindamira you came Fresh into my mind (H MS 250).

[6] arriv'd at Paris] arriv'd happyly at Deipe and from thence to Paris (H MS 250).

I spoke the language before and found the Court Very Agreable.[1]
I saw Fontainebleau and Versailles but dare Not speak of either after
your description of the first.[2] Wee found Phylomont with a Nephew
of his call'd Theander. Hee was a Gentleman not then 22,[3] very well
made, had the best air in the world, a peculiar art of charming in
Conversation and an Agreable wit without Affectation, but I scarse
took anny Notice of him, so much I Thought of Cleonidas. But my
Dear Lindamira, observe the Capriciousness of my fate. Phylomont
told us hee had contracted a freindship with him but that t'was
2 months since hee had quarrell'd with a French Marquis who
Challeng'd him. Hee was Victor and gave the insolent French man
his Life.[4] But Duels are there unpardonable, the unhappy Conqueror fled, and Phylomont was intrusted with his Flight to
Holland, but[5] the sea prov'd as fatal to him as the Land,[6] the ship
Sunk and there my faithfull Cleonidas [was] lost.

Ah Lindamira, in what terms shall I exspress my Greife at the sad
relation? I swooned, allmost Dy'd, 3 hours lay motionless and when
I recover'd t'was to fill the house with cries and raveings, call'd on his
Lov'd name and did a thousand exstravangcies. Amestris in vain
argue'd to moderate my Greife, all she cou'd Gain was to make mee
leave of[f] Loud Complaints and fall to Silent weeping—and I had
ever wept but that they Gave mee a stupifying Drug that took away
the Sence

of your
Indamora.

Letter fourth

Whole 2 months my Dear Lindamira I remain'd so malencholy I was
Scarse to bee known and all the Consolation of Amestriss, Phylomont and Theander signify'd nothing. I spoke little but Mus'd and

[1] H MS 250 adds 'And full of magnificence and Gallantry'.
[2] Both royal seats near Paris, respectively a Renaissance hunting-lodge (whose charms
were described by Lindamira's cousin Doralisa: *Adventures of Lindamira*, letter xiv) and the
nerve-centre of monarchy.
[3] In H MS 250 he is Altamont, '25 years of age, very accomplished'.
[4] i.e. spared his life. In H MS 250 the challenge was given 'on some Slight Affair'.
[5] H MS 250 adds 'them that are Destin'd to be miserable are always soe'.
[6] Did Lady Mary suppose that to reach another country *must* involve a sea crossing, or did
she plan a voyage down the Seine and through the straits of Dover?

read much. All my thoughts was of Cleonidas and my reading some
sad tale of unhappy Lovers.—Amestriss was vissited by most of the
Great Ladies in France, they wondred exstremly at my continued
sadness and was soe obligeing to strive all they cou'd to devert mee.
The[y] show'd mee all that tempts the Curiosity of Strangers[1] and
spite of my resistance carrie'd mee to all the Balls, Opera's and
Comedys[2] but I saw the most Charming things with indifference
and there was a perpetuall Chagrine in My Eyes.

The 3d month after this Affliction I began to Hearken to the Sage
discourses of the Prudent Amestris, who was Continueally[3] showing
mee the folly of exstravagant Greife. At Last (my dear) her
Conversation and time wore away great part of My Malencholy but
the immage of the faithfull unfortunate——was too deeply graven
in my heart to bee ever wholly remov'd. However my eyes reasum'd
their usuall Liveliness and my cheeks and Lips their Lost Colour
and I Look't as before—Versailes Seem'd more agreable to mee and
I discover'd a thousand Beauties in it I had never took notice of.—

One evening as I sat at work Theander came into my Chamber,
but soe alter'd and an air soe different from his Accustom'd Gaity, I
cou'd not help asking him what hee ail'd. Hee made mee no answer
but chang'd the discourse and wee talk'd of severall indifferent
[things]. Hee paus'd some time, and then with a Disturb'd Countenance and a[n] irresolute Gesture[4] crie'd out, 'Oh madam what
unlook't for misfortune—I Love.'—I burst Out a laughing at the
Serious [air] wherewith hee pronounce'd these words. 'Is this, said I,
soe exstrodinary a misfortune? for my part I don't find you have any
reason to dispair. You[r] estate and person are neither dispiscable
[*sic*] and Your Uncle will, hee declares, make you his heir. But pray
let mee know Who this killing Beauty is.' 'Ah madame, continue'd
hee with a sigh, Phylomont is my persecuter and I must forfeit his
esteem if I refuse Amarante.'[5] 'Hee is indeed (added I Smileing)
very Cruel, to oblige [you] to marry a Lady that has Soe much
wit, good nature and Soe great a Beauty, besides an Heiress great
enough to make her have a 1000 Admirers if She had no other

---

[1] that . . . Strangers] the Beaux Endroits there (H MS 250).

[2] H MS 250 adds 'and all most every Day some or Other force't me to the Aggreable Walks
of the Thuilleries.'

[3] who was Continueally] who when Wee was alone was Continually preaching to me
moderation and (H MS 250).

[4] Disturb'd . . . Gesture] sort of start (H MS 250).

[5] Named, perhaps, from the never-fading flower amaranth; in H MS 250 'Elliorante'.

Accomplishment'—[1] 'But, cry'd hee, I Love, and I Love the most
charming Person in the world. Under Freindship's Specious name I
have till now even from My Self conceal'd my Pasion, but when
Phylomont propos'd this marriage to mee, I found, too Lovely
Indamora, twas no longer in my power and that you alone is Mistriss
of my Destiny. On my refuseing to obey him[2] hee Threatens to dis-
inherrit mee, but madame (continue'd hee) t'is not that causes this
disturbance in my eyes, t'is the fear to displease you with this bold
declaration of a Love it is imposible for mee to conceal, and—'

Here I Hastily Interrupted him (and t'was only my Surprize
hinder'd mee from doing it before), 'I beleive, said I, that this is Only
to show mee what fine things you can say—but Theander such
railleries are very offensive.'—Here hee begun to swear the Sincerity
of his pasion. 'Grant you Speak Truth (added I stopping him), can
you have soe mean thoughts of mee to immagine anny thing Can
make mee forget Cleonidas? No! (said I, pointing to my breast) here
hee still reigns. Therefore Theander (persued I more calmly), forget
this foolish weakness, Obey your Uncle and I'le forget it.' 'Madame
(answer'd hee with a Languishing Air) I can never cease my Love and
your eyes make no Impresions capable to bee efface'd,[3] but I can
cease to Live and soe cease to offend.' Hee withdrew with a Submissive bow.

This Amarante was very Vertuous, witty, fair, rich, and I must
needs say hee sacrifice'd to mee a very Charming Lady, who really
lov'd him, and hee resisted all the threats and Importunitys of
Phylomont. The Lady found (as is usuall) her Love and dispair
Augment together and went into a monastery.[4] Theander never gave
mee any more trouble[5] but his Silent pasion encreas'd soe as to bee
visible to every body. Amestris and his uncle quickly perceiv'd it
while hee Endure'd all a repuls'd Lover is capable of suffring and fell
into a Languishing Distemper which concluded in a feavour which
brought him very low, and tho' the Doctors dispaird not of his recovery hee pleas'd himself with thinking hee shou'd die. Hee told his

---

[1] great enough . . . Accomplishment] vastly rich (H MS 250).

[2] Under Freindship's . . . obey him] yes (continued he) t'is Indamora that I love but I was
ignorant of My Pasion till Palamede talk'd to me of this Lady, then I found my heart was not
my own. I told him soe but Conceal'd the Devine Object of my Flame (H MS 250).

[3] This clause is new in H MS 251.

[4] A word used at this date for religious communities of each sex; H MS 250 reads
'Convent'.

[5] Theander . . . trouble] Altamont spoke Nothing to me (H MS 250).

Aunt and Phylomont (who was continueally at his bed side) the true Cause of his Sickness¹ with Looks that mov'd them Soe much they sent for mee and I went without knowing why they ask't my Company. My freind and her Husband beg'd mee with tears to give their Nephew some hope, and I must own my dear Lindamira the Sight of the poor pale Theander had some effect on mee. I Approach'd his bed weeping and trembling, hee said a thousand Pasionate things to Mee and (in Compliance to Amestris) I desir'd him to Live² and he reply'd hee wou'd for ever obey Mee. To bee short, in a fortnight's time (such prodigious effects has hope) hee was wholly recover'd. What follow'd I'le inform My Dear in my next, resolveing no Longer to defer Saying

> I am ever your most Obedient faithfull
> Indamora.

Letter Fith

Theander (my dearest Lindamira) was no sooner recover'd then hee renew'd his adresses to mee, Amestris and Phylomont joyn'd their prayers with [his],³ this match was very advantagious to mee, and all my Relations beg'd mee to accept of it—I Married him and must own hee was ever Complaisant and Obligeing nor ever gave mee cause to Complain of him.⁴ I pass'd 2 months with great Tranquillity, Theander was Very dear to mee tho' I Lov'd him not with all that Fondness I had done Cleonidas.

Our happiness was Mightily disturb'd at an Accident which exstreamly Trouble'd us. Phylomont dy'd of a pestilental feaver. Hee left us his estate (which I have said was very Considerable). Wee had a great Deal of reason to regret the Loss of soe Tender a relation and wee mingle'd our tears with those of Amestriss. I beg'd her never to Leave us and she Accorded it to my earnest Intreaty.⁵ Theander had business in Holland which oblig'd us to goe thither, but wee had not

---

¹ told . . . his Sickness] accus'd mee of his Death (H MS 250).

² In the code of heroic love, a significant sign of softening: H MS 250 reads, prosaically, 'to take Care of Him-self'.

³ Reading from H MS 250.

⁴ nor ever . . . of him] I do not remember he ever Contradicted me (H MS 250).

⁵ In the earlier version Palamede/Phylomont does not die yet; it is on his business, not that of Indamora's husband, that they go to Holland. The first five sentences of this paragraph replace H MS 250's 'I was of all the Parties of Deversion and pass'd my time very Agreably.'

been at Amsterdam 3 days when going in my Coach with my Aunt[1]
and Woman I saw (oh Amazment) Cleonidas standing at a window.[2]
I, not able to bear Soe great a Surprize, swoonded in Amestris's
Arms.[3] Florimel saw him and not doubting but t'was his Apparition
shreik't out with Violence. My Aunt was all wonder (knowing not
the Cause) but Seeing Mee half dead and wee far from our Lodgings
she resolv'd to have into the first publick house which happen'd to
bee the Cabarette[4] where hee Lodg'd. She had mee Laid upon a bed
without yet my Showing any signs of Life.

(Admire this strange[5] Adventure) t'was his chamber (as the best
in the House) they brought <me> into. I begun to open my eyes
when Cleonidas (who immediately knew mee) Came into the Room.
I was unable to speak and my Woman, perswaded she Saw his Ghost,
run Squaleing under the table, and this had Certainly been a very
pleasant[6] Scene to any uninterested Person. Amestriss was
exstreamly Amaz'd and thought Florimel either possest or distracted. Cleonidas Approach't the bed where I lay, and seeing mee
show Signs of Disturbance, 'How Madame, said hee, have You forgot mee? then would to Heaven I had been Drown'd with the rest of
my poor Freinds—and You Florimel (Said hee, turning to her who
had Now a Little recover'd her fright), have you alsoe No remembrance of the unfortunate Cleonidas?'—Now I begun to See it was
no fantome and wept to know t'was hee. My Aunt perceiv'd the cause
of this Disorder and my woman show'd abundance of Joy for the
safety of that unhappy Lover, who seeing my Tears said 'doe you
greive madame at my Life?'

'No, said I, Trembling, all my vows have been for your happyness
but I beleiv'd you dead, and you are Lost to the wretched Indamora.'[7]
'How, cry'd hee, in the Last you honour'd mee with You inform'd
mee Diphilus and Eurinoe both are dead, who then obstructs my
bliss?'

'A more formidable enemy, reply'd I riseing, Honour hinders mee
from being ever yours.'—[8]

---

[1] Amestris stands in this relation to Indamora by marriage.

[2] H MS 250 adds 'He look't on me with no less Astonishment.'

[3] swoonded . . . Arms] fell half Dead into the Arms of the Amaz'd Dalinda (H MS 250).

[4] Inn.   [5] Admire this strange] See the odeness of this (H MS 250).

[6] i.e. amusing, comic.

[7] doe you greive . . . Indamora] are you then so sorry I am alive? No, I reply'd, I am Sorry
I have for ever lost you (H MS 250).

[8] This splendid riposte and the following sentence are absent in H MS 250.

I Stop't here, haveing not the Courage to proceed farther, and
Florimel continue'd. 'Yes Sir, said she, my Lady ****[1] Is ever Lost
to you.'—

'How,' cry'd hee hastily, 'how did you Call my Love? has she
change'd her name and is she Married—?' At the end of these words
hee Sunk into a Chair[2] and t'was visible how nearly his heart was
touch'd.

Amestris was mute with wonder, I durst not look that Way and ris,
saying faintly, and trembling that I cou'd Scarse Stand, 'Aunt let us
goe.' And that moment leaning on her Arm I went quick into the
Coach and drove home without any of us opening our mouths all
the way.

Theander wonderd to see mee when at home doe nothing but
weep (for I cou'd not command[3] my tears and 'spite of mee the[y]
flow'd), hee ask't mee tenderly what I ail'd and I complain'd of a
Violent pain in my head. I Laid down upon the bed and Lock't the
chamber Door, there t'was (Dear Lindamira) I gave vent to my Sighs
and tears. Amestris said nothing of What had past and my woman
had the discretion to bee Silent. Next morning I saw a Note on my
Toilet derected to mee by a hand I too well knew, I cou'd not forbear[4]
opening it and found these words.

Are you then marry'd madame?—but why doe I fondly ask what I'me too
well asur'd of?—oh Indamora had I but known you was no Longer mine, I
had not Swam to shoar but careless of my Life resign'd it to the fury of the
waves. Curst bee my stars, my self, My fate that sav'd but to distroy mee[5]—
but on My Indamora fall all blessings and bounteous Heaven give her all the
bliss that I must ever want, and oh thou faithless charmer if you can pity
Grant one Interveiw and I'le forget t'is you have ruin'd

Cleonidas.

I had no sooner read these lines then I call'd for Florimel and chid
her for Receiveing this billet (for I guess'd t'was she had Laid it
there) and She confess't his footman Gave it her. I sent for my Aunt,
show'd it her, and how I answer'd it, which was thus.

---

[1] She uses, correctly, Indamora's married name.
[2] Sunk into a Chair] fell against a Chair and had much adoe to hold himself up (H MS
250).
[3] cou'd not command] was not master of (H MS 250).
[4] forbear] resist the Temptation of (H MS 250).
[5] my stars . . . distroy me] the Howr I was saved (H MS 250).

Sir

Your Note caus'd my tears, and had I thought you Liv'd Nothing shou'd
have hinder'd My being ever Yours, and I confess my weakness that t'is not
without doing a force to my self that I refuse to see you,[1]—but I am now another's and I beg you to[2] goe where You may never bee seen by

The too tender
Indamora.

'You are too severe, said Amestris, and you might suffer a Visit without injureing your virtue.' But I persisted in the resolution I had
taken not to see him. I sent that Billet very privately and hee reply'd
hee wou'd Allways obey mee. Next week hee took shiping for England resolving to Lose a life which was no longer dear to him,[3] but
(observe the strangeness of his Destiny) hee was no sooner come to
London then his freinds came to Congratulate his return, saying it
was 3 Days since[4] they had got his pardon and admir'd hee shou'd
bee soe Soon inform'd of it. Hee thank't them but had been better
pleas'd if they had been less importunate. A month after this
Theander dy'd of a Pleuresie which soon rob'd mee of him, I greiv'd
exsesively and staid my year there,[5] and then return'd With Amestris
to my Native Country, Cleonidas renew'd his Adresses and I cou'd
no longer deny to crown the Wishes of so constant a Lover and I
married him with the Consent of all my Relations who aplauded my
Choice and my Lindamira I am entirely happy and have Nothing to
fear but your just displeasure for tireing You with soe tedious a
Letter,[6] and All I have to hope is a pardon for this trouble, which I am
almost asur'd the Goodness of my dearest Lindamira will Grant

To her most faithfull
Indamora.

---

[1] Nothing . . . see you] I never woud have Married but Myrtillo, you may easily immagine
how sorry I am to Refuse your request (H MS 250).

[2] I beg you to] what wou'd it signify Therefore (H MS 250).

[3] Lose a life . . . to him] Dye (H MS 250).

[4] H MS 250 adds 'by their Continuall Importunity' (H MS 250).

[5] A month after . . . year there] A Fort-night after this Palamede fell ill and Dy'd in 5 Days
to Great Greife of us all. He left My Husband his heir, but I had a month after a far Greater
Affliction, for Altamont had a malignant Feavour which quickly kill'd him. I never Stir'd from
his bed side and was exsesively Greiv'd at his Death. He left me Sole Executrix of a Great
Estate. My Aunt and I staid our years out in Holland (H MS 250).

Periods were prescribed for mourning: six months for a sibling, for a husband a year of full
mourning (i.e. wearing entirely black). Cf. below, p. 167.

[6] Letter] Hystory (H MS 250).

The Sultan's Tale

Textual note. This untitled fragment among the Mar and Kellie MSS (Scottish Record Office GD 124/15/1505/1), in MWM's hand (unusually neatly written, in carefully spaced lines), begins with her own ellipsis, and breaks off unfinished. She numbered it twice: at top middle of the pages as 1–[28], and at top right as [24]–52, presumably reflecting its place in a larger whole. On page 1/[24] is noted 'Fragment' (probably in MWM's hand), and '(Ly M. W. M.)' and '(no [?] that pretty)', both in hands other than hers. An attached scrap of paper reads 'Free Edw: Montagu', to mark papers sent franked through the post while Edward Wortley Montagu was a Member of Parliament. EWM sat in Parliament for most of his life, and the handwriting is hard to date. If the reference to Iphigenia targets Elizabeth Chudleigh (p. 25, n. 2 below) then the date is after 1749.

'. . . What stuff, interrupted the Sultan, but pray, Madam, can you who understand, or think you understand every thing, can you tell me the Reason, I mean the natural or supernatural cause of Flowers retaining their Freshness in the Bosom of a Vestal, and fading on that of a married Woman?'

'No really, replied the Sultana Queen,[1] my Philosophy does not reach so far, but common Sense would make me question the Fact, even if dai\<ly\> Experience did not shew the Falsity of it; yet I confess I have often wonder'd and wish'd to know what could give rise to so ridiculous a Saying.'

'Oh mighty ridiculous, to be sure, say'd the Sultan, *Your* common Sense tells you so, because Your \<e\>xperience shews you that all the Nosegays which your Maids of honnor deck themselves with, dye before they have worn them a couple of hours, from whence you are so charitable or so wise as to conclude that the Saying is without Foundation and absurd: others less goodnatured or less incredulous

---

[1] MWM probably means a *Valide Sultan*, or mother of the sultan, who, says Fanny Davis, stood at 'the apex of the harem', her authority extending 'officially over the entire harem and unofficially sometimes far beyond' (*The Ottoman Lady: A Social History from 1718 to 1918* (1986), 1). The gender politics of the story are interestingly complicated if the Sultana and Sultan are mother and son.

might draw another Conclusion[1] from such an observation, but no matter for that, <I> know what I think on't and that's enough for me, <I> am very willing, for the credit of your female Courtiers, that other people should think it only a ridiculous saying, of which, however, I can tell you the Rise, if you please, which I shall not be sorry to do, that once in my Life I may have the pleasure of making you own I knew something you did not. Besides, I have now nothing else to do and am tired of hearing the Vizir's Nonsense,[2] and tho' I don't remember that any of my ancestors condescended to relate a Story themselves, I don't see why I should not set the example of it to my Successors, and I fancy when a Sultan will take the trouble of it, nobody will dispute his doing it better than his Vizir or anybody else; but I shall forget what I have to relate if I don't make haste, for without Vanity, I may say my Memory is very bad and it is allmost a Week since I read the curious Anecdotes I am going to entertain you with, to satisfy your Curiosity, Madam. But I would have you and the Vizir beware of interrupting me, for if once you break the thread of my Narration, I can not promise to go on again, like those who are used to make stories out of their own head: be silent therefore and attend.

'Some Ages ago, the Goddess of Chastity, Diana I think her name is, quite tired with the Din of Juno's Tongue and offended at the scandalous Lives of many of the Gods and Goddesses, resolved to quitt the Skies and visit the Earth for a while; but not to demean herself too much by keeping Company with mere Mortals, she went first to the gardens of Flora, whom some call a terrest[r]ial Goddess, others say she was a mortal and no better than she should be.[3] But no matter for that (only I like to communicate what I know) and be that as it will Diana had a very good opinion of her, was fond of her Company and admired her Gardens, tho' she prefer'd the Woods of [*sic*] to any other Retreat and thither she invited Flora in her Turn, who accepted the Invitation and to shew her Sense of the honnor Diana did her in admitting her into her Company, she cover'd the ground with Primroses and Violetts and a multitude of other Flowers unknown before, and twined the fragrant Woodbine round the Trees, which have perfumed the Air ever since.

[1] That they are not chaste ('married Woman' above is a euphemism).

[2] The vizier was the sultan's chief minister. MWM owned François Petis de la Croix's *Histoire de la Sultane de Perse et des visirs: Contes turcs* (1708) ('Catalogue Lady Mary Wortleys books Packed up to be Sent Abroad July 1739', Wh MS 135).

[3] Flora was Roman goddess of the spring, of flowers, and of youth; sometimes confused with a courtesan of the same name.

'In return for this Favour, Diana prevail'd on her Brother Phoebus[1] to allow some Flowers to open in his Absence, Flora having lamented to her their closing up in the Evenings, the Time that Zephirus generally chose to walk out with her;[2] and not satisfied with only obtaining this Boon for her Friend, Diana promised that for her sake, she would sometimes return to the Skies and would shine on her Parterre[3] from thence for several Nights in every Month of the Year, to render it more agreable and lengthen the time of Zephir's visits. Flora, full of gratitude for such Favours, consulted with him in what manner they could requite them, but being but subordinate Deities nothing in their Power appear'd to them worthy the acceptance of Luna. I suppose you know she's the same with Diana, for I do not affect to shew my learning.

'But to return to Madam Flora, She recollected that Diana had often complain'd to her of the Limitation of her Power in some Things and particularly of her being Lyable to be deceived in her Opinion of her Nimphs and therefore concluded that a Charm that could discover to her their Breach of her Laws, would be extreamly acceptable to the Goddess. She talk'd of it to Zephirus at his next Visitt, which happen'd in a fine moonlight night, at which Time, according to my Author, he was less sensible than he ought to have been of Luna's goodness;[4] he declared to Flora that his Power was not great enough to assist her in so impracticable a scheme and advised her to give it over. But She, either picqued at his refusal, or like the rest of her Sex, more bent on having her will by her Husband's opposing it, exerted all her divine skill and cull'd the choicest Flowers, on which she conferr'd the Virtue of continuing a whole Day in their Bloom if worn by a Virgin but to fade and dye in a few hours if any other presumed to wear them.

'These dread Flowers she presented to Diana, who received it [*sic*] with inexpressible Pleasure and flew with it to Olympus, which was immediately in an uproar upon it. All the Gods but Hymen and Vulcan (who grin'd but shook his head)[5] were displeas'd at this

---

[1] The sister (goddess of the moon) and brother (god of the sun) were Cynthia and Phoebus in Greek, Diana and Apollo in Latin.

[2] Ovid relates how Flora was abducted by Zephyr or Zephirus, the west wind, later her consort (*Fasti*, 5. 209–30).

[3] A formal flower-bed.   [4] That is, less inclined to value chastity.

[5] Hymen as god of marriage and Vulcan as husband to the unfaithful Venus would favour this tool for exposing unchastity; Vulcan uses buffoonery to defuse strife between Jove and Juno at the end of *Iliad*, book 1.

exertion of Flora's Power, which they term'd intolerable Presumption. The Goddesses too were divided about it. Minerva was silent and would not declare her Opinion, dubious as the Commentators say whether the effects would prove good or bad. Juno tho' she envy'd the Present and was vex'd to see it in the Possession of Latona's Daughter, saying with an Ironical Smile the Mother would never have been so thankfull for it; yet she stood up in Flora's Defence, hoping with her assistance to render the failings of Wives as conspicuous as those of Maidens were now likely to be,[1] if Flora's Cause prevail'd. Venus opposed it with all her Might; she pretended this Nosegay was an infringement on her Prerogative, and design'd to abridge her Power.

'Jupiter, for Reasons best known to himself, tho' not hard to be ghess'd at, sided with Venus and gravely told his beloved Daughter, that she ought to be satisfied with the Reputation her Chastity procured her, and content herself with recommending it to others by her example; then order'd her with a stern Countenance to throw away a Nosegay the scent of which was far from gratefull in his Nostrils, and which he forbade her ever to bring up to the Skies again.

'She obey'd with a Sigh, presageing that the Rebuke she now mett with would encourage her Nimphs to swerve from her Laws. Juno seeing the discarded Flowers fall from the Heavens, before they could reach the Earth pronounced a sentence not only to preserve them unhurt but to communicate their Virtue to all others that grew.

'Allarm'd at this and vowing Revenge against Flora, her antient ally, Venus flew down to Paphos,[2] where she made an Edict to forbid any of her Votaries from gathering a Flower, [and] sent out her little Cupids to watch the effects and defeat the Use her Ennemies intended making of the Flowery Tribe. No sooner was the Rumour of their rare Virtue spread over the Earth, than Jealous Bridegrooms presented their future Brides and old Rakes their daughters, with the finest Nosegays, which to many Toasts[3] proved of still worse consequence than killing the Lillies and Roses on their Cheeks, and Those whose Nosegays retain their Freshness became so proud

---

[1] Minerva had her reputation to keep up as goddess of wisdom, and had not been born, but sprung fully armed from Jove's or Jupiter's head. Latona was mother, by Jupiter, of Diana and Apollo. MWM's first juvenile album opens with a poem about her flight from Juno's jealousy (H MS 250, fo. 1; Grundy, 'The Verse of Lady Mary Wortley Montagu: A Critical Edition', Oxford D. Phil. thesis, 1971, 244–5). Juno was a strong patron of marriage.

[2] A town on the island of Cyprus, centre of the worship of Venus.

[3] i.e. beauties who are much toasted.

and overbearing that the Men who rejoiced most in the Discovery, soon wish'd it had never been made.

'Many other Damsels exclaimed against the Injustice of such Suspicions and refused, thro delicacy of Sentiment no doubt, to submit to a Tryal so injurious to their Fame and too ridiculous, they sayd, to be depended upon by any but Fools, for it seems they were of your opinion Madam (bowing to the Sultana, who shrug'd up her Shoulders) and no wonder therefore if they prevail'd and talk'd poor Flora and her Flowers out of Repute. They were every where neglected and exploded; Evergreens took their Place and not a Flower was to be seen except in woods and desart Places,[1] from whence alone any could be had to offer to Flora on her Birthday, which was no longer celebrated but in some remote Country Villages.[2]

'The neglected Goddess saw with Vexation her altars go to Ruin in all the Courts where she was wont to receive Incense; All Nature mourn'd with her and shared her grief, till Diana, who had been the innocent Cause of all her Misfortunes and was forbid by Jupiter to interfere any more in the Affair without Venus's Consent, obtain'd it on condition she should use no Power but that of Persuasion to restore Flora to her former Renown. For this She was obliged to quitt not only the Heavens but her more favourite Woods, and to live some time in the World, where her Eloquence long proved ineffectual.

'At last, in the year——, (for I love to be exact)[3] she came to an Island where the fair Emma kept her Court:[4] this beautifull Princess was a Mirror of all Perfection, a professed Votary of Diana and like the Goddess (who now assumed the shape of one of her favourite Ladies called Bettina) was not only chaste herself but desireous that all the Ladies of her Court, should, if possible, outshine her in this

---

[1] As early as 1685 Sir William Temple declined to advise on growing flowers because they were 'more the ladies' part than the men's' (*Upon the Gardens of Epicurus* (1685), 24). They fell further out of favour with the rise of landscape gardening: at Woburn (bought in 1735 by Philip Southcote, inventor of the *ferme ornée*) the flower-beds were said to 'hurt the eye by their littleness'. Sir William Chambers, who is credited with bringing flowers back into fashion, was an associate of MWM's son-in-law (Laurence Fleming and Alan Gore, *The English Garden* (1979), 106; Derek Clifford, *A History of Garden Design* (1962, 1966), 93, 162–3; Miles Hadfield, *Gardening in Britain* (1960), 199).

[2] MWM may be conflating the Roman festival of Floralia (28 Apr. to 3 May) with English traditions of decking country churches with flowers once a year.

[3] MWM leaves a blank for the crucial date.

[4] The island must surely be Great Britain. Emma's name may come from history (daughter of Richard of Normandy, she married successively Ethelred the Unready and Canute) or from Matthew Prior's *Henry and Emma*, a romantic ballad which so 'charm'd' Lady Mary in youth that she still knew it by heart at 65 (*CL* iii. 68).

Virtue, and nothing was a greater vexation to her than to see how ill her Laws were observed in this particular. What can I do, say'd she one day to Bettina, more than I have done, to preserve both their Virtue and their Reputation? I had once resolved to have none but unmarried Women to attend me, but finding this was attended with some Inconveniencies,[1] I thro' your persuasion allter'd my Resolution and allowed any of them to marry that pleased, tho' you know Dear Bettina with what Reluctance I consented to your being led to Hymen's Altar. This Liberty and your Example will, I hope, keep my Familly free from Pollution and Slander, but the rest of my Court is impure, or may be so for ought I know; why can not I distinguish by their Looks, those who have forfeited their Title to their White Robes? (for such you must know, she obliged them to wear as long as they continued unmarried).

'Diana seiz'd this lucky opportunity of relating the wonderfull Property of Flowers, which she say'd, she had heard from her Grand Mother, a Lady of undoubted Veracity.[2] The Princess was at first as incredulous as some Philosophers[3] of my acquaintance would have been, but after hearing of several experiments which her confident assured her consisted with her own knowledge, she was persuaded by her to have a Parterre made and as soon as the Flowers were in Blow,[4] to institute an Order of unmarried Women,[5] of which the Princess was to be the grand Mistress: the Badge was to be a Nosegay of fresh Flowers, without which, none of the Order was ever to appear at Court.

'I like your Scheme extreamly, say'd the Princess, but—will it be proper for the grand Mistress to wear the Badge too? Certainly Madam replied the counterfeit Bettina, but to distinguish it from the rest, it may be composed only of Flowers of the purest White, such as Lillies and Tuberoses.[6]—Merci cried the Princess, do you want to strike me dead? what head is[7] able to support such strong Scents? I beg pardon, Madam, return'd the frighted Goddess, my own are so strong that I had forgot the Delicacy of your Highness's, but there

---

[1] i.e. love affairs of the unmarried.

[2] Diana's grandmother, mother of Latona, was Phoebe (who confusingly shares one of Diana's names), one of the Titans; but presumably Bettina's human grandmother is meant.

[3] i.e. natural philosophers; scientists.　　　　　　　　　[4] i.e. in bloom.

[5] On the model of the all-male orders of chivalry: the Order of the Bath, for instance, was awarded to Sir Robert Walpole in 1726.

[6] Bulbs grown in warm conditions, with white, scented flowers.

[7] Alternative reading, 'Nerves are'; neither is struck out.

are other Flowers, which, tho' less stately, are of as pure a white and a less offensive smell, the Jessamine for instance—oh as much a Perfume as any—the Lilly of the Valley?—too faint and not of a pure white—the Daisie then and snowdrop—very paultry indeed, answer'd the Princess scornfully. Besides, they are not allways to be had, and what an Indignity would it be for me to appear any one day without the Badge of an order of my own Instituting,—after once I had begun wearing it!

'Bettina who had never seen her Mistress in so bad a humour,[1] began to be affraid she had offended her undesignedly, and that it might overthrow all her Designs in favour of her Friend Flora. After muzing a little she told the Princess, She did not see it was absolutely necessary a grand Mistress should wear any Badge at all. Your Royal Father, Madam, does not wear those of all his Orders, except on great Festivals. Why that's true, replied the Fair Emma with a smile, and if there are any snow Drops to be had at the Time, I could wear them on Flora's Birthday, but let us consult your Husband; he's my Friend and near Relation, you know, for his grand Mother's Father was my great grand Mother's Cousin. I dare trust his Discretion, and if I did not, I know you would, so pray send for him—

'This put the poor Goddess under a new difficulty. The true Bettina whose shape she had assumed, was all this time in the Country with her Husband; to pass upon him for his Wife would have been as easy for Diana as it had formerly been to Jupiter to deceive Alcmena,[2] but it was not agreable to her Principles. For her to disappear and send the Husband without the Wife, she thought not fair to poor Bettina. In this Dilemma a thought occurr'd to the Goddess, which sat [*sic*] all right. She recollected that Pallas at their last Interview had made her a Present of some artificial Flowers of her own work,[3] which no mortal had yet ever seen or heard of and were so well imitated as not to be distinguish'd from natural Ones by any human Eyes. She flew to fetch it and presenting it with all the Art of a court Lady, told[4] a plausible story of the way she came by it and of the impropriety of a Princess's exposing herself to the hazard of her nosegay's fading, which must happen to Diana herself if she sat

---

[1] Emma's chastity here falls under suspicion.
[2] Jupiter came to Alcmena in the form of her husband, Amphitryon, lengthened the night to three times its normal duration, and begot Hercules.
[3] Pallas was patron goddess of arts and crafts.
[4] Alternative 'made' left in place.

up late and the Flowers had been gather'd early, as none had the Priviledge of keeping their Freshness above 24 hours.

'Having thus happilly got over that knotty point (which let me tell you required no small address, in such circumstances) and all Things being settled between the Princess and her Favourite, publick Notice was given of the new Order and as the treacherous Design was not yet known (the Tradition of the wonderfull property of Flowers being entirely lost) all Parents and Guardians of unmarried Ladies and The poor innocent girls themselves hasten'd to make Interest to be admitted into the order of Flora, as it was called. The Princess graciously granted it in the most affable Manner to all who ask'd it, which gain'd her the greatest Applause till after the first drawing Room,[1] where she was surprized at the fading of some young Ladies Nosegays and the lasting Bloom of others, quite contrary to her expectation; but out of the latter the great Number of which gave her much satisfaction, she selected a Partie to sup with her; 'tis true they were many of them so much younger than herself that she could not have much pleasure in their Conversation. This obliged her to declare she did not intend to restrict herself to those of the order and she admitted[2] by Turns all the married Women whose Husbands appear'd satisfied with her Conduct.

'At the first of these Suppers The Princess could not forbear dropping some hint of the Virtue annexd to Flowers and the Secret once getting Vent, soon became publick. For many drawing Rooms no Lady appear'd whose nosegay had been seen to droop, but in a little while, All came as usual and stay'd to the last without one sprig's withering. The Princess and Bettina stared at each other with Looks of amazement, and when they were alone, and talk'd it over, allmost persuaded themselves They had been mistaken in the former day's observation and had doubtless wrong'd many innocent young Ladies. But the next drawing Room made them change that opinion and encreased their Wonder, for not only all the[3] order were there, but many married women with Nosegays as big as Brooms, which remain'd unfaded the whole Evening. The first they had taken notice of was the Lord Adm[ira]l's Wife, at which the Princess burst out o' laughing, nor could Bettina with all her Divinity forbear it; but how great was her Astonishment when in a group of wives, she saw her own that is the true Bettina's Sister, with as blooming a Nosegay and

---

[1] A court reception.   [2] Alternative 'invited' left in place.
[3] Alternative 'those of' left in place.

unconcern'd a look as her young Daughter the lovely Cara. Impatient to know the Mistery, which she suspected Venus to be concern'd [in] contrary to their agreement, Diana or Bettina call'd her Sister into another Room and beg'd of her to tell her the meaning of it, but all she could get from her was that it was a Secret which she had promised not to reveal, but assured her there was no Inchantment in it.

'Diana who was bound by her promise to Venus not to exert her divine Qualities on this occasion, was forced to have recourse to Female Arts alone to find out this Mistery, which was likewise no more than a human Device, as Venus has since protested. After a whole day's Flattery to several Ladies and their Confidents, Diana at last prevailed upon one of them to discover her Friend's Secret. The Story was This. A Young Beauty who had long resisted the Attacks of an [*sic*] Lover and had prided herself on the remarkable Freshness of her Nosegay, was at her Return from Court[1] betrayed into his embraces, from which she no sooner disengaged herself, than, recollecting the Disgrace she was sure of meeting with at the next Drawing Room, she fell into the greatest agonies of grief, and vowed never to appear in publick again till she could do it without fear of Reproach.

'Moved at her distress, the Lover say'd all he could think of to comfort her; marry her he could not, having as many Wives allready as the Law allow'd of, but he assured her he would not rest till he had found out some way to save her Reputation. A little quieted with this Assurance, she composed herself, and pretending a fit of low Spiritts, she shut herself up and would see nobody for a week, during which the pious Lover never ceas'd imploring Venus's Assistance, who answer'd him in a Dream that all she could do for him in this Emergency, was to shew him the materials with which he might deliver his Mistress from the danger he had exposed her to, but must leave the manner of it to his Ingenuity to find out, unless he could get some Friend to assist him. Upon This appear'd a sheet of Tin, a chisel and some other Tools, a vial of Water and a piece of green Silk. When he awoke, he ruminated a great while on this strange Vision, but thought Venus had sent it at her Sons desire to mock his grief and punish him for his many Infidelities.

'To divert the melancholy with which this apprehension fill'd his breast, he went to take a Turn or two in a Temple called the

---

[1] Alternative 'in an unguarded hour' left in place.

Rottunda¹ where many Goddesses were worship'd under Various Forms. There he met with the fair Iphigenia, so celebrated for the Interpretation of Dreams that some thought her an Inchantress:² he ran to her and beg'd of her to explain his, for old acquaintance sake, which she generously did without insisting to know the Lady's³ Name and bade him bring her such materials as he had seen in his Vision, of which (the Tin) she soon made a flat kind of Vase, to which she gave the name of garde fleurs,⁴ poured as much Water in it as would keep a nosegay fresh 24 hours and cover'd it so artfully with the green silk that it look'd like the stalks of the Flowers.

'With this he ran to his Mistress, who hook'd it on her stomacher and hasten'd to make a Tryal of it at an Assembly which she had luckily been invited to that very evening: the Success proving answerable to her wishes, she appear'd with it the next day at Court in high Spiritts and with equal Success, and being extreamly good natured, She in a day or two communicated this valuable Discovery to a dozen or two of her intimate Friends, to whom she thought it might be of use, tho' she was too well bred to hint any such thing and too prudent to trust them with her own Secret. She was no Fool you see, and she soon persuaded her Friends, that for all the Fuss the Princess made about Flowers, their effect was not owing to any occult quality in them but to some charm which she had and bestow'd only on her Favourites, that she might have a Pretense to exclude all others from her private Parties. She did not pretend to know what the Charm was, nor did not desire it, for Flora had reveal'd to her in a Dream the best and surest way of preserving Flowers from fading, which she was glad to oblige them with, having got some Vazes, but added she, to mortify the Princess and her Favourites thouroughly, I wish we

¹ The low-domed, symmetrical shape of the Roman Pantheon and other ancient temples was copied in Andrea Palladio's Villa Rotonda (1566–7), in Lord Burlington's Chiswick House near London, and in the Rotunda in Ranelagh gardens, opened 1742.

² Iphigenia, sacrificed by her father Agamemnon, was miraculously preserved in one version of the myth, and became priestess to Artemis/Diana, indistinguishable from the goddess. But this would put her on the wrong side in this story. Elizabeth Chudleigh (1720–88), later mistress to MWM's nephew the 2nd Duke of Kingston and a fitting patron of extramarital love, made a sensational appearance as Iphigenia at Ranelagh on 1 May 1749.

³ Alternative 'his Mistress's' left in place.

⁴ After this phrase, three lines at the bottom of the page are left blank. I have not found the word 'garde-fleurs' in either English or French, though French portraits from the 1730s show fresh posies being worn. By the 1750s an object holding 'bosom-flowers', called a 'bosom-bottle', was worn tucked into 'a pocket made in the top of the stomacher [the garment visible under the lacing of the bodice], between the breasts' (information from Aileen Ribeiro; Doreen Yarwood, *The Encyclopaedia of World Costume* (1978), 47).

could persuade all the married women of our Acquaintance to follow this Fashion and keep the Secret.

'The undertaking would no doubt have proved fruitless in our Country, but the Women of that Island were remarkable, says the Commentator, for their Secresy, which renders what I before told you less incredible, that only one of the number was overcome by Diana's Flattery, who as soon as she had learnt the Secret which had so much excited her chaste Goddesship's Curiosity, flew to the Princess and discover'd it to her with all the particulars she had heard of the whole Story, and concluded with assuring her that if she would once more follow her Advice she would have the pleasure of seeing their Antagonists punish'd and brought to open Shame. The Princess say'd she would be guided by her Counsels and accordingly a Ball was appointed and every body invited without distinction or mention of the Nosegays, there being no fear that any Lady would now come without them, as they had got so infaillible a way of preserving them, unknown as they thought, to the Princess and her Favourites.

'The malicious Diana, for I will not now call her Bettina who was innocent and ignorant of all these Artifices, Diana I say had industriously spread a report that there was to be a most extraordinary [*sic*] Waterwork or firework, some say'd the one and some the other, play'd off in the garden after the Ball, which occasion'd the gardefleurs being filld fuller of water than usual, as the entertainment was to last so long, and made the Ladies[1] extreamly impatient for <t>he last Dance. The Princess say'd she would lead it up her self and desired all the Women to do every step exactly as she did, which they punctually obey'd. The Beginning was solemn and nothing but minuet steps; then a little brisker and some gentle pas de Rigaudons,[2] but at the close the Princess cut such a Caper as she had never been seen to do and all striving to outdo her, particularly those who bore the gardefleurs, the Water spurted out and form'd the most diverting Jets d'eaux[3] that can be imagined and the disconcerted Damsels who had trusted their Reputation to this new Device had as much water thrown by it into their Faces as might have recover'd 'em out of a Sound,[4] if their Fright had put them into one, and many had their eyes allmost put out by it for some minutes.

'The Princess and her Confident put on Looks of Astonishment

---

[1] Alternative 'company' left in place.

[2] The rigadoon, as it was generally called in England, originated in France with Isaac Rigadon.   [3] Fountains.   [4] Alternative 'Swoon' left in place.

and concern and with an officious kindness enquired of all the drip-
ping Sufferers, who look'd like so many Naiads,[1] what could be the
Cause of their Disaster and whence the Water had sprung. Some
pretended they had a smelling Bottle in their hand with some kind of
Water for the head ach and that the stopper had flown out; others
that they had been seiz'd with a violent fit of sneezing, and many
such pittyfull excuses, but Bettina's Sister who never could disguise
the Truth and now thought herself disengaged from her Promise of
Secresy in an Affair which she had been drawn into unawares, declared the whole Mistery and pulled out the wonderfull Engine from
her Breast. The Princess smiled and soon observing many of the
Nosegays to be dying, which she had the goodnature to say was no
wonder after such a Dance and wonder'd how any had stood it, She
carried the Company into the Garden, (while the Rooms were a dry-
ing) and began to gather fresh Flowers for those who wanted them
and to present at Flora's Statue, who to their inexpressible Surprize
appear'd in Person and with a sweet but rather melancholy Countenance declared that Jupiter had decreed She should be adored in every
Garden of the Island, but had in effect taken from Flowers the Virtue
they were before endowed with and which had caused so much Disturbance, for he had now order'd that none should presume to wear
a Nosegay without any gardefleurs, under Penalty of appear<ing>
old and ugly or being thought a Prude, and that to appease Venus,
he had also given her leave to reward her greatest Favourite and to
punish her bitterest Foe, of which they would soon see the effects;
but that he had granted the same Priviledge to the chaste Diana.

'At these words all trembled and turning to Bettina, whom they
expected to see fall a Sacrifice to the rage of Vulcan's wife, could
hardly believe her [*sic*] Eyes when they knew her to be Diana and saw
her gradually assuming the Goddess's Person and Dress. The Wings
of her Cap turning up form'd a Crescent; her mouchoir[2] was
changed into a deerskin Mantle and her Fan into a Bow; her hoop
drop'd off and became a triumphal Carr; two of her lapdogs were
transform'd into milk white Stags. Before she took her leave of the
Court, She recommended the faithfull Bettina to the Princess,
assuring her that as long as she continued to favour her and follow
her Counsels, she might depend on the Love of all who approach'd
her. On the Princess she conferr'd, with a gardefleurs of the finest
Diamonds, the Gift of charming all her hearers, and after [. . .]'

[1] Water-nymphs.   [2] Handkerchief.

Court Tales I
Mademoiselle de Condé

Textual note. H MS 78, fos. 11–12; 80, fos. 386–7, 382–4, 379–81. The sequence of the story provides the page-order. The two leaves of dedication, H MS 78, fos. 11–12 (written, like the rest, in MWM's mature hand), look like an actual letter. I have supplied the accent on 'Condé' where MWM (occasionally) omits it.

You will be surpriz'd my dear Mademoiselle[1] after so long having taken Leave of Follys of this nature, that I return to the little Amusements of my Childhood. But I am alone, tis ill weather that I can find no Diversion abroad,[2] and tis necessary for me to make some to my selfe, or my melancholy, which you know to be too reasonable, would not fail to throw me into an ill state of Health, which must always be an addition to any Misfortunes. I find these little works of fancy employ my thoughts more, than any triffling Book, and I would not indulge my selfe in being too attentive on a serious one. I chuse to dedicate my follys to you, since I know you have the good sense not to expose them.

The Prince of Condé is [*sic*] one of the most considerable of the Royal Family of France;[3] he had the sentiments worthy of his Birth, and was scrupulously affraid of the conduct of his children. But

---

[1] While living at Avignon MWM had addressed a letter in French to the Dutch scholar Anna Maria van Schurman as 'Mademoiselle' (*E&P* 165–7). Nevertheless her addressee here must be Anne-Marie-Louise d'Orléans, duchesse de Montpensier (1627–93), 'La Grande Mademoiselle'. She exemplified the 17th-century 'femme forte', wearing male dress as a leader of the Fronde. In exile she formed a writing coterie, producing *Nouvelles françaises, ou Les Divertissements de la princesse Aurélie* (1656) (together with her 'scribe' Jean Regnault de Segrais), and her own *Memoires* (pub. 1728). MWM owned both (Joan DeJean, *Tender Geographies: Women and the Origins of the Novel in France* (1991), 28–9, 37, 52; Wh MS 135). Suitors for Mademoiselle included each contemporary prince de Condé (father and son). She visited England in 1685, and was the heroine of Marie Madeleine de Lafayette's tale *La Princesse de Montpensier* (1662).

[2] This suggests 1746–56, her years in North Italy.

[3] MWM plays fast and loose (presumably by intention) with historical fact, writing of an imaginary prince de Condé. 'Le Grand Condé' (Louis II de Bourbon, 1621–86) died before the events of this story (set in the 1690s, see p. 33 n. 1 below). His son Henri-Jules de Bourbon (1643–1709) was known as duc d'Enghien during his father's lifetime, and had daughters; but his son (Louis III, 1668–1710) was never known as duc d'Enghien; and *his* son (Louis-Henri, 1692–1740) was born too late to fit.

Love has no regard to the Distinctions of Fortune, and those Young Princesses was [*sic*] not inexorable because they were great.[1] It was indeed a considerable peice of temerity in Monsieur Fontenelle to lift his Eyes that way.[2] But when he met those of Mademoiselle Condé he saw something so soft and inexpressibly charming he had reason to apprehend his presumption would bring him death from her Hand. It was far remov'd from the Prince of Condé's imagination that he was capable of a thought so presumeing. Monseiur Fontenelle had no Advantages of Birth or Fortune, his Admirable Pastorals had introduce'd him with successe to Madame the Dauphine who he celebrates under the Name of Victoria; her favour made him well look'd upon at Court, and procur'd him the Glory of being chose of the Academy;[3] his agreable Wit made him the Delight of those capable of tasting . . .[4]

. . . perswaded that she had wholly overcome her Passion, and extreamly satisfy'd with her own strength of Mind. Next day Letters came from Versailles. Mademoiselle de Condé saw with surprize a Letter directed to her in an unknown hand. She open'd it the first, and was yet more surpriz'd at these words in the cover.

[1] Of the daughters of Henri-Jules, prince de Condé from 1686, Marie-Thérèse (1666–1732) married (1688) her cousin François-Louis, prince de Conti; Anne-Marie-Victoire, Mlle de Condé (1675–1700), died unmarried; Anne-Louise-Bénédicte, Mlle de Charolais (1676–1753), noted for intellectual brilliance and recklessness, married (1692) the duc de Maine; Marie-Anne, Mlle de Montmorency (1678–1718), married (1710) Louis Joseph, duc de Vendôme. MWM mentions her heroine's marriage (below, p. 41), but gives her the title of the only sister not to marry.

[2] There is no record of any such temerity by Bernard le Bovier de Fontenelle (1657–1757). He frequented court circles (not always harmoniously), had various affairs, and translated a Latin poem in praise of Le Grand Condé in 1676. He wrote of himself, 'il aimait les plaisirs, mais point comme les autres. Il était passionné, mais autrement que tout le monde. Il était tendre, mais à sa manière' (Alain Niderst, *Fontenelle à la recherche de lui-même (1657–1702)* (1972), 58, 68, 136–7). Letter 4 in his rakish *Lettres galantes* (1683) advocates choosing a woman for physical beauty, not noble blood. MWM's lover Algarotti was later judged to have attempted for Italian thought what Fontenelle had done for the French (Enea Balman, 'Fontenelle en Italie', in Alain Niderst and Jean Mesnard (eds.), *Fontenelle: Actes du colloque tenu à Rouen du 6 au 10 octobre 1987* (1989), 586).

[3] Fontenelle was presented in 1686 or 1687 to the dauphine, Victoire de Bavière, who was a polyglot reader of novels and poetry. On arrival in France she had been snubbed by the King for trying to play a political role, and perhaps persecuted by Mme de Maintenon. Fontenelle wrote an eclogue to her and celebrated her and her husband in an opera, *Énone*, in 1688, the year also of his *Poésies pastorales* (which MWM owned in an edition of 1698). The dauphine intervened in his favour when the Academy rejected him (he was elected in 1691), and wrote words to his music (Wh MS 135; Niderst, *Fontenelle à la recherche*, 339–40).

[4] Part of the story has been lost between H MS 78, fo. 12, and H MS 80, fo. 386: ellipses editorial.

Open me alone.

She blush'd, she was pleas'd, she did not doubt she was going to hear from monsieur Fontenelle, and made haste to her closet where opening it with precipitation she found these words.

> Why Albisinda would your Eyes
> So slight a Conquest make?
> Why wound a Heart you must despise
> And which dispair must break?

Charm'd with these lines which she knew to be his hand, she forgot all the lectures of Seneca,[1] she forgot the Princesse,[2] she forgot every thing, only to remember she lov'd and was belov'd by the most lovely of his Sex. She never debated whither she ought to answer it, but with a mixture of Joy and Fear writ the dictates of a young lovesick Heart in these words.

> Cease to persue a triffling Heart
> You may with Ease deceive.
> Young and unskill'd, I know no Art,
> But what I wish, beleive.

Monseiur Fontenelle, who writ allmost against his Will, compell'd by an invincible power, had no sooner sent his Letter but he repented of that temerity a thousand times, and was thinking of what submission, what excuse to form for his madness, when he receiv'd this favourable Answer. I can not pretend to represent what he felt at that minute, or repeat his Soliloquys on this Occasion. He thought his Happyness too great to be real, and after his first transports were over, industrious to lessen his pleasure, he begun to fear mademoiselle de Condé entertain'd him in sport, and perhaps only meant a diversion in her present Solitude by his Passion. This thought cut him to the Soul, which thô he sometimes rejected as too injurious to her, yet it perplex'd him so much he knew not what to write, which at last he did in this confus'd manner.

Could you see me at this time, I know not whither Mirth or pity would first rise in your breast. If I could express what I feel it would be unworthy of you, and (give me leave to say it) of me. If I could see you, the Eyes come the nearest to explain the Heart, thô even they can but imperfectly represent

---

[1]   Mademoiselle de Condé must have been presented, in the part of the story now missing, as learned. MWM owned an edition of *Seneca's Morals Abstracted*, i.e. by Roger L'Estrange.

[2]   i.e. forgot she was a princess.

my thoughts—I would neither write uninttelligibly nor obscurely, yet I am forc'd upon both, but I hope I am understood—you are not one that can deceive me. When I refflect on my selfe I mistrust every thing, but when I think of you, I dare beleive even impossibillitys. I can forget my selfe to think of you, O make me allways do so, Let me ever be lost in this sweet dream of transporting Joy, and expressless Gratitude.

I know not but this Letter may seem very unworthy the Author of the Poesie Pastorals, and the Dialogues to the Dead,[1] but Mr Fontenelle was not now endeavouring at applause but expressing Sentiments which were too passionate, and too sincere to be capable of the Ornaments of Art. The Princesse was more pleas'd at these undoubted marks of her Lovers sincerity than she could have been with any Flourishes of his wit. Whatever some people imagine, in Love, Love only ought to speak. She had not been without repentance after her short kind billet. That Modesty so natural to her sex, and so powerfull in those well born, reproach'd her easynesse, and gave her all those severe corrections she might have expected from the Prince, her Father. She could not resolve, to cease this delightfull Correspondance, or resign a Heart of more value to her, than all the Crowns upon Earth, but this Letter of his seem'd to give her a Hint to save her modesty and yet preserve his tenderness. She determin'd to affect an Air of raillery in her Answer, that might not either break off with him, or confess her Love.

I am very sensible I offend at this minute against the rules of custom, but I am not conscious of any Intention that should make me condemn my own manner of proceeding. I desire nothing more, nor will think of no farther engagement, than that of Freindship. Let this freindship of ours be unattended with those passions that serve only to render a commerce tiresome and displeasing. I am not so unreasonable to desire that you should have no Goddesse of your Poems; I would only have some small share of your esteem. These are at present my thoughts, and I hope there is nothing dangerous in wishing the Freindship of a Man whose merit I am (I fear) too sensible of—this fear makes me tremble, without well knowing why. Alas, must I renounce so innocent a pleasure or run the risque of all my repose?

The last words of this Letter restor'd Monsieur Fontenelle all the easyness that he lost at the light beginning of it, and he answer'd in these Lines—

---

[1] The *Dialogues des morts* appeared in 1683; MWM owned *Nouveaux Dialogues des morts* (1st pub. 1694).

How happy they that can their passions chuse,
And Love or Freindship, proffer, or refuse:
How easy, and how cautious is that Heart
Which ere resolv'd to meet, forecasts to part!
Where such Indifference or such care appears
How needless, Albisinda, are your Fears!
Esteem you say, is all you must approve,
You dare no more; nor can I less than Love.

After raising my Hopes, why will you again sink them? am I guilty of any thing to deserve this cruel usage? can you make sport with the most ardent passion in the world? I am every other way unworthy of you. I know you are a Princess. What is far more considerable, you have a wit and Beauty that perhaps never met before. I have no merit to plead, but I have [a] heart fill'd with truth, that adores you, and only You, nor can never fall so low, as any other object.

Thô the letters of Monseiur Fontenelle and Mlle de Condé can never be tedious to the reader, yet I can give no more of them, the rest having never come to my hands.

This is certain, before mademoiselle return'd to Court he had the pleasure of so far overcoming her scruples, he had leave to Love, to tell it, and to believe that she was not wholly unmov'd by it. When the young Princesses return'd to Versailles, their first visit was from the Prince.[1]

This took up great suspicions of the Intteligence between her and Monseiur Fontenele, and being determin'd to know the Truth, he pretended a great Freindship for him, which was so well acted that with all his Wit, he did not discover the snare under it. During the Absence of Mademoiselle it was easy for a man of the Duke's experience,[2] to remark a certain negligence in Monsieur Fontenelle, and after her return a new Air of Sprightlynesse that diffus'd it selfe over his whole person. To be better assur'd, he often prais'd him before his sister, brought him to sup with her, and with all their premeditated

---

[1] Fo. 387 ends here; if something is missing before fo. 382, then the Prince is (as above) Mademoiselle de Condé's father. If the story proceeds without a break, then 'the Prince' and 'This' refer to her brother, the duc d'Enghien.

[2] The likeliest candidate as MWM's duc d'Enghien is Louis III (1668–1710), who never bore that title. He was also (like his father) ugly and malevolent, with none of the magnetism MWM depicts (Anne-Marie-Louise de Montpensier, *Mémoires* (repr. 1985), ii. 191; Vita Sackville-West, *Daughter of France: . . . La Grande Mademoiselle* (1959), 68; Eveline Godley, *The Great Condé: A Life of Louis II de Bourbon, Prince of Condé* (1915), 587). The nearest relative to exhibit these characteristics at this time was a cousin, François-Louis (1664–1709), who became prince de *Conti* in 1685.

Discretion, he needed not much observation to perceive the Mutual Love between them. Who having now overcome all their Fears, enjoy'd the Pleasure of the most perfect union of 2 inttelligent minds. The Princesse (as by degrees a Woman in Love is brought to say any thing) confess'd she Lov'd. Transported with the dear confession, his passion redoubled with his Pleasures and twas in these happy hours he writ the Opera of Diana and Endimion, where he described the growth and success of his own presumptious Love.[1] This opera which was universally admir'd as one of his best peices, pass'd at Paris as the Effect of a lively imagination beautifully express'd, but the Duke of Enguien made no doubt who was the Diana of the Opera, and saw in every Line the transports of a happy Lover. He waited only for some proof that he might produce to his Father to ruin them both.

Charlot was the most belov'd of the princesse's Women. She had wit and address and a share of Beauty that render'd her very agreable. The Duke of Enguien did not doubt she knew all the secrets of her mistrisse, and attempted her Fidelity by flattery and magnificent presents. But it was impossible for him to make her accept of any Jewels, she refus'd all, and he observ'd she never made the least hesitation in her refusal; but when he proffer'd, (as what he call'd a mark of his freindship) his own picture enchas'd in Brilliants, she return'd it, but with a sigh that shew'd her reluctance. 'Beautifull Charlot (said the artific[i]al Prince, who immediately saw into her heart), in what have I offended you, that you will keep nothing for my sake? I ask your pardon in pretending to attack your heart, like that of another Woman. Alas, I did not then know its value. Permit me to make you a present not alltogether unworthy your acceptance, 'tis a heart wounded by your Eyes, and that will be yours for ever.'

Poor Charlot, who had not regarded his complements and presents while she thought he sought only to know what the Princesse had intrusted her, was easily perswaded to believe them an Effect of her Charms, and in a short time he triumph'd over at once her chastity and Fidelity. Tis a rule without an exception, after a Woman has once given a man a certain Favour she refuses him nothing. Without examining the reasons of his Curiosity, she put into his hands the Billets of Mademoiselle de Condé and Monseiur Fontenelle, and

---

[1] Fontenelle's heroic pastoral *Endymion* was composed in 1692, published in 1698: called in MS *Diane et Endymion*. In it Amour says that as Diana once favoured Endymion, so a young beauty today will be pleased by a shepherd (Niderst, *Fontenelle à la recherche*, 419).

betray'd a mistriss to whom she ow'd every thing. He chose the most passionate amongst those of his sisters writeing, and enclos'd it in these Lines writ by an unknown hand to the Prince of Condé.

My Lord,
   tis with a great deal of Displeasure I send your R[oyal] H[ighness] this Letter of Mademoiselle de Condé, yet my passion for your service would not suffer me to conceal it.

I am my Lord &c

It is impossible to express the Surprize of the Prince of Condé. He would fain believe this some artifice to trouble his repose, but he fear'd the hand could not be so exactly counterfeited; he felt all that an affronted haughty mind could suffer from indignation, and a fathers tendernesse could feel for an erring child. He sent for Mademoiselle de Condé, who was at that very time in her Closet writeing to Monseiur Fontenelle. She came into his Apartment with her usual Gaity, but what did she think when without speaking he presented to her the fatal Letter? Perhaps, had she been able to have look'd upon it with an affected surprize, and read it over without concern, he might have been perswaded it had been a Counterfeit, but her concern was real, her astonishment was beyond disguise. She no sooner cast Eyes upon the Letter, but she fell back into a swoon, which was very far from moving the compassion of the Prince her Father. Confirm'd in all his Suspicions he scarce restrain'd his passion from putting an end to her Life, which in her present misery would hardly have been cruel.

She was carry'd halfe dead upon her Bed, where she tore off her beautifull Hair in a rage of Greife approaching to distraction. The Prince having orderd her Women to leave the room, came near the Bed. 'Infamous wretch (said he in a furious Tone), what expiation canst thou make? to what Dishonnour hast thou expos'd the house of Bourbon? what fellow have you pick'd out? tell me his name, that at least his Blood may satisfy my resentment, and assure the secret. Tell it me, or you shall suffer the death I prepare for him—'

I admire how mademoiselle outliv'd the hearing of these words. The very idea of monsieur Fontenelle, the Lovely, the Innocent Mr Fontenelle suffering for her, fill'd her Heart with that Horror, she took up a resolution of suffering all things rather than betraying him. What she? she betray him, doom him to death in Whom alone she liv'd?—Fortify'd by these thoughts, she made no answer to the rage of the Prince of Condé, but throwing her selfe at his feet, 'I am ready to die Sir,' said she wetting the Floor with her tears. Enrag'd by this Answer, 'tis possible he had put his threats in execution, if the Duke D'Enguien her Brother had not enter'd, whose advice he resolv'd to take in an affair of that Importance.

He shew'd him the Letter. The Duke, who came prepar'd with arguments to moderate the resentment of his Father, represented to him, that silence and secrecy were the best Guardians of Women's honnour, and the blood of a man upon that occassion stains for ever that Reputation for which it is shed. He spoke with so much reason, he calm'd the transports of the Prince of Condé, especially with a promise that he would find a way of punishing the offender perhaps more cruelly than by Death. Depending on this promise he pass'd into the Garden, and left the Duke to return to his Sister. He threw himselfe on the bed by her with a great appearance of tenderness. 'My dear sister (said he) I am sensibly touch'd with your misfortune, and thô it is entirely proper you should never more see monseiur Fontenelle yet—'

This word struck mademoiselle de Condé to the Heart. She burst into yet more violent weepings. 'By whatever Secret you have found his name (said she allmost in agonys of passion), if you would save my Life Brother, if you would not see me dye, dye miserable and in tortures, do not disclose that name, do not expose that poor unhappy Youth to the Resentment of my cruel father. Let me conjure you, pity your Sister, pity my youth, pity my wretched passion. We are allready miserable in this hopeless Love, now lost to all our Innocent endearments. Does there need any Accumulation of misery? yet if your cruel Honnour, your inhuman Pride is not satisfy'd with the Sacrifice of all our Happynesse, in an eternal Separation, if only Blood can attone your savage rage, satiate your selfe with mine, strike this breast which I make bare to your Sword, plunge it into my bosom, and know that I, alone, am guilty. I lov'd Monseiur Fontenelle, I did not wait his courtship, but follow'd him with mine. His obligations to my Father and to you, were powerfull enough in his Gennerous gratefull mind to resist my first Efforts. At length he yeilded, he yeilded to be my Lover, or rather, he made civil answers to the extravagancys my passion inspir'd me with.' The Duke of Enguien, who knew from Charlot the whole progress of the Intrigue, stood astonish'd at this new and wonderfull Effect of Love in his Sister, which I believe the first and last instance of a Woman, who not only expos'd her Life to save her Lover's, but her Honnour and that in a point in which all women are tenacious: that she would be willing to be thought the Pursuer, and her Charms not only neglected but slighted, instead of excusing her frailty as another would have done, by the weakness of her Youth, and the force of his Solicitations.

The Duke of Enguien found his vanity touch'd that any man but himselfe should be capable of inspiring such delicate sentiments, and Interrupted her as soon as her impetuosity would give him leave. 'It depends wholly on you sister whether I ever disclose his name (return'd the Duke), there is a condition, by which you may make me swear never to disclose it, nor shall he himselfe ever have the pain to believe I have discover'd it.'—Mademoiselle was very attentive, and he went on, 'Since your Indiscretion (I will not speak more harshly) has thus given occassion to his vanity to think he was belov'd by you, You must retreive your Honnour in his opinion by a Letter to tell him, that you have only diverted your selfe with his Folly, and are now grown weary of a Jest that is no longer new to you. I will write such a Letter which you shall copy and send to him. Nothing else can save his Life, for I would not suffer a man to live that could think you capable of so low a thought.'

Mademoiselle, who was prepar'd to consent to any condition for the safety of monseiur Fontenelle, melted into Tears at the hearing of this. The Duke D'Enguien did not expect an Immediate answer, and saying 'Well sister, I leave you to consider of it,' left the room, and sent Charlot to her. Poor mademoiselle with a Heart oppress'd with Griefe, pour'd all her thoughts into the bosom of this false Creature. 'Ah my Charlot (said she), what shall I do? Good Heaven, can I renounce my vows with my own hand? tell him, I've triffle'd with his honest heart! can I write this, with the same hand, that swore eternal Truth? when he shew'd any doubt, how have I invok'd the saints to wittness for my Soul? how have I vow'd, and reproach'd his Incredulity? till he has quite forgot his fears, lull'd and secure and easy of my Faith—Can I abandonn, not only abandon his Esteem, that confidence, that value for me which I even prefer'd to his passion, but be contemn'd and loath'd! contemn'd by him! Oh, I can never bear it—but can I bear to see him pale and cold, and know then when I see him dead, know I might have prevented the inhumane blow!—No, let me rather write any thing—Yet, this way I kill him too. Ah Charlot, you know not how he loves me! I have seen him gaze

'till tears have falln from his eyes! Then that respectfull passion!
his Love in all its transports one severe look would moderate,
would throw him trembling at my feet, and when excess of Fond
Desire hurry'd him on to ask what I not dar'd to grant, even then he'd
tremble with submissive Fears, shrink from the <?feirce> resentment of my frowns,[1] fall at my Feet, and weep away my anger—'

Mademoiselle de Condé had proceeded in her transports, if
Charlot had not begun the artifice she was sent in for. 'You know
Madam (said she forceing out some false tears), I am wholly devoted
to your highnesse. Oblige monseiur the Duke, and write the Letter.
You may let Mr Fontenelle understand by another, that force you
was under, and I will take care to convey it.'

I won't say this proposal appear'd to Mademoiselle like a twig to
catch at, to a man drowning, because tis a simile so constantly us'd
on these occasions, but like a door to get out of, in a room on fire.

The Duke of Enguien came in presently with the letter which he
had form'd in these words.

I will not be so injurious to your wit, Monseiur, to suppose that with all my
endeavors I have deceiv'd you, but I begin to grow weary of this diversion.
Thô your Letters are very entertaining, let me have no more of them, and
return all mine. I don't doubt you understand better than to think there was
any thing serious in this innocent peice of raillery.

What were Monseiur Fontenelle's thoughts when he receiv'd this
letter copy'd out in the hand of Mademoiselle! The perfidious sent
it, and kept back the other writ by her unhappy Lady. He read it over
several times without being able to believe it was her hand, he turn'd
the words to every seeming sense, to try to deceive himselfe. At
length confirm'd (as he thought) in his misfortune he fell back into
his chair with the Letter in his hand, without speaking one Word.
His Valet de Chambre came into the room and seeing his master pale,
and seemingly faint, undress'd and put him to bed, which he suffer'd
without resistance, or makeing any Answer to his repeated asking
him how he did.

There he had full Leisure to think over his misfortunes. When he
refflected on the youth and Quality of Mademoiselle de Bourbon,
this falsehood was too unnatural to her youth, too base and low for
her Birth. He recollected all the innocent marks of her unaffected
fondnesse, the soft Encourragement of her Glances, that tender

[1] MWM added later these eight words, making one of several iambic pentameters.

inimitable concern in her Lovely Eyes not to be Counterfeited. All these instances of Truth, would have perswaded him, twas impossible it could be all design, a barbarous design of makeing miserable a Man that doated on her. He read again the Letter, he compar'd it to her others and saw too well there was no difference in the Characters. After passing a Night in Agitations not to be describ'd, suffering all that Love, and greife, could do to oppresse the tenderest and most sensible Heart, he writ in the Morning this Letter.

Yes Madam you have deceiv'd me. I own my folly. In spite of the Vast distance between us, in spite of the little merit of a Man who has nothing irreproachable but his honnour, thô I know Fortune has plac'd me in a condition to be the Object of your Mirth, thô I knew all this, I was deceiv'd. I thought it possible that you might look with pity on my passion, which never had offended you, but you, how artfully you tore the secret from my bleeding heart, expos'd its inmost weaknesse to your Veiw. Even then I should have refflected how improbable it was for me to please the greatest and the fairest princesse upon Earth. I did refflect upon it, I did not act without my reason, but against it.—You are now grown weary—Good God!

　　Here Madam are your Letters. Tis certain I am so much yours, you may treat me as you please. This cruel, this Perfidious, still is charming, still mademoiselle de Condé, and Oh forgive my breaking Heart, forgive the Insolence, I still must love you. I must remember there was a time, great and Royal as you are, you suffer'd me to tell you so without a frown. Then (As my last words I swear it) I swear that Royalty and greatnesse was no charm to me. This Fontenelle, this wretch so much below you, was not to be mov'd by shew or titles. It was that Beauty, that artlesse natural Wit, that dear engageing Innocence enslav'd my heart, and now—Oh Princesse, why did you force the fond confession from my torture'd Soul? Thô I had dy'd, I had dy'd without reproaching my selfe of Vanity or an unbecoming Boldnesse, and witnesse Heaven I had resolv'd to dye, without disclosing the secret cause, but you would have it thus.—How have I deserv'd it? Even to your selfe with all your Cruelty, I dare appeal, if all my Madnesse, all the Ensnareing oppertunitys you gave me, then when you fann'd my flame to fury, could produce one Action in which I did not ever shew, that my first care was you, and the highest Satisfaction that I aim'd at, pleasing you. Did this respect deserve—

　　But oh, no more. It is your pleasure, and I will not murmur. I will not tell you what I suffer. May your highnesse blesse some Prince whose Greatnesse and whose Virtue may deserve you, may you live long and happy, and may death soon close the Eyes of the unhappy

Fontenelle.

Monsieur Fontenelle made up this Letter in a pacquet with those he had receiv'd from the princesse, and gave them to his most intimate Freind, directed to Charlotte with orders not to send it, till he had left the Kingdom, which he did as soon as it was possible, abandonning the fair Veiws he had of makeing his fortune, his Interest at Court, his Freinds and Reputation, and went to finish his Life in the Solitudes of America where some of his Relations were establish'd,[1] secure of lesse barbarity amongst Savages than (he thought) he had met with in the fairest princesse of France.

Charlot deliver'd the Pacquet to the Duke D'Enguien but his Revenge had not been compleat, if he had not caus'd it to be deliver'd to his sister. She saw thus at one Veiw, the Perfidy of her Confidante, and the irreparable losse of her belov'd Lover. No Expression can come up to what she felt. She knew not how to convey a Letter to him. Would she venture one to New France, (which was very hazardous) all her servants were spys, and she knew they would carry any letter they should be trusted with, to the Prince of Condé. Yet she resolv'd to write thô she was forc'd to burn it afterwards. She sat down in her Closet, her Eyes halfe blind with weeping, in a confus'd Character these words flowing from an Aching Heart.

Can you know me so little, can you believe it possible I can be false? Base, treacherous, deceitfull, all that is detestable, for such I am, when I love no more monsieur Fontenelle, or when I love another.

By what curs'd means I know not, my father knew our correspondance, spoke to me of it, with bloudy threats, swearing he would know my Lovers name or I should be the Sacrifice. Oh with what Joy could I have dy'd to save you! not all his Threats, racks, fires, or worse, a parents curses[2] could have made me reveal your name, dear to my Soul. But my cruel Brother, by what Instrument of hell inform'd I know not, told me your name, and vow'd with horrid Imprecations he would expose you to my fathers fury if I refus'd to write the Letter which he dictated. Oh could you guesse the torments that I felt, the Labour of my Soul, you would pity what I felt, till the Perfidious Charlot with counterfeit compassion, hir'd to betray me, promis'd to send instead of it another which I writ giving an Account of our misfortunes and my miserable State. Thus to save your Life I comply'd with my Brothers will, persuaded that the cruel Letter would not reach you.

Oh Monseiur what since have I endur'd? Restraint, Reproach, all that is hard to youth to bear, but I could bear it all, if you was safe. Heaven! Oh I

---

[1] Cyrano de Bergerac visited Quebec, and made it the refuge for his hero in *États et empires de la lune et du soleil* (Jean-Pierre Collinet and Jean Serroy, *Romanciers et conteurs du XVIIe siècle* (n.d.), 141).

[2] This last is what weighs heaviest with Richardson's Clarissa.

must call you cruel: was I born to destroy this man! this charming—do not hate me. For me, was I now suffering the Agonys of the most exquisite tortures (as sure I think I feel a pain to equal them) I still would blesse the lovely cause of all. Methinks there is even a sweetnesse in suffering for you, Oh depend on it, where ever fortune throws me, what ever Seas divide us, still monseiur Fontenelle shall fill this faithfull Heart, which never shall admit a second Inclination. I speak your name with tendernesse not to be told. Wretch that I am! while I indulge my fondnesse, we are parted for ever. Oh whither my dear Wanderer are you fled? that I could bribe some Angel to whisper to your Soul my spotlesse truth, unutterable Love, I could with Joy shake off this train of pageantry, and follow you, through all the hazards of your voyage, did I not fear my fathers cruel power might be fatal to you. No, let me still preserve that dangerous secret, but parted as we are I'll ever love you.

Oh in what words then can I say farewell! Oh my Ador'd, imagine some expression for my passion, something to signify my agonizing Greife, that cold dead damp I feel about my heart at that sad word, Farewell.

After mlle de Condé had writ this Letter she knew not which way to convey it. She durst not trust any of those about her, and she lay on her Bed, weeping and revolving a thousand vain contrivances, when Charlot came in and told her Monsieur de St Albé, her singing master, was in the next room. His coming at that instant jogg'd a thought that made Mlle dry her Eyes, and bidding him wait, pass'd into her Closet, and takeing a purse with 100 Lui D'ors [*sic*] in her pocket,[1] she commanded his Admittance. The thought of the confidence she was going to repose in him, the fear of being betray'd, and the confusion of discovering a secret so dangerous for her fame, threw her into a disorder not to be express'd. She blush'd and hesitated, sigh'd, and at last with difficulty brought out—Monsieur I have—something—to say to you. The Colour mounted into his face, very visibly in his fair complexion; he tremble'd, and with a Joy that he could not conceal answer'd, 'Is it possible Madam that I can be of any service to you?'

'Yes Monseiur (said she with a more assur'd Voice), you may do me the most important of all services, I confesse with some hazard if it be known, but I dare hope you will venture to serve me. Convey this Letter to Monseiur Fontenelle, and till I am able to shew my gratitude in a Better manner accept of—' and presented him at the same Instant the Gold and the Letter. He chang'd pale as Death,

[1] The louis-d'or, minted under monarchs from Louis XIII to Louis XVI, was in 1717 legally assigned the value of 17 shillings (*OED*).

leaning against a Scrutore[1] that stood near him, cast down his eyes with a melancholy capable of forceing pity, putting back the gold with a tone mix'd with some little disdain, 'You do not know me, Madam (said he sighing). Can you think so meanly of a Man you dare trust? There is no hazard could hinder my serving you, but this way is the only one I would refuse.—But no matter (added he hastily) I am ready to serve your Highnesse with my Life. Give it me,' and took the Letter from her Hand, which she gave him in hast, for the perfidious Charlot was entering the room, and gave her no time to pay thanks to Monseiur St Albé for so much surprizing Generosity. He obey'd her commands, and sent the Letter according to the Direction Monseiur Fontenelle had left with his Banker, but whether he ever receiv'd it, Mademoiselle de Condé was never so happy as to know, for she receiv'd no Answer.[2]

Cruel Afflictions and the mortifications she receiv'd from her family, made her retire into a convent pretending a strong Vocation to that Sort of Life. But the Prince of Condé did not intend to carry his Resentment so far. He would not suffer her to be proffess'd, but it was a year before she could be prevaild on to come out, and marry as we since all know.

[1] Escritoire or writing desk.
[2] The following paragraph survives, crossed out, at the beginning of 'Louisa', a story following this one in sequence (H MS 275). I assume that MWM *may* have intended to resituate rather than to suppress it.

Court Tales II
Louisa

Textual note. This long story occupies an album, H MS 257, written in MWM's hand, with minor revisions of which only the significant ones are noted here. She numbered the pages. The album opens with two paragraphs later cancelled, which link it to 'Mademoiselle de Condé'; the former paragraph is here attached to the former and the second to the latter tale.

After mademoiselle de Condé was retird, the Duke D'Enguien thought of her no more and pass'd his time in other Amours till she was marry'd. About that time, the whole Court talk'd of a new star that threaten'd to eclipse the most celebrated Beautys.[1]

All the world has heard of that Seminary of young Women founded at St Cyr by Madame Maintenon, for the Daughters of Officers kill'd in the War.[2] She is her selfe the Governesse and gives them portions, or makes them Nuns, according as their Inclination determines. It hap\<pens\> sometimes that those poor Virgins by her favour marry very considerably, and there is gennerally one or other Among them that she honnours with her particular distinction. This Charitable foundation is scandaliz'd by the Mallicious as a sort of Seraglio where Madame Maintenon trains up young Creatures for the Diversion of the King or the princes of the blood, whom she finds it her Interest to oblige.[3]

A young Orphan whose mother had dy'd in childbed of her, and her Father was kill'd at the Seige of——, was educated here from

[1] The next paragraph, after the two struck out, has a note in margin: 'Commencez ici.'

[2] Françoise d'Aubigné (1635–1719), daughter of the poet Agrippa d'Aubigné, was born in debtors' prison and grew up partly in Martinique. She converted to her father's Protestantism, then back to the Catholic Church. As widow of the crippled satirist Paul Scarron (whom she married at 18), she became governess to the royal bastards; she was created marquise de Maintenon in 1675. Probably she was not the King's mistress but secretly his wife, perhaps as early as 1684. Female education in France was entirely in the hands of nuns; at Saint-Cyr (where proofs of nobility were required for entry) the 250 pupils were to dress as young ladies; money was available for dowries for twenty of them annually (Madeleine Marie Louise Saint-René Taillandier, *Madame de Maintenon: L'Énigme de sa vie auprès du Grand Roi* (1923), 171, 175, 179).

[3] René-Louis de Voyer d'Argenson said that Mme de Maintenon, knowing the King's appetite for women, founded St Cyr to 'lui administrer selon ses besoins' (*Journal et mémoires*, quoted in Gilette Ziegler, *Les Coulisses de Versailles: Le Règne de Louis XIV* (1963), 243).

the age of 6 years old. Even then she shew'd an early Wit, and promiseing Beauty that engag'd Madam Maintenon in her favour, who usd frequently to call her, her Lovely Child, and often brought her little presents of toys and sweetmeats. As she grew older, her Beauty and Wit encreas'd with her stature, and Madam Maintenon begun to shew her a kindnesse, that attracted the Respect of the Whole Nunnery. She had from her Childhood a particular attachment for reading, and being suffer'd to employ her time much after her own fancy, she pass'd whole days and nights in that Diversion. Poetry, and the softest part of poetry, was her belov'd study. She had an Inclination for Learning. An Admirable Apprehension surpriz'd all her masters, by attaining the Languages in an Age when few people are acquainted with their own.[1]

Nature had given the Beautifull Louisa the necessary Qualifications to make her the most miserable of her Sex. With the softest Soul naturally susceptible of the most tender and violent Passion she had a sense of Honnour and innate Virtue more rigid than that of the Catos and Scipio's of Rome.[2] She had a delicacy of sentiments, and generosity of principles no<t> to be found but in Romances, with the sweetest of tempers and a warmth of Constitution that expos'd her to all the Attacks of passion. Her Education improv'd these unhappy Qualitys; the Solitude of her Life remov'd from the commerce of the World, had hinder'd her of Experience to defend her selfe from its Injurys, and she was so sincere, that it has been often said of her, the only thing she could not do was to dissemble. The Vivacity that shew'd it selfe the first part of her Life can hardly be believ'd by those that only knew her, when her misfortunes had drawn upon her allmost an habitual melancholy.

Her person was not tall but her shape clean and easie, her Hair a Light Brown soft as her virgin Heart. Her Complexion, unsully'd by Art, without being of that surprizing White which allways gives Suspicions was Lively, and had a bloom that invited the touch. Her Eyes were Large, and full of fire; their glances peirced to the very Soul. When she was gay, a little wandering wildnesse scatter'd flames to the hearts of those that saw her, but there was a[3] softnesse in them

---

[1] Apprehension is understanding; 'the Languages' are the classical ones.

[2] MWM thought Cato 'perhaps the greatest character amongst the Romans' and used him as a type of Stoic virtue in 'Epistle from Mrs. Y[onge] to her Husband' (*E&P* 62, 231). Among the Scipio family, she may have in mind Scipio Africanus Major (234–?183 BC) or Scipio Aemilius Africanus Numantinus (184–129 BC), the highly cultured conqueror who wept over the ruins of Carthage.   [3] Altered from 'an inexpressible'.

that in some moments is not to be express'd. Her mouth gave an Air of Sweetnesse to her whole face, but her Air is not to be describ'd, which made it so impossible for the most celebrated painters to succeed in attempting her Picture. In different Days, she differ'd so much from her selfe, she sometimes alarm'd the Soul with an uncommon Vivacity, and her Eyes had a fire, her whole person an Air of Life and Gaity that inspir'd pleasure, and rais'd the most stupid Spirits; when she was melancholy (as the misfortunes of her Life gave her too often occasion to be) she had a Beautifull Languishment, a killing softnesse that stole away the Hearts of all that saw her, and softened the coldest and most insensible Bosoms.[1] From this Reason, we have seen her Inspire such violent passions in such contrary Minds, that have never before like'd the same thing. The gayest Wildest Rakes have been touch'd with that expressless modest sweetnesse, and the coldest most Philosophic Reasoners fir'd by that Brightnesse of conversation, and air of Wit.

Such as I have describ'd her, at the Age of 16, all that visited St Cyr spoke of her as a Miracle. Even her own Sex, to oblige Madam Maintenon (who was fond of being told there was more Beauty in her convent than at Court,) was Lavish in her praises. The Duke of Enguien, who heard every where of the charms of this fair devote,[2] shew'd a good deal of Curiosity to see this Wonder, thô his Heart was at that time deeply engag'd, while she pass'd all her time with her Books, Innocent of the noise that her Beauty made in the World. She had indeed heard the Characters of all the great men of the Court, and she admir'd that of the Duke of Enguien. She heard from every one that spoke of him, that he was the bravest General and the Handsomest young prince in Europe, that he had Wit, and his conversation enchanted all the Ladys that were so unhappy to be acquainted with him, but at the same time she heard he was the most dangerous of all Mankind, too Amorous not to attempt, too Lovely to be resisted.

This character made some little impression on her Mind, and without knowing why, she was allways asking little Questions about the Duke D'Enguien, when an Extrodinary Accident gave her Occasion to hear a great deal of him. The Duke had after a long courtship, and much Assiduity, had the good fortune to gain the Heart of Madame La Marquise de Nerville who was without doubt the finest woman at the Court of France.[3] She had beside the Advantages of a

---

[1] Altered from 'Beholders'.   [2] Pious person, or bigot.
[3] The name Neufville (not Nerville) occurs in Mlle de Montpensier, *Mémoires*.

Beautifull Face, gracefull shape and good proportion'd Height, a
Wit delicate and well turn'd, and a Soul but too sensible of the
softest passions. She had been marry'd very young, and liv'd in perfect agreement with the Marquis de Nerville, who was an honest
man of much merit, but she had never been sensible for him, of that
tendernesse which can only render such a Union pleasing. The
Duke of Enguien soon learn'd her the difference between the
Complaisance exacted from Duty and reason, and the Impetuositys
of a violent Inclination. She was not able to resist the Artfull Attacks
of the Lovely Duke and her own heart that spoke to her in his favour.
A tender Correspondance was established between them, but as
Women of her Quality have great measures to keep, she was forc'd to
depend on a Confidante to whom all his Letters were directed, and
at whose house they met.

This was Mademoiselle de Canaple, a young Lady of great Wit
and Beauty, but naturally mallicious, and too apt to envy the good
fortune of her Neighbours, but she hid these ill Qualitys so well, with
her agreable Wit, there was hardly any person more aimable. The
Marquise de Nerville tenderly lov'd her, and was not at all afraid of
trusting to her the most important Secrett of her Life, but she could
not see so often the charming Duke, without a desire of stealing from
her freind so considerable a conquest. The Complaisances that he
shew'd her, and the obliging things which he often said to her, for the
good offices she did him, flatter'd her Vanity, that it was not impossible to make some Impression on his Heart, and that perhaps allready
her charms had a greater Effect there, than he durst tell her. In consideration of the vow'd freindship between her and the Marquise de
Nerville, she resolv'd to help his Scrupules, and to that purpose
made him a thousand Advances which he would not understand.

One day when he waited at her house the coming of the Marquise,
mademoiselle de Canaple entertain'd him in the mean time. 'I know
not what to make (said she) of this delay of the Marquise; this has
very little the Air of a Lovers impatience, I can hardly beleive she
can grow cool to such a Lover as you are. Is it not rather (added she
smiling) that she has reason to complain of your Highnesse? You
have lost something of your first Ardour, and she is resolv'd to shew
some Indifference in her turn, thô against her Inclination.'

'Madame la Marquise (reply'd he) would be very unjust to use
me in that manner. Tis certain my heart feels all the fires of a first
beggining passion; her goodnesse for me instead of Lessening, has

fix'd her Empire in my Soul for ever. For gods sake Mademoiselle suffer her to have no cruel suspicions of my Faith; assure her, that tis impossible I should not be her's for ever. Even at this minute I Languish for her Appearance, I dye with Impatience, and I protest to you, with the same eagernesse as if it was the first dear Assignation.'

These were not the protestations she expected from the Duke D'Enguien. She blush'd with Spite, and when the Marchionesse came in, Lookd upon her with Eyes flaming with Envy. She left them together, and retir'd into her Closet, where after a shower of spitefull tears, she took a resolution of ruining without remorse her unhappy freind, whom she now perfectly hated, and since she found it impossible to make the Duke sigh for her charms, she found some pleasure in Imagining it in her power to make him sigh with rage and Dispair. This was very Easy for her to do: the very first Letter of the Marchionesses writeing that pass'd through her Hands, she sent to the Marquis de Nerville enclos'd in a Letter from an unknown hand.

The Marquis who passionately lov'd his Wife, and had till that minute a great Esteem for her Conduct, was struck to the Heart by this fatal Letter. However his reason did not abandonn him on so nice an Occassion. He would not see the Marchioness, being sensible of the power she had over him, that he should be melted by her tears to some shamefull Indulgence. He sent her word to retire to some convent, till he had consulted with her Relations what to do with her. The Marchionesse de Nerville, who fear'd some more fatal Effect of his Just resentment, retir'd that very night to the Convent of St Cyr, in the Affliction that may be imagin'd, Love, Shame, greife and fear oppressing her Mind at once.

No peice of Scandal can be a secret. All Paris knew the cause of her retirement, and when she enter'd the convent there was not one person ignorant of her misfortunes. She staid there 2 months, having many great Relations, some of which were willing to excuse her, and endeavor to perswade the Marquis de Nerville to forgive the folly of her Youth, which perhaps had not carry'd her so far as he apprehended. During this time, the fair Louisa, who was by Nature all softnesse and compassion, pass'd all her Evenings in the Chamber of the Beautifull Penitent. She even at last took the halfe of her Bed. The Marchionesse was charm'd with so much good sense in so young a creature, and soften'd by her tendernesse (Louisa often mingling her tears with her's) she made her the confidence of her most secret thoughts.

'I am ruin'd, I am undone, my dear Louisa (said she weeping), but, suffer me to own my weaknesse, I cannot yet repent. I would be still undone for the Duke of Enguien. You would not be surpriz'd at this Extravagance was you acquainted with that great Charming Man. He is all that can be lov'd, or esteem'd; his person inspires admiration wherever he passes. His Air, his Shape, his Eyes, good God How they can Languish! they speak ten thousand namelesse things, and with a softnesse, that tender fond respect, and yet that passionate eagernesse, blindnesse only can resist him; nay was I blind, his tongue would charm a Saint, would tempt an Angel to seek for Heaven only in his Arms. Nor is it my Love that makes me partial to him. Was I a Man to chuse a freind, or serve a Master, it should be the Duke of Enguien. How brave, intrepid in War, how good, how tender, and gennerous to his Enemys, then what is he to his freinds! he seems to take a Joy in going through the greatest Difficultys to serve them, yet insensible of Interest or any design of advanceing his Fortune. You know with what slavish attendance the rest of the Nobillity wait the Smiles of the King; they watch whole hours for a glance of Madam Maintenon. When the Duke D'Enguien enters the Court he appears the only prince in it, and the other [*sic*] of his Rank seem only his Attendants. He approaches the King with a Noble Air of conscious Merit, and greatnesse of Birth, and he neglects Madam Maintenon notwithstanding all her endeavors to engage in her Interest a prince whose great Qualitys are capable of every thing.'

Thus Madam de Nerville run on, and gave by degrees the highest Esteem of the Duke, to the young Louisa, thô she all ways stop'd her, when she made the Least refflection on Madam Maintenon, whom Louisa lov'd with the filial tendernesse due to a mother, and all the Gratitude and reverence for her Patronesse, and benefactres<se.> During the Time of Madam de Nerville's stay at St Cyr, the Beauty of Louisa who was now 16 made a great noise at Court, and the Duke D'Enguien was not without some Curiosity of seeing this Miracle, but he durst not approach the Convent for fear of destroying all hopes of the Marchionesse's reconciliation with the Marquis de Nerville, who would without doubt have imagin'd it a design laid to see her. However this caution did her no service. After many fruitlesse meetings, and negotiations, the Intercession of her Director and all the Endeavors of her Relations, the Marquis remain'd firm to his first Resolution of not takeing her again, and her family at length leaving her to his disposal, he remov'd her from a convent so near the Court, and sent her to an obscure Monastery in Normandy to passe the rest of her Life without hopes of seeing again the Duke d'Enguien.

Louisa parted with her unhappy freind with a great deal of tendernesse, and some little Astonishment that such cruel misfortunes could not lessen her fondnesse for the cause of them, not being able to apprehend those extreme Effects of violent passions, which are allways look'd upon as unnatural before they are felt. This extrodinary adventure could not fail of makeing her curious to see a Man capable of inspiring such sentiments, and it was not long before that curiosity was satisfy'd. Madam de Nerville had not been gone ten days, when madam de Maintenon brought with her one Evening the Duke d'Enguien, the Marquis d'Hailly, and the young Marquis de Genlis, Madam the Countesse de La Sale, and Mademoiselle des Cars. Madam Maintenon, who intended to oblige the noble Company with a sight of the Lovely recluse, gave them the Liberty of the Parlor, which is often enough permitted to people of the first Quality, and could not be the least scandalous in the presence of such a rigid Prude Governesse as the Devout Madam Maintenon who sanctifys all things by her appearance.

She sent for the Lovely Louisa, and 2 or 3 others of her most beautifull pensioners, but they were hardly observ'd near their fair Compannion. She enter'd the room with the modest unassur'd Air of a young Maid unus'd to Assemblys. A little blush which the curiosity of seeing the Duke of Enguien and her natural modesty spread over her face, heighten'd her charms, that twas impossible to see an object more dangerous. Her dresse was a good deal negligent, and her fine hair play'd carelessly about her face, with an Air easy and unaffected. She saluted the Ladys with the respect due to their Rank, without shewing any want of the politenesse of the Court, and seem'd neither to look on the Men with that eager curiosity common to those Educated apart from their company, or to receive any pleasure in the Surprize and admiration which it was easy to read in their Eyes. She seem'd ignorant of the Advantages she possess'd, and not desirous of the reputation she had attaind of the greatest Beauty in France.

The Duke d'Enguien allways magnificent in his dresse, had taken care that Day to <set> off his handsome Shape and mein, with the most becomeing Habit. He wore a fine white Cloth, richly embrodier'd with gold, but his Air seem'd to give those charms to the Galantry of his Dresse which other people receive from it. He

Look'd upon Louisa when she first enter'd with that eager applica-
tion, it was easy to see that she more than paid his Curiosity, and his
Eyes did not fail of giving her those praises, and marking his Surprize, which decency exacted from him to keep in Silence.

Madam Maintenon, who was willing that day to lay aside her
Gravity, soon put an end to the formality of first visits. A noble Collation was serv'd in, and the conversation soon became free, Galant
and entertaining. The young Marquis de Genlis was seated next
Mademoiselle de Cars, and as he would have said some soft thing to
her in a low voice, ' 'tis dangerous to hearken to you (said she aloud
laughing, having a mind to make the discourse general); you have the
Reputation of a Wizard. They say tis in vain to conceal our thoughts
from you, you penetrate into our very hearts, and there is nothing
even of the past or the future, but is known to you.' The whole company knew Mlle meant to railly the young Marquis on an Adventure
then very much talk'd of. To serve one of his freinds in an Amour, he
had consented to personate the Astrologer. Madame de Lascuris, who
was the Lady in Question,[1] and naturally superstitious, had been
perswaded to go to him, as the most Learned man of the Age. He plaid
the part perfectly well; he describ'd her Lover exactly, and told her
however she might disguise it, he saw very well she was in Love. She
sighd and confess'd that his science was admirable; 'but, said she, am
I belov'd?' This Question open'd his Eyes, he saw his freind was not
the happy Man in her favour, and answer'd Ambiguously that she
was certainly belov'd, but the Man she lov'd, had some reasons that
check'd his Addresses. She interpreted this her own way, and made
answer, 'I know he is the most Intimate Freind of my other Lover—'

To make short of the story, the Marquis of Genlis under the
appearance of a fortune teller drew from her artfully the whole secret
of her heart, and learnt that himselfe was the favourite. He made
such good use of this discovery, the disguise which he had assum'd
at the desire of his freind with an Intent to serve him, was the
Occassion of his possessing his Mistrisse. His freind complain'd of
the Infidelity, and for his complaint was only railly'd for trusting his
mistrisse with a man so well made as Monsieur de Genlis. The story
being very pleasant was soon known to the whole Court, and when
Mademoiselle de Cars made him this Raillery, the whole company
had something pleasant to say on the Occassion.

---

[1] A similar name, Lascaris, occurs in *Nouvelles françaises* (1656) by Segrais and la Grande
Mademoiselle (ed. Roger Guichemerre (1990), 139).

'I know not Ladys, said he laughing, how you may despise my Science, but I dare engage that if you will give me the Liberty of Looking in your hands, you will find a great deal of truth in my Predictions.' The countesse de La Sale gave him her hand with an Agreable Air. As soon as he had done speaking, and after he had predicted her all sort of good fortune, he took that of the fair Louisa who sat next her, and being willing to say something galant, 'I am very much afraid Madam (said he affecting to examine her hand nicely) that you will be guilty of a very great Crime. By this Line, I see plainly if you do not abate something of your Indifference you will murder the most passionate of your Lovers.'

The Duke d'Enguien who had listen'd very attentively to what he should say to Louisa, intterupting him earnestly presented him his hand, casting a passionate Look on the fair Devote, 'Marquis, tell me if I am not threaten'd with some cruel Death.' This was speaking plain enough, but the Company look'd on it only as a peice of Galantry common to the Duke d'Enguien.

They stay'd in this agreable place as long as Madam Maintenon thought it consistent with her Severity. The Lovely Louisa did not fail to make some Refflections on the Galantry and good Mein of the Duke d'Enguien, whom she easily distinguish'd from the other men of Quality, and without being sensible of any Inclination she had for him, did not alltogether wonder so much at the Extravagance of Madam de Nerville. The Duke of his side was charm'd with her Beauty and Sweetnesse. He pass'd the whole Night in contrivances to see her again, and thô he was sensible that he lovd her, he perhaps allready lov'd better than he Imagin'd.

He told the Dutchesse the next day, that most of the considerable Ladys at Court had paid Madam Maintenon the compliment of going to see her fair favourite at St Cyr, and he thought she should take some oppertunity of waiting on her. That Princesse, who was all softnesse, and submission, promis'd to do it, without apprehending his Design.[1] That very afternoon she made a party for that end, and carry'd with her some Ladys of Quality and the Count de Belforrest. This Count was a Gascon,[2] who having his Lands near Spain and having pass'd the greatest part of his youth in his own Castle, had at

---

[1] If MWM had in mind Louis III de Bourbon as d'Enghien, his wife was Louise-Françoise (1673–1743), legitimated daughter of Louis XIV and Madame de Montespan.

[2] MWM does not follow the French fictional tradition of type-casting the Gascon as boaster.

least as much of the Spaniard as the Frenchman. He was now nearer 50 than 40, he had serv'd in the Army with much courrage, and had lost a leg in the Service, but being of a temper haughty and very little complaisant, he had made his court so ill, that he had never attain'd any considerable Imploy. Having the displeasure of seeing younger Officers put over his head, he had retir'd from the Camp, and with a sullen pride which had something noble enough in it, he chose rather to live upon an Estate very unsuitable to his Birth than solicite the ministers for any thing. He had marry'd 16 years since a Daughter of the Marquis de Migneu, who was the finest Woman of her time, with whom he had been passionately in Love, but having discover'd her in some criminal Gallantry, he carry<d> her into the Low Languedoc where the report commonly run that he had poison'd her. From that time, he shew'd some Aversion to the fair Sex, and he did not scruple declaring publically that he would never marry again because he did not beleive it possible to find a Woman that would comply with the rules that he should think necessary for his wife. Yet this Stoic sower'd by Age and Disapointment, could not defend himselfe against the Inevitable charms of Louisa.

He return'd back from the visit pensive and unquiet. He had sense enough to know, nothing could be more ridiculous than for a Man of his Age and figure to project the Conquest of that young Beauty. 'Tis true her fortune was so low, twas an honnour for her to be his Wife, but when he imagin'd himselfe her Husband, he was shock'd at the Raillerys that he must endure, and he trembled at the consequences which seem'd not to be avoided. He repeated to himselfe over and over all the considerations that could turn him from so Ridiculous a Design, without abateing any degree of his passion, and the conclusion of all his fine Reasonings was, that 'twas much more easy to be ridiculous than miserable.

Louisa was not at all trouble'd with Refflections concerning him; she hardly knew he had been there, and all her thoughts were employ'd on the Dutchesse D'Enguien. She admir'd her Beauty and sweetnesse, but yet she seem'd to think that she had not all that delicacy of Wit which seem'd necessary to entertain agreably the Duke d'Enguien. She could not help sighing when she refflected on the happynesse of that Princesse. She had never before perceiv'd in her selfe any Envy for persons of that Rank; she had been hitherto contented with her Humble Birth, and she felt with surprize certain Emotions that seem'd to murmur at the Felicity of the Dutchesse, and the injustice of Fortune. She could not feel any sentiment that seem'd repugnant to her native goodnesse without a deep Melancholy. 'Alas (said she to her selfe, melting into tears) is it the Fortune and elevated Birth of the fair Princesse that gives me pain? is it those advantages she has over me? is it not rather another peice of happynesse, which those advantages have procur'd her? Oh my heart, if thou art capable of so criminal a weaknesse, at least let me hide it from all the World.'

She went into the Garden and gave up her mind to the most melancholy refflections, but with what surprize did she find there Madam Maintenon and the Duke d'Enguien! The blood mounted into her face, as he approach'd her. 'I come, madam (said he with an Air of respect), as Madam D'Enguien's Ambassador. She is ambitious of the honnour of waiting on you to the Opera to Morrow, and if you please to take a supper at my House afterwards, I will have the Violins and some company to entertain you.' Louisa answer'd with the respect due to the Dutchesse, and they continu'd their Walk, Madam Maintenon commanding her to give her hand to the Duke, who trembled as he touch'd it. That trembling told her more, than the most passionate declaration of Love could have done. She cast down her eyes, her young Bosom heav'd with artlesse sighs, and she had hardly strength to support her selfe. The conversation seem'd only on Indifferent Subjects, but the Duke made several pauses, unable[1] to talk of trivial things when his whole Heart was full of a violent passion. He was oblig'd to wait on Madam Maintenon when she thought it convenient to retire, but his Eyes bid Adeiu to the Lovely Louisa with a Glance more significant and more touching than the tenderest Words could have.

Madam Maintenon saw with vast pleasure, the progresse her young pensioner had made in his Heart. She did not doubt but Louisa's Eyes would give her that power over the Duke which all the Honnours in her disposal could not acquire; in the person of that fair Devote she had a Bribe which he could not resist, and she flatter'd her selfe allready with those agreable Idea's. But to preserve her Character of Devotion, she entertain'd the Duke in his return to Versailles, with the praises of his Dutchesse, adding that she was very glad a Lady of her Highnesse's exemplary Virtu and piety would take the young Louisa into her protection, that for her part, she tenderly lov'd the Girl, and would not trust her with any other

---

[1] Altered from 'as if unable'.

Lady about the Court, but she could not deny her the advantage of being oft with the Duchesse D'Enguien where she was sure she would learn nothing but what was commendable, and whenever she pleas'd to send for her, she should certainly wait on her.

The Duke easily understood all this precise Jargon, and that it was telling him in other Words, she sacrifice'd to him the young Louisa, and there should be nothing wanting on her part to gratify his Love. He made Answer he was very sensible of the good Opinion she had of Madam D'Enguien, that he would shew his gratitude all man<ner> of ways, and the rest of his Life should be devoted to her service; which was just what Madam Maintenon desir'd, and without makeing any Verbal compact, they parted perfectly satisfy'd with one another.

The unhappy Louisa past the night in a far different manner. She could not forgive her selfe that irresistable Inclination she found at the bottom of her Heart for the Duke; in vain she combated it by all Efforts of her Reason and Virtue. She wept, and wish'd a thousand times she might never see him more, yet at that very instant she felt a certain pleasure in the necessity of seeing him the next day.

Madam Maintenon came her selfe to see her dress'd for the opera; she presented her some Jewells, and took care there should be no advantages wanting to make her altogether charming. The new desires she felt in her heart had given a Lovely Languish to her Eyes, and she seem'd the most perfect peice of artlesse Beauty. When she went to the Hotel D'Enguien, the Duke met her himselfe, and gave her his hand to help her out of the Coach. 'What massacre is it you design, madam (said he looking on her tenderly), you seem prepar'd to let no heart escape you, that sees you this day,—do not cast down your Eyes, let me look on them, thô to kill me.' It was well for Louisa she was allready near the Hall; it was impossible for her to make any Answer, and the Duke who easily penetrated into the soft emotions of a beginning passion, saw the Effect which he had made on her Innocent Heart.

The Dutchesse carry'd her to the Opera, from whence the Duke led her out, and from thence they went back to his Palace where there was an assembly of persons of the first Quality, a Supper magnificent enough to have entertain'd the King and the whole Royal Family, a Splendid Ball, and an entry of Masques richly habited. The Duke caus'd the Ladys names to be put into a Hat, and the Men drew their partners, but it was allways so well contriv'd, that Louisa fell to the

Share of his Highnesse. Without saying any thing that shock'd her modesty, he acted all that Night the part of a Man passionately in Love. Tis easy to imagine what Effect it must have on a Girl of 16, just taken from a convent, to find her selfe in a Palace, her sight charm'd with the most Luxurious Objects, with the Advantage of a vast number of Wax lights in Chrystal Lustres, magnificent Furniture, Beautifull Paintings, and fine tapistrys, her taste tempted with rich Wines, her Ears surpriz'd with the finest softest Airs, and at her Feet a Royal Lover, in all the Bloom of youth, tender, eager, respectfull and passionate. What change from a melancholy cloister, early mattins, and a midnight Bell!

Tis all that a long experience and the coldnesse of age can do, to harden our hearts against the soft insinuations of Pleasure, and the natural Propensity human Nature carrys with it to Luxury. What then must it be to the young and Innocent Louisa? she could not look indifferently upon a Man, that with so vast an expence gave her the pleasure of so many new and Lovely Objects, yet nothing she saw touch'd her so much, as the Looks of the Lovely Duke, and in the midst of that magnificence she whisper'd to her selfe, she could be happy with him in a Cave, remote from humankind. She check'd this wish as soon as form'd; she cast her Eyes on the Dutchesse and refflected he ought only to be hers. Her Bosom heav'd with unbidden sighs, and in spite of her Endeavors to suppresse them, tears filld her Eyes. When the Ball broke up, she retir'd full of this disquiet, so little mistrisse of her selfe, she hardly knew what she did. She threw her selfe into Bed, without being able to sleep. The more charming she found the Duke, the more Necessary she thought it to avoid him. But how could she avoid him?

Madam Maintenon came to her in the morning, and more laughing than chideing, 'You are very carelesse (said she), you left your fan last night with the Duke d'Enguin, and he was so discreet, he would not send it to you, but sent to me to bring it you,' and gave the fan into her hands. It had only round it a little Bandage to keep the sticks close, that seem'd too small to be of any other use, but it was a Billet, the most galant, and the most respectfull in the world, and yet writ in such a manner, as if he felt more passion than he durst expresse. Voiture never writ more agreably than the Duke;[1] he express'd what he would in Italian, French and Spanish, and was master of the Stiles

[1] Vincent de Voiture (1598–1648): MWM owned his *Œuvres* and his *Familiar and Courtly Letters* (3rd edn., 1701) (the latter now at Sandon Hall).

of those different Languages. Louisa was but too sensible of what was finely writ. She open'd this billet before Madam Maintenon; her heart heav'd at every Line, her Eyes grew moist, and the Letter drop'd from her hands. Madam Maintenon took it up, seeing the disorder she was in, and read it, returning it to her with a gay air. 'You are a little fool, Louisa (said she laughing), you are unacquainted with the manner of Living with men of the Dukes Galantry. What need you look so much alarm'd, I see nothing in this Letter of any ill Design. The Duke has a mind to divert himselfe, in my opinion he writes very well. Let us shew him that the Education of my Convent does not produce a Genius inferior to his. You have the prittyest stile in the world. Write my dear Louisa.'

—Louisa cast down her Eyes without any reply. She had a great Inclination to answer this Letter, and would fain perswade her selfe she might do it, with as much Innocence as Madam Maintenon made her beleive. Who could suspect the Advice of so religious a Matron? Louisa retir'd to her Closet where she writ a Letter of wit and raillery, in which she utterly disclaim'd all correspondan<ce> with him but in that manner. This Letter both pleas'd and disapointed the Duke. He was charm'd with that Lively Wit, surprizing in her Youth, but he fear'd so agreable a Letter could only be writ by an Indifferent Heart, and that if she felt all the tendernesse he hope'd she had, it had been impossible to write in so easy and gay a manner. He did not fail to reproach her with it in his Answer. This 2d Letter was infinitely more serious and more passionate than the first. He prais'd her Wit, but tenderly assur'd her, she had pleasd him better by 2 or 3 lines dictated from her Heart. To remove her Scruples, he told her she knew him very little, if she Imagin'd his pretensions would ever be what she could reasonably be offended with; that he desir'd no more than the pleasure of sometimes hearing from her, and the glory of being permitted [to] approve him the tenderest and most faithfull of her freinds; that however as the World was made, it was necessary to preserve their freindship a secret from the mallicious, who had not wit enough to comprehend so delicate a commerce, and was for bringing all things to the Grossnesse of their own Ideas. Therefore to hinder all ill interpretations, and impertinent observations of her Companions, he would ask leave of Madam Maintenon to send her the new Books as they came out, and his Letters should be neatly pasted in the first leaves.

Louisa in her turn complain'd of the Duke, he seem'd to carry things much farther than she design'd. She told him, how innocent soever her Intentions were, such a correspondance would injure her in the Opinion of the World, and might give uneasynesse to the Dutchesse, who had a Merit that exacted the Respect of all that knew her. She did not doubt but her Highnesse had a nicety that made his Heart more valuable to her than any other Consideration; to her only his tendernesse, and his freindship was due, and she would not accept of any Vows in her wrong. Thô Louisa did not refflect upon it, this was tacitely telling the Duke if he was free from any other Engagement, her Heart found no repugnance to that tendernesse he demanded of her. He was charm'd with this Letter, his impatience did not suffer him to answer it, he hasten'd to the convent, and demanding only to see Louisa at the Grate,[1] she could not deny it to him. She came thither in her undresse, the disorder of her mind, and all the working passions there visible in her Eyes. He look'd on her with a passionate eagernesse peculiar to him. 'Beautifull Louisa (said he) how cruel you are to me! your Scrupules are indeed very gennerous, but they are wrong founded. I give nothing to you, which I take from Madam D'Enguien. I respect her very much, and I would displease her in nothing, but there is a certain tendernesse, an Expresslesse fondnesse which we can feel but for one person. Till I saw those Lovely Eyes I was ignorant of the meaning of it. I have lov'd before, but I never before felt these soft namelesse Emotions which dilates my soul at every dear Glance of yours, and diffuses a pleasure not to be describ'd in every vein of my heart. Do not be afraid of me, I have no Intentions that are not pure as your own Spotlesse Mind, innocent as the Visits of Angels. Suffer me only to approve my selfe your freind, and let me flatter my selfe that you have some pity for a man that Devotes his Whole Life to you. It is no longer in your Choice whither or no you will accept of it. Use me as you will, you may make me miserable, you may kill me, but you cannot make [me] otherwise than yours.'

Louisa's own heart echo'd to her every tender word she heard from his tongue, and if she had suffer'd her's to expresse her thoughts, she had at that minute made him a thousand fond pro-testations of Eternal Love. But her Virtue check'd her fondnesse,

---

[1] A barred window at which enclosed nuns received visitors. MWM wrote of the Laurenzerinnenklöster in Vienna that the grate was 'not one of the most rigid. It is not very hard to put a head thrô and I don't doubt but a Man a little more slender than ordinary might squeeze in his whole person' (*CL* i. 277).

and with a sigh, that assur'd him he was not very unhappy, she made answer, perhaps his Highnesse had a mind to divert himselfe, and as poor a Maid as she was, she could not suffer to be the Object of his Raillery. 'But (continu'd she, seeing he was going to answer to that) if it be true that I have made some Impression on your heart, I have yet a better Reason for seeing you no more. I should look upon my selfe with Horror, as enjoying a tendernesse only due to the Dutchesse. No, no, Monseiur, let me dye rather than Injure that Aimable Princesse.'

Tears came into her Eyes, at the End of these Words, and she put up her fan to conceal them, when the Duke answer'd, 'you can no way injure her but by this cruelty to me. Inhumane as you are, why will you drive to Despair a man that adores you? Do you beleive I can ever suffer a Woman upon whose account I am ruin'd? I shall revenge upon her, the outrages you do me, I shall hate her whom I now Esteem. I shall fly from her and tis to you that she will owe the most cruel misfortunes of her Life.'

How pleasant is it to find an Excuse for yeilding to our Inclinations! How easily are we induce'd to believe that they are consistent with our Virtue! after some other expostulations, the Duke allways remaining firm to his Resolution, Louisa yeilded to suffer him to write to her, upon condition he pretended no farther. He seem'd all transported at this permission, and gave her thanks for it in the most lively expressions. She was disatisfy'd with the grant she had made; she blush'd, and fixing a tender look on the Duke, retir'd from the Grate, full of confusion, leaving him charm'd with the progresse he had made, knowing very well, that a Maid who consents to hear, is not far from being won.[1]

The next morning a Gentleman from the Dutchesse came to St Cyr, desiring the fair Louisa to go with her Highnesse that afternoon to Marli, which Louisa had yet never seen. She return'd an Answer full of submission, and the Duchesse carry'd her in her Coach with Madame de La Sale, and Mademoiselle de Canaple. Some other Ladys follow'd in Chariots. They were waited on by the Duke on Horseback, and a galant troop of young Nobillity. The Duke never mov'd from that side of the Coach where Louisa sat, perpetually saying agreable things with an Air of Life and Gaity only he was master of. There <could> not be a more Lovely Figure than the Duke

---

[1] MWM had expressed these sentiments in 'Written ex tempore in Company in a Glass Window the first year I was marry'd' (*E&P* 179).

D'Enguien on Horseback; he recall'd to the Memory of young
Louisa the Oroondates, and Aronces, of Scudery, and she found that
Nature in him excell'd the noblest flights of fancy.[1]

I need not describe the Gardens and Palace of Marli; they are
known to be some of the finest in France.[2] Here was a magnificent
Collation, a consort of Music with the finest Voices from the Opera,
and the Evening was concluded with a Ball. The Duke dance'd with
Louisa, and found a way of slipping into her Pocket a Billet which
she found in these words.

If I was not deceiv'd in those charming Eyes last Night I am the Happyest
of all Men. Yes, my Lovely Angel, I prefer one tender thought from you to
all the fondnesse of any other woman. Let me but gaze upon those Eyes, and
suffer me to see in them, that enchanting softnesse which I saw last night,
and I am happy. My Heart yet flutters with the dear Remembrance, my
Head swims, and I faint over the paper—do not make thy selfe uneasy my
tender maid by imaginary Scrupules: to make my selfe worthy of you, I
shall endeavor to be Honest to all the World. I shall act every where with a
design of gaining your Esteem. You shall govern me in the Camp and the
Councel. Can an Ardour like this, which only serves to make me better, be
criminal? I will behave my selfe to Madam D'Enguien with the Respect due
to her Rank, but my tendernesse, my fondnesse, shall be etternally yours,
they can be no others. I should hate my selfe if I could look with pleasure on
any other Face. No, no, my Louisa, my Goddesse and my Freind, I must be
only thine.

Louisa was now so well convince'd, or rather so madly in Love, she
no longer scrupule'd to answer the Dukes most tender Billets. She
cover'd her Love with the specious name of Freindship, and by slow
degrees was brought to receive his fondest expressions without confusion. He often ask'd for her Picture, and at length (as to her Freind)
she gave it him, and he return'd her his, set with Diamonds of great
Value. He omitted no Assiduitys to fix her Heart, by the Means of the
Dutchesse, and often of the Princesse of Roche sur Yon, his Sister.[3]
When Madam D'Enguien was not of a Humour to be so complaisant,
he carry'd her to a thousand different Partys of pleasure. It was
allmost every day, Balls, consorts, and Splendid Entertainments, till

---

[1] Heroes of romance: Oroondates actually appears in *Cléopâtre* by Gauthier de La
Calprenède.

[2] MWM visited this royal residence in 1718, and later hoped to see it imitated in
Buckingham Palace (*CL* i. 440–1, iii. 291).

[3] Louis III de Bourbon's sister Marie-Thérèse was married to François-Louis de Bourbon,
prince de La Roche-sur-Yon, later prince de Condé.

they became mutually so entirely charm'd with each other, it had been impossible for the Duke to live a day without seeing or hearing from his Charmer, and the fond Louisa grew sick of Life it selfe in his Absence.

They continu'd some months in this commerce. The Duke had no opperturnitys of seeing her alone, but with a grate between them except some little snatch'd moments, in Walks or Balls, where he kept to Articles most religiously. He sometimes kiss'd her Hand with a good deal of struggling on her part, and that was the highest favour he had obtain'd, but his hopes, and his desires, were much bolder. He waited till he had an Interest so well establish'd, in her heart, it would be easyer for her to dye than break with him, before he durst let her know that he had any Designs that were Criminal.

Tis true Louisa was Vertuous enough not to be thorroughly satisfy'd with this Correspondance, such as it was. She never look'd upon the Dutchesse, but she made her selfe a thousand reproaches in her Name, and she often went from the Entertainments, to throw her selfe into Bed, where she wept over a Weaknesse, she knew not how to conquer. She made resolutions of breaking off this freindship so fatal to her repose, and which cost her such cruel remorse. She even made some faint Efforts towards it, but one soft Glance from the Eyes of the Duke melted her best resolves, and she found all things easy to her, in comparison of giveing pain to the lovely thing she lov'd.

She endeavor'd to be oft with madam Maintenon. She hop'd her sage discourse would fortifye her Resolution. Without saying the thing directly, she gave hints enough of her weaknesse to give madam Maintenon oppertunity of adviseing her, but this was poison to her; she only heard in return, Lavish Encomiums on a Man which was allready but too meritorious in her opinion. Madam Maintenon repeated over, and over to her, his truth, his Generosity, the natural sweetnesse of his temper, concludeing nothing was to be apprehended from him, and no man upon Earth so much to be depended on in any Engagement. Louisa felt that pleasure in hearing his praise, that all the World feels when their own Judgments are applauded. She flatter'd her selfe she was but doing Justice to extrodinary Merit, and that there was nothing criminal in the tendernesse she had for him, but she had too soon reason to suspect this tendernesse.

The Princesse of Roche sur Yon seting her at St Cyr one night from the Opera, the Duke D'Enguien being in the Coach, he perswaded Louisa to be set down on the Garden side, adding that the

Moonshine which was then very bright would make the Walk pleasant crosse the Garden. She was not very averse to a short oppertunity of talking with his Highnesse, and he led her, without reluctance above the halfe of the Garden, but then whither he before intended this tryal of his interest in her heart, or that the stillnesse of the night, the Brightnesse of the Moon which shew'd her Beautys to advantage, and powerfull Oppertunity, fir'd him beyond the possibillity of forbearing, he snatch'd her into his Arms, and before she could struggle from them, printed ten thousand kisses, on her mouth and eyes, with short breath'd sighs, and reiterated whispers, 'my Life, my Soul, my Goddesse.'

—Young Louisa could not be insensible of pleasure at the transporting touch of the dear Man she Lov'd. His kisses diffus'd¹ a new pleasing warmth in her soft bosom, her unexperience'd Heart beat with nimble motions, but her virtue alarm'd even² by the pleasure she felt, gave her strength to get from that Enchanting Embrace, and she made such haste to the door of the Convent, she shut it after her, before the Duke could overtake her. This precipitate silent flight told him the whole state of her heart. He saw that she durst not trust her Virtue with so dangerous an Assault, and yet her Love preserv'd him from the Anger that he apprehended. She pass'd that Night in inexpressible³ inquietudes; she saw too plainly that the Duke was allready weary of Platonics,⁴ she could not think of breaking a commerce that made all the Happynesse of her Life, of seeing no more a man she tenderly lov'd, and she trembled at the apprehension of any attacks inconsistent with her Virtue. Her Apprehensions were encreas'd by this Letter the next morning.

This whole Night has entertained me with Visions of my Angel Louisa. What made you so cruelly break from me? I would have given my Life to have had you in my Arms. You have ten thousand times more Wit than any of your Sex, you ought to be above their common Notions. You have too exalted a Sense to be frighted by vulgar Shadows. I do not say this my charmer, to make you think I would neglect the care of your precious Honnour. No my lovely Maid, let us humour the World in their nonsense. I would rather sacrifice my Life, more than my Life, my fondest wishes, rather than hurt your fame. I will preserve it with care; but in recompence for all my fondnesse, do not rob me of all the Happynesse that Life can give me. You have wrought up my passion to that excess of height, I live all in

---

¹ Altered from 'gave'. ² This word added.
³ Altered from 'undescribable' [*sic*]. ⁴ i.e. love without sexual expression.

you, and I dye without you. I must dye, or you must be mine. My heart, my soul, my fortune all are yours, and by Heaven I swear (Heaven strike me dead this Instant if I lie) if ever it is in my power, I joyn my fortune with yours for ever. Use me then Gennerously my charmer; depend upon it, your Bounty now (which is of absoloute necessity to save my Life) will fix me yours for ever. I shall love you (if possible) with more passion than I do now, I shall trust you as my freind, and honnour you as my sister. It will be a tye, not to be dissolv'd by time. I never will think of any other Woman. I shall then be yours by obligation and gratitude, as I am now by passion and Inclination. You cannot seriously believe that there is any thing criminal in a commerce of this kind. No body whose Esteem is worth having, ever dis-esteem'd a Woman but for Multiplicity of Lovers, where her tendernesse appears to be the Effect of her Constitution. I will use Madam D'Enguien with the respect due to her Rank, but do you think, because the King force'd my hand at the Age of 17,[1] either God or Nature obliges me to be etternally wretched for a few hasty words, compell'd and frighted from my timerous youth? You have no tye upon you, no claim is laid upon your heart. Bestow it then thou Lovely Maid; no man can doat, and languish for the dear possession, with the Warmth that I do. Who will be Injur'd by the Genner-ous Gift? and you will make Everlastingly happy the most amorous of all Mankind.

Do not be offended my Louisa at the Liberty I take of sending you the Enclos'd. You would have reason to be so if I pretended any merit from it. No my Angel, I know too well the value of your heart to barter for it, but I would have all the priveleges of your Freind, and as such, I would put you above the necessity of the Assistance of Madam Maintenon, or the tempta-tion of accepting any Husband which must be disagreable to you, if it be true as I hope that you are not without some Inclination for me. I chance to have this paper about me, at this time, but I beg, I insist upon it, if all your vows of freindship were not feign'd, that you will permit me as your freind, to be of use to you. You can not have so low a thought of me to fear, I should think I had obligd you. Tis you that oblige me by accepting of my Freind-ship, and tis an Obligation I shall think not to be repaid by all the Services of my Life. I am with all the violence of Passion, and the most entire Esteem Etternally Yours.

He enclos'd in this Letter a Bill of 5000 pistoles.[2] Louisa with the Lownesse of her Birth and fortune, had the most exalted sentiments of Gennerosity and honnour. If she had been a princesse of the Blood, she could not have been more offended at the present made her by the Duke. She flung the Letter on the Ground, in a passion that for

---

[1] Louis III de Bourbon was 19 at his marriage.
[2] This was a French name for (at various dates) various coins, including a louis-d'or of 1640.

some moments made her hope she hated him, but tendernesse re-assuming its empire in her soft Bosom, she burst into a flood of tears, and took up the Letter, which she read over again. The respectfull Manner in which he made his Offers, abated part of her Resentments. She even felt some gratitude for the Gennerosity with which he treated her, but when she consider'd over those parts of his Letter, that press'd for Happynesse, and recollected his behavior the Night before, she saw her selfe under a fatal necessity of either abandonning him, or her Virtue. She resolv'd to dye rather than part with her Hon[ou]r, but Oh 'twas cruel Death to part with the Duke of Enguien. He had gain'd her Innocent heart by ways so subtle she knew not how to drive him thence, that constant Idol of her tender thoughts. She wept without being able to resolve upon any thing.

Madam Maintenon came into her Chamber as she was lying all in tears upon her Bed, and with the tendernesse of a parent sat down by her, and embraceing her, 'My dear child (said she) what makes you weep? tell me—can my Advice, can I any way be of service to you? There is nothing I would not do to make you easy.' Madam Maintenon spoke this with an Air of goodnesse and Insinuation peculiar to her selfe, which peirce'd the very Soul of Louisa, and she took a Resolution of disclosing to her the real state of her Heart. She threw her selfe at her feet, and embraceing her knees, weeping, 'Forgive me Madam (said she). Look with indulgence upon my crimes. I confesse I have very ill answer'd the care you have taken of my Education, a wretched copy of that Virtue your Example has set before [me]. I have forgot those principles of Piety, and rigid Modesty you taught my Youth—Oh forgive me, look with pity on my Blushes, pity my breaking heart, and streaming Eyes, while I con-fesse with Shame, I love—Nor is that passion halfe my crime—I love a man allready engag'd, marry'd to a princesse who loves and who deserves him. I love the Duke D'Enguien. There was no triffling with a Man like him. I begun this correspondance in raillery, and play'd away my heart before I knew twas gone. I am now ravingly in Love, I doat, I dye for him. But oh believe me Madam, to Heaven and you I swear, I'll dye rather than live a Dishonour to you. The Duke who knows his Empire in my Soul, presumes upon it to undo me. I dare no longer continue a correspondance so dangerous. To you, here to your feet I fly for shelter, and beg you would permit me to take the Veil, and put it out of my power ever to see this Lovely Ruiner of my Virtue.'

Madam Maintenon look'd a good deal surpriz'd at this confession, which she could very well have spar'd. She all along hop'd the Duke could bring about his wishes with Louisa without her appearing to aid him farther than by a little connivance. She was however glad that Louisa had no suspicion of her relasching any part of her Severity. She took her up in her Arms, and even wept for her misfortunes, 'which I fear (said that artfull Woman) I am in some degree the occassion of, in permitting the Duke to see you so often. But his pretences fool'd me. He has sworn to me, a thousand times, that he admir'd you as the most Accomplish'd young Creature in the World, and that he would endeavor the Establishment of your fortune. I never knew him other than nicely just to his word—but no wonder a Beauty like yours has surprizing Effects—I begun to suspect his freindship carry'd him farther than he pretended, by the Indifference he shews to the most lovely Ladys of the Court. He has no longer that Gallantry which gain'd him so many Hearts, he is pensive in the most beautifull Assemblys, and only Gay where you are— You are very young, my Dear. This unlucky passion may wear off, and a Beauty like yours was not made to be conceald under a Veil. Think seriously upon it, but if you persist in that Resolution, you shall lose no part of my freindship, and I will do every thing I can do for you, in that station.'

Madam Maintenon thought it became her not to consent too readily, but she was very well pleasd to hear her speak of confining her Selfe to St Cyr, which was putting her Beauty entirely in her power for the rest of her Life. Louisa gave her a 1000 thanks for her goodnesse and kiss'd her hands with tears of Gratitude, calling her her Protectresse, and Preserver, assuring her with Blushes, that it was absolutely necessary for her to avoid the tempting Duke, since she fear'd the weaknesse of her Heart, and had too much reason to think she could not resist him.

This was very agreable news to Madam Maintenon, who after several consolatory Embraces, and praises of her Virtue, exalted to her the happynesse of those devoted to Religion, and run over very readily the Works of that Divine Theologist the Pere Bourdaloue,[1] concluded with giving her the key of her Little Oratory,[2] in the Grove at the south End of the Garden of St Cyr, where she assur'd

---

[1] Louis Bourdaloue (1632–1704), Jesuit preacher, famed at court and among the literati, regarded as having refuted Pascal.

[2] Altered (here and below) from 'Library'.

her she would find many Books, proper to fortifye her Pious Resolutions. But Louisa was so long writeing to the Duke and enclosing to him his Bill, that it was allmost Evening before she went into the Oratory.

That Oratory is an Enchanted place. It stands in the midst of a thick Grove of Trees, divided into irregular walks, to preserve the Beauty of its natural Wildnesse. A large canal terminates the veiw from the windows of the Oratory, in the Middle of which the Books are in fine Glasse Cases, on the one end a closet with a Bath, and at the other a day Bed of green damask with furniture suitable. Louisa was laid on the Bed, with a Book in her hand. The door was lock'd on the Inside. Nothing could equal her Surprize to hear a key in it, and allmost at the same time, the Duke d'Enguien enter'd. She shreik'd out with surprize but she was too far remov'd from the convent to be heard.[1]

He approach'd her with an Air of sadnesse and submission that allmost reassur'd her. 'What have I done? (said he kneeling at her feet), what have I done to deserve the cruel Letter I receiv'd this morning, and the return of that paper I sent you? Is it not contrary to those dear promises of Freindship which I can never forget? why do you tremble, my Angel (said he, takeing her hand gently), can you fear a Man who you may command with a look? By Heaven, by thy dear Lovely Selfe which is dearer to me, I will not hurt thee—'

'If you would have me believe you, my Lord (said she sighing, when she had recover'd her selfe enough to speak), leave me this moment. Thô I durst trust my selfe with you, yet consider how much you hurt my Reputation. What must the sisterhood think, when they know I am here alone with the Duke D'Enguien and that I suffer him to stay with me?'

'You need not apprehend that, reply'd he, I came over the Wall. None of the House know that I am here. I stole the Impression of Madam Maintenon's key, and had another made by it.'

Louisa made no Answer to this part of his discourse, (from his first entrance she had suspected he had receiv'd the key from Madam Maintenon, but she knew he would not confess it, and therefore

---

[1] This reads like a composite of several seduction scenes in Delarivier Manley, *The New Atalantis* (1709). Diana de Bedamore, discovered in a delightful garden retreat near a canal, shrieks in surprise, 'but there was none in hearing'; Charlot, presented by her seducing Duke with the key to the gallery he uses as a library, is discovered by him with the book dropped from her hand (*Novels*, ed. Patricia Köster (1971), i. 760, 334, 336). Neither, however, resembles Louisa in resisting (thanks to Elizabeth Hollis Berry for these references).

made no Enquiry). Her fears made her repeat again to him, that she beggd his Absence. She spoke with so much unfeign'd concern, her Lovely Face pale as death, and tears standing in her Eyes, as mov'd the Duke, and allmost entirely alter'd his first design. He threw him-selfe at her feet. 'Do not be so unjust my fair one (said he, kissing her hand which he still held). I will do nothing to displease you. There is nothing brutal in the passion I have for you; I could not be happy, except at the same time I made you so. Let me confesse (don't turn away your Eyes, my lovely Maid) I can<not> see that heavenly form without ten thousand fires in my heart. I cannot touch this soft, this powerfull hand, but my pulse beats high, my most ardent desires are rais'd, Nature her selfe commands me to make my selfe happy. Can I be so near my wishes and forbear? but yet my Charmer, yet, see the Empire you have over me, you can calm all these wild desires, throw this Ravisher at your feet, all tame and trembling. Tis in my power to clasp you in my Arms, to throw you on this bed which seems to invite the Pressure. Your crys could not reach the House, no humane help is near you, your little Strength would soon be overcome. You have no guard but those delicious Eyes, them speaking tears, a surer guard than a crowd of Armed Men. A pistol at my breast, death in my Veiw should not make me forgo my Lovely prize. But rather than offend you, I will sacrifice all my hopes, my wishes, suppresse this raging flame that drinks my blood, stiffle my sighs, and confine my roving hands, these eager trembling hands that burn to grasp you. But in return my Angel! what can you pay me for this unpresidented sacrifice? Will you not own that I deserve your Love? will you not permit me the innocent pleasure of seeing you thus sometimes?' He spoke these words with all the fondnesse yet all the respect of a Man truly touch'd.

Louisa had however reason to apprehend the Fire which she saw in his Eyes, and the yeilding softnesse she felt in her own heart. Looking on the Ground, she made Answer, 'If you would have [me] think I have indeed some power over you, leave me, my Lord Duke, leave me this moment. Oh be assur'd I would not lose my Virtue for an Empire—'

'I obey you, rigid as you are too Lovely Maid, reply'd the Duke riseing from his knees, I leave you, now that my heart beats high with transport, and every pulse alarms my glowing blood. But you with all your coldnesse won't deny me one dear parting kisse if I must leave you.' Allmost before he had ended these words, he snatch'd her in his Arms, kiss'd her soft eyes, and suck'd her Balmy breath,[1] press'd her white Bosom close to his panting heart, with so much trembling transport as left him no longer master of himselfe. But Louisa frighted to death, rallying all her scatter'd Resolution, started from his Arms, fell on her knees, too plainly perceiving to what this Embrace tended.

'Look upon me Monseiur (said she), look on me kneeling at your feet. I own your cruel Power; my crys would not avail me, you may if you please triumph over the Virtue of the poor Louisa; but oh depend upon it, you also triumph over my Life. I can-not Live and know my Virtue stain'd. I shall dye raving, and hateing you, I shall hate you as the Author of my Ruine. If you have greatnesse of Mind enough to Sacrifice your desires to my tears, Ages of Service could not make so much Impression on my Heart. I shall add the highest Esteem to that tendernesse I have for you. My Morning Orisons, my Evening Prayers, shall be for you. I shall dare to trust you as my Freind, and ever blesse you as my Benefactor.'

'Do not suspect me capable of any Violence against you (said he, tenderly raising her). I would be happy, but I would only owe it to the tendernesse of your heart. I hope my continu'd service, this mighty Sacrifice, my everlasting Passion, will at length overcome your Cruelty; your Scrupules will vanish, and that I may one day be happy. Suffer me this hope, permit me to see you sometimes alone. Hear my Vows, and listen to the Arguments proper to combat your too scrupulous nicety, and I swear to you by every sacred name, I will, never will, attempt any thing displeasing to you.' He let go her hand, while he spoke these words, and she gain'd the door without daring to stay to answer, and flew to her Apartment with as much swiftnesse as ever Daphne or Syrinx fled of Old.[2]

Possibly many men who read this Novelle will think they would have made another use of this Opertunity, but the Duke D'Enguien both by her Silence, and the tendernesse he knew she had for him, made no doubt, after so great an Instance of her Power over him, she would no longer scruple giving him private meetings, and that by soft degrees, he might attain that Happynesse, which now he saw perfectly well, he could no way obtain but by the last degree of Violence. Favours forc'd lose (at least a great part) of their Sweetnesse,

[1] Manley's Duke 'drunk her Tears with his Kisses, suck'd her Sighs' (336).
[2] Daphne and Syrinx fled from Apollo and Pan respectively, and were saved from rape by metamorphosis: Daphne into a laurel and Syrinx into a reed.

especially to a Man sincerely in Love as the Duke was, who trembl'd to disgust her, and was naturally of a soft temper.

Louisa gain'd her Apartment, so well pleas'd with her Escape, she hardly perceiv'd for some Moments the sorrows in her Heart. But when she refflected she found her selfe a miserable freindlesse Orphan, betray'd by her Freind and her Protectresse, tempted to Ruin by the Man she Lov'd. Whatever the Duke pretended, she was very well convinc'd he had the key of the Oratory from the hand of Madam Maintenon. The care she took to perswade her to go thither, her own innocent confessions to her, that she did not believe she could resist the Attacks of the Duke joyn'd with oppertunity, her Artfull Praises of him: ten thousand things that she recollected from the beginning of this fatal acquaintance confirm'd the Horrid thought. She remember'd now that Madam de Nerville had told her, Madam Maintenon try'd all sort of ways in vain to engage the Duke in her Interests, and that since she had brought him to St Cyr he appear'd complyant to her in all things. Unhappy Louisa could not make these Refflections without being allmost ready to dye with Greife. She no longer wonder'd to see Madam Maintenon hearken with so little reluctance to her Desiring the Veil; she saw, she would be very glad to keep her allways in her power, to oblige the Duke, and when he was sated with her Beauty, any other Nobleman she found it her Interest to oblige. She knew Madam Maintenon could easily introduce who she pleas'd even at midnight to her chamber and her Bed. And after she was profess'd, all complaints were vain: there was Discipline for Disobedience. Oh how she wept. She saw nothing round her, but Snares and Ruin. Whom could she complain to? The King was Madam Maintenon's, the Laws were his; there was no way, no earthly path to scape impending Destruction.

She turn'd her Eyes to All powerfull Heaven. She spent that whole night out of her Bed in tears, and prayers, and in the Morning found her selfe so much disorder'd, she went to Bed not without hopes of a Fever to put an End to her Life. But she was not so happy. Madam Maintenon came to see her, and finding her feverish, her Eyes all Swell'd with tears, and her Mind in a deep Melancholy that hardly permitted her to take notice of any thing, she did not doubt the good successe of her Hellish Enterprize, and with a malignant Joy which she could not dissemble, enquir'd after her Health.

Louisa made her very short Answers, and seem'd to desire Repose, complaining she had not slept all night. Madam Maintenon, with consummate hipocrisy, affected a mighty concern for her Illnesse, and would give her a sleeping Draught with her own hand. She had but Just left her, when her Woman brought her in a Letter from the Duke. There was enclos'd in it a Bill of ten thousand Pistoles. He left nothing unsaid to remove her scruples, he tenderly reproach'd her Crueltys, which he said would be his Death, and finally begg'd to see her once more, with Oaths of being entirely govern'd by her. She put this letter under her Pillow, she wept a long time, and at length, Stupyfy'd by Sorrow and the composing Draught she had taken, fell into a Sleep of 4 hours, which with her Youth so well compos'd her, she wak'd without any Symptoms of her Fever; but the Name of Madam the Dutchesse D'Enguien allmost threw her back into it. She was come to see her. Louisa could not refuse that Hon[ou]r from her Highnesse, and she came into her Chamber, tho she was yet in bed. After the first complements were over, and the Dutchesse had with great goodnesse shew'd a concern for her Indisposition, 'I am sorry (said she with a smile) to find you in a condition that makes it allmost improper to mention the proposals I have to make you, but I shall not be forgiven if I return without some Answer to them.' She proceeded and propos'd to her the Count of Belforrest for a Husband. He had often seen her with that Princesse, his Love increas'd to a degree that no longer left him Master of his Reason, and thô it was easy enough to perceive that the Duke D'Enguien had an Inclination for her, yet the Count depended so much on his own good conduct in securing her after his Marriage, that he fear'd nothing from that side, and only made use of that discovery, by applying to the Dutchesse, whom [*sic*] he very well guess'd for that reason, would leave nothing undone to put him in possession of the Beautifull Louisa.

The Dutchesse never was better pleas'd in her Life than when he gave her this commission. She aplauded his fair choice and assur'd him again and again nothing should be wanting on her Part to make him happy. Louisa heard this Proposal, as the only possibillity of escaping the Artifices of Madam Maintenon. She thought Heaven whom she had so earnestly supplicated, presented this only way to save her. She knew very well the Severe temper of the Count; she had heard how he had poison'd his first Wife, and she did not doubt if he marry'd her, it was to make her a Prisoner for the rest of her Life. These reasons, which would have deter'd any other Woman, made her resolve on the Match, without refflecting on the disproportion of their age, and the disagreableness of his humour and person. She return'd thanks to the Dutchesse for the Care she was pleas'd to shew, for her establishment, and said she had no objection against the Count de Belforrest, who honnour'd her very much, 'but (added she) I fear your H——will not easily induce Madam Maintenon to it, who intends me for the Veil.'

'Madam Maintenon (reply'd the Dutchesse) is too reasonable to impose the Veil on so young a Creature as you are. Depend upon me for gaining her Consent. If you will give me leave, I will tell her you have confess'd to me your Aversion to a Recluse Life and that you have some inclination to accept of the Count de Belforrest, for I would not appear to have too much perswaded you in his favour, being unwilling to disoblige Madam Maintenon, who would un-doubtedly take it very ill, if it be true, that she intends to keep you in her Convent.'

Louisa easily apprehended it was the Resentment of the Duke that she fear'd, and made Answer, she left it entirely to her Highnesse, to make use of any method she judg'd most proper. The Dutchesse embrac'd her with promises of Freindship and made haste to let the Count de Belforrest know his successe. She even flatter'd him that the fair Louisa had some Inclination for him, but the Count did not know himselfe so little. He was mortify'd to hear of so easy a consent, and his suspicious temper begun to suggest to him very disagreable reasons for it. He receiv'd the news with so much coldnesse, it was easy to penetrate his thoughts, and the Dutchesse begun to fear that he would make some sorry excuse. To remedy her Indiscretion (which she saw had caus'd his Coldnesse) she let him know that Madam Maintenon intended to impose the Veil on her lovely pen-sioner, and that perhaps the Aversion Louisa had for that sort of Life, had some share in her consenting so readily to the proposals had been made her. This restord to the Count part of his Quiet, thô he laugh'd to himselfe at the Simplicity of the Girl, who would find the rules of his House yet more severe than those of the Convent.

The Dutchesse to lose no time, immediately sought out Madam Maintenon, while the unhappy Louisa was refflecting on the rash consent she had given. She easyly foresaw to what miserys she expos'd her selfe, and it had been a thousand times easyer for her to put an end to her Cares, by the Poison, or the Dagger, but her Reli-gion forbid her to think that way, and she could not otherways live and preserve her Virtue. She ris up and writ a Letter to the Duke in these words.

Yes, my Lord Duke, your cares, your assiduitys are Answer'd. I own your power, I can no more defend my heart, I love you. I love you with a passion not to be express'd. I doat on you, I rave, I languish, and I dye without you. You have made me unhappy for ever—this is all your conquest—you shall not make me guilty. All your Arts, my own Desires, the Stratagems of Madam Maintenon can only make me miserable, but never criminal. I am not to learn that she acts in concert with you; that meeting in the Oratory too well convince'd me, whence you had your Inttelligence, and tis in vain you would give it another turn. I see I am not only expos'd to your persuits, and my own Inclinations, but all the Artifices of a Woman, in whose power I am. You had compassion on my tears, your Gennerosity was mov'd, you suffer'd my flight. I own the mighty Obligation, which touch'd my Heart more sensibly than all your charms and vows; but oh my Lord will it be allways thus? I can't deny you oppertunitys, your confidante is too much mistrisse here, and who can answer but in some fond minute, some unguarded hour, I may forget all things but that I love you. I own it to you with ten thousand blushes, you are all powerfull in my heart. That doating Heart pleads allways in your favour. Tis a sort of heaven to be near you, and when you look upon me, my best resolves melt fast away, and I can think of nothing, but of pleasing you. All things tell me the fatal necessity of seeing you no more—oh God can I live and see no more the Duke D'Enguien? No matter, Life's not the Question now, 'tis Glory.

I gave you back my Lord your vows, carry them to the Lovely Princesse to whom they are due, a thousand times superior to me in every charm. Pay to her the tendernesse you owe her truth and Beauty, and forget the unhappy Louisa, I will not complain of you for my undoing. Forget me, and that you may do it, and I may see you no more, I have resolvd—I shudder at the thought—but 'tis past, 'tis done, and I have promis'd—I faint to speak it—to marry—marry Another, one whom you can't suspect of being capable to move my heart—I marry the Count de Belforrest—and now what shall I say, where shall I find words to bid you farewell, words expressive of my tendernesse? Oh, there is none.—Pity me too Lovely Prince, Pity this Victim, this undone, this lost Louisa. I may ask your Pity without offending what you owe your princesse. Oh that my Life was to end with my Letter! but I must live and must be wretched long—Oh Pity me—

She enclos'd in this the Bill he had sent her. The Duke read it over with a mixture of Resentment, Sorrow and tendernesse that even his own Expressions come short of. This was his Answer.

Is it then possible? Louisa false, that Angel Innocence perjur'd? Why Madam did you ever flatter me with your Love, why did you play with this fond honest heart, why did you smile when you resolv'd to ruin me? you bid me forget—you can do that, but I have lov'd too truly, my whole Soul was yours, nor can I carry those vows to any other Object. But you, false as you are—Good God must I see you anothers? A man every way unworthy of you, must he possess those Charms for which I dye!

'Tis certain you may do what you please; you know you have nothing to fear from my Resentment or you durst not use me thus.—Another perhaps would—but I am too much yours, I can't offend you. Yet give me leave to argu with you. Let me plead a little for my happynesse, or if that is (as sure it is) of no Consideration with you, think on your own. Do not in one rash Minute sacrifice that lovely person to a Monster. If tis me you fly from, the object of your hatred, take this Bill (I furnish you with Arms against my selfe), go with it to Venice or to Rome. Let me see you no more, but suffer it to be possible for me to hope to see you one day mine, and if tis ever in my power, in whatever part of the world you retire, there I will seek my Louisa and lay my fortune at her feet. Don't give thy charming selfe away from me, let me not see—tis Madness to imagine—Good God was it for this? tis certain I knew very well in what manner to make use of the oppertunity that I had of makeing my selfe happy! I knew what use another Man would have made of it, and how I my selfe would have mannag'd it with any other Woman, but the respect I had for you, that expressless tendernesse that melts me to an infant's fondnesse made it impossible for me to hurt my Lovely Maid. I could not offend you to make my selfe the happyest of Mankind; it was easyer to me to sacrifice the Dearest desires of my heart, than give a pain to yours. Have I by this Submission merited this usage? Is it thus you pay me this unpresidented fondnesse? Can you stab me to the heart in return? Do, kill me, sacrifice me to your honnour or your hatred (call it which name you please) but do not wound your selfe to torture me. I dye to see those heavenly Beautys possess'd by any other, but I should find some ease in Death to think you happy, blest with some Man sensible of your Charms, and deserving your Love. But you (too unthinking fair one) you give your hand to a Man whose age, and whose ill humour will be insupportable to you, and whose circumstances are so strait, you involve your selfe in numberlesse ills and hardships. His Revenue is so small you can live no where but at his castle in Languedoc, a Desart Country, remote from all Conversation, allmost from humankind; and if his Fortune was more ample, his humour is too capricious to suffer You to live in Paris. All your Virtu will not secure you from his vile Suspicions.

—Good God can you endure the ill natur'd constructions that he will put on the most Innocent Actions, the cutting reproaches? Can that lovely Innocence bear the treatment only fit for the most profligate? can you who meet with Adoration and praise from all about you, can you suffer stinging refflections, and sharp upbraidings? can you who enjoy all the Delicacy of Affluence, who are accustom'd to the brightest conversation where you shine in all your Beauty, who have a soul sensible of the Charms of

tendernesse, and capable of the most delightfull Union of 2 hearts equally
touch'd, loveing and belov'd, is it possible you can submit to the low cares
and drudgery of a scanty fortune, the Society of rude unpolish'd clowns, to
hide those charms amongst rocks and woods, and suffer under the haughty
tyranny of a rigid Master? For such you will find the Count de Belforrest,
this happy Count for whom you forsake the most faithfull and most
passionate Lover upon Earth. But if notwithstanding what I have said, if
you can resolve upon makeing entirely for ever miserable, a Man that
Adores you, if you are determin'd and all my prayers are vain (for Oh I see
too well how much my Interest is decaid in that dear changing Heart), Yet,
keep this Bill; let me beg it as a freind, the name of Lover is what I must not
mention, it may serve as a retreat for you, when his ill temper forces you to
think of one, or it may be a way to make your circumstances more easy with
him. You may use it in such a Manner, he need not know you have it, or you
may call it the Gift of Madam Maintenon. Leave me this pleasure to imagine that I have some way contributed to your happynesse. I would make
you happy thô tis in his Arms while you give Death to the Wretched

D'Enguien.

P.S. I send you this which is all I have at present in my cabinet, but my fortune is yours.

He enclos'd the Bill of 10000 pistoles. Louisa allmost effac'd this
Letter with her tears. The gennerosity of it touch'd her to the Soul.
She allmost halfe resolve'd to accept his offer, and notwithstanding
the advances she had made, break off with the Count de Belforrest,
but she knew too well the Duke D'Enguien, with all his gennerosity,
would persue her to Rome, to Venice, or wherever she retir'd. She
could not refuse to see a Man from whom she receiv'd her bread.
If she saw him—that seem'd to include a train of consequences
too dreadfull to be look'd on. She wept again, and fortify'd her
selfe in the Resolution which seem'd the only way to preserve her
Virtue.

   She was in these thoughts when Madam Maintenon came in. The
Dutchesse D'Enguien had allready ask'd her consent for the marriage of Louisa, representing to her that it was very hard to cross the
Inclinations of that young Woman. Madam Maintenon could not
decently oppose the Dutchesses reasons, and coldly answer'd, that
certainly if Louisa own'd her selfe engag'd to the Count de Belforrest,
she would not intterupt her Love, thô she did not think it so good a
Match as she might have elsewhere. The Dutchesse appear'd contented with this answer. Madam Maintenon had learn'd from the
Duke the ill success of the garden Adventure, and surpriz'd at what

the Dutchesse said went to Louisa's chamber. 'I hear (said she with
an Ironical air) that your Love for the Count de Belforrest has made
you lay aside all thoughts of the Veil. I suppose you know I give but
500 crowns to those Girls that chuse for themselves, and tis as much
as his Estate deserves,—'

Louisa sigh'd, and made answer, she was allready so much indebted to her Bounty she had no reason [to] complain if she receiv'd
no more from it, and whatever she pleas'd to bestow, she receiv'd
with all submission. Madam Maintenon could hardly contain her
Spleen at this answer. 'You do not then deny your Engagements with
the Count de Belforrest,' said she to her.

'I am ready to marry him,' reply'd Louisa.—Madam Maintenon
left her so much provok'd at her Behaviour, she was allmost at the
End of her hipocrisy.

The Dutchesse D'Enguien, who had the Charge of this Negotiation, hasten'd all things with so much Diligence, the contract was
sign'd the next day, and the wedding celebrated 2 days after to the
astonishment of the whole Court, who not penetrating her Reasons,
could not comprehend by what Magic the Count de Belforrest at the
Age of 55, with one Leg, and otherways not handsome nor agreable,
could engage the affections of a young Beauty of 16 whose Wit had
been the admiration of all the World.

The day before her marriage she had sent back to the Duke
D'Enguien his Bill, enclosd in a Blank paper. His Rage was so great
that for some Moments he hop'd he lov'd her no longer, but time too
soon convince'd him, tis but a feeble passion which cannot survive
hope. The Impossibillity of gratifying his Love, rather serv'd to
encrease it, and he felt all the complicated pain that Love, Jealousie,
and disapointment could give to a tender and passionate Heart,
while the Object of his Envy the Count de Belforrest was not more
happy than himselfe. He had indeed the possession of one of the
most charming Beautys upon Earth, with whom he was passionately
in love, but what is possession where the heart is wanting?

Louisa swooned in the chappel after she had given him her hand.
He found her cold and weeping in his Arms. The lovely form was
there, but all the Life was vanish'd. The Youth who enjoy'd a Marble
Venus had allmost as warm a Mistress, perhaps a more pleasing
one, since she could show no signs of Reluctance.[1] The Count
de Belforrest knew very well this was something more than Virgin

---

[1] Presumably Pygmalion before the answer to his prayer for the statue to come to life.

coldnesse, and thô he trouble'd himselfe as little with Delicacy as another it did not fail to give him mortal pangs. Without know<ing> where to fix it, he enter'd into a most furious Jealousie. The 2d day after their marriage, he bid her prepare for Languedoc in 24 hours. He expected and had prepar'd himselfe to resist all her tears and Expostulations, but he knew little of her Heart. All things were become indifferent to her, and she was too unhappy to make any Distinction of place. She made no answer but, with a softness capable of raising compassion in any breast but his, she was ready when he pleas'd.

When they were a League from Paris, on a rising Ground from whence it was possible to survey that great Town, the Count order'd his coachman to stop. 'And now Madam, said he, addressing himselfe to the fair Countesse, look back upon Paris, for tis the last time you shall see it as long as you live.' She made him no Answer but by a great Sigh, and they proceeded on their Journey. The Count, who had a Serpent in his Breast that turn'd all things to poison, was even uneasy at the Indifference with which she left Paris: the little Inclination she seem'd to have for company, and her Desire for retirement, so unnatural to her Youth, perswaded him some secret passion was the Cause of it. He expected at every Inn to meet with some Lover, that he fancy'd she had appointed to follow her, but all things seem'd to contribute to his repose, if he had been capable of any. The fair Countesse shew'd him an Entire Obedience, and if she was melancholy, he had never seen her otherwise, and might have suppos'd it her natural temper.

After ten days Journey they arriv'd at the Chateau de Belforrest. Twas situated on a high Hill environ'd with woods, cheiffly compos'd of fir trees. At the Bottom of the Hill, a Large River with a gentle course water'd the Vallys. Art had had no hand in Beautifying this Situation; there was no regular Walks, or Plantations, but Nature had made it yet more charming in its native Simplicity. The Castle it selfe had been built in the time of Phillip the Fair,[1] when the family of Belforrest was one of the most considerable in the Kingdom. It had been very large with regular fortifications but was now above halfe ruin'd. What remain'd had thick walls of stone, after the Ancient manner of Architecture, and being a place more Intended for strength than Pleasure had little Windows, and was low roof'd as you see old castles. The furniture was not much more modern than the building,

---

[1] Philip IV (1268–1314), styled 'Le Bel'.

a good deal musty and moth eaten. Louisa shew'd no dislike of any thing she met with. The Count, who narrowly watch'd her, could not perceive the least disgust in her Countenance. She did not ask any thing to be chang'd, and enter'd into her Apartment with an Indifference that hardly suffer'd her to observe the Ancient figure it made. She found there an old Housekeeper, a good deal with the Air of a Duenna. The young Countess instead of shewing any dislike at the frightfull Attendant that was assign'd her, spoke to her with all the Sweetness in the World, and seem'd to take no notice of her impertinent persuing her, whenever she walk'd out.

The Count, whose natural ill humour was encreas'd by his Suspicions, had allready said upon a thousand occasions ill natur'd biteing things to the Countesse, thô it was difficult enough to find oppertunity to do it, for she never answer'd his most stinging words, nor ever spoke to him but with the utmost respect and Submission. He sometimes ask'd her if her Heart was not at Court, and whenever she sigh'd, to which of her Lovers that sigh was sent? These cruel peices of raillery mov'd her not at all, and she bore her sufferings with a patience that would have tir'd any other persecutor. Her only pleasure was in those pathless solitary woods, on the banks of the River, but the old woman constantly follow'd her thither. She neither ever forbid her, or shew'd any uneasyness at it, or pretended to ask for Henrietta, her own Maid, Whom the Count allways look'd on with an ill Eye, often commenting the wise mannagement of the Spaniards who never suffer'd a ser[van]t about their wives that was not of their own placeing. He had laid his measures so Just, all the Letters the Countesse writ was to fall into his hands, and all those directed to her; but she had been there allready 2 months without ever having ask'd for Pen and ink, or having receiv'd one Letter. The Count had taken the same way to read all those of Henrietta, but his curiosity was only paid with one that maid writ to her mother, and the old woman's answer.

All this did not convince the unhappy Count that Louisa had not left some engagement at Paris thô he knew not with whom. Never man took more pains to confirm his own suspicions or had less foundation for them.

Mean time the Beautifull Countesse gave up all her time to Devotion,

—But oh what Pious Art?
What vows avail to cure a bleeding Heart?

It was in vain she strove to drive from hers the Duke D'Enguien. Time lessen'd that Resentment his attempts had kindle'd; he appeard no longer to her in the form of a Ravisher; solitude and these Romantic Scenes recall'd all her softness to her Bosom. He was lovely, he was adorable, he was the Duke of Enguien. The Soft vows, the gentle Whispers of his Love recall'd themselves to her remembrance, and all the force was vanish'd. Her Virtue, which allways struggled to oppose her Love when he was near her, now was hush'd and calm when she no longer apprehended any Danger from indulging her Inclination. She could now love the Duke D'Enguien innocently: it did not violate her honnour to be miserable for his sake, and she even found some Sweetness in being so.

She had preserv'd his Picture, which she wept over, whenever the Count and his Deputy left her. In this manner she pass'd 2 months, more in love with the Duke D'Enguien than when he was every day at her feet, encreasing her passion with new Vows and assiduitys. The Count de Belforrest was summon'd to Paris as a Wittness for one of his best freinds in a very considerable Lawsuit. He left strict orders to continu a constant watch with his Duenna, and took post with a promise (which the Countess did not fear he should break) of a quick return.

The Night after, the young Countess, pleas'd with the Oppertunity of looking on that dear Picture, after she undress'd her selfe to a loose Nightgown[1] retir'd in her Closet within her Bedchamber, leaving Henrietta and the old Woman (who genneraly saw her in Bed) in her Dressing Room. She had one candle in her Hand and had just open'd the Picture, when a Noise in the Window behind her oblig'd her to turn her head. She saw a man coming in, which she had first took for a theif, and was riseing hastily up, when she saw him fling open his course coat discovering the order of the St Esprit,[2] and heard a soft voice she was too well acquainted with cry—'Hush my Angel.'—Her first thought was a Joy she could not resist, but immediately refflecting it was not for nothing that he came thither, she gain'd the door with so much precipitation he could not stop her, and thô she saw him fall on his knees with that Suppliant Air capable of disarming all her fear, she clap'd the door after her, and giving a great Cry, both Henrietta and her Duenna came to her Assistance. Some of the Men servants below run up, thinking

---

[1] Informal dress, not for sleeping in.
[2] An order instituted by Henri III in 1578 and limited to 100 knights.

Theives had broke in, and allmost all the family was assembled in her Chamber. She lean'd her back against the Closet door to prevent their going in, and give time to the Duke D'Enguien to make his Escape. Looking pale as Death, she tremble'd so, it was sometime before she could give an answer to their repeated Enquirys, what was the matter?

'As I was at my prayers (said she with great presence of Mind), a snake came out of the wall and glided just by me.' As it is common enough in that Country for Snakes, and those Venemous, to breed in old walls, no body doubted that was the cause of her fright, which she pretended had affected her so much it was necessary for 2 servants to sit up with her. As she gave these Orders in the Duke's hearing he was forc'd to retire, full of Admiration of her Virtue. For her part she pass'd the Night in agony hardly to be express'd; thô her Virtue forbid her to see the Duke, yet she could not but take it kindly of him to leave the pleasures of a Court, to follow her into the solitude of a Desart. She could not comprehend[1] how he could fly ten days Journey from Paris, and be at Belforrest the very Night after the Count had left it, who had not resolv'd to do so above 3 days. But she was not long in this Incertitude. There came to her from Tholouse, as by her Order, a piece of rich Brocard, and writ on the outside in the Duke's hand '30 yards of Brocard for the Countess of Belforrest.' She easily comprehended there was some mystery in this, and without appearing deconcerted when she receiv'd it before the Old Spy, she call'd her, and opening it, ask'd her opinion of her Fancy. The Old Woman without any Suspicion admir'd the beauty and richnesse of the stuff, and the Countess with an Air of Indifference bid her lay it in the Closet, where she soon after made some pretence to go, and locking the door, carefully unlapp'd it, till she came to the Board on which it was roll'd, which according to custom was cover'd with a White paper, between which and the board she found this Letter.

How can you use me so cruelly? I doat on you, and you will cause my Death. I left Paris the day that you did, and went to my seat in Normandy, from whence only attended by one ser[van]t I cross'd the country hither. I have been this 6 weeks in a private Lodging at Tholouse, waiting an Oppertunity of seeing my Louisa (Oh let me forget that you are the Countesse de Belforrest). Do not apprehend any danger to your Reputation (more valuable to me than my Life). I am entirely unknown here, and at court they

---

[1] Altered from 'conceive'.

believe me in Normandy. I did not think so much softnesse as I once thought lodg'd in that dear bosom capable of giveing me the shock you did last night. Where was the Occasion of that hasty flight? was it needfull to call your Ser[van]ts to assist you against a man you know you might command with a look? What pangs did you give me? Suffer me to see you once, there are ten thousand ways of contriving it, in spite of all your Guards. I am not to learn in what manner you are treated, 'tis no more than what I foresaw. Oh Why—but let us forget the past. I will forgive the giving away Your Selfe, let me but see you. Take my most Solemn Oaths: by all things sacred, you shall command my very wishes, I will not dare to think that you are Mortal, but as a Goddesse let me offer up my Vows. One sigh will pay me for all this Lavish Love, this tedious 6 weeks waiting. Let me conjure you by all I have suffer'd, and shall suffer, for I must love you for ever: by all my restless days and wakeing nights, by all the Agonys your Losse has cost me; by the dear hopes that once your Eyes have given me, thô now forgot and vanishd, let me see you. Is it a Crime to see me at your feet? is it too much to grant a Man whose Life and Soul is yours? But Oh, I plead in vain: my heart forebodes me, tis no longer to Louisa that I speak. You have forgot that name, and all your tendernesse. Yet can that Angel be capable of Levety? have you not vow'd you lov'd, and can you ever grow Indifferent? Do not suffer me to have a thought so Injurious to your Virtue. No, you are all perfection, you have none of the little weaknesses, nothing but the sex and lovely form of Woman, Oh my Louisa!

I will walk every Night from 12 till 2 under your Closet window, and if you ever will hang your handkercheif out of it, I will fix my Ladder and enter, with what Joy—unutterable transport.

The unhappy Countesse read over this Letter with Emotions only to be felt by one as much in Love. The tendernesse of it soften'd her to an excesse of Fondnesse; his reproaches fir'd her with great Inclination (so natural to us) of Justifying her selfe; so considerable a proofe of his fedelity rais'd her Passion and Esteem; and she could not do otherwise than think it a mighty proofe of boundlesse Love. For the great Duke D'Enguien to leave the Court, to live conceal'd six weeks in a cottage only to see her, she could not refflect without some degree of pleasure. It [*sic*] represented to her, she had now more tyes, more Obligations not to see him: the very mention of his Name was criminal. She was marry'd, her love was vow'd away, and if her heart was not in her power, at least her Actions were. These Refflections determin'd her: she made it a Law to her selfe not so much as to go into that Closet, but with a violence that allmost lost her her life. Her thoughts were continually there, and wherever she went the Duke D'Enguien seem'd present to her Sight, who continu'd to walk a fortnight under her Window without Intermission, during which time he sent her allmost daily Letters, by different contrivances, in Pieces of Lace etc. He try'd alternate Reproaches and intreatys, he left nothing unsaid to move her Heart, he allways mov'd it, but she was fix'd not to see him, not withstanding her own Desire pleaded strongly in his favour.

The Count de Belforrest return'd, and the Duke took post for Normandy after writeing to the Countesse all that Despair could dictate, and repeating to her that she would be the cause of his death. Love seem'd to take pleasure in revenging on the Duke D'Enguien all his Infidelitys. He now felt a passion he had hitherto been unacquainted with: 'twas no longer a Love that could be cur'd by Absence or another Face. He return'd to Court so much chang'd, he was hardly to be known. The Remembrance of Louisa, the Enchanting Louisa, haunted him without ceasing. He endeavor'd to lose it by plunging himselfe in Diversions. He play'd deep, he even dran<k> to excesse, thô he naturally hated it, without any other Effect than makeing him yet more miserable. A constant Melancholy, and an unusual Quantity of Wine, with Late hours, enflam'd his Blood and caus'd him a fever which lasted[1] ten days, and had probably been fatal if Youth <and> a great Strength of Constitution had not got the better of i<t.>

The unhappy Countesse felt all his sufferings doubled in her Bosom. The Count de Belforrest was as much out of humour at his Return, as if he had known she had seen the Duke D'Eng<uien> every night, tho his faithfull Spy assur'd him she had never stir'd from her Side. His Jealousie and Spleen suggested to him a thousand uneasynesses, thô he could not well assign any reason for them. Wretched Louisa, doubly miserable by the Assiduitys of a too Aimable Lover that her Virtue forbid her to Love, and the ill usage of a Disagreable Husband, which her Duty exacted from her not to hate! Twas impossible to bear up under so many Afflictions. She fell into a Languishing Melancholy, that daily impair'd both her health and beauty. Her bright Eyes lost all their fires, her Complexion faded, and she lost both her strength and appetite. The Count, suspicious of a Design in every thing, believ'd her sickness feign'd to carry her to Paris. She suffer'd him to remain in this opinion, and

[1] MWM wrote and rejected a very different fate for the Duke: 'but ten days. Thus dy'd that Duke D'Enguien, a Man of Merit, who had made a much more considerable figure in the World, if his passions had had less Empire over him.'

with pleasure felt the decays of her Health which promis'd her soon
an end of her miserable Life.

She was allready far gone in Consumption before the Count
apprehended her in any Danger, but when he thought her realy very
ill, his Passion reviv'd for her. He saw he was going to lose that
adorable Beauty, and thô he had not been happy in the possession of
it he could not without exquisite greife think of being depriv'd of it
for ever. He sent for Doctors from Tholouse. They Advis'd her to
have recourse to the Waters of Bourbon,[1] but twas too late. The night
before her design'd Journey thither, she fell into fainting fits.
Henrietta sat up with her, and calling the faithfull maid, she took a
small Box from under her Pillow and squeezing her hand gave it to
her, and immediately swooned. The Maid gave a great Cry, and the
Count whose apartment was next to it, ran thither, but Henrietta had
had the precaution of putting the box in her pocket. He came too
Late to say any thing to the Dying Louisa. She open'd her eyes but
once more, and then clos'd them for ever, Leaving behind her an
Example of Inimitable Virtue. Thus dy'd the greatest Beauty of
France a Sacrifice to the Ambition of Madam Maintenon.

Henrietta found in that Box the picture of the Duke D'Enguien.
Thô her unhappy Lady had given her no order about it, and the
Diamonds was a present considerable enough to a maid of her rank,[2]
yet with an uncommon fidelity, she took care with the utmost Secrecy to carry it, to the Duke D'Enguien. He receiv'd the News of
the Death of the Countess of Belforrest with transports of greife,
that one would have imagin'd too violent to last, and yet he remain'd
above a year in a Melancholy that nothing could Dissipate. At length
time and the busynesse inseparable from the figure he made in the
World, if it did not banish from his memory the Idea of Louisa, at
least it made his Sorrow supportable to him.

[1] The little town of Bourbon, high in the Massif Central, a long and difficult journey from
Gascony, did indeed have mineral springs; but the doctors' choice of it may be an ironic play
on the Duke's surname.

[2] Perhaps the very picture that was reluctantly refused by Mlle de Condé's maid, Charlot
(above, p. 33)?

Italian Memoir

Textual note. Original in Italian (Wh MS 510; p. 193 below), in a scribal hand which, from its occurrence elsewhere in MWM's papers, may be that of her secretary Dr Mora. Once safely out of the province of Brescia, at the end of August 1756, she planned to prosecute Count Ugolino Palazzi (1714–after 1765) 'for swindling her' over 'a house in the Mantouan' [*sic*]. The Imperial Ambassador, Philipp Josef, Count von Rosenberg, helped her to draw up an 'account' which is probably this document (William Graeme to Lord Bute, Valdagno, 30 Aug. 1758, Bute MSS). Eight lines in her commonplace-book may be notes towards it (CB, fo. 22). The scribe's habits of punctuation differ from MWM's, and are followed closely only in the original.

My stay in Avignon had become very troublesome to me, and I longed to return to Italy, but I did not dare undertake such a journey, since Italy was then a Theatre of War.[1] Count Palazzi, who had by then arrived in Avignon, had been presented to me in Venice by Signora Pisani Mocenigo as a young man under her patronage, whom she had recommended to the service of the Prince of Saxony; for this reason he had left Venice a few days later.[2] This was in the year 1740, and after that I heard no mention of him until his arrival in Avignon, which was in the year 1746.[3]

He then came to pay me a visit, and I was very pleased to talk with him about my Friends in Venice, and I mentioned to him in conversation that I should have very much liked to be able to return there. He replied that he was going to Brescia to visit his Mother, and begged me to allow him to escort me at least as far as Brescia.[4] He

---

[1] MWM had lived in Avignon since May 1742. As papal territory it was neutral in the War of the Austrian Succession, but from July 1745 she had complained about its Jacobite activity and counter-espionage. In July 1746 her plan to travel to Italy with Sir James Caldwell fell through (*CL* ii. 358, 361, 375).

[2] MWM had boasted in Oct. 1739 of knowing Pisana (Corner) Mocenigo (d. 1769), the recent bride of a Procurator and future Doge. At the house of this 'most considerable Lady' of Venice she also met Prince Frederick Christian (1722–63) of Saxony, who left Venice in June 1740; Palazzi became gentleman of the bedchamber to him (*CL* ii. 155–6, 162, 192; *Life*, 236).

[3] Palazzi reached Avignon in late July 1746, bearing a letter of introduction to MWM from an old friend of hers, the Prince of Saxony's tutor (*Life*, 236; *CL* ii. 166, 192–3).

[4] Brescia lay within the Venetian dominions. Palazzi's mother, a widow, was Giulia (Fenaroli) Palazzi (1697–1751) (*CL* ii. 375).

added that his Mother would most certainly not allow me to sleep at an Inn, but that she would consider herself much honoured if I would stay at her House. I told him he need not think of such a thing, as I would never go to a Lady's House without having been invited. As for the journey, I understood that he wanted to save on expenses, and I therefore considered whether or not to assume them myself.

A few days later he came to bring me a letter from his Mother, apparently an answer to one that he had written her. In this letter she told him that she was relieved that he had become discreet enough to be accepted into the company of such a respectable Lady as myself. She made me a thousand grateful compliments, and begged me, as the greatest honour I could pay her, to stay at her house.

In the end, having a great desire to leave Avignon, I took this opportunity as the only one that had offered for a long time. I made my preparations to leave, paid the necessary visits to Friends, and ordered our post-chaise. On the eve of my departure, the Count told me that he was truly mortified, but that since all his property was in his Mother's hands and since he had a very small allowance, he had been obliged to run into debt, and that he could not leave Avignon without three hundred sequins,[1] for which he would give me a note which his Mother would not refuse to pay upon our arrival. I had some doubts about making such a loan, and saw too that he set too high a price on the escort he proposed to give me; nonetheless, having many strong reasons to leave Avignon, I gave him the 300 sequins, and took his note. I confess that his escort was indeed very necessary; we were obliged to cross the path of the Spanish army, and it is indubitable that if I had not been able, thanks to his Company, to pass for a Venetian Lady, I should certainly have been in great danger.[2]

I was received by Countess Palazzi with all imaginable politeness.[3] She took me into her confidence and told me that her Son had ruined the Family by his extravagances in Saxony; from this I understood that she would not be inclined to pay his debts, and so I judged it would be useless to present her with the note from Avignon. I was planning to continue my journey as far as Venice when I was overcome with a malignant fever which immobilized me. I remained bedridden for two Months, which left me feeling weak and depressed, so

---

[1] Two Italian zecchini or sequins were worth one English pound.

[2] She encountered both Spanish and Austrian armies on 16–19 Aug. 1746 (*CL* ii. 376–7).

[3] MWM arrived at Brescia on 20 Aug. and was received in the Palazzi house in today's Piazza del Foro (*CL* ii. 377, 378).

that I believed the doctors who told me that Country air was absolutely necessary to re-establish my health.[1]

The Count offered me a House of his in the Country; I agreed to
go there, although I was so weak that I had to be carried in a Litter;
Countess Palazzi accompanied me. I found the House so run down
and in such bad condition[2] that if I had known the state it was in, I
should never have gone there, but it was too late to change my mind.
I went to bed and the fever seized me again. I was given quinine, and
in the morning the fever left me, so that I was able to get up. Countess
Palazzi made me a thousand apologies for the necessity she stood
under of returning to Brescia for some important business. She left
with her Son, who came back after a few days and told me that his
Mother would not be able to return for some time, but that I was mistress of her house, and of everything in his power. The fever meanwhile had become intermittent; I told the Count I was mortified
about putting Madame Palazzi to so much inconvenience, and distressed to think of the embarrassment and expense that she had suffered on my account, so I begged him to tell me frankly what gift I
might make that would please her.

He hesitated a while and after much ceremony told me that his
Mother was the most self-seeking Woman in the World,[3] although
very ambitious, and that if she were to receive a gift from me she
would feel obliged to make me another in return, and that she would
find this very embarrassing, but that if I were to insist on making a
payment, she would not make any scruple to receive cash, as long as
I paid her secretly, and that he would undertake to ensure she received it. I therefore gave him two hundred sequins for this purpose,
and he left in the morning in order (as he said) to take it to her.

During this time I received many visits from Ladies in the vicin-
ity, most of whom were relatives of the Palazzi Family. Among them
the Countess of Cigole paid me a thousand courtesies. I found meanwhile that the country air was very beneficial to my health, which I
hoped would soon be perfectly restored, although I was not yet able

[1] She did not recover until late November, having lost a lot of weight and been thought in
danger of death (*CL* ii. 378–9).

[2] MWM's note says '1746 went to G[ottolengo] from [*something crossed out*] Torbule.
Sought Houses all Winter' (CB, fo. 22). She implied in spring 1747 that she had only recently
taken this house, at Gottolengo, about 18 miles south of the town of Brescia. At Torbole, 3
miles south-west of Brescia, Palazzi had a villa (*Ville della Provincia di Brescia*, 1985, 411). She
said the Gottolengo house was 'not much more than the shell of a Palace', built early in the century for an owner who died leaving it unfinished (*CL* ii. 383, 388, 389).

[3] An awkward, unidiomatic construction in Italian (information from Patrizia Bettelli).

to leave my room. Count Palazzi returned, bringing more compliments from his mother, and renewed apologies for not being able to
leave Brescia to come and keep me company. It was then the month
of November. He invited me on behalf of the Countess of Cigole to
share the St Martin's Goose at her House.[1] The entire Family and
many Friends were to be gathered there. He represented that the
good Lady would be severely disappointed if I were unwilling to do
her this honour; that it would give her the greatest pleasure to receive me at her House, and that I would meet there the most distinguished People of the Neighbourhood, who were most desirous to
make my acquaintance. I replied that it would be a delight to me to
confer pleasure on the Countess of Cigole, his Aunt, but that I feared
I would be risking my health, for the fits of fever were still frequent.
He argued that it was no more than two miles away,[2] that I could go
in a well closed Carriage, dressed as I pleased, and that it was a
beautiful day. I therefore consented, thinking that, warmly wrapped
in a Fur, I could risk exposing myself to the open air. I gave orders to
my Maid not to leave my Apartment, and got myself ready to go out.
The Count said that it was Customary in the Country for Ladies to
take their Maids to wait on them; that if I should happen to be taken
ill again, mine would be necessary to look after me; and that my Man
would be needed to serve me at table. I had only these two Persons in
my service, and it displeased me greatly to leave the custody of my
Room to People I did not know. To this he replied that he could
vouch for the trustworthiness of his Man-servant, who would be
assigned to guard my room since there were neither keys nor locks in
the House.

At Cigole I found many People of quality and enjoyed a magnificent dinner. We dined in a Salon where the air was so grievously cold
that I was obliged to leave the table and to call for my Carriage to return home. Madame Cigole came out with me, but she would not
permit me to leave [her house]. A Doctor was found, who having felt
my pulse, confirmed that I was having a very severe fever, and advised me to put myself to Bed. The Countess had a bed warmed for
me with all imaginable attention. Count Palazzi left with his Brother
the Abbé. I stayed in Bed until two hours before noon, sleeping
peacefully all the morning, and when I awoke, the doctor found me
free of fever.

[1] Goose was traditional in England too at Martinmas, 11 Nov.
[2] Cigole is two or three times that distance from Gottolengo.

I wished to leave, in order not to inconvenience the Countess. Count Palazzi came to escort me, and I returned to Gottolengo. I was astonished upon entering my Room, to find many things out of their places, and to learn that the Servant who had been assigned to guard it was out Hunting. I looked for the boxes containing my jewels. I kept the keys to them in my purse, and I had put the said boxes in a velvet bag under my Bed. I could find neither the bag nor its contents. I had the Count informed of the loss I had sustained. He pretended to have difficulty believing it, but when he was convinced, he flung himself in Tears at my feet, inconsolable, as he said, for the dishonour brought upon his House. I replied merely that he must find a way of getting them back; and the fever returned, and I went to bed again. In the morning he came back to say he had searched the entire Castle without result,[1] and that in order to make further enquiries he would need some money. I counted out forty sequins for this alleged search, and so he went off on Horseback to look for the Thieves. He stayed away for three days, and then told me with Tears and sobs, that he had found no trace of them, and that if I did not take pity on him, he would be a lost Man: that he would become the disgrace of his Family, and that his Mother, who was already dissatisfied with him, would use this pretext to disinherit him. He said he had suspicions about his Brother, the Abbé, who was a very bad man,[2] and might have committed this theft. I silenced him, saying he ought not to entertain such a suspicion, but in the absence of solid proof he must bury it deep in his heart, and consider that he might be doing wrong to a Churchman, and his own Brother. 'Oh God!' he answered, with bitter tears, 'I must be mad, I don't know what I am saying. Have pity on a Wretch, who knows he is dishonoured by this cruel mischance.'

In spite of all this display of grief, I could not get rid of a secret suspicion that he himself was the thief, of which, however, I determined not to show the least hint without first having valid evidence to confirm it; and I thought it would not take long for such evidence to emerge if in fact he was guilty. I imagined that he would follow his own bent and go back to Poland, where he could set himself up splendidly with the aid of my jewels. But instead of that I saw him eternally coming and going, in despair, ready to put the servants to inquisition if I would have permitted it.

---

[1] MWM often later called the house her castle: it stood on the site of one.
[2] Alessandro Palazzi (b. 1719), *abate* of Pontevico, was indeed criminal.

Madame Roncadelli, his Father's Sister,[1] came to visit me. She is a respectable elderly Lady who had lived honourably and had the reputation of a saint. She wept at my Bedside, and obliged me to give her a List of my jewels, for her to send away to all the Jewellers of Italy. I believed this to be quite useless, but I allowed her importunity to overcome me and dictated the list to her, being in no state to write since I was running a fever at the time. For this reason the List was incomplete, although it did record the principal items. Madame Roncadelli had it printed, and sent round all the largest Cities. I discerned such candour and good breeding in her conduct that I conceived a real esteem for her, and she has always shown great friendship towards me.

The quinine cured my fever, but Winter was so far advanced, and my health so shaken, that I saw I should be compelled to stay at Gottolengo until the Spring, to my great displeasure. I bought a dilapidated old armchair for which I had to pay very dear. The Count assured me it was the only one in the whole village, where they had nothing in their houses but wooden [armless] chairs.[2] I had locks put on the doors, and glass in the windows. I complained that the walls were damp, and the Count told me that a certain Count Martinengo wanted to sell his old tapestries, but he did not want to divide the set. I was unwilling to commit myself to such a large quantity, but my Furnishings were still at Avignon, and I was much incommoded by the cold. I therefore made the purchase, and had the whole house covered, and was able to stay there comfortably.

My health was becoming daily stronger; everyone remarked on its improvement, and fully expected that I ought to be satisfied. Nevertheless I resolved to leave in the month of April, not wishing to renovate a House which would cost me as much as a new building. Meanwhile all the Relations of the Count came to visit me, and he used my Horses to come and go, which I permitted as a small favour that I thought not worth the trouble of refusing. When I told him I designed to leave, he began once more to enact despair, and said that I was destroying his honour, and would leave an eternal stain on his Family. His conduct appeared to me in every way so unbalanced that I ceased to suspect him of cunning, and considered him an object of pity. I felt myself still obliged in some way to expunge a disgrace

---

[1] Madalena (Palazzi) Roncadelli, widow of Giovanni Battista Roncadelli of Cremona, and sister of Federico Palazzi (1687–1731) (*Aspetti della società bresciana nel Settecento*, 1981, 68).

[2] In MS 'careghe', a regional word.

which he had incurred on my account, even though its cause was his own imprudence. It was easy to see that great expense would be needed to make his House habitable, and it had no garden, which is necessary and agreeable for a Country House.

A few evenings after this Conversation he came to tell me that he had made a discovery that could in some sort make up for the damage done: that an old dying Priest wanted to sell a little piece of land to pay his debts, that I could have it for a very low price if I would let him occupy the House until the end of his life, that there was a large Garden which could be embellished to suit my own taste, that it was near enough to the Castle to meet all my needs, and that in any event I should be able to sell it for a profit whenever I might wish to do so. I had these matters examined into by competent people, I went there myself and found it quite a beautiful spot, and I bought it for eight hundred sequins in cash. I diverted myself with the garden, and decided to spend another two hundred sequins on it. This was in the year 1747.[1] I did this even though I had not yet decided to stay on in Gottolengo. I had left my heavy baggage at Avignon in the house of the Vice-Legate.[2] I thought it would be very difficult to convey it in time of War, and before having it sent I was waiting for peace to arrive; also I was still uncertain where I should settle. Little by little I became accustomed to the solitude of Gottolengo; I enjoyed the walks, the air agreed with me, and I let myself be talked into making improvements to the old House. The Count returned from Brescia, where he had seen, so he said, Signor Bettoni, a great Merchant who was about to travel to Avignon. He said that Signor Bettoni had great obligations to his family, and would therefore undertake to arrange for my Baggage to come. I knew Signor Bettoni's reputation, and had no doubts about his trustworthiness, and since the Count insisted I allowed him to put Signor Bettoni in charge of the transaction. My Baggage arrived in a terrible state. Many pieces of my furniture were missing, also some of my china and four fine snuff-boxes, one of them set with diamonds and rubies. I was very displeased about this,

[1] MWM's letters home (above, p. 83, n. 2) elide her first winter at her 'castle' in Gottolengo, sounding as if she settled there only at the time she acquired the garden, which she describes in detail in July 1748 (*CL* ii. 402–5, 407–8). Her notes provide, apparently, a name for the garden house: 'Spring [1747] took Legere, staid little . . . 1748 pass'd between Legere and G[ottolengo]. 1749 Ditto etc' (CB, fo. 22).

[2] A new Vice-Legate had arrived at Avignon in June 1744: Pasquale Acquaviva (1719–88), 'Young, rich, and handsome, and setts out in a greater Figure than has ever been known here' (*CL* ii. 320 n. 2, 331).

and the Count appeared to be angry. He cursed all merchants as Thieves, and offered in all seriousness to have Signor Bettoni shot. I laughed at this extravagance, and begged him not to murder the reputation of such a respected Man of Business, saying that no doubt this had been caused by the dishonesty or negligence of one of his Agents.

This was what I believed, and I diverted myself with my Books, which had all arrived safe and sound,[1] and I paid the 200 Sequins that the Count requested in Signor Bettoni's name to cover his transport expenses. The Count made his House at Gottolengo over to me by a deed signed in the presence of Witnesses, and I had it repaired, and enlarged, and fitted up with my Furniture. Two months later he arrived from Brescia with joy painted all over his face. 'God be praised, he said, I have found a way to repair, at least in part, the loss you have suffered in my House, which is always present with its attendant horror in my mind. There is a Decrepit Old Man at Trenzano, a few miles away from Brescia,[2] who is Childless. He has offered to sell his Property for a Life Annuity of two thousand six hundred sequins per annum. He is ninety years old, as you can verify from the Baptismal register, of which I will bring you a certificate. His land is worth at least seventy thousand ducats. I have had it examined and valued by experts in these matters. I have seen it and fallen in love with it. The poor invalid cannot live more than six months, and the profit will be all yours.' I replied that I was not a Person greedy for Property, and did not want to involve myself in land ownership in a foreign Country. At this he shouted at me that I wished to deprive him of his only chance of restoring the value of my jewels, and that in doing me this service he would have proved that he was incapable of wronging me; that he had flattered himself that I would have had Compassion on a Wretch who would choose to die to repair his honour, and that he had assured Signor Castelli that I would accept the bargain, that he would be coming to Gottolengo next morning with the deed ready for signing, and that if I were to cause him to break his word, I should have shown such injurious mistrust of him that he would be the laughing-stock of the whole

---

[1] This suggests she had not yet parted with the 300-odd titles listed in her book-catalogue in 1739 which are no longer among her surviving books at Sandon Hall, Stafford (Isobel Grundy, 'Books and the Woman: An Eighteenth-Century Owner and her Libraries', *English Studies in Canada*, 20 (1994), 1–22).

[2] About 10 miles away.

Country, and especially of his Mother, who had flattered herself they had found in this a means of making up the loss of my jewels.

Castelli (or somebody else calling himself by that name) arrived. He was a white-haired Old Man, bent and trembling. He brought with him the valuation of his Property calculated by public Appraisers and the deed of sale to me on the above-mentioned conditions. I signed it in the presence of the Notary of Gottolengo and of two witnesses, and paid the first annuity in advance. This was in the year 1749.[1]

I continued to occupy myself in my solitude with my Books and my Garden. The Count came seldom, which I was very glad about, because he had been spoiling my Horses and breaking my Chairs. In the Month of March 1750 I took a chill while out walking; I was taken with fever and many aggravating symptoms. I had Doctors come from Brescia and from Cremona, and recuperated with great difficulty and very slowly.[2] The Count came to visit me, and brought me a thousand compliments from his Mother, assuring me that she would have come herself to take care of me, if her health had not been so delicate, and the roads so damaged by the excessive rain, on which account she dared not venture out. Two days later he asked permission to enter my Room looking very frightened; he told me that he had received an express letter from his Mother, telling him that it had been represented to the Podestà of Brescia, Angelo Contarini, that he was holding me Prisoner in his Castle,[3] that this was undoubtedly the doing of the Rodenghi, hereditary Enemies of his Line, that this accusation would spell the ruin of his whole Family, and he besought me with Tears in his eyes to save him. I replied that

---

[1] On 27 May [1749] MWM for the first time complained in a letter about the distance between her Gottolengo house and garden. She was at Lovere on Lago d'Iseo, 40 miles away, in 1747, from late July to Sept. 1749, and in 1750 and 1751 (CB, fo. 22). Gottolengo had two notaries in 1750 (Leonardi Mazzoldi, *L'Estimo mercantile del territorio, 1750*, Brescia, 1966, 184).

[2] On 24 May she wrote to her friend Lady Oxford (see below, p. 97, n. 6), 'I have had the severest illness I ever had, and heard Sentence of Death pronounce'd against me. I am now told I am out of Danger.' Next month she elaborated: infection of her teeth and gums had turned to 'gangrene' (perhaps abscesses?), but she was saved by 'the most celebrated Surgeon in all these parts', fetched from Cremona, who applied first red-hot irons and later caustics to her gums (*CL* ii. 454, 460–1).

[3] As Podestà of Brescia, Angelo Maria Contarini (1693–1772) administered Venetian justice in the province. On 8 June 1750 François-Zacharie de Quinsonas Lauberivière, Knight of Malta, filed a deposition saying that on his travelling to Gottolengo to take MWM a letter from John Anderson (tutor to her son), he was surrounded by Palazzi's minions, threatened, and shut up for two hours in a cellar, while Palazzi impounded the letter (Venetian Archivio di Stato, Brescia, Busta 21. 14).

nothing could be more just than for me to do this, and that I was ready to testify that I was staying there of my own free will, and that he had never shown any lack of respect for me. Indeed, two hours later an Official of the Podestà arrived with orders to speak with me privately.[1]

I was ensconced on my Couch, still weak from my recent illness; I assured him, as was the truth, that I had received nothing but courtesy from the Palazzi Family, and I wrote personally to Signor Contarini to thank him for his concern, and at the same time to repeat the aforesaid testimony to him.[2] The Count went to Brescia, and returned two days later with a closed Carriage sent for me by his Mother, who besought me for pity's sake to come to her House, to silence all the false rumours still in circulation, which only my presence could quash. The doctor assured me that I could make the journey without risk, and I made it in such a state of weakness that my Maid had to support me in the carriage, and the Count and his Brother the Abbé could hardly get me to the Apartments which were my destination. In their House I found their Aunt Signora Roncadelli, their Mother, and their Sister, who is now a Nun. They treated me with all possible honour and respect. I slept well, and in the morning I was well enough to receive visitors. I was therefore visited by a large number of Ladies and Gentlemen. I laughed at the idea that I was kept at Gottolengo by violence; it seemed to me very natural that a Lady of my age should choose retirement, and so I said to everyone that I saw.[3]

The whole Family begged me to stay in Brescia until the arrival of the new Podestà, who was every day expected, so that I could repeat the same thing to him. I agreed the more willingly to this, because

[1] Contarini wrote on 9 June asking MWM to come to Brescia and give her side of the affair (Busta 21. 16).

[2] She told Contarini that she was too ill to travel to Brescia, that Quinsonas Lauberivière was a madman, that he had shown her a letter from an unknown, perhaps non-existent, lady (which she had returned to him), and had drawn a pistol against her servants (10 June 1750, *CL* ii. 456–7).

[3] Lauberivière (who had been at Avignon when MWM was there, and was rumoured to have left the town at her representation to the authorities) may have been an emissary either from her faithless lover, Francesco Algarotti (she jotted their names side by side a few years later, CB, fo. 21), or from her errant son, Edward Wortley Montagu, jr. (1713–76). She had last seen him (in order to report on him to her husband) in 1742. After performing creditably in the army and at the Aix-la-Chapelle peace talks, he was now in England, probably against his father's will, since only his status as an MP prevented his arrest for massive debt. Lauberivière claimed to be bearing a letter from John Anderson, young Montagu's ex-tutor: falsely, since Anderson arrived in person at Brescia in July, to quite a different reception (Busta 21. 11; *CL* ii. 285–6, 367–8, 397 n. 2, 462, 465).

Signora Gradenigo was the new Podestà's wife, and I was eager to see again a Lady to whom I was indebted for many courtesies received in Venice.[1] My strength returned, but the elderly physician Dr Guadagni advised me to take the waters at Lovere, and I prepared to go there once I had made my compliments to Signora Guistiniana Gradenigo. The Count continued taking his usual walks, and came to tell me that there was a very beautiful Palace, and a Garden in the most perfect taste, that I should be able to buy for a trifle, and he begged me at least to go and and look at it. I did not want to listen to talk of this kind, and I made what haste I could to travel to Lovere.[2]

On the eve of my departure the Count warned me that I should have to traverse a very dangerous Forest, and that if I had any money I should do well to leave it in the hands of a Banker. He strongly recommended Signor Francesco Ballini: he told me his Father had made this man's fortune and he therefore considered the family as his Patrons; besides, he was a man of unblemished integrity, and of great wealth. I asked to see him. He replied that the banker had the gout, but that he would take him the money and bring me back the receipt. I have actually forgotten the exact sum I entrusted to him, but I think it was two hundred sequins. I left. The Count would have liked to accompany me. The Ladies made me visits of leave-taking, and to wish me a speedy recovery of my health, which in fact was entirely restored, thanks to the waters and the good air of Lovere.

I found it a most agreeable place, inhabited by people of rank, and I should have made a longer stay if I could have found a more comfortable House, but I had such poor lodgings that I lamented the fact to my Physician, Dr Baglioni,[3] and told him I could make no promise to return in the Spring unless he could find me a House. He searched for a long time without success. In the end, shortly before my departure, he told me there was one for sale, small, and in bad condition, which for those reasons was being sold for three hundred

---

[1] In Venice in 1740 Giustiniana (Morosini) Gradenigo (b. 1705) broke with tradition to make 'a great Supper' at Carnival time for the foreigner MWM, and she and her sister-in-law accompanied her in the Bucentaur when the Doge wedded the sea that year (*CL* ii. 170, 172, 180). Girolamo Gradenigo became Podestà in 1750, but Contarini seems to have dealt with MWM's case to the end.

[2] Nevertheless, her letters to England gloss over a brief absence from Brescia in Palazzi's company, before she finally left it for Lovere (*CL* ii. 464; Contarini to the Venetian Governor, 21 June and 12 July 1750, Busta 235. 1, 7). Dr Gian Francesco Guadagni (1704–94) was younger than she was.

[3] Probably Antonio Baglioni, 'medico condotto' (Mazzoldi, *L'Estimo mercantile*, 132). She had put herself under his care on her previous visit to Lovere, in Aug. 1749 (*CL* ii. 436).

scudi; but I could enlarge and improve it. It was positioned above the lake, and had a beautiful prospect. I gave Dr Baglioni a note on Ballini for this sum, with my instructions to purchase.

Meanwhile, at the time I intended to leave Lovere, the Count arrived from Brescia. I thought I had to go via Brescia, not knowing that there were other Routes to Gottolengo, but he had me travel through another canton to avoid, so he said, the terrible roads.[1] He took me to see the Mansion he had mentioned to me, which was at Solferino,[2] and which I found just as lovely as he had depicted it. I must admit that it astonished me.[3] He told me it had been confiscated by the Empress Queen, but that if I were to write to General Stampa I would no doubt be favoured with permission to purchase it.[4] I therefore did this, and then returned to Gottolengo; and divided my time between Gottolengo and Solferino [*sic*] until the Month of May 1754.

I had often wished to make a journey to Venice to see the Friends I had there.[5] Three times I had Post-Horses brought from Brescia with this purpose, but sent them back again for various reasons: because the roads were infested with gangs of Bandits, or because the rivers were impassably in flood,[6] or another time it was asserted that there were contagious diseases at the Inns. If the Count had told me these stories I should perhaps have deemed them false, seeing clearly the advantage that accrued to him from keeping me at Gottolengo;

---

[1] A mountainous section of the Roman Via Valeriana was abandoned in 1850, when a route was constructed through tunnels. MWM called the road 'one of the worst I ever passd, being all over precipices' (*CL* ii. 466).

[2] From her letters, this is a mistake (though a consistent one) for Salo, on Lake Garda (*CL* ii. 467). Salo is about the same distance from Brescia westwards as Lovere is to the north-east; Solferino is south of Salo, half-way between that and Mantua, not on a lake.

[3] The estate, MWM says, belonged to the Martinengo family: its current owner, 'having spent a noble Estate by Gameing and other Extravagance, would be glad to let it for a Triffle'. Her letters mention only renting, not buying (*CL* ii. 468–9, 470). Bartolomeo Dominiceti, MD (who later had a flamboyantly self-publicizing career in London), claimed to have discussed smallpox inoculation in detail with MWM in 1749–51, 'both during her residence in my neighbourhood, at the *Palazzo Rovea*, at *Salò*, and during her stay with my unfortunate friend *Count Augulino Palazzi*' (*Medical Anecdotes, of the Last Thirty Years* (1781), 431 n.).

[4] Maria Theresa (1717–80); Count Cajetan von Stampa (1716–73), of an old Lombard family.

[5] This had been her intention on leaving Avignon. Quinsonas Lauberivière wrote *c*.27 June 1750 that he had hoped to escort her to Venice (Venetian Archivio di Stato, Brescia Busta 21. 11). On 28 Apr. 1754 she expressed herself 'quite sick with vexation' at the failure of letters to travel safely between London and the province of Brescia (*CL* iii. 50).

[6] She wrote to her husband of floods, broken bridges, and 'scarce practicable' roads (22 July [1753], *CL* iii. 33).

but it was not he, it was the Doctor, the Parish Priest, and all those I spoke to, who assured me of the same thing. I was also told a thousand stories of Houses broken into, and of their Owners who were murdered, which alarmed me so much that I Resolved to keep nothing of value by me except the money necessary for everyday Household expenses.

The Count advised me to remit everything I received from England into the hands of Signor Ballini, who would take care of my Bills of exchange, and render me exact and faithful accounts. I did this, and he sent me his receipt for two thousand four hundred pounds Sterling.[1] I was still determined to go to Venice. I had my Trunks packed, and was only waiting for fine weather. The Count came to collect his rents. He had had a serious illness, he said, and he certainly looked like it, for he was crippled in his feet and his hands. He was carried to a small Room far from mine, and there he remained Bed-ridden. Two months later, as I was planning to leave for Venice, when I was out late walking I was seized with a discharge above my cheek which became much inflamed, prevented me from sleeping, and was accompanied with a slight fever. The Count sent his Doctor to me, who assured me I was dangerously ill. I despised him, and was unwilling to take his medicines; however, my ailment persisted, and caused me much pain. Two days later I found Dr Baglioni had arrived post from Lovere. The Count sent a message by my Maid, to ask pardon for the Liberty he had taken, but that since his own doctor had assured him that I was very ill,[2] and that I had no confidence in him, he had accordingly sent for Dr Baglioni, with whom I had appeared satisfied[3] on other occasions.

She used her opportunity to embroider upon the concern the Count had for my health, which I did not doubt, knowing that my life was very profitable to him. Dr Baglioni swore that I was in great danger, that if the discharge had got to my chest I would have been dead in two days, and that I needed to begin my cure with a change of air, that the air of Venice would be downright adverse to me,

---

[1] It seems that MWM was receiving £800 annually from her husband, plus £180 interest from her father's legacy, which replaced the dowry she forfeited by eloping (*CL* ii. 177 n. 1, 227 n. 1). In 1748 she had hoped to double her capital by farming ventures (*CL* ii. 404).

[2] In MS 'che io ero malissimo': both unidiomatic and ungrammatical. Again, 'a discharge above my cheek' translates 'una flussione sopra la guancia', but sounds unlikely: possibly an abscess high in the mouth from an infected tooth? The doctor may be Dominiceti.

[3] Also unidiomatic.

whereas I had found benefit at my little House at Lovere, which was in order for my reception, and he would accompany me there. In the end he persuaded me to leave with him next morning. I found the House barely habitable but my discharge was gone in a few days.[1]

He persuaded me to take the waters, and to bathe, and I found myself much improved in health. Since I should need to stay for some Months,[2] I amused myself with improvements to the House, and I decided to enlarge it, so that I should no longer be obliged to lodge my Domestics elsewhere. I put my plans into the hands of a Man much renowned for his experience in building, and I had pleasure in watching them carried out.[3] I went out frequently in a boat on the Lake, and enjoyed perfect health. Baglioni spoke of it as if it were a Miracle and often said that if the Count were willing to come and entrust himself to him, abandoning the Ignorant people he frequented, he would regain his health. The Count came in the Month of August,[4] and lodged in a House near mine, where Baglioni had found him Apartments.

He was moving with difficulty, supported with Walking-sticks, and seeing him in this state made me pity him. He told me he had received a letter from Signor Hermann, Banker to the Duchess of Guastalla, written at her commands, to tell him she had ordered some furniture and chinaware in England, and that if he could get bills of Exchange for that Country from me it would be doing her a great favour. He had often spoken to me of this Princess, of whom he claimed to be a Favourite, and told me he had spent much of his time at her Court. He had often invited me there in her name.[5] I doubted

---

[1] To her daughter she wrote that before Baglioni arrived she 'prepar'd my selfe for Death with as much resignation as that Circumstance permits', that when he advised Lovere the 'other Physician asserted positively I should die on the road', that her bed was placed on a litter (later in a boat) for the journey, and Baglioni and her cook rode ahead each day to prepare for her reception 'at Noblemen's Houses which were empty' (*CL* iii. 52).

[2] 'You may imagine I am willing to submit to the orders of one that I must acknowledge the Instrument of saving my Life, thô they are not entirely conformable to my Will and pleasure. He has sentence'd me to a long continuance here. . . . and would persuade me that my illness has been wholly owing to my omission of drinking the Waters these two years past. I dare not contradict him.' She follows this with an encomium on his character and practice (*CL* iii. 52–3).

[3] She now confessed the purchase (for £100, free from ground rent or local taxes) to her daughter, emphasizing the house's 'tatter'd circumstances': she had left the state rooms 'for the sole use of the spiders that have taken possession', and fitted up six others, 'with Lodgings for 5 servants' (*CL* iii. 55, 59).

[4] In late July Baglioni advised her to stay another month (*CL* iii. 69).

[5] MWM recorded a visit in 1748 from the Duchess, who complained politely of MWM not having visited her (*CL* ii. 415). There were two widowed duchesses of Guastalla: this is probably Eleonora of the Holstein-Wiesenburg family (1715–60).

the high favour he boasted of, but I did not dream he would have the audacity to make use of her name without some basis, and I was delighted to render this small service to the Princess. I gave him bills of exchange to the value of two thousand sequins, which he promised to have paid to me in Venice, or wherever I might decide to spend the winter. Dr Baglioni insisted on my taking Asses' milk for two Months, and then heavy rains came on at the end of autumn, and the season was so severe that I was easily persuaded of the danger of taking a journey, and so not knowing what better to do I stayed at Lovere. I had a stove put in my Room, I had Books brought, and I contented myself with the Conversation of those Few People who came to visit me. The Count's health became steadily worse. He was constantly surrounded by Doctors and Surgeons.

In the new year 1755 he sent Dr Baglioni to tell me that he had taken into his employ a secretary, who had the reputation of great learning and integrity, and that he flattered himself that I should find his conversation agreeable. The Doctor added that he had recommended him because he supposed I was truly likely to kill myself with my perpetual studying. I replied, laughing, that I never felt better than when I was alone, that I did not study, but diverted myself; that I was nevertheless relieved that he had found himself an honest man, never having seen any but Knaves in his service. The man he spoke of was Dr Bartolomeo Mora, who arrived the next day. I found him to be a Man of wit and learning, proving on experience to be gentle and sincere.[1]

I had some time ago ceased making annuity payments to Castelli, fearing to pay him more than the whole value of his land. I informed the Count of my doubts, and he confessed with an appearance of frankness that it was quite possible that he might have been gulled, that it would be all right if the old Ruffian (that was his expression) were to die soon, and that at the worst, what I had given him must be reckoned as Credit. I did not trust his judgement, but had the contract looked at by Dr Mora, who examined it, and told me that indeed, as was too evident, I had been deceived, and that he had no doubt I could legitimately demand my money back. The Count in the meantime led the most ridiculous life imaginable. Dr Baglioni

---

[1] Graeme (see below, p. 98 n. 2) reported in 1758 that her household was 'derected by the abby Mora who was formerly Chaplain to the Comte Palazi' (to Lord Bute, Valdagno, 30 Aug. 1758, Bute MSS). Mora remained in her service for the rest of her life, accompanied her back to England, and was left £500 in her will: her only substantial money bequest (*CL* iii. 295).

related me a hundred good stories about him, and told me seriously that he feared he might be going mad. He ran a gambling Assembly in his House, and invited me to attend his Basset game, but I declined. In the month of February I prepared to leave. My personal Maid, whom I had brought from France,[1] fell ill, seriously as I was told. She was necessary to me for the journey, and I decided to wait till she recovered, which happened very slowly; she got well after a Month.

The Month of March is so severe in that mountain Country that I heeded Dr Baglioni's forbidding me to start the journey, unless I wanted to risk my life, and when in the Month of April I thought of leaving, an indisposition overcame me which rendered it impossible. I had diarrhoea intermittently for six weeks on end. The Count let me know that he was going to take the waters at Bormio[2] on his Doctor's orders, and humbly entreated me to let him bid me Farewell at the lakeside. I saw him Embark, and wished him a good journey and the re-establishment of his health. When mine was re-established I thought once again about leaving. Dr Baglioni told me that the thawing snow had broken up the roads so badly that I should find the steeps impassable in a chaise. He, however, would charge himself with finding me a closed Carriage, which he would have sent from Bergamo.[3] This Carriage had left with a Great Lord for Milan, but its return to Bergamo was expected daily. In the end, on one pretext after another, and in spite of all my efforts to leave, I found myself still there when the Count returned, as he said, from Bormio. He appeared surprised to see me there, and this was in the Month of September.[4] I was firmly resolved on leaving for Venice, and he besought me humbly to pass through Gottolengo to take possession of the Furniture which I had practically abandoned on my sudden departure. My Maid put me in mind that she would have to pack up the linen. This would not mean a very long detour, and I was persuaded to make it.

The Count wanted to come and escort me, against my wishes. He told me the roads were unsafe, because of Robbers, and that although

---

[1] Presumably the successor to her English maid Mary Turner; MWM was 'very well satisfy'd' with her in 1745 (*CL* ii. 360).

[2] With thermal springs, in the Alps 50 miles north of Lovere.

[3] Thirty or forty miles south-east of Lovere.

[4] Only two of her letters reached her daughter between January and September 1755. On 22 Sept. she wrote from Lovere, mentioning no journeys, actual or intended, but ordering watches with enamelled dials and shagreen cases to present to Baglioni and to '2 Priests to whom I have some obligations' (*CL* iii. 86–90).

his personal escort was worth nothing because he was carried in a Litter, the appearance of being a large party would be an insurance against being attacked. He added that the state of his affairs made it necessary for him to inspect his property immediately. We left, therefore. I wanted to travel through Brescia in order to consult my banker, Ballini, whom I had never met. When we got to Iseo,[1] the Count, with expressions of sorrow, reported that a Bridge was broken, and we should be compelled to go via Delo. There we stayed for ten days on account of the heavy rains which had flooded the Countryside. We arrived towards the end of October at Gottolengo. I intended to stay for two days only, and to pursue my journey, but the rain continued, and that Country, which is marshy, was so muddy that I allowed myself to be persuaded that it was impossible to get away.[2] I sent back the Postilions with their Post-Horses, paying for those of the Count, and indeed the whole cost of the journey, which was most extravagant. I let this sponging pass, as I had many other instances. I believed him to be poor and observed him to be stupid, and supposed that he too was being swindled as he was swindling me. His health declined more than ever, and he remained Bedridden for almost two months. I sent to enquire several times how he was, and the usual reply was 'that the Door was closed.' Then he sent me word that a Friend of his, a Merchant, for whom he could vouch, was going to England, and that if there was anything I wished to send, he would deliver it personally into the very hands of any Person I should direct.

I remembered a ring, the only one that remained to me of my jewels, because I had had it on my finger[3] when the others were stolen. I sealed it in a Box, and sent it to my Grand-daughter.[4] It was safely delivered by the hand of Signor Prescot.[5] A few days later a Letter from the Duke of Portland informed me of the Death of his Wife's Mother, a close Relative and dear Friend of mine.[6] She had

---

[1] At the southern end of the lake of the same name, about two-thirds of their way to Brescia. Tenses are incorrectly used here and later in the tale.

[2] In MS 'uscire', an odd choice of word.

[3] The MS might possibly read 'nel letto' (in bed); but 'nel detto', for 'dito' (finger) makes better sense.

[4] The courier was a Signor Pitrovani, the recipient of the ring her second god-daughter among Lady Bute's children, Lady Jane. A long letter dated 20 Oct. went with the ring (*CL* iii. 91–8).

[5] George Prescot (*c*.1711–90), merchant and future MP, was offended at the reception he received in the Bute household, and declined to act as a regular channel for letters (*CL* iii. 106).

[6] i.e. a few days after 1 Apr. [1756], when she heard the ring had arrived. MWM had been 'play fellows in the happy days of ignorance' with Henrietta (Cavendish Holles) Harley,

left me a Legacy in her memory, of four hundred sequins. Her death afflicted me so deeply that I spoke of my grief to everybody I saw. The Count, for his part, sent me his compliments of condolence.

A Month after this he had himself carried to my Antechamber to tell me that the same Merchant who had served me so faithfully, his Friend and agent, needed a certain sum of money in London, which he could have repaid to me in Gottolengo. I resisted his importunities, but after a month of his continual insistence, I wrote a note to the Duke of Portland asking him to make the two hundred sequins payable to the person who would present a note in my name.[1]

Spring was well advanced, and so were my preparations for making the journey to Venice, when I realised that I was a Prisoner. Every kind of ruse was employed to make me stay. My chaises were broken, my Horses lamed, my Maid taken ill, the rivers in flood. While these stories were being manufactured I had the good luck to receive a visit from General Graeme, a Relation of my Son-in-law,[2] who had been requested by my Daughter to seek me out, because she had heard no news of me, even though I had written nearly every week. I also complained of silence on her part, for it had been many months since I had received letters from England, and had begun to believe that they were being intercepted.[3]

The Count had had himself taken to Cremona, and returned to find me unmoved by all the tricks he had used to make me stay in Gottolengo, and that I laughed at the doctor who threatened me that I should die on the road. He mounted another stratagem. He sent me word by a certain Priest, his protégé, named Don Geronimo Zarza,

---

Countess of Oxford (above, pp. x–xi). Both descended from 'Wise' William Pierrepont (1608–78). Though dismissive of her as a young woman, MWM found her friendship and correspondence with Lady Oxford outlasted all others. Margaret Harley (1715–85), Lady Oxford's only child and a close friend of Lady Bute, married William Bentinck (1709–62), 2nd Duke of Portland, in 1734 (*CL* i. 114–15, iii. 17). In 1738 or 1739 an engraving was made uniting Zincke's portraits of the Duke, the Duchess, and MWM (see cover of this volume).

[1] She described this transaction defensively to her daughter: Pitrovani wrote that 'he heard I had a Legacy to receive in England, and as he was oblig'd to pay a sumn of money and should lose by the Exchange, he hop'd in consideration of his care and faithfull delivery of the Ring I would favor him with a Bill on the Person who was to pay it. I made answer I would not draw a Negotiable Note on the Duke of Portland as on a common Banker, but on his pressing me, I wrote a respectful Demand payable to the Bearer' ([22 Aug. 1756], *CL* iii. 110).

[2] William Graeme (d. 1767), Commander-in-Chief of the Venetian forces.

[3] Six letters survive from Oct. 1755 to May 1756 (none from June or July 1756), and an Italian translation of excerpts from letters (H MS 81, fos. 299–302; Lady Mary Wortley Montagu, *Selected Letters*, ed. Isobel Grundy, forthcoming from Penguin).

to come to his Chamber for a Moment, saying that he begged pardon for this liberty, but that he was not well enough to get up. The Priest added that he had been suffering violent pain all night, and that he believed his end might be near. I found him in Bed, propped up on Pillows, his face pale and distorted. He made a sign to Don Geronimo to remain at the Door, and told me in a low voice that it was important to preserve great secrecy in an affair of this kind: that he thought he might be able to retrieve my Jewels, which had been pawned to a great Ecclesiastic, a Relative of the Pope, and that it would take twelve thousand sequins to redeem them. This story seemed to me so ridiculous that it made me laugh. I answered that I had never owned jewels worth that amount of money, that I supposed he meant to coin a few sequins by this trick, that I had long since given up the search, and that I wouldn't give a farthing for such information.[1] I went out laughing, supposing that the poor man must be dreaming, or else that he had made up this fine fiction to delay my journey under the pretext of expecting news from Bologna.

In the afternoon he had himself carried to my Antechamber and complained to me, weeping, how little regard I had for his honour, which was a thousand times dearer to him than his life, that he would give all he had, either now or in the future, to remove this stain from his Name. He said my jewels were in pawn to a Marchesa from Bologna, a great Lady who was Related to the Pope, that the Thief, being about to die, had revealed the fact in the Confessional, and that a Monk, who had been charged with the restoration of my property, was even now in the House, but that he did not wish his name to be given. He begged me to be so good as to see him. Quite thunderstruck by this story, I agreed. The Count was carried back to his Chamber, not being able to stand (as he said before). He sent the Monk in to me, and I saw to my great surprise that he was carrying a case[2] which I recognized as belonging to the Count. He opened it, and pulled out first a beautiful embroidered Indian shawl, and then many other items which I had believed to be stolen by the Agents of Signor Bettoni: some of my furnishings, the diamond and ruby snuffbox lost at the same time, and then many of the jewels which were stolen two years before my Furniture came from Avignon, but these were damaged and in the condition they are in now. I knew then what I had to believe, and recognized also the danger of being

---

[1] The word in MS is 'soldo': the twentieth part of a sequin.
[2] In MS 'valise': one of the French forms found in north Italian dialects.

in such scoundrelly hands. I concealed my thoughts from the Friar, a fine fellow to have had a hand in such roguery. I pretended to be satisfied at having my jewels restored, at least some of them. Examining them, I found a large Cross of Emeralds surrounded with small diamonds, and a ring of the same stone which I thought looked like an Episcopal one. I said, 'these are not mine, but I shall guard them until a claim is put in for them, since they must be stolen.'

The Monk, who kept his face hidden the whole time under his Hood, made a great deal of difficulty about leaving me my jewels, but I spoke to him in such a tone that he durst not reply, and withdrew with muttered complaints. An hour later the Count sent to tell me that the Cross and ring were his; he asked me for them, and I handed them over without hesitation. In the evening he sent Don Geronimo Zarza to tell me he had pledged all his present and future possessions to this Marchesa of Bologna to get my jewels back, and he feared she would foreclose on him, and that I was obliged as a matter of honour to get him out of this most difficult situation, in which he had placed himself out of zeal for my service. I replied that such an Action would be so groundless that there was nothing to fear, that I had never till now taken pleasure in anyone's suffering, and that assuredly he was not going to be the first. I sent for the post-Horses, which arrived very late that evening. I proposed to leave in the morning. The Count sent word that the Rodenghi, his Enemies, had circulated a rumour that he was keeping me at Gottolengo by force and threats. He begged me to write a letter to the effect that I had no complaints about his behaviour towards me. I understood what he was asking, and so I wrote a letter which contained some of the truth, and did not satisfy all his demands. It was, however, so polite that he durst not ask for another. Once it was written Don Geronimo Zarza came to tell me (with an appearance of being offended at such insolence) that the Postilion had got tired of waiting at my Door, and had left. I asked Doctor Bartolomeo Mora to run after him; he had wit enough to understand the danger I was in, and energy enough to find a way to save me. He caught up with the Postilion, and compelled him to await my orders.

Twenty-three hours elapsed before I was able to leave the House. I found the Count in his Armchair in the Courtyard, where he had had himself carried to bid me Farewell. This he did in the most respectful manner, although he tried to terrify me with stories about Bandits. When he saw that this had no effect, he requested me as a last favour to call in at Signora Roncadelli's Country House; she had invited me (he told me) very pressingly, and would be sadly disappointed if I were to leave the Country without seeing her, and that her house was in fact very close to Pontevico.[1] He reminded me of the obligation I was under to her for having had the Notice printed about the loss of my jewels, and for having had it circulated throughout Italy, without which they would have been lost forever. I replied that I was well aware of all this, and I gladly promised to pay her a visit. Ballini had continued to act as my Banker. I had kept an exact account with him, and he had in his hands more than four thousand sequins of mine. The Count asked me where I wished to have them paid, and I replied that I intended to pass through Brescia and would leave him my own orders. 'At this very time (he added) he has written to tell me that since he is obliged to pay out a considerable sum in London, you would do him a great favour by sending him a bill of exchange for that City.' I replied that I would talk to him myself. 'Oh, he cried, my Aunt loves you too much to permit you to leave her until after several days, and this good man is very hard pressed. It seems to me a small sum of money will be of no consequence in Venice.' I gave him a note for four hundred sequins.

I left, then, accompanied by my Maid in the Carriage, by Doctor Mora, by my old Manservant on Horseback, and my Footman, to whom the Count insisted on adding some armed Peasants, and his faithful Don Geronimo Zarza on horseback, for my protection. The Postilion drove so badly, and found, or pretended to find, the roads so bad, that it was already night when we arrived at the villa of Fianello. The Postilion avowed that he had never travelled so bad a Road, and told me that it would be worse as we went onwards and that he did not want to run the risk of taking me. Don Geronimo said that I could sleep at the House of a Merchant at Alfianello,[2] who had already been informed that I might be in need of this, and he made a great deal of the attention offered me. I stopped. My Swiss Manservant was lost on the road, having proved easy to seduce into a Tavern. The House seemed to me above suspicion; but on our entering it my Maid was seized with an attack of vomiting so violent that she was unable to wait on me. I was obliged to undress on my own, and Don Geronimo told me that he had to leave us in the morning to

---

[1] Pontevico, 10 miles east of Gottolengo, lies in the opposite direction from Mantua and Venice. [2] Two-thirds of the way to Pontevico.

attend the Fair at Brescia. He asked me if I had any commissions to give him. I wished him a good journey, and asked him to carry a Letter for me to Ballini, saying that if he wished to set out before day-break I could write that evening. He begged me not to fatigue my eyes by candle-light, saying that he would wait on me at breakfast time, since a few hours would suffice for such a short journey. My Maid could not sleep in my Chamber on account of her sickness; my Manservant, who returned drunk two hours later, settled in the Antechamber. The Priests both slept downstairs. I had had two large leather bags made. In one I kept my jewel-cases, in the other a purse, tied up, where I placed my receipts, from my Bankers and from Castelli, his Contract, and in short all my important papers.

The agitation I had gone through, both of body and mind, in these travails, made me sleep very soundly. I had placed the bags on a table, and there I found them in the morning. I was so glad to have got out of Gottolengo that I felt myself in perfect health. I got up before any of my Servants, dressed myself, and had the others roused. I was astonished when Dr Mora told me that Don Geronimo had left two hours before dawn, after having promised to wait for my Letter. I blamed his rusticity, and ordered the Horses to be harnessed. Dr Mora found one of the wheels broken. Then I realised that a plan had been laid to keep me there; he shared my suspicion. He summoned a Master-Carpenter and had a new wheel made and attached in spite of the Postilion, who appeared displeased at this operation. It was the evening before I was able to set out, and the Peasants whom the Count had provided for my escort took themselves off. A mile away from Pontevico I sent my Footman to notify Madam Roncadelli of my arrival. As soon as he had left us I saw an Officer, a young Man, approaching at full speed with a large Arquebus.[1] This terrified Dr Mora, who was a few steps ahead of my Carriage; he came to its window with his eyes staring and hair on end; he confessed to me later that he thought he had come to the last moment of his life. He presented me with a Letter from the Count, addressed to him, in which was a mandate with the seal of the [Venetian] Republic, by which the Marchesa of Bologna seized possession of all his property; and he had written that in order to save it he had been forced to cash in my money, and that he begged Dr Mora to obtain my pardon for him, failing which not only he but his whole Family would be dis-honoured for ever, and that he would pistol himself. This last article

[1] An obsolete type of gun which had to be placed on a stand or tripod for firing.

was so ridiculous that when I had looked at the papers I hurled them at Dr Mora and directed the Postilion to move on. A few moments later I saw Madam Roncadelli's fine carriage approaching with many of her Servants. I was invited, on her behalf, to make use of them, and she sent many apologies for not coming herself to meet me, being indisposed. Nevertheless I found her ready at the door to receive me. She embraced me cordially, and led me into a Hall where was a Gentleman of Cremona, her Friend.

I had my head full of the encounter with the Officer, and I naturally related it, saying I could not understand what money the Count could have taken, as I had left none in his hands; that my Bankers' bills were payable to none but myself, and at my orders. To show them to her, I pulled out of my bag the purse where I kept them, with the title-deeds for the lands I had bought; and I found they had been replaced with blank paper of the same size. Madam Roncadelli appeared just as outraged as myself; she promised me to have restitution made, and begged me as a favour to stay at her House until her infamous Nephew should arrive. He did arrive next day towards evening, in such disorder, whether real or assumed, that he went straight to Bed.

Madam Roncadelli besought me to hear his case, which I refused to do otherwise than in her presence. She wept, and took my hand and kissed it, and led me to the Chamber where he was. He tried to make a long speech punctuated with sobs; I cut his oration short, and told him that I had not come to listen to his excuses, but to demand the return of my papers. 'They are burned (he replied, weeping), and even if they had not been, they would have been just as useless to you, because they were all forged.' His Aunt apparently fell in a swoon, and I left the Chamber saying, 'You are a worthless Thief.' I locked myself in my Room, to reflect upon the situation in which I found myself. My position seemed to me one of grave danger; but I had a good opinion of Madam Roncadelli, who was a Lady universally esteemed, and I believed myself to be safe in her House. But I had to pursue my journey, and I faced a desperate Man capable of any Crime, who kept in his service Villains of every description, and who would no doubt have me assassinated on the road if he believed that I intended to prosecute him at Law. I resolved to keep my resentment hidden.

In the Morning I received Madam Roncadelli with the appearance of calm. She was weeping bitterly; I felt genuine pity for her grey hairs. She assured me that she had not closed her eyes all night, and implored me to listen to some compromise to save the honour of her Family. She said it was impossible to restore me all my money, because he had spent some at Turin, some at Milan, and in many other Places, and that she was not rich enough to refund it. 'Even if you were, Madam (I interrupted) it would be unjust that you should pay for his dissipations. I ask nothing from you, and will take nothing from you.'

She extolled my generosity highly, and proposed to draw up new deeds for the properties at Fornace[1] and Solferino [*sic*]. As for the House at Gottolengo, that was entailed; I was Mistress of it if I wished to stay there, but if I had decided to vacate it, it would be best to allow him to occupy it to hide his shame in a Country where his Ancestors had lived with honour. She said that the note for four hundred sequins, which I had given him before leaving, would be returned to me. I left it to her to look after my interests, and did everything that she thought fit to propose. I did not leave my Chamber, and I ate alone, from one dish only. There were great comings and goings of various relatives, in which I wanted no part. In the end Madam Roncadelli informed me that the Count, although much indisposed, had had a document drawn up which he implored me to sign, and that he had the money ready that was specified in the final note, which would be restored to me with the title-deeds of the properties. She brought the Notary to me, who presented me the document in the presence of the above-mentioned Gentleman of Cremona, two others whose names I have forgotten, and Dr Mora.

When I read it I found the statement, obscurely expressed, that I admitted to having lived for ten years at his expense. I tore the Paper into a thousand pieces, saying in a loud voice that they meant basely to swindle me. Dr Mora drew near me, all trembling, and said in a low voice, 'Madam, be less hot-headed; think of your danger.' I replied, raising my voice, 'I would rather die than sign such a foul lie, which would dishonour me.'

The Lady and all the witnesses left in confusion, and I went to bed. In the morning she came back to ask my pardon for having a document presented to me which she had not seen; she said she would have another one drawn up, in which I would agree to be satisfied with the restoration of my properties and of the four hundred sequins, which she gave me her word of honour that she would keep

---

[1] Eight miles from Trenzano.

in her custody, and would never hand it over to her Nephew as long as I kept possession of the lands. I was content to sign to these conditions, thinking that unless I did so I should never be permitted to leave. I pretended to have forgotten past events; but I did not see the Count. He sent to beg me as a last favour to permit him to escort me as far as Mantua, where he had Relatives. I agreed to this.[1] Count Ignazio, his Brother,[2] accompanied me on Horseback.

I bade Adieu for ever to Madam Roncadelli, who used a thousand obliging and tender expressions to me. I left the Count confined to Bed at Mantua, and continued my journey. I was surprised to learn at Vicenza that he had taken a Room at the same Inn where I was staying. I thought it unwise to demand that he explain his reasons for this, and pursued my way to Padua without seeing him. I met him again a mile short of this City, and he informed me that he had prepared a Lodging for me. I understood that he intended to keep his wicked proceedings concealed from the Public, and took the Lodging. I stayed two or three days, during which time I took a House in Padua, and then went to Venice. The Count had again prepared me Lodgings; I stayed there three days, and then returned to Padua.

Here I found the Count, who had settled himself in my House, in my Swiss servant's Room near the Door. I had him informed that I was not running a boarding-house, and I begged him to leave. I demanded that he surrender to me the title-deeds of my properties, and tell me the name of the Merchant who had received the Legacy from the Countess of Oxford. He refused both one and the other, and departed for Gottolengo. He returned some weeks later, but he has not handed over the deeds, nor will he tell me who received the money from the Duke of Portland.

[1] She thus apparently gave up her intention of visiting Ballini at Brescia. She wrote to her daughter from Mantua on 22 Aug. 1756 (*CL* iii. 109–10).

[2] The youngest brother, the only one to marry.

Princess Docile I

Textual note. The original Part I (untitled; in French) runs through H MS 80, fos. 310–21, 324–33, 369–77: mostly in MWM's late hand, though a scribal hand (which she corrected) wrote the first thirty-eight words, and a few later passages. She numbered the pages and usually left wide margins (perhaps for revision), some of which are marked or scribbled on by others. Original p.211 below.

There was once a Queen of some Kingdom or other, who was the favourite of an aged fairy, not for any good reason, since She was perhaps the least deserving person in the world; but it is common enough to see caprice or chance determine the favour of the Great. The Nurse of the Queen had become chambermaid to the Fairy. She was a Peasant, a simple soul who talked all the time about her nurseling, for no other reason than the pleasure she took in recalling the years of her youth, and the vanity she felt in having suckled a Queen. Her artless remarks had made such a deep impression on the Fairy, that she reserved privileged access for the Queen, who was often at her bedside when her door was denied to all that was most respectable or amiable upon earth. In fact this good woman had assumed the upper hand over her Mistress, without either one or the other realising it. The Fairy was always scolding her, and never spoke of her without the epithet, that poor chatterbox; yet since it was she who sat up with her when she was ill or fancied herself so, and who gave her her potions, she had imperceptibly acquired the right to say whatever she wanted, and her perpetual babbling had more effect on the Fairy's mind than the greatest Eloquence could have had.[1] All this turned to the Queen's advantage. The Nurse was ignorant of the influence which she could perhaps have Exerted quite otherwise if she had wanted to.

The behaviour of the Queen of Contrary (that was her name) strongly enforced the Idea the Fairy had formed of her Merit. She visited her very seldom and said little. The fairy, accustomed to see nothing but people demanding favours and assistance, and who was overwhelmed every day with ten thousand petitions, was relieved to

---

[1] Scribal hand resumes.

find one person who never asked her for anything. She had no doubt that this resulted from great modesty, or great disinterestedness. There were even moments when she flattered herself that she pleased the Queen to the point of making her forget all else by the charm of her conversation. This idea so softened her as to make her say, one evening when she was with the queen, 'Good heavens, Madam, how different you are from all others I see. You cannot be ignorant of my Power, which is almost boundless. Instead of pestering me like a thousand others who have no reason to count on me, you have never asked me for the slightest favour, despite all the proofs which I have given you of my good will. Therefore I am resolved, as reward for your restraint, to grant you the first thing you ask of me.'

'Well, what do you expect me to ask? replied the Queen with an air bordering on impertinence. I am accustomed to granting favours, not to asking them. Am I not the greatest Queen in the world? (but she was only queen of a little island, quite poorly situated) My husband, who receives addresses every fortnight from subjects struck to the heart by his wisdom (her husband was King Imbecile), defers to my opinion just as he should. I have no complaints against Nature, neither for my looks nor my mind (she was squinting and hunchbacked). I should not care to be upright and pinched in figure like a Bourgeoise; and a sidelong glance becomes a Queen, who must not distinguish any person with a direct regard. I can safely say that I am yet more distinguished for my virtue than for my rank or my talents. My severity has never slackened for one moment of my life.' (It is true that, born without taste, with a hard heart and cold imagination, she had never felt either tenderness or Inclination.)

The Fairy, whose eyes were beginning to open to her Character, replied in a dry tone, 'Indeed I see that there is little I can do to serve you. Since it is not permitted me to contradict myself, I grant you whatever request you make, but I swear to you, Fairy's honour, never to grant you another, even if you should become less contented with yourself or your situation than you seem to be at present. You are pregnant: have you nothing to wish for your Child?'

'I ask nothing but Docility, replied the Queen. Although good breeding does not permit me to undergo the fatigue of instructing the child myself, I shall be able to choose persons of merit who will not fail to render it perfect, as long as it submits itself to their lessons.'

'Right, said the Fairy, I grant you a perfect Docility. You will bear a Daughter, and you may Confidently name her Princess Docile.' The Queen retired well satisfied at having sustained her Rank with appropriate Haughtiness. The Fairy went to bed cursing her stupid Chambermaid for having given her such a ridiculous Acquaintance, and three days later she took on another Favourite, who was clever enough to profit by her favour and play a very important Role in the World, although her sole merit was to have a Footman in her service who was highly pleasing to the good Chambermaid.

But let us leave the Fairy Court, and return to that of the Queen of Contrary, who was brought to bed of an extremely pretty Daughter. Everyone at Court killed themselves to assure her that they were as like as two peas; she was so well convinced of this that she resolved to omit nothing to render the Princess the most accomplished in the World. She was barely beginning to talk when her mother had her taught 5 or 6 different Languages; the poor child strove to remember them all, and at seven years old she could express herself in none. She had a naturally good ear and charming voice: this was a fine field for the Queen, who wanted her to learn, all at the same time, to sing in all the various national styles and to play every kind of instrument.

She gave her an old maid for Governess. This lady was irreproachable, having been, all her life, respectably ugly; Prudish, sanctimonious, and stupid beyond belief. For Colleague she had a white-bearded Hermit, torn from his desert, where (with the best intentions in the world) he had spent thirty years eating Roots, and being eaten by Fleas. He had lost an Arm to honour the Gods, by having it stretched above his head for ten years in succession, to recommend himself to Brama, by whom he believed himself favoured, in consideration of which he had had himself whipped regularly twice a week, since the age of puberty. These individuals were precisely the wisest choice for instructors of a Princess pre-ordained to rule.

She was born very lively, with the acutest memory, her Heart perfectly well disposed, and a great capacity for tenderness.[1] It should not be surprising that, dowered with that extreme Docility, she gave herself up entirely to the sentiments of her instructors. To obey in everything, and not to reason in anything, were the fundamental

---

[1] In MWM's briefer autobiographical fairy-tale, 'Carabosse', this last gift, tenderness, is described in exactly the same French words, and is bestowed by the bad fairy (*E&P* 155).

maxims of her Education. The good Hermit wept ten times a day, to see the happy progress of his precepts; he came close to believing her inspired as she improved on her lessons, surpassing him in the acts of Devotion and austerity which he recommended to her. At eleven years old, she took a vow to remain for seven years sitting cross-legged in honour of the Goddess Vishnu.[1]

Her Governess, frightened by this unlooked-for Resolution, reported it to the Queen, who had been so much occupied raising Canaries, that she had not seen her daughter for six months. She entered her Apartments, and was even more shocked by her omitting to rise and pay her the reverence which was due to her, than by the extravagance of her religious Devotion. She began by treating her as Disobedient, then as a Madwoman and a Revolutionary. The Princess, already pale and thin from fasting, perfectly resembled an Idol, her hair thin and badly dressed, her Headdress crooked,[2] her eyes cast down. She replied in a modest tone, that she had been taught, that her first Duty was to the Gods; that if she was pleasing to Vishnu it concerned her very little to be pleasing to others; that she clearly saw that her Vow had been accepted, since the Goddess deemed her worthy of suffering Persecution; that she regarded all the Hardships which it pleased H[er] M[ajesty] to heap on her, as signs of the favour of the Goddess; that she had always feared a path strewn with Roses, which leads only to certain perdition, while it is through thorns that true happiness is to be reached.

She would have finished giving us a very fine Dissertation on Mortification, if the Queen, who was infuriated to find that she made so light of her resentment, had not ordered her to be silent, and that in a peremptory tone.[3] She turned to the Hermit, who was in ecstasy at the fine things his disciple was saying. 'So these are your hellish doctrines! she cried. Listen, if you do not remove this Lunacy from my Daughter, in twenty-four hours, you will be hanged next Tuesday. Work at it, and if you succeed, I shall reward you with permission to return to your desert, and die of hunger there if you think best.'

The poor man was naturally the greatest Coward in the world, and although he had often said that he was assured of his place, under

[1] The Hindu deity Vishnu is male. MWM owned fictions set in India, but she uses eastern religion chiefly as a stalking-horse for aspects of Christianity.

[2] In the original 'travers', which is also the kingdom's name.

[3] Here begin several paragraphs which MWM redrafted on another sheet of paper. I have followed the apparently later version (H MS 80, 314 ff., her own hand), with a few torn words restored from fos. 312–13 (scribal hand).

the little toe on the left foot of Brama, he was not at all in haste to assume it. This glimpse of power made him tremble. The same cowardice which had made him a Saint, made him very unlikely to be a Martyr. He prostrated himself before the Queen, swearing that his Religion exacted unreserved Obedience to all her orders, and that he did not doubt he could persuade the Princess that she could do nothing so agreeable to the Gods as blindly to obey a faultless Queen, who was the living image of the Goddess. He so well converted the mind of his pupil, that she went next Day early in the Morning to throw herself at her mother's Feet, weeping bitterly for the Sorrow she had caused her. She dared not request her dear Instructor's recall; he did not much wish it himself. The idea of the Hangman was still in his head, and he believed himself safer among the Bears and Wolves, than near an absolute and capricious queen.

A successor had to be chosen. The Queen dug up from the depths of a College a Philosopher, a good Geometrician, a great Mathematician, suspected of being unorthodox or even something worse. He had jested on several topics of veneration; had appeared to doubt whether the Great Brama, great as he is, could please sixty thousand Goddesses at the same time; and he had written a Book to prove that Vishnu had never metamorphosed herself into a Fish. It is true he had withdrawn this book, and had seen it burned with great sangfroid, but it was believed that that was from Fear of being burned himself; and it was not at all clear that he was sincerely penitent for having originated the sect of Doubters, who threatened a terrible schism which made all true believers tremble. He was otherwise of great Probity, austere Morals; there was nothing to reproach him with but the mania of wishing to be an honest man without interference from the gods (an innovation which the Clergy were most eager to suppress). The Queen commanded him to springclean her daughter's Brain, and he found the task much easier than he had hoped. She loved to reason; it was her natural bent; she had stifled it only by her extreme Docility. Virtue as represented to her by the Philosopher seemed more pure and noble than under the farrago in which the hermit had swaddled it; she loved Reading,[1] and became indefatigible in studying.

Her Master, charmed by her gift for the sciences, Complimented the Queen on the astonishing Genius of the Princess. She was not

---

[1] The revised passage ends here.

over flattered, having never thought much of the mind; she replied drily to the Philosopher, that she feared this History, this Geography, and this Philosophy which he spoke of, would make her too serious, and since she wished to read he ought to choose her diverting Books.

'She has her hours of recreation, he replied, when she is learning *Télémaque* by heart.'[1]

'That is yet more history,' said the Queen in an angry manner which prevented him from answering. 'I intend to send her *The Princess of Cleves* to brighten her spirits.'[2] Her Governess had already given her *Pamela*, to form her Heart.[3] Soon the poor Princess became quite stuffed with Sentiment. She ardently accepted the Imprint of Heroism; she was enchanted with Telemachus, especially when he chose to perish with all his friends, rather than disavow his Name (without reflecting that one Page later, he let an Innocent person die in his place, without making the least attempt at rescue),[4] and she vowed that all her life she would possess the Silent Modesty of Antiope,[5] the Sincerity of the Princess of Cleves,[6] and the disinterestedness of Pamela, without realising that this would be to renounce all hope of pleasing or of growing respected or great.

She had no Idea of any one of these ambitions; her Governess had accustomed her to neglecting her appearance as beneath her attention, and had always assured her that no one but Coquettes and

---

[1] MWM owned a copy of François de la Mothe de Fénelon's *Les Avantures de Télémaque* (1699) (Wh MS 135). She commented on its moralizing and its '*clinquant*' or tinkling style (*CL* ii. 73, iii. 215). H. Hillenaar finds it antifeminist (*Le Secret de Télémaque*, 1994).

[2] On the contrary, Marie Madeleine de Lafayette's *La Princesse de Clèves* (1678) is historical (reigns of Henri II and Queen Elizabeth) where *Télémaque* is mythical, and is no very cheering tale: its heroine's honour forbids her to marry the man she loves even after her husband dies. In vol. ii of her copy of *La Princesse* (Paris, 1741), MWM pinned a piece of paper bearing fourteen lines of Italian verse in Francesco Algarotti's hand (now at Sandon Hall).

[3] Samuel Richardson, *Pamela, or Virtue Rewarded* (1740). MWM 'heartily despised' Richardson, yet 'sob[bed] over his works in a most scandalous manner'; she thought *Pamela* would teach scheming and artifice (*CL* iii. 75, 90), and strongly objected to the moral voiced in its subtitle.

[4] Telemachus rejects advice to save himself from a tyrant by giving a false name, but allows the tyrant's mistress to substitute for him in prison and death an effeminate youth who has scorned her advances. A moral is drawn: 'les dieux se servent du mensonge des méchants pour sauver les bons, qui aiment mieux perdre la vie que de mentir' (book iii: Fénelon, *Œuvres complètes* (1851–2, repr. 1971), vi. 417–8).

[5] In book xvii Mentor bestows lavish praise on Antiope: when she speaks, it is only 'pour la nécessité', and impeded by her blushes (*Œuvres*, vi. 551).

[6] The most famous scene in *La Princesse de Clèves* is that of her confession to her husband that she loves another.

Fops considered their own or other people's, and that nobody shone in the eyes of sensible People excepting only by charms of soul and spirit. The governess persuaded the princess the more easily because she was firmly persuaded of all this herself, and it was her sole consolation for her Ugliness. The Hermit and the Philosopher had both inspired her with contempt for Empty Greatness, without perceiving that the contempt which was very necessary for them to accept the obscurity of their condition, was melancholy indeed for a great Princess, whom it cheated of all sweet Enjoyment of the splendour which surrounded her. She had reached such a point of perfection that she could not taste the most precious gifts the Gods can give: in vain was she one of the most beautiful women in the world, and Heir to a Throne, envying the condition of a Shepherdess or a Vestal. Alas, she did not know that true Wisdom would extract Pleasure from all good things in one's possession, and despise only those which are unattainable.

Her Beauty, useless as it was to herself, became troublesome enough to others. The Queen, who had never thought her pretty enough at four years old, thought her far too pretty at thirteen. She could not in justice reproach her with the vivacity of her eyes when she did everything she could to extinguish them: she strove to lose the bloom of her complexion by Reading all night, and she tried to ruin her posture by writing ten hours at a time. But Nature, more powerful than she was, had created all these things perfect, and the Queen could not discompose her inwardly although she remarked every day that she was pitifully changed.

It was necessary to set up a Household for her, and her mother, who had so Delicately searched out admirable Persons to whom to confide her Childhood, felt very Indifferent about the choice of those whom she would place about her as Ladies in Waiting. Without Reflection or Discrimination, then, she Gave her the Countess of Good Sense, and the Marquise d'Artifice, the first only because she bored her in her own Palace, and the second because she had caballed busily for this charge.

The King had sent to the Princess (following Court etiquette) an assortment of magnificent Jewels, and they allotted her for her Residence quite a fine Old Castle, 4 leagues distant from the Capital, where she was almost banished, much to the Pleasure of the Queen, who could no longer see her without regret and without being personally offended. The Philosopher made her value it as a mark of her Mother's tenderness, that she would rather lose the pleasure of seeing her than hazard her innocence amid Luxury and Tumult. He was himself charmed with this retirement; he had sense enough to perceive that he made a very poor figure at Court; the Pages played Tricks on him, the fops and the agreeable Ladies (who are always the strongest party), overwhelmed him with mocking compliments and amused themselves pitilessly with his Trustfulness, and his Philosophy. He was much wounded [?] by this conduct.[1] Despite all his contempt for society, he was the most sensitive man in the world to the least slight upon his appearance, and he even sometimes lost his temper in a manner to scandalize Philosophers and make all the ignorant people laugh. The Governess too was well content to be removed from a Court where her Prudishness was so little valued that she often saw horrid little Coquettes treated with more respect than a Chastity invincible for 50 Years.

Lady Good Sense was perhaps a little displeased with the Solitude to which she was condemned, but she was accustomed to saying nothing, and she could even find amusement where others found irritation, in what was ridiculous. The Marquise was the one who most missed the Court, but she too knew how to hide her feelings, and flattered herself that she would compensate herself most splendidly for the constraint she had chosen. She had had her plans when she had asked to be placed about the Princess, and she did not swerve from them for a moment. She sought to make herself loved, and it was very easy to succeed; the poor Child had never seen anyone around her but those who meant to instruct her and had no thought of pleasing her. Seeing distrust as a sentiment unworthy of a Generous soul, she gave herself up wholly to the lures of the Marquise with a Trustfulness that would have brought remorse to a Heart capable of feeling it. But Lady Artifice was not given to Weaknesses of that kind; she was lively, insinuating, complaisant, teasing or tender according to the Princess's mood, and knew so well how to profit from every emotion that in a few days she could not do without her.

It was most natural that the sweet and attentive manners of the marquise should make a great impression on an untried Heart, which up till then had been tyrannized by pedagogues. The Queen had never relaxed her lofty maintenance of royal and maternal Dignity;

---

[1] A word illegible or deleted; a marginal X perhaps signifying that something was to be added.

the hermit had announced his visions as authoritatively as divine Inspirations; the Philosopher was harsh and dry in his communications, and the Governess, for a thousand reasons, was always in a bad temper. The Lovely Docile had by nature so great an impulse towards tenderness, that she would have bestowed it (for want of any other object) on a Chambermaid, if the Governess had not always dismissed them as soon as she distinguished them, and reprimanded her very sharply if she lowered herself by saying the least agreeable word to them. She was therefore thrown back on herself, and I believe it was to escape from that that she had formed that bizarre vow which became so notorious, preferring to belong to Vishnu rather than to nobody.

This fantasy having passed, she felt a void which plunged her in despair. She waited only for the first object on whom to bestow the finest feelings in the world. Love had been represented to her as a Passion so shameful that she dared not so much as think of it, but lovely Friendship is the crown of virtue.[1] Telemachus, who was proposed to her as model, felt it to such a point that he wished to kill himself when they took his beloved Mentor from him, and Minerva herself made friendship her delight.[2] This was quite enough to decide the Princess to give herself up to these amiable sentiments[3] which satisfy both Heart and Reason. The Court which Lady Artifice made to her, seemed to her the effect of the most tender Sympathy. She would have thought herself insulting her if she had refused her her entire esteem; she was touched by gratitude for her flattery; the preference which the Marquise showed for her company, finished by making her entirely her own. The Marquise was too much a connoisseur to be blind to the ascendant which she had acquired over the innocent Princess. She influenced her as she pleased. Her first step was to separate her from Lady Good Sense, who watched all these scenes coolly. She was not made for the Court. She feared equally to be Favourite or to be disgraced, and in simply performing the duties of her station, with neither zeal nor negligence, she ensured against becoming either.

---

[1] In her copy of Montaigne's *Essais*, MWM wrote 'true & just sentiments' beside his disquisition on true friendship which seeks its friend's good before its own ((Geneva, 1727), iv. 288; now at Sandon Hall).

[2] In Homer's *Odyssey* Telemachus hears from Minerva about her friendship for him and his father before him (2. 286–8); in *Télémaque*, Mentor is actually Minerva in disguise. When 'he' is enslaved, Télémaque threatens suicide if not allowed to share his slavery (book iv).

[3] MWM at first called these sentiments delirium (App. II, p. 217).

For several months, Tranquillity, Peace, and even pleasure reigned in the Castle. The Mystery which these tender friends were obliged to adopt in their communication to escape the envy of the Governess, made it yet more precious. Everything was working together for their happiness, when that of the Princess was troubled by perceiving in the face of her beloved Marquise an air of Sadness, which seemed to increase every day, although she did her best to hide it. She forced herself to appear gay but it was easy to see that these efforts cost her dear and that she had some source of Melancholy which neither the presence nor even the caresses of her adorable Princess could dispel. What sorrow for that tender Friend! She was dying to learn the cause of this mournful change, but did not dare enquire, in case it might embarrass her. She was delicate enough to fear giving her the suspicion that she was presuming on her rank to try to extract her secret, and she suffered for several days everything that Curiosity could make her suffer without seeking to enlighten herself, convinced that the Marquise would not refuse her least desire, but that she doubtless had very pressing reasons for her silence since she did not confide her disquiet.

This Discretion of the Princess was even more a burden for Lady Artifice. She wanted to be importuned, she even wanted her secret to be dragged from her. She redoubled the colouring of Sadness which she had applied to her features, and made no gesture which did not discover it. Sometimes she fell into so profound a reverie, that she would be spoken to at least twice before she answered; sometimes she had tears in her eyes, and when the Princess surprised her in that state, she tried to smile with an air of Languor which pierced the Sweet Docile to the soul. She often wept in her private room for sorrows which she did not understand. 'How can I tell, however (she thought one evening when her dear friend had appeared even more sad than usual), if I cannot assuage this affliction, at least I can weep with her. Perhaps it is only fear of troubling me that makes her conceal the pain with which she is overwhelmed. How little she knows my overflowing tenderness! I will sacrifice everything to save her from the least difficulty; I can bear any suffering but that of seeing her suffer.'

Full of these ideas she wrote a billet which she slid into her Hand, in which she tenderly begged her to come down the hidden stair to her bedside after her Governess was in bed. Though the billet had only these few words, it was enough to tell the Marquise that her project would succeed as she wished. She did not fail at the rendez-vous. The first quarter of an hour passed in expressions of the liveli-est gratitude for the Honour which she was receiving. She threw herself on her knees beside her bed, she kissed her beautiful hands and bedewed them with tears which seemed to come from a Heart touched by her indulgence. The Princess, moved by her tenderness, mingled her own tears.

'But my dear Marquise, she said in an uncertain tone, despite all these proofs of your friendship, I have a complaint to make about you—'

'About me! cried the marquise, interrupting as if beside herself: am I so unhappy as to have displeased you for a single instant? what do you need as proof of my zeal and my attachment? I should count myself happy to shed all my blood at your feet, if you would confess that never devotion equalled mine.'

'I want to believe it, replied the Princess, but can I not then make you happy? You are hiding from me something that touches you most nearly, and when one loves fully one keeps no more secrets from the beloved object. I know that I find pleasure in developing all my thoughts to you, and I should hold it a Crime to conceal from you any of my sentiments.'

—While the Princess was speaking, Lady Artifice assumed the air of someone who sees her greatest secret discovered; from being sur-prised she passed to being thunderstruck, then she interrupted her with her sobs. The Princess embraced her, begged her to confide in her, and renewed her protestations of eternal and unvanquishable friendship. At length the Marquise submitted, as if unable to with-stand her commands, and opening with some stifled sighs, she began the sad recital of her woes.

'You are the judge, my lovely Princess, she said, whether I could care about anything except as it relates to you; you cannot be ignor-ant with what ardour I solicited the honour of your service. I saw you, and can anyone see you without wishing to see you every day? All the steps I took would have been useless, if I had not addressed myself to the Queen's favourite Groom of the Bedchamber. You do not know, perhaps, that he is the most miserly and grasping of all men, all favours pass through his hands, and he profits by the needi-ness or the ambition of all who have business with the Court. Mine was limited to attaching myself to your highness, but it was too lively to escape the penetration of a man accustomed to studying all those who present themselves before him. He demanded an excessive sum for his recommendation, giving me to understand I had a positive rejection unless I gave it. Everything I had to sell or pledge did not amount to half of what he had demanded. I took the course of borrowing the rest from Merchants who trusted my Word. My past Conduct had given so advantageous an Idea of my trustworthiness, that they made no scruple of trusting me. I stood to receive in a few months sufficient to meet my obligations, but while I was waiting, I heard that my Husband had seized upon it to pay a gaming debt. My Creditors are becoming importunate, they will make loud complaints, I shall be regarded as unworthy to be near you. The man who took my Money is one who will deny it, I shall be accused of shameful dissipation, my Reputation so stainless heretofore will be besmirched, but the summit of my Misery will be to be parted from you: when I imagine that sorrow, the others become invisible.'

She ended in a burst of tears, half of which were shed quite unnecessarily: the princess was already so moved that she would have plucked out her eyes if they were needed to save the Marquise from the troubles which threatened her. She embraced her tenderly. 'Do you believe me so unfeeling (said she) as to leave you in this dreadful state? Even if I did not love you, could I deny myself the heavenly pleasure of helping a virtuous person, whose good Heart has brought her misfortune? It is true I have no money, that my Governess[1] has control over all I receive, and sometimes she refuses it to me, although I never ask for any except in order to do good. I dare not speak to her about this, you know how jealous she is of your charms; she would surely refuse me. But here is the Key of that casket which you have seen on my Toilet. My Jewels are bestowed there. Take them, you know I hardly care for them; I have never dared hope they would bring me so lively a pleasure, a joy as incomparable as[2] that of being serviceable to a Friend for whom I would lay down my life if that could assure her happiness!'

After Lady Artifice had feigned surprise at the unheard-of Generosity of the Princess, and omitted none of the praises which would naturally Confirm her in her glorious action, she absolutely declined to accept her offer; she argued that, since noble hearts are rare, the Story could not fail to be given shameful Implications when it became public, and she would be driven from the Court with

---

[1] The wide margin here bears scribbles in another hand.
[2] See App. II, p. 220.

ignominy. The Princess was almost offended to discover that she did not believe her capable of keeping a secret; she vowed to her that no persecution could compel her to reveal a matter in which her honour was concerned. This developed into a fine Sentimental Scene.[1] Only with the greatest reluctance could the marquise resolve upon an action which might be suspected of self-interest. Although she allowed that it is Sweet to owe an obligation to somebody one loves, she also gave her to understand that, by a refinement of Generosity, between perfect friends the greater proof of friendship is perhaps given by her who receives;[2] that this is the higher sacrifice of self-love, and that it takes unbounded tenderness for a well-born person to do such a humiliating thing as to accept a benefaction of that Nature. Docile was deeply struck with these reasonings, which seemed to her the most correct in the World, and she never wearied of thanking her generous Friend, for offering such proof of her devotion. When Lady Artifice was so good as to empty her Casket, she left the Princess admiring her virtue, and very pleased with herself for having so promptly seized the first opportunity that had offered for performing a Heroic Action. She went to sleep with these pleasurable Ideas, and had never appeared so gay as she was for several days afterwards. The Marquise had recovered all her vivacity; she had become twice as dear to her young Mistress since this adventure, and the days went by, threaded with silk and gold. But Happiness is seldom lasting.

The King's Birthday was approaching; all the Court would appear in great Festivity; the Princess could not be excused from attending, and everyone was much astonished to see her without Jewels when all the Ladies were decked out in mutual emulation. Conclusions varied on this occasion; some thought it a remnant of her religious Devotion; others attributed it to the Philosopher's influence; and there were some who imagined that it was a dawning of Coquetry, that the Princess wished not to obscure any part of the finest Breast that was ever seen, or weight her delicate little ears with Pendants which would disfigure them. King Imbecile took extraordinary offence about it; and the Queen, who had found her daughter increased in stature and Beauty in a manner to irritate the best Mother in the universe, was not slow to suggest to her Husband that

[1] See App. II, p. 220.

[2] A tenet of sentiment, cf. 'The conferrer of an obligation stands in a superior light to the receiver of it' (Sarah Scott, *The History of Sir George Ellison* (1766), book 1, ch. 5).

the princess had failed in respect to him and deserved at least an exile of some years to teach her good behaviour; and that since she so little valued his gifts he should take them back. She demanded them, for her part, very Harshly; the Princess replied, blushing, that she had not got them.

'So what have you done with them, you madwoman? cried the Queen. You answer nothing, you turn pale, you lower your eyes— can it be possible? But no, no one of my blood can forget herself so far; no doubt you have been robbed, and I shall have all your servants put to the Torture.'

'Alas Madam, said the Princess, falling at her feet and bursting into tears, do not accuse innocent people; I have disposed of them.'—

'You! you! interrupted the Queen in fury, to Whom? on what occasion? what service could deserve so munificent a recompense?'

'It is not permitted to me to explain, answered Docile, but I am sure that you would have done the same that I have done, if—'

'I! cried the Queen with redoubled Anger, you believe me then as Stupid as you, as capable as you are of shameful aberrations, for I am not deceived by your modest air; nothing but a perverse Passion could induce such an act of Folly, and I am so unhappy as to have given birth to a degenerate Daughter, unworthy to be owned since she has lost her Virtue.' This reproach pierced the poor princess to the Heart, and she fainted, without arousing the least Pity in her mother, who could not forgive her daughter for having supposed her capable of loving anything in the world more than her jewels.

The princess was taken, half lifeless, to a Tower reserved for state Criminals, accompanied by no one but her frightful Governess, who had orders to make use of every method to induce her to confess the details of her misconduct. This violence alarmed the Court and made a great Noise throughout[1] the Kingdom. Thousands of extravagant stories were uttered; some said that the Princess had conspired to dethrone her father, others added that she had drawn a dagger on the Queen; some asserted that she was 7 months pregnant. Women who feared a Beauty which eclipsed them, and a Virtue which set a threatening example, let fly against her; but it was Generally agreed that, as Heir presumptive to the Crown, she deserved that her Crime, whatever it might be, should be made known,

---

[1] Here (following MWM's p. 8) 'Docile' is interrupted by two sheets of unrelated material (H MS 80, fos. 322–3).

and that she should not be imprisoned without a session of the states general.[1] The provinces sent Deputies, and the magistrates made representations to the King, who would listen neither to the one nor the other. The Queen made him understand that he must uphold the Royal authority, and she treated with so much contempt and Disdain all those who dared enquire her reasons, that her firmness and her Policy began to be respected. Her extreme views triumphed even while they were most exaggerated, and she kept the whole nation in respect and silence.

This is not the first time that extreme and credulous Virtue has attracted infamy, and it is common enough to see bold, audacious folly steal the good opinion of the Public. This is a fine Ground on which to deploy my erudition; I could cite four hundred and fifty-eight passages from ancient and modern history to enforce this truth; but I shall bow to the impatience of my Reader,[2] who is doubtless most anxious about the fate of the Princess.

After the first surprise was over, she armed herself with Philosophy, wrapped herself up in her Virtue, and even found some sweetness in suffering for so glorious a Cause, and so perfect a Friend. Her only sorrow was the sorrow she believed herself to be causing the Marquise; she imagined her sunk in the most violent grief, and her greatest care was to assuage it, by giving her news of herself. One of her Guards, touched by her Beauty and sweetness, risked his life to furnish her with writing materials, and undertook to deliver her Letter. She spent half the night pouring out her tenderness to this dear Object, at the same time taking great care not to touch on the part which she had played in her disgrace. She told her more than once that the happiness of loving her could recompense her for everything, and ended by assuring her that as the cruellest Tyranny could not erase her Image, she had always something with which to console herself, amid the most grievous persecution.

Lady Artifice was much alarmed when she received this Letter; it might perhaps be discovered whence she had had it; that would be enough to expose her to the Fury of the Queen, and perhaps to make

---

[1] This title was given to the French representative assembly of clergy, nobility, and people (summoned by the king for important decisions of state), and to the body of delegates of the various United Provinces of the Netherlands. Both were generally concerned in raising money.

[2] See App. II, p. 222. MWM used this technique in 'The Reasons that Induced Dr S[wift] . . .': 'Here many Noble thoughts occur | But I prolixity abhor, | And will persue th'instructive Tale . . .' (*E&P* 275).

her suspected of a criminal conversation[1] with the Princess, who was classed as a Prisoner of state. She chose the action of a skilful Woman, and took the Letter to her Majesty, who, delighted with this sacrifice, condemned the Guard who had carried it to be hanged, and sent back the letter to the tender Docile, loading her with all the reproaches which she supposed due to her obstinacy and lack of respect for her anger. The Princess never doubted that her Unhappy messenger had been captured, and was far from imagining the Marquise's Treachery. But her Governess, following orders, enlightened her, and added that the marquise was appointed Overseer of the Queen's Household as reward for her noble Action.

It may be asked, perhaps, what became of Lady Good Sense during all this? She retired from the Court, where she has never since then reappeared.

I leave to lively and tender imaginations to picture to themselves the affliction of the Princess at this event; mine is too susceptible to find expression for it. But after having wept, groaned, sighed, and talked for hours and hours to the walls of her Castle,[2] she remembered a maxim of her Philosopher, that it is better to be deceived by a thousand Rogues than to refuse one's aid to a single person who truly deserves to be pitied.[3] She felt herself very much consoled by this Reflection, and consequently made a vow to be a dupe all her life. Anybody else would have written to tell the Queen the true history of this affair, and thereby justified her innocence, and revenged herself for the perfidy of the Marquise; but she was bound by her solemn word, and no consideration could have tempted her to violate it.

Her imprisonment lasted six months, and would have lasted much longer, if the King had not killed himself with mushrooms and Barbados rum Punch.[4] The Queen had made herself generally hated by all her subjects, and perhaps a strong desire to revenge themselves for the taxes she had piled on them contributed largely to the eagerness of the states to deliver the Princess from her mournful castle

[1] A term generally used for adultery or seduction.

[2] Cf. 'Talk to the Stars, to Trees complain | And tell the senseless rocks my pain' ('Ballad to the Irish Howl', *E&P* 304).

[3] Johnson's *Rambler* 79 (1750) concludes: 'it is better to suffer wrong than to do it, and happier to be sometimes cheated than not to trust.'

[4] The notion of a monarch dying of surfeit seems to be a very old joke. Alexander the Great died of the effects of a drunken debauch; among English kings, the death of Henry I was attributed to lampreys, and that of John to peaches and beer.

and proclaim her Queen.[1] Nobody doubted that she would begin her reign with the impeachment of her Mother, who was expected to be condemned at least to exile or to Imprisonment for life. She feared something worse. The King was hardly dead before she took refuge in a temple, not forgetting to take with her all the Crown jewels and the royal strongbox, which was the means to enlist the High Priest in her Interest.

Her Precaution was not necessary. The New Queen wrote her a respectful and affectionate Letter, begging her to return to the Palace and to occupy the same apartments from which she had fled; in short she professed more submission than she had ever done in her life. But all this could not win the mother's Confidence; she believed that, not daring to violate the sanctuary, her daughter meant to trick her out of it; she insisted on remaining there, and would not even see her daughter, though the latter came in person with few attendants, to offer her duty to her. Lady Artifice, who had far greater cause to fear her resentment, had better studied her character; she did not dream of fleeing, or hiding herself; she carried her effrontery so far as to come among the other Ladies to congratulate her on her accession to the Throne. Docile contented herself with viewing her with contempt, and did not deign to reproach her; by this conduct she played into the Marquise's hands, who did not fail to point out to everybody the slender reliance one could have on her favour, since she was capable of so quickly forgetting a person to whom she had been so attached.

The People, who had hoped to see a treason Trial[2] (a Spectacle whose opening always gives a great deal of pleasure), were shocked by this Philosophical clemency, which was not well judged to make her authority respected. The Priests, bribed by the Queen Dowager's treasure, did not fail to plant a thousand Calumnies against the Queen Regnant. The story of her alleged Gallantries[3] was revived; she was informed of it, but instead of punishing its authors, she forbade the pursuit of them, saying openly that one must never take revenge for personal injuries. This maxim, spread abroad, entirely abolished any Fear of offending her. She snubbed her Flatterers, which deeply disgusted those who paid Court to her.

---

[1] See App. II, p. 223.

[2] In the original 'un lit de Justice': originally the ceremonial seat occupied by the French king at sittings of parliament.

[3] Love-affairs.

She declared that, finding the Treasury empty, she would retrench all superfluous expenses, to spare her Subjects, whom she did not wish to load with taxes. There were obviously no Fortunes to be made out of her; her rewards were destined to virtue or to heroic actions. People were not inclined to undertake these painful routes, they were too accustomed to growing rich by easier methods; but what completely sank her in the mind of the People was the indifferent air with which she attended at sacrifices. The Queen of Contrary had always appeared very religious, and perhaps, among all her vices, truly was so. Her daughter detested Hypocrisy, and since she had lost her enthusiastic faith, she was unwilling to appear to entertain any faith at all. This turned the Nobility, the Clergy, and the general mass of her subjects against her; they only waited their moment to overthrow the Form of her Government.

They opened negotiations with King Wildman to deliver their Island up to him. He was the most powerful of their neighbours. Ambitious, and accordingly quite unscrupulous, he did not hesitate to conspire with evil affected subjects against a Legitimate Queen who had no fault but her Virtue. He sent his son, Prince Sombre, to put himself at the head of the conspiracy when the time for action should come. He covered the true purpose of his voyage by proposals for a Marriage between the Prince and the young Queen, who had reached her sixteenth year. He supposed it would be easy to persuade her, that the Prince, already struck with the Fame of her Beauty, wished to pay Court to her in person, being impatient to see those charms which had been so much talked of in the World. He was received with all the politeness due to his rank, and the Queen made him most obligingly welcome at the very time that he was seeking her fall. Her Innocence, her sweetness, and that air of goodness which accompanied all her actions, nevertheless touched him with Compassion. He had not a bad Heart, despite the savage customs of his Country; he had honour and probity, and detested Baseness; he had accepted this commission only with great repugnance, and only in obedience to a violent and absolute Father. Although he believed most of what had been told him to the Queen's disadvantage, the sight of her was almost enough to exonerate her. She was, at least, a very amiable monster, and from their first interview he Resolved to serve her interests instead of damaging them. For this plan to succeed, it had to be concealed, and this he did with all possible artfulness.

He had all the Qualities of an upright man, and no single quality of an amiable one: with direct, rigid Reason and impenetrable secrecy, he was impervious to flattery, unshakably firm, but so Jealous as to be perpetually mistrustful, true to his word, ungracious in his actions, tall and well-built but with a proud air and no charm. Even in his Conversations with the Queen he thought less of pleasing her than of studying her; therefore he did not please her at all, and this he perceived too acutely for his quiet. He was not accustomed to the company of Ladies. Characters like his are well distanced from Gallantry, his Rank excused him from certain assiduities towards them, and he had always treated them with a coldness verging on Contempt. He had no fear of their charms, and exposed himself every day to those of the Queen, who had made a great impression upon him without his suspecting it. The interest which he took in her he called Generosity, and he might perhaps have remained long in ignorance of his passion, in spite of thinking about her, if he had not felt himself stung to the quick by her quite casual praise of a young stranger who had appeared at her Court for the past few days.

It was hard to see him without praising him. He was a cavalier aged about twenty, whose figure had been formed by the hands of the graces, and whose traits seemed to have been fashioned by Love itself: a modest, shy air, seeming not to know the charms he possessed, and a noble, natural demeanour.[1] Politeness mingled with Dignity set off his attractions; he spoke little, but always to the point, and never took sides; he avoided praise, without discourtesy to those who offered it. The most determined Coquettes became timid in his company and did not dare set out to seduce him; they respected, in spite of themselves, a modest Wisdom which, without affectation, never contradicted itself. Yet his eyes gave assurance that his Heart was not formed to be insensible; they were full of a sweet softness which inspired softness in all females who beheld them. He singled out none of them, and this restraint occasioned the praise which gave such pain to Prince Sombre.

He discovered his love in feeling himself Jealous. A pious Prude in love with her Stableman could not have been more outraged by his own passion; he was almost at the point of hating the person he loved; he could not forgive her for her Conquest, and so he did everything he could to break his chains. He recalled to memory all the Stories he had heard of her Misconduct, he tried to persuade him-

---

[1] X in margin.

self of their truth; he reproached himself as if for the deepest baseness, for the slightest sentiment in her favour. He arrived at flattering himself that he despised her, and with this happy Idea he went to Court with the intention of speaking incivilities to her in order to draw from her retorts in kind which might finish by ridding him of a taste that he regarded as a blemish on his honour. He turned the conversation to the foreign Cavalier, watching the Queen with a malice which she did not understand; she replied to his insolence with so much sweetness, and such ingenuous Innocence, that he found her more amiable than she had ever been, and he left her presence with redoubled Love and Fury.[1]

This Love, far from being attended with playfulness and laughter, brought nothing in its train but vexation and sorrow. He felt it as a Humiliation that she was necessary to his happiness, and his Pride would have wished to be self-sufficient. But such passion customarily triumphs over Pride and Prudence; he was already its slave, and it exerted all its power.[2] Given over to new thoughts, and occupied in internal Warfare, he appeared cold and abstracted among the conspirators. These assembled sometimes at his apartments and sometimes at those of the High Priest, an Aged and consummate Politician, who had designs of his own. When he had opened negotiations with King Wildman, he had been impelled neither by zeal for the Faith, nor by Fear of the innovations which he claimed to dread; he aimed to be Prime Minister at least, and he could not hope for this from the Queen.[3]

She had offered this post to her Philosopher; he was wise enough to refuse a function which he felt himself incapable of exercising with honour, and he was mad enough to desire, as reward for his service past, permission to go to Lapland to carry out experiments on air. He was frozen to death there in 1709.[4]

Despairing of satisfying his ambition through Docile, the High Priest conceived the bold Project of dethroning her, and he counted it little to sacrifice his country to his Ambition. He had insinuated himself so well with the Queen Mother, that she joined in everything he wished, and he used his influence to blacken her Daughter in the

---

[1] See App. II, p. 226.

[2] This seems to be the meaning, although the wrong gender is used.

[3] The next paragraph, and the opening of the next, were added in the margin.

[4] Algarotti celebrates in *Newtonianismo* a learned company then leaving France in the cause of science for the gulf of Bothnia, or deserts of Lapland (transl. as *Sir Isaac Newton's Theory of Light and Colours* (1742), ii. 193).

people's eyes. Everything was moving towards imminent revolution, and everything was halted by the Bizarre behaviour of Prince Sombre. He caused Difficulties to spring up, he hindered plans, and it was easy to see that he did not wish for success, without being able to divine his motives. Indeed, so little was he in agreement with himself that it was impossible to guess his Aims, which were not yet settled. He saw too much coolness in the Queen to be able to flatter himself that he pleased her; he feared she had a secret Inclination for some Object formed to inspire it. With these beliefs he did not wish to marry her, but he wished even less to see her shut up among the Vestals, as was resolved in the Plan of the conspirators.

The proud and discontented air which he maintained at their meetings, and the brusque manner in which he often opposed the High Priest, had inspired in the latter a Fear of him, which ended in the most violent Hatred, which he concealed under the deepest submissiveness. But he sent a Confidential courier to King Wildman, to inform him of the extraordinary conduct of the Prince his son. He accused him of the Design of seizing the Kingdom for himself, and professed to prove it by a thousand circumstances, true or alleged. The King, violent and cruel by nature, without examining closely into the case, sent him a commission to arrest the Prince the same day that he took the Queen prisoner, and to hold him captive until further notice, naming as his Viceroy the High Priest, who now dreamed of nothing but of hastening the moment which would crown his Ambition.

The lovely Docile suspected nothing of what was brewing against her, but she had anxieties of a different kind, which gave her much livelier alarm than any which self-interest could have caused her. A Heart as tender as hers could not remain entirely empty; the perfidy of Lady Artifice had not disillusioned her about the charms of Friendship; she blamed only her own failings, and little knew that in seeking a faithful friend she was seeking, morally, the Philosophers' Stone.[1] She thought she had found it in the person of one of her maids of honour, about her own age, who had an air of innocence and modesty which might have imposed on a person of wider experience than the young Queen. Her attention and obligingness succeeded in gaining the queen's confidence, which she bestowed entirely on the

---

[1] The imagined substance which can turn base metals into gold. MWM annotated as 'Natural' her copy of Sarah Fielding, *The Adventures of David Simple*, whose subtitle is *In the Search of a Real Friend* (1744, 1753) (at Sandon).

amiable Emily, who, under an appearance of naïve timidity which the graces of youth seemed to confirm, was the most dangerous coquette at Court. The Queen freed herself as often as she could, and oftener than she should have, from the crowd which Besieged her, to taste the pleasure of sharing her thoughts with her.

One evening, walking in the Maze in beautiful moonlight, leaning on her arm, 'Have you observed, my dear Emily, she asked her, this stranger whom they call Philocles?'[1] Emily would have believed that the Queen was going to reproach her for her coquettish behaviour towards him, and which she did not forgive his having ignored, if she had not observed a note of tenderness in the Queen's voice which conveyed to her some reassuring Ideas and inspired her with this flattering reply.

'Yes Madam, she replied smartly, no one else is observed ever since he arrived, and he has eyes for no one but Y[our] Majesty.' The Queen blushed, and changed the subject with a promptness which better explained her sentiments than the most detailed Confession would have done; but Emily had too much wit to appear to notice. The conversation lasted not much longer, the Queen became dreamy, and retired early to go to bed and give herself up to the monologues she longed to compose there.

Any Prude who reads this story will be scandalized that this Docile, with so rigid a virtue,[2] should be capable of dreaming (for one may well suspect the subject of her dream) of a young man whom she hardly knew, and who seemed to be of a rank well below her own; but remember if you please, my Ladies, about sympathy. You have almost all felt its force on certain occasions; it is enough for the Queen's virtue that she should fail to recognize her own sentiments, and that she should struggle against them in proportion as she began to understand them. Her Confidante's answer had made her feel a pleasure mingled with shame which she had never experienced. After having spent a very unquiet Night, she got up strongly resolved to pay no more attention to this Cavalier, whose face troubled her repose. She went to the temple in this mood; the first object which struck her sight was himself. She turned away in a confusion which would have flattered him very much if he had had experience or Self-conceit. Modest, timid, and sincerely in Love, he was fearful

---

[1] The name, meaning 'lover of fame', suggests a Scudéry romance. Lady Mary had used it elsewhere (above, p. 3).

[2] Someone else's illegible scribbles in margin.

and trembling in her presence; he observed her with too much attention for any of her movements to escape him, but he thought he saw displeasure, and perhaps Anger, in the pains she took not to meet his eyes. He imagined that she had received some impression to his disadvantage, and he suffered so cruelly from this imagination, that he found himself indisposed, and sought to retire.

The Crowd was thick, the Queen turned her head as she heard the noise that was made as people made way for him; she saw him Pale and discomposed, she turned red and became confused. Prince Sombre was by her, and interpreted her looks in a manner very unlike that of Philocles. His suspicions became certainty, and he meditated plans of revenge, which vanished on his return to his Palace. There he found a spy, Skilful, whom he had enlisted from among the confidants of the High Priest, whose true Character was not unknown to him. This man had had the presence of mind to make off with his master's Strong-box, and had brought it to the Prince, who opened it eagerly. He found there the King his Father's thunderbolt of a <dispatch>, and by a Copy of the High Priest's answer he saw that the next night was appointed for a general uprising and the enactment of the blackest Treason ever to be planned. There was no time to be Lost; he requested an Audience with the Queen, who with her customary goodness granted it to him. Pity and love possessed his soul when he saw her, and, joining with his natural Generosity without vanquishing his Jealousy, transformed all his intentions. He conceived, all at once, that of sacrificing everything in order to rescue her; he expounded the frightful situation she found herself in, and laid the evidence for it before her. 'It would be vain, Madam, he added, to have the Guilty men arrested; they are too many, and too powerful; perhaps they would like nothing better than a pretext of self-defence to cover their rebellion. You have only one course to follow: flee. I offer myself to conduct you to a place of safety. I shall take you to an Island of which I am the ruler; it was the dowry of my late mother. No one can challenge my right to it without an Injustice by which the whole world would be repelled.'

'But sir, interrupted the Queen, astonished at such extraordinary and overwhelming news: whatever my Danger, ought I to escape it at the expense of my Honour? Will not that be tarnished for ever, by giving myself up to the Conduct of a Prince who. . . .'[1]

---

[1] The ellipses here and two paragraphs later are MWM's.

'Say, Madam, he cried, of a Prince to whom you will have given your hand, and who will make you sovereign of his territories.'— The Generosity of this offer in the present circumstances struck the Queen with intense gratitude. She remained Silent, her eyes cast down, for several moments; then she lifted them, sighing.

'Alas, my lord, she said, I am too much touched by your conduct not to wish to be worthy of your attachment. I should like to be able to make your happiness, but if it is my emotions which must do so, I confess that I am unable to feel any others but those of esteem and gratitude. I cannot compel my Heart, which recoils from entertaining a tenderness which I have no doubt that you will inspire in some Princess more well-judging than myself.'

'I understand you Madam, he replied, I do not need this moment to teach me that I am the object of your Aversion; I know also that another. . . . no matter, you are lost if you refuse me, and perhaps one day I shall be acceptable to you for having saved you from a people that betrays you, and from an Inclination that dishonours you.'

These words (pronounced with an air that would have decided anyone but the innocent Docile never to put herself in the power of a Lover so disrespectful, not to say Brutal) made a quite different impression on her heart. It was the first time in her life that she had reproached herself. She felt in the depths of her Heart that the Prince's reproach was justified; she felt herself so much to blame, and so humiliated, that she felt she ought at the same time both to punish herself for her Weakness, and to reward the tenderness of the most generous of men. She extended her hand to him, tears in her eyes. 'Since you desire, she said, to become responsible for a miserable woman who has nothing to offer you except gratitude, I put myself under your protection. I plight you my troth, and you have only to order in what manner you wish me to conduct myself.'

One might perhaps expect to observe transports of joy from the Prince at this almost unexpected success; but he was accustomed to criticize everything, and always to look on the dark side. His Jealousy became half as strong again; he came close to repenting the proposal that he had just made. He kissed her hand quite coldly, and without any pretence of thanking her for the Favour she was bestowing on him he merely informed her that she must repair to the garden at nightfall, accompanied by no more than one woman, that he would provide a Priest loyal to her, that once the Ceremony of their marriage was performed a post-chaise would convey them to the nearest

Seaport, where he would have a Shallop[1] ready to sail. The rebellion ought not to break out until after midnight, when they would already be out of reach of all pursuit. He went out without waiting for her reply, and I believe he would have waited for a long while if he had stayed; she had become dumb with Confusion and bursting with Ideas which she could not disentangle. She was torn from her dream by the arrival of Emily, who told her that Philocles was in the ante-chamber, and that he was begging for an audience with so much eagerness and so bashful a manner, that she did not doubt he had come to seek her protection, or to inform her of something truly out of the ordinary.

His Name made the Queen tremble. Her first impulse was to refuse to see him; but then why refuse to see a stranger who appeared to be of distinguished rank, who had never failed in respect for her, who came to implore her Aid, or perhaps to give her some important information? These hastily-made reflections decided her to permit him to enter. He appeared, and Emily retired into the bay of a distant window, whence she studied every least one of their looks.

He flung himself at the Queen's feet, and begged her to listen to him in a tone which commanded her whole attention. 'I should not dare to present myself before you, Madam, he said in a trembling voice, having noticed that the sight of me is disagreeable to you, if it did not concern your interests, which are a thousand times dearer to me than my life. I have just received some information from the Genie my Father, who is the intelligence which presides over the planet Venus. He is virtuous, and nobly protects Virtue, and yours is not unfamiliar to him. His knowledge is boundless, though his power owns limits; he can do nothing to serve the inhabitants of the Earth, but he can withdraw you from it. For a long time he has felt pity for your situation, and admiration for your person. Do not be astonished that he knows you; he has Telescopes of his own invention, infinitely more perfected than those of the most celebrated instrument-makers upon this Earth. You seized his attention; he wished for me the Glory of pleasing you. I am his only son. He sent me here, incognito, with this intention. Fatherly feeling gave him this hope, which I feel to be presumptuous, and I would not dare mention it to you, if he had not written to tell me that through his Telescopes he has discovered a universal disaffection among your subjects. Your very life is in danger; preserve this precious life, and

---

[1] A large, sail-driven canoe: related to *sloop*.

preserve the most passionate and respectful of Lovers from eternal mourning, for my Essence does not permit me to die. Speak, divine Princess, but remember that you will be deciding your Fate and mine. Consent to make my happiness, and you will enjoy immortality with me, a Cloud can convey us in a moment to my Father's Palace and you will reign over a Planet which is not the least agreeable in the system of the universe.'[1]

The judicious Reader has doubtless divined the more than illustrious birth of my hero.[2] Young and handsome without vanity, possessed of wit without the urge to show it off, joining to all the graces of nature a modesty which did not let him see that he pleased: never has a mortal like this been seen. But the Queen had too little experience to make this reflection.

She was so astonished that she lost her Tongue for some time. She recovered from this Astonishment only when she began to feel all the Suffering by which a Soul can be torn. Only an hour before, she had plighted her troth to a petty Prince who was unworthy of her in every way; now she was offered the most brilliant station with someone she adored. Reason, ambition, and love (which pictured a Heart newly submitted to his laws) solicited for him. But her Word solemnly given was a Barrier which resisted everything; she resolved to sacrifice to her virtue both her happiness and that of her amiable Lover. But how could she find expressions to soften this cruel sentence? She had not the strength to pronounce it, and she melted in tears, in a silence which the unhappy Philocles interpreted as a pronounced Aversion to his person. Settled despair made him bold. She had one hand languishingly disposed on the arm of her Chair, while the other held her handkerchief to her eyes. He dared to take this lovely hand and print a thousand kisses upon it.

He would have kept himself scrupulously from such hardihood, if he had believed himself loved: he would have feared offending the Queen's delicacy and modesty, or giving the impression that he presumed she had an Inclination for him. But imagining himself detested, he thought himself at the nadir of Unhappiness, and that she might of her goodness forgive the last farewell of a miserable

---

[1] Interplanetary travel had been used in fiction since the Greek satirist Lucian (owned by MWM in three versions: Wh MS 135), 2nd cent. AD: notably by Francis Godwin, *The Man in the Moone* (1638) and Cyrano de Bergerac, *Histoire comique contenant les états et empire de la lune* (1657).

[2] See App. II, p. 230. The passage following is marked in the margin with emphatic lines and 'fin' (not *the end*, but *subtle* or *witty*).

Lover who would for ever adore her. If there is in the World a girl of seventeen, tender by nature, whom no man has ever approached but at excessive distance, and who is just feeling the first warmth of a dawning passion, it is for her and only her to judge the emotion which Docile experienced when she felt the impress of Philocles' trembling lips on her hand. She did not think of withdrawing it; could she think of that in so delicious an <instant?> Intoxication of Pleasure suspended all movement. Then her Virtue roused her; she compelled herself to call Emily, and said Feebly to her, 'Conduct this Gentleman—'

She went to her Closet, and flung herself more dead than alive on her Sofa. Emily could understand nothing of this scene in which she had heard nothing; she could see that the Queen loved passionately, and that she was beloved; but why these Tears and this despair? She imagined that her pride was combatting her Love, and believed that it would not resist for long. Already enraged with Philocles for his coldness towards the advances she had made him, she swore to revenge herself at the first opportunity. She returned to the Queen to attempt to uncover her secret, but found her without strength to utter a word. Nothing ensued but tears, and sobs, and fainting, until the hour appointed for her fatal rendezvous with Prince Sombre.

She came down to the garden, followed by Emily; the marriage took place in a Summer-house, and the ladies immediately entered a post-chaise escorted by the Prince and six of his officers. All this took place in profound silence. For the Prince, the sight of her arriving all disfigured with tears, barely supporting herself with her maid of honour's assistance, augured very badly for his Marriage, and he pronounced its words of mystery[1] almost with regret, and without giving her a single caring word. During the Ceremony she was too overcome even to articulate, and Emily, amazed at these proceedings, assumed that she must have decided to equip herself with a Husband in order to protect herself from an irresistible Lover. This precaution seemed to her very uncertain, and she already imagined an Intrigue developing between the Queen and Philocles. She believed herself destined to be the Confidante of it, and resolved to leave no avenue unexplored to evade this unbearable Function.[2]

She revolved various plans in her thoughts during the three hours that they travelled towards the sea. When she saw they were to

---

[1] Especially, perhaps, 'With this ring I thee wed, with my body I thee worship . . .'
[2] Some of these readings are doubtful: see below, App. II, pp. 231–2.

embark, she decided to abandon her mistress there. She assumed she would be going to the Court of King Wildman, of whom she had formed a very gloomy opinion, and she did not mean to share the Queen's unhappy fate. Even less did she mean to permit her to sweeten it by the Presence of her Lover. She did not doubt that he would be sufficiently in love to follow her and she meant to warn Prince Sombre of this. She begged him to step aside and listen to her, which he very willingly granted; he had already formed the plan of corrupting her with bribes, so that he might learn the Queen's very thoughts.

She began her discourse by begging him to permit her to retire, giving him to understand that she had most Vital reasons for quitting Docile's service. She allowed herself to be much pressed to relate them; persuading her took nothing less than a very costly Diamond. At last she informed him of the interview between the Queen and the handsome stranger. Her tears, her Despair, the kissing of her hand: no detail was omitted, and the entire story was poisoned. 'Be the judge, my Lord[1] (she said, sighing and wiping her eyes, which were perfectly dry), whether a young Lady of my Birth can remain with a Princess who forgets herself to the point of permitting Liberties of such a kind. I believe her, however (she added with an air of charity), to be at bottom most virtuous, but imprudence is as damaging as vice to one's Reputation. Mine is extremely precious to me, and obliges me to return home to my Father. I should not be capable of doing this, had I not the Consolation of leaving her happily united with a Prince who cannot fail to make her happiness, once she has lost the recollection of this little Gentleman with whom she is infatuated.'

The Prince was too much struck by what he heard to reply to it. He contented himself with giving orders that she should return in the Chaise, while he boarded the Shallop with the Queen, who only said to her, 'Are you leaving me, Emily!' and fell fainting in the arms of the Prince's officers. He was too incensed against her to offer to assist her in so touching a condition.

They set sail, although the weather was darkening; and Emily returned to the Court,[2] where she broadcast, while urging everyone to keep it secret, that she had long been shocked by Docile's

---

[1] H MS 80, fo. 333, ends here: the sense goes straight on to fo. 369, despite irrelevant material having been bound between them.

[2] Note in margin: 'comence la'—[begin here? begin the . . .?]

excessive taste for Gallantry, that she had tried every possible means to cure her of this shameful bent, that at last this Abduction, planned without her knowledge, and carried through with unparalleled effrontery, had disgusted her to such a point that she had refused the most shining offers, and preferred to remain in an obscurity which exacted no price from her Innocence.

This speech was a marvellous success for her. Of six marriage treaties which she was negotiating, she achieved the most advantageous, which would never have fallen to her lot without this adventure. The delicacy which she had shown in spurning fortune to preserve her honour, erased all the impressions made by her former Coquetry; it was the more plausible since the Conspiracy did not become known until after the Queen's flight. The High Priest, who was its leading spirit, was not so unskilful as to be without spies; a Page informed him of Docile's every movement. He knew about the two Audiences which she had granted; he did not doubt that they would have some extraordinary sequel, and he hoped for a pretext which would give his Rebellion the appearance of a generous-minded revolution against a Princess unworthy to reign. He postponed his enterprise, and it did not break out until Docile's absence had plunged the whole city in Tumult; all kinds of stories were in circulation, when Emily's return revealed that she had fled with Prince Sombre.

Poor Philocles[1] became so distracted by this Bizarre event that I have no doubt that he would have run mad had not, happily for him, his All-knowing Father had the Telescope that moment to his Eye. He saw his beloved Son tearing his lovely locks in Desperation; he transported him in a moment to his side. His wise Counsels, the Brilliant Beauties of his Court, time and distance, all contributed to curing the Prince of his unhappy passion. He forgot Docile, and vowed never to revisit that planet, where an honest man is exposed, all his life, to Warfare as unequal as that of the naked Americans against the Spaniards armed with swords and Guns.[2]

---

[1] This paragraph is attached on a separate slip of paper.

[2] At 14 Lady Mary had created another discarded lover who responds by abjuring love and the scene of love: Strephon in 'The Adventurer' (I. Grundy, ' "The Entire Works of Clarinda": Unpublished Juvenile Verse by Lady Mary Wortley Montagu', *YES* 7 (1977), 106). Compassion for the invaded 'naked Americans' had been voiced by Swift in *Gulliver's Travels* (1726), book 4, ch. 12, and Montesquieu in *Lettres persanes* (I owe this point to John Rempel).

The High Priest appeared at the head of the Clergy and the Nobility; he assembled the estates, he made a touching Harangue; even while preserving his respect for the royal prerogative, he tore the Queen in pieces with the most atrocious Calumnies. And yet, in measured terms, with eyes frequently lifted to Heaven, making his Moderation admired, he expatiated on the Wisdom of the late King, the Piety etc. of the Queen Mother, the rational education she had given to the daughter whose aberrations she had never been able to correct, who had finally abdicated from her realm to go wandering the world with the object of her deranged Passion. 'It is well known (he continued) to what point we have carried submission to our Masters, always more eager to demonstrate that than to preserve our most legitimate rights. I should still be zealous to nurture in you that Loyalty owing to our sovereign; but it is she who now abandons us. King Wildman, redoubtable in arms and respected for his Prudence, will doubtless seize this opportunity to mount an Invasion; are we in any state to resist him? An empty treasury, maladministered Finances, a small number of inadequately paid Troops! Can we flatter ourselves that we shall not be compelled to yield to his Forces, and would it not be to draw on us his legitimate Vengeance to offer him a resistance in which we cannot persevere? Let us implore his Protection; I have no doubt that he will grant it, his Generosity will be interested in preserving our Privileges. I believe that our tutelary Gods have inspired me with this Idea, as the only means to avert our total destruction. May their goodness open your eyes to your situation, and give you courage to come to a Resolution which will be expedient for the state, and necessary to spare the people's blood.'[1]

This speech (like all speeches in the world) had different effects on different tempers, but a majority of voices supported it, in conformity with the sentiments of the High Priest, who hurriedly dispatched Deputies in the name of the assembly to King Wildman to implore him to come and take possession of their Island, abandoned by their Queen, and exposed to the insults of their neighbours.

The unhappy Docile, during these negotiations, was sailing towards the little Island which belonged to her new Lord. Never was there so unpleasing a voyage. When she had tranquillized her spirit so far as to order her thoughts, she devoted them entirely to pleasing Prince Sombre, and even to loving him. She constantly presented to

---

[1] MWM may intend Docile to parallel Christ, of whom the high priest Caiaphas counselled 'that it was expedient that one man should die for the people' (John 18: 14).

herself the obligation which she believed she owed him for his disinterested conduct; she sought to make the most of all his good Qualities and turn a blind eye to his faults. Finding herself unable to force her Inclination, she exerted herself to offer him at least the forms of tenderness which ought to content him. Her object was not that of appearing otherwise than what she was, but that of striving to become what she wished to be. This Intention, which would have charmed a reasonable man, completed the alienation of the Prince. He was too penetrating, and she dissimulated too badly, for him to fail to perceive the constraint she was under to conceal a sorrow which gnawed at her. He gave the reins freely to his ill humour, sometimes in reproaches, sometimes in biting jests, with never a single moment of Confidence, or esteem, or tenderness.

His Insensibility gave him no compassion for a young Princess Delicately brought up at a magnificent Court, who was suffering all the fatigues and inconveniences of shipboard without a murmur. Her sweetness, her patience, were lost on him; he did not perceive them, concerned solely with weighing the emotions of her Heart, and always finding something to complain of. If, exhausted by continual constraint and sick of his insulting remarks, she let her depression become visible, he reproached her with dwelling on the memory of a cherished Lover, giving her brutally to understand that he believed she had granted him the last favour.[1] If she made an effort before her People to hide her Melancholy under the appearance of a borrowed Gaiety, he was so persuaded of her Gallantry that he enquired which of his officers had the honour of pleasing her. In short, his conduct would make an observer believe, from the pains he took to disgust her, that his happiness depended on making himself hated by a wife he adored.

He encountered a trouble of a different kind when he arrived in sight of the Island where he claimed to reign. He saw the Port occupied by his Father's Fleet. Contrary winds had retarded his voyage enough for King Wildman (who suspected he would retreat there) to seize it, and there was no safety in landing there. He needed to seek another asylum; but where could he find one? The territory of King Goodchild[2] was not far away; he was an enemy to King Wildman,

---

[1] i.e. gone to bed with him.

[2] There seems to be no adequate English expression for 'le Roi des Bons Enfants', with its implications of naïve open-heartedness. (A *bon enfant* is an adult who is liked if not deeply respected.)

and would have been happy to entertain his disgraced Son, if the latter had been willing to request his protection; but he would have regarded this as a blemish on his honour, and perhaps he feared to show the Lovely Docile at a Court so amiable and so gallant as that.

He followed the course of landing at an unfrequented port, in the guise of a private person of modest Condition; he dismissed most of his retinue, and distributed half his jewels among them as payment for their Fidelity. He sold the rest in a nearby town, and bought a little house which was clean enough inside although the exterior looked like a cottage. Its situation was charming, on the skirts of a Forest, near a brook which flowed from a spring of the finest water. A Hill clothed in Woods protected it from Wind. The prospect, wide and varied, was of well-tilled Countryside and beautiful skies, the house surrounded by modest grounds which abundantly furnished all the necessities of life. Their household was reduced to two Menservants and two women.[1] This solitude was made to inspire Tranquillity, and anyone else but Prince Sombre would have found it in the company of the amiable Docile, always attentive and obliging; but he was not formed to enjoy it. His continued Caprices made their time in this place as troubled as the most tumultuous Court, without the opportunity for Dissipation which that supplies. The only periods of relaxation for the unhappy Docile were those which he spent out hunting, which were plentiful.

She was walking in the Forest on one of those days, attended by one of her women, to whom she never talked. Her reserve did not arise from her sad experience of the unhappiness which her Confidences had brought on her; but she would never have forgiven herself if she had uttered the least complaint against a Husband whom she still regarded as the object to whom she owed the most inviolable attachment. Her abstractedness had led her quite a long way from her house, when a loud noise of hunting Horns, the cries of whippers-in, and the chiming of a pack announced the approach of a magnificent hunt. She tried to slip away to her retreat, but the Stag crossed her path with the hounds in close pursuit. She saw, halting in his tracks, a Cavalier of handsome appearance, richly dressed and mounted on a fine horse, at the head of a numerous and brilliant retinue.

[1] See App. II, p. 235.

A straw Hat,[1] a fine linen bodice, and a plain gown in light taffeta made up her whole costume. Such simplicity perfectly set off the charms of a young woman whose freshness needed no help from Art. Docile looked far more beautiful than among the reflectors[2] of her Royalty. King Goodchild (for, you may well believe, it was he), struck by an appearance so far out of the common, forgot the ardour of the Chase to converse with her. The people in his train would not have been surprised even if her Beauty had been less interesting: he was the most familiar King that was ever seen, never inhibited by his Rank. His old Courtiers accused him of too frequently forgetting it; he laughed at their Formality, and was never so happy as at a Table where the company was distinguished for wit alone, and he flirted with all Beauties equally, without troubling himself with their Lineage. With the greatest good nature in the world, he preferred to inspire joy rather than respect.

He was absolutely determined to escort Docile back home; she dared not say that she feared her Husband's Jealousy, and other reasons proved incapable of deflecting him. He accompanied her, followed by about thirty of his lords, to a stone's throw from her House, where they met Prince Sombre. His air, noble but proud, transmuted the compliment which the King had intended for him. 'I feel certain (said he) that you were not born to inhabit the cottage I see here. The charms of Madam your wife had already taught me what to think of this; I do not wish to enquire your secret, but I cannot permit persons like yourselves to remain in a state so unworthy of them. You are strangers. If I cannot right your fortune, at least it is more fitting for you to be at Court than in the obscurity of this Forest; I require you to leave it this very hour.' Without waiting for his reply, he ordered a carriage to convey them, and himself walked Beside it, entertaining Docile with gallant politeness which threw the Prince into despair. The latter remained in doleful silence, which the Courtiers interpreted as excess of joy for the unlooked-for happiness which had befallen him.

The King paid no attention to this; he was too much occupied with the charge of amusing the Beautiful stranger. He was quick to receive all pleasurable impressions, and he had never experienced anything more pleasurable than being at her side. He was born for

---

[1] Labouring women's wear, cf. Richardson, *Pamela*, letter 24.

[2] This word, illegible in MS, seems to be 'ab<atj>ours', reflectors, but might be intended as 'ab<at>is', trophies.

joy, free-handed, gay, and (which will appear incredible to some people) in his first vigour although 25 years old.[1] Everything at his Court betokened pleasure. He provided for the strangers apartments magnificent enough to have been suitable even if he had known their rank. From that very evening they ate at his table. He proposed cards after supper, and retained them with him long enough for Docile's apartment to be prepared according to his orders. She found there a superb Dressing-room furnished with a screen set with Diamonds, Wardrobes full of the richest stuffs and lace of the latest mode, agreeable young Ladies detailed to wait on her; nothing was forgotten that might mark his intention to render his Palace pleasing to them.

One can imagine how Prince Sombre savoured this magnificence. He began by quarrelling with Docile about her walk, which had drawn this adventure upon them. He carried his injustice so far as to say that it was clearly the result of premeditated design, that she had written to bid the King present himself, and that she had already agreed the price of the honours with which he was crowning them. She was well enough inured to insults not to be surprised at this one, and replied with a submissiveness that would have converted any other Heart but his. 'When I gave you my hand, my Lord, she said, I submitted myself unreservedly to your will. You have only to order; you will always see me obey.'

'I will not constrain you, Madam, he replied in a dry tone: if the King pleases you, you have only to remain here. For my part, I shall withdraw, even if the most cruel Death should be the consequence. If you wish that I should believe you innocent, contrary to all appearances, request that you may retire from court in such a manner as to obtain your request without my having anything to do with it. I should blush to contend for a Woman light enough to waver between a Lover and her Husband.' She promised to carry out his wishes, and agreed with him to take the risk of Flight if it proved impossible to obtain leave to go.

All the Great or amiable of each Sex presented themselves next Morning at her Toilet, and set at work every idea that ingenuity and the desire of pleasing could inspire, to make themselves agreeable to her. The men lauded her beauty, the Women loaded her with caresses, and with proffers of Friendship which were not so insincere as might be suspected. It is usual for Courtiers to fashion themselves after the Model of their King. Frankness was his favourite virtue; he

[1] MWM implies that modern young gentlemen ruin their health early by dissipation.

so strongly disliked envy and teasing that they had gone out of fashion. Even a woman would have made herself so ridiculous by wounding someone else's character, that no one dared to do so. The prudes and hypocrites had been forced to retire to the provinces, and Gallantry was so well established at Court that there was no Mother or Husband foolhardy enough to find anything to blame in it.[1] It is true that this was not the Nation for Sentiments; they looked for nothing but painless pleasures; taste and convenience governed all their relationships; they mocked at languishment and had scant respect for sighs. None of those Novels preaching delicacy were to be seen there; Libertine Tales, Comic Operas, and light Comedies made up the whole business of their Poets, who never failed to be duly rewarded if they proved successful as entertainers.

The King openly admitted that he valued a sweetly turned drinking song above a volume of Metaphysics; General panegyrists were exiled, as tending to trouble public Pleasure by the boredom they induced; Philosophers and Astronomers were free to study in private, but forbidden to publish anything unless it could be found useful or amusing. Any Theologians, Casuists, or Controversialists would have been sent to the Galleys[2] if they had dared to reveal themselves. Priests existed only for services at the Altars, and as the practice of Religion (according to their doctrine) demanded great simplicity, they were prohibited from learning to read or write.[3] Exquisite Music was the sole Ceremony in the Temples, and it was for the sake of varying his pleasures that the King attended them frequently. Victims were presented decked with Garlands, but none was sacrificed. They burned the most rarefied perfumes; beautiful Young people danced in honour of the Gods; a sacred Pleasure expanded in every Heart, and when people had thoroughly enjoyed themselves they believed they had rendered acceptable homage to the Deity, who delighted (according to their system) in seeing happy people, and turned his face with horror from those Monsters of ingratitude who refused to enjoy his gifts. They shunned excess, for the sake of preserving Health, the foundation of Pleasures; but they sought it

[1] This suggests MWM's account of Venice in 1739–40 ('Fragment to ***', *E&P* 301).

[2] Galleys were rowed by slave or convict oarsmen: a form of punishment still used at this date by France as well as Islamic countries.

[3] The Hindu religion includes certain doctrines that cannot be written down, only communicated by word of mouth (*The Hindu World* (1968), s.v. 'Secrecy'). MWM, however, is probably reversing the Catholic Church's historical opposition to translating the Bible into languages accessible to anyone *but* the clergy.

only by means of Bodily exercise and Gaiety of mind. They almost never turned to remedies; of all the arts of Medicine, only the study of herbs was permitted.[1] Their Laws were few in number, clearly phrased, and had never been the subject of commentary.[2]

Such were the manners of this singular people, who were more envied than feared by their neighbours. They never embarked on Conquests, but contented themselves with a defensive stance, united among themselves. King Wildman, although much stronger, had always come to grief in his operations against their nation; their King was not ashamed to mock all Conquerors of the past, present and future. 'Life is too short, he said, for monumental projects. My Friends, let us enjoy the benefits which lie within our reach, and allow others to enjoy those which the beneficent Gods have given them for their share.'[3] Such maxims do not make a Hero; they make something better, they make a truly honest Man and a kingdom which, he boasted, abounded in all the Virtues of humanity.

His Court was a refuge for all good people persecuted by Fortune. Talents or beauty passed current with him for titles of nobility. He had therefore founded an order,[4] whose requirements for admission were those of disinterestedness, Generosity, and friendship. His courtesy and attentions to Strangers who appeared to merit them surpassed anything imaginable. Imagine then how he behaved towards the Lovely Docile. He came in person to entreat her to honour his Court with her presence; he spoke graciously to Prince Sombre, although the latter replied lamely enough, and withdrew himself several paces with a discontented air, while the King advanced towards Docile, who seized this opportunity to beg his permission to return to her retreat, while assuring him nevertheless of the gratitude which she owed to his goodness.

He appeared quite astonished by so whimsical a request. 'Are you so quickly weary, Madam, he asked, of being the ornament of my Court? has anyone failed in respect for you? or do you fear (he added, lowering his voice) to find me too susceptible to charms which

---

[1] See App. II, p. 238, n. 1. MWM had been sceptical of medical claims even before her support of inoculation brought her numerous enemies among the doctors. She owned two books by the herbalist Nicholas Culpeper; in Italy she studied 'Simples' and apparently made up remedies (Wh MS 135; Arents Collection, New York Public Library, S. 383; *CL* iii. 32–3, 168).

[2] In Brobdingnag the laws were 'expressed in the most plain and simple Terms . . . And to write a Comment upon any Law is a capital Crime' (*Gulliver's Travels*, book 2, ch. 7).

[3] MWM used the same sentiments in her fable 'The Turkey and the Ants' (*E&P* 156).

[4] Cf. Princess Emma, above p. 21.

eclipse everything that is most worthy of love? I confess you have vanquished me, but in losing my Liberty I shall not lose my respect. Since I have seen you, you have only gained one slave more. I shall never speak to you in any other tone; you will make me happy if you judge me worthy to be your slave. If you find another better able to please you, I shall strive to find my Happiness in yours, and shall never hinder it.—Could it be that my Lord your Husband obliges you to retire? It is not natural that at your Age you should wish to bury yourself in the Woods, and to hide a Beauty formed to triumph over all Hearts. Husbands are often inconvenient.—We must win him over.'

He turned away from her without waiting for her reply, and advanced towards Prince Sombre, with that frank air which is so becoming and so rarely seen in princes. He made him the most magnificent and the most attractive offers, to persuade him to establish himself in his company. Prince Sombre, who wished to put Docile to the final test, replied with a forced air of respect that he appreciated the value of the honour which the king did him, and would be happy to spend his life in his service; that it would be easy for him to give up a retired life, whose idleness was disagreeable to him and which he had chosen only in Compliance with his wife; that if his Majesty could alter her unsociable humour he would be delighted; that if he dared, he would take the liberty of entreating him to do so.

The King, quite astonished, turned towards her and said, 'Is it possible, Madam, that it is you who insist upon choosing to abandon us? What Reason can be found for so wild a penchant in such flower of youth? Is it Contempt? we will try to win your esteem. Is it melancholy? you must cure it by occupying yourself with the amusements proper to your age. Out of Consideration for your husband, at least, you ought to restore to the world that merit of his which has been buried for too long. I am not surprised that you can be a whole world for him, but be generous in your turn; bow to our wishes, and quit that solitude which renders useless two people whom the Gods designed to contribute to Mortals' happiness.'

The unhappy Docile kept her eyes cast down during this speech, and when she lifted them she saw those of Prince Sombre fixed on her. This too well informed her of what he wished her to reply. She insisted upon her request, without entering into any discussion about it, and this with so profound a melancholy, that the King had not a moment's doubt as to her extraordinary Humour. His love was half cured by it. He left, remarking that he would have to wait some time for her to adopt a more favourable decision, and left these two people in a condition difficult to describe.

Prince Sombre was the first to break silence. 'I clearly see (said he) that the King desires to retain us here. In spite of that feigned Compliance which does not deceive me, he apparently flatters himself that you will find such violence attractive. Entreaties will be no use with him, one must take a bold Resolve, and carry it through with firmness. They are not spying on me; I shall take a post-chaise which will be ready two hours after midnight. If you wish to keep yourself for me, you will enter it, and take the road to the sea. I shall follow you the next Morning. If I come with you, I shall be accused of having abducted you; we shall be pursued, perhaps taken; I shall be exposed to the Resentment of a Monarch both absolute and infuriated. The forwarding of his Amour demands my destruction, and the pretext would be plausible enough to justify it. Appear in the Circle this evening, to avert suspicion of your intention; wear the jewels he sent you; I should be delighted to have disappointed hopes set the final touch to his mortification when he sees he has lost you for ever.' She replied simply that he would be obeyed, and went to her closet to give way to the tears which she had suppressed with difficulty while he was speaking.

Docile's Character was the topic of conversation for the whole Court. They praised her Beauty but found fault with her Heart. The Ladies who had made advances of friendship to her complained of her coldness, and the men marvelled endlessly at the abstracted and unmoved manner in which she had received the King's Attentions. They generally concluded that she had a hard heart, and they pitied her Husband for having to suffer caprices which were so obviously disadvantageous to his Fortune. She appeared, and her presence put an end to all Criticism. No one thought of anything but her Beauty, highlighted by her Finery and even more by the natural Graces of her person. The King appeared enchanted; he forgot that she had wished to leave him, and flattered himself that she had forgotten it too. She supped in Public with him, and affected an Air of satisfaction which convinced everybody that she had taken pleasure in deciding to stay at a Court where she was adored.

Her flight was not noticed, till 4 hours after her departure. Prince Sombre was the first to announce it, and seemed in despair about it.

He assured the King that there could be no doubt she had taken the road to her Hermitage; that if she might possibly be persuaded to return, she would yield to entreaties rather than to violence. He begged permission to follow her alone. This the King quite Willingly granted him. Urging him not to constrain her in any way, 'Assure her from me (said he) that she will always have my Protection, and that if she takes pleasure in her Forest I shall never oblige her to leave it.'

The Prince did not know what to make of the coolness that the King showed in Circumstances in which he had expected to see him in despair. He suspected in his usual manner some secret communication between him and Docile. If he had not kept her constantly in sight, he would have had no doubt that satiated Love was the source of the tranquillity in which he saw King Goodchild. It was nevertheless very simple. The King was not of the humour to languish at the feet of a cruel beauty. He never pursued his pleasures in the teeth of Obstacles. He frequently said that the truly Wise man awaited pleasures in the arms of indolence, and that they never failed to present themselves to those who were willing to wait for them; that delicacy poisoned Happiness; and that Constancy unrequited was a Banality unworthy of mankind, invented perhaps by some decrepit old man who was willing to spend his last days adoring an Insensible object, in order to disguise the Decrepitude that could no longer render homage to a tender, favourable Beauty.

The Court wore themselves out in speculations on the extravagant behaviour of the lovely stranger. Her conduct was seen as treachery, and those who treated her the most favourably spoke of her as Mad and unfeeling, even while she was making a sacrifice to her Virtue of her repose, her happiness, and her honour. Even she herself felt acutely how prejudicial to her was such inconsistency of Behaviour. But she obeyed, for that she considered an indispensable duty.[1]

---

[1] The end of the section is marked by lines across the page; a blank leaf follows (H MS 80, fo. 378).

Princess Docile II

Textual note. The original Part II (untitled; in French; MWM's hand) occupies H MS 80, fos. 344–67 and 334–42. It begins (numbered p. 1) in larger writing than Part I, and from the second side is written in a narrow column, leaving generous space for revision; but the alterations are slighter than in Part I.

Prince Sombre directed his steps towards the Port where he had appointed Docile to meet him, by unfrequented ways which added several leagues to his journey, and it was dawn before he arrived within sight of the town.[1] From some distance away he noticed a Body of troops coming away from it. He observed them with the greatest attention, and his Imagination, which had a singular fertility in producing ideas to torture him, pointed out to him that they were escorting a Chaise. He doubted not a moment that they were taking Docile back to the Court. He believed he had found the explanation for the indifference the King had shown when he told him of her departure. He remembered the submissiveness with which she had carried out his orders, and concluded that she had made a Pact with the King, who was to carry her off, in order to shield her Honour. He saw her Obedience to him as the final insult. Absolutely resolved not to be duped by her Hypocrisy, and still fearing that orders were out for his arrest, he plunged into a nearby Forest, with emotions so painful and confused that he did not know where he was going, and still less where he wanted to go. However, the troops which had so much alarmed him were nothing else but the Garrison which was changing its Quarters.

Let us leave him being driven hither and thither, driven distracted by the Demon of Jealousy, and return to Docile, who was so much overcome by Fatigue and by her thoughts, that she went to bed on arrival at the inn, where her husband had assured her that he would join her the same evening. She was much astonished to hear not a word of him, neither that evening, nor the whole of the next day. She had never suspected him capable of breaking his word to her, and had only a very little money, which in two days was all spent. She

---

[1] A briefer version of this stage of the story survives as Fragment I (below, p. 188).

expected him every moment, but the Landlady was not of a humour to wait for her money. She demanded it with Vigour, having no very good Opinion of a young woman travelling all alone in this manner.

The poor Princess found herself in the most embarrassing situation. She had no other resource but to put into the Landlord's hands a beautiful Ring which Prince Sombre had given her when he wedded her etc.;[1] she begged him to take it as a pledge, saying that her Husband would not fail to come and redeem it. He believed nothing of this; he even thought the Diamond too large to be genuine. He took it, however, having decided to allow her to stay a few more days in his house. Beauty always exerts its rights over the most rustic Hearts, and it was no mean effect of Docile's beauty to soften a Soul like that of her Host.

At midnight that very night, a Vessel arrived at the Port, and from it there disembarked a Cavalier with all the trappings of a great Lord. He came to demand lodging at the inn, followed by his whole train of pages, Gentlemen, and servants. The Landlady was in despair because Docile was occupying her finest Chamber, and had been in bed for a long time. She would have had the Brutality to wake her up and make her vacate it, if her Husband had permitted it, but he contented himself with making his excuses to the newcomer, because he was not able to give him his best bed for that night, adding that if he was willing to make do that night with an inferior room, he would tomorrow throw out the person who was sleeping there and who certainly had not the means to pay for it.

'Perhaps it is some lousy beggar you have put there, said the cavalier, laughing, and I shall be certain not to take his place.' The Landlord's honour was touched, at being accused of lodging people of that kind. He painted Docile's portrait with all the eloquence he was master of, and finished by showing the Ring she had entrusted to him, saying that he could see very well that it was Paste, that in any case it might be worth one or two Louis,[2] but having no Jeweller in that town he didn't know its exact value. The Cavalier, who was an excellent connoisseur, judged very differently. He ordered him to have it placed on the Lady's Dressing-table before she rose, together with a Purse which he drew from his pocket, in which he had

---

[1] The 'etc.' suggests 'wedded and bedded', and that the ring is a gift after the first night together.

[2] A gold piece worth 24 livres. (The livre, also called the franc, was reckoned equivalent to the US dollar of 1968: Theodore Besterman in Voltaire, *Œuvres complètes* (1968), lxxxv, p. xix.)

more than a hundred louis. The Host took it, saying in a grumbling tone, 'Ah, my lord, I see very well that it is not the Ring that you wish to buy.'

'Listen, My Friend, replied the Cavalier with an air of severity, learn to speak respectfully about persons whom you do not know. This is perhaps a Woman of Quality, reduced by Misfortune to a condition unworthy of her. Follow my orders Faithfully, and you will receive your reward. If you dare to deceive me—' The Landlord interrupted by swearing perfect obedience to him, and to prove to him that he could be trusted began a Litany of stories which could have lasted all night, if the Cavalier had had the patience to hear them. He went to bed as soon as his servants had set up for him a Magnificent camp bed which he had brought with him.

Docile was very far from passing such a tranquil night. Her past misfortunes, and those that she had to fear, occupied her mind too much to allow her to sleep. She tried to hope she would see her Husband again; she remembered (in spite of herself) all the harshness she had suffered from him, and she feared to be abandoned by him, although she rejected that idea as too unjust to him, and contrary to the trust which she believed she owed him. Sunk in these reflections, she fell into a slumber towards morning. She had not enjoyed this repose for an hour when she heard someone opening the door of her room, and looking out through her curtains she saw the landlady gently placing on her Table the Ring and the Purse. She called to her, to ask her for an explanation of this action, by which she was quite stupefied. The Landlady was not sorry to be caught in the act, in order to have an excuse to talk of the Cavalier, whose air of breeding and magnificence had furnished her with a host of conjectures which she was burning to share.

'Ah Madame, she cried, in a tone far more respectful than before, We had an unexpected pleasure last night. There arrived at our unworthy house the most handsome Lord in the world, with a prince's train, a superb Turn-out.'

'And what has all this to do with my ring?' interrupted the unfortunate Queen. 'Oh, plenty, Madame, continued the chatterer. My husband spoke of you (I make bold to say you are obliged to him for that). The prince needed no entreaties to serve you; he made haste to order that the Ring should be placed on your Table, with this fine purse, which is well freighted, I'll answer for it. He forbade us, though, to let you know whence it came, but I love you too well to hide anything from you. Besides, it seems to me that when someone does a generous action they ought to be very glad for all the world to know of it, and I don't understand by what Singularity he wanted to hide something that does him honour.'

'*I* understand him, said the Queen. Leave me, child,[1] I wish to consider what I should do.' The landlady, who wanted to get on the right side of her, obeyed.

Docile admired the stranger's Generosity, but she felt herself capable of doing likewise, so she did not regard it as so marvellous an adventure as a person of greater experience would have done. She did not fail to entertain the liveliest gratitude, mingled with that shame which touches every generous Soul who is reduced to receiving an Obligation.[2] She condemned the latter feeling as an effect of self-love, and made a Resolution to see the stranger, deciding to make him keep the Ring, at least until she could return him his Money. With this intention she sent to beg the honour of his Company. He understood from this message that she knew from what quarter this unexpected assistance had appeared. He had already taken care to dress himself in the very pink of gallantry, set off by an Air of negligence, and hastened to satisfy his curiosity with the sight of this Beauty of whom he had heard such wonders.

But I believe I have too long delayed to satisfy that of my Readers, who are doubtless on tenterhooks to know who this extraordinary Cavalier was. I do not know exactly how to answer, because he did not know the answer himself. No-one had ever spoken to him of his Birth. A Bourgeois living out of the world had brought him up: he had sent him at six years old to a celebrated school, where he had made such good progress that at Twelve he was in the highest Class. It was then that his Protector withdrew him from school, in spite of the assurances given him by the master of the college, that with the accurate memory, sound intelligence, and taste for Literature that this Child possessed, he could not fail to become an ornament to the university, if he would be willing to let him continue his studies. The Bourgeois listened to his eloquent Speeches with a Stolidity unknown outside his Region, and without offering any reason for his decision, articled him to a pleader[3] much renowned for his Expertise

---

[1] A term of endearment, usually to a social inferior.
[2] The true version of the doctrine falsely espoused by Lady Artifice (above, p. 118).
[3] The legal profession here described is Continental, not English.

in the mysteries of Chicanery. Though he was so young, he did not fail to find it extraordinary that his benefactor had taken such pains to nourish him on the Classical Authors, who seemed to him useless enough in the profession to which he was assigning him. But he had sufficient sense to understand that his part was to obey, and not to reason why. He had no friend but the old Bourgeois. He could not say that he came of any family, having never heard of any name that he had except that of Janot. The old fellow never treated him with a Father's tenderness, or with the disdain of a superior. He had spoken very little to him all his life, and always with great seriousness, which forbade the child to dare to question him about anything.

He understood that his present Advantage rested solely on pleasing him, and perfect submission seemed to him the only way to achieve this. He entered, uncomplainingly, the firm of the Pleader, who soon realized that he had a Genius for making money: subtle, accommodating to others, capable of great concentration. He resolved to cultivate these rare Talents, which might be of use to him one day, and instructed him with greater Care than he gave to his other pupils. Janot had stayed with him two years and had made astonishing progress in his profession, when his Patron removed him from there, to send him to the Indies with one of his friends, a Merchant, who had made an immense fortune there by his trafficking skills, which he undertook to teach the young man in return for a considerable sum which the Bourgeois gave him. The merchant stayed two years in China,[1] and returned in triumph with a Vessel loaded with rich merchandise. He brought Janot back to his Patron (somewhat tanned, much grown, and of a handsome appearance) and assured him that he had never been so well satisfied with any Boy in his life. He was tireless in praising his prudence, his Modesty, and his Industry.

The Old fellow listened to him, as phlegmatic as ever, received his pupil home, and soon afterwards bought him a lieutenancy in a Regiment which was leaving for War, bestowing upon him the name of Fortunate.[2] He was naturally brave, and, even if he had not been, he had so completely accustomed himself to regulating his actions

---

[1] MWM uses both '[les] Indes' and 'la Chine', presumably for French Indo-China, which included present-day Vietnam and Cambodia (see E. Hammer, *The Struggle for Indo-China* (1954); G. Taboulet, *La Geste française en Indochine* (1955–6); Le Than Khoi, *Histoire du Viet Nam* (1955)).

[2] The name 'Fortuné' occurs in several French fictions of this time or earlier. Delarivier Manley uses 'Fortunate' for a seducer (*New Atalantis* (1709), i. 52–7).

according to his immediate interests that his reason would have con-
quered a natural timidity. He found himself at two battles and one
Siege[1] during this campaign, in which he brought himself into
notice by his gallant conduct. He had succeeded in gaining the
goodwill of his whole Regiment. The Soldiers had never seen
such a sympathetic officer, attentive to all their needs and sparing
them in every possible way. His Comrades were charmed by his
Obligingness, and Officers of the highest rank spoke favourably
of a Young man who could make his Court to them without self-
abasement. Peace was made a few months later, and Sir Fortunate
was given permission to return to his relations: that is to say, to the
old fellow whom he did not dare call a relation. He received him in
his Ordinary manner, without either blame or praise, in spite of the
good things which all the world were saying of him. He left him one
Year more in the army.

It was then that for the first time in his life he dared to think of
amusing himself. But it was without excess, whose unhappy effects
he noted in the majority of his Companions. They took him sometimes to their Haunts of Debauchery, but he went there only out of
Compliance, without ever compromising himself. He felt a lively
enough inclination for pleasure, but he wanted it with more Taste,
and less Risk. He tried introducing himself into genteel Company.
His Friends were delighted to present him to their Wives and their
Sisters, and he took advantage of the goodwill of all those ladies who
encouraged him. He had learned in the army that easy air that is so
seldom acquired elsewhere, without losing a disarming Modesty
which adorned all his Attractive qualities, and made him, for the
Hearts of the fair Sex, dangerous to Know. He found hardly any who
resisted him, but far from sowing Discord in Families, he always
brought Peace into them. His first Lesson to those Beauties (to
whom he had the right to give lessons) was, to put themselves on a
perfect footing with their Husbands, and it often happened that he
established harmony in households where people had despaired of
seeing it. Husbands and wives were equally satisfied with him. He
had no scruples, however, about fidelity or Constancy, and was not
so much in love with anyone as to inspire them in her. He regarded
woman as a kind of Game animal made for man's amusement, to
divert himself with, not to be bound to.

[1] MWM would have read and heard about plenty of battles and sieges in the War of the
Austrian Succession (1740–8), and perhaps by this time in the Seven Years' War (1756–63).

Far from spreading these maxims, even among his Comrades, he never spoke of Gallantry but in a serious tone which sometimes drew on him the mockery of young people, but which ensured him the Ladies' Confidence. Indeed, they had no reason to complain of him: he had total Discretion, and as much precaution on behalf of those he abandoned as of those he pursued. He endeavoured to transform their lost Lover into a useful friend. When they were reluctant to accept this exchange, he withdrew himself, still speaking well of them, with such gentle and honest conduct that they were ashamed to be his Enemies. When some mistress left him (which happened very rarely) he made no reproaches or threats, and remained a Friend to her who had once favoured him. He had wit enough to make an Observation which is not within everyone's capacity, which is that Vanity is the source of almost all our sorrows. He knew how to stifle its first stirrings; he never entertained any about the success he had with Beauties. He never aimed at anything beyond the favours which their Hearts chose to grant him, or looked for a Profit as so many others do.

Loved by the Ladies and sought after by the Men, he was high in general esteem when his Patron thought fit to retire him from the Troops, having bought him one of those little Court positions which make no noise but in which one sees much more of the inner work-ings than in those which have a higher status. It cost him a lot to obey this new Caprice of the Bourgeois. He even wondered whether he ought to do so. He had hopes of advancement through the favour of his colonel, and regretted leaving the pleasures to which he had given himself up. But the Old fellow was failing badly, and he did not want to give up the hope of an inheritance, a hope which, although uncertain, seemed to him as well founded as any that his circum-stances allowed him; and as so far he had pursued his Advantage without any distractions from that purpose, the only one he was fixed in, he resolved to shape himself according to the instructions of the Bourgeois, with his usual Submissiveness; and he took up his place a few days later.

He did his duty with an assiduity which the King himself re-marked. No one could ever accuse him of stirring up trouble or tale-bearing; he observed everything, without appearing to see anything, with so simple and natural an air that the most experienced Court-iers were mistaken as to his Character. He paid all the Ladies the Re-spect that was due to them, without distinguishing any. He saw in them an eye to Politics, a Party spirit, and an ambition which over-powered all their passions. He avoided their Confidence as the most Dangerous thing that could befall him. His observations allowed him to discern the first glimmering of Favour or of disgrace, and he made his court so early to those who were beginning to enjoy the Minister's good graces, that it was impossible to tell whether this was a consequence of their Fortune, or a Desire to serve them. He was no less prompt to withdraw himself from those whose credit was in decline. He always left them a Crowd of less enlightened Followers, and he was often the only one whom they believed they had no reason to complain of, for abandoning them as Fortune did so. He had never made in all his life either a Friend or a Mistress of the Heart. He did not allow himself to be carried away by his Taste, and never enquired into anybody's merit, but into the advantage which he might find from acquaintance with them. He was seldom dogmatic, and never contradicted anyone. In Conversation he sought to please and not to shine, believing that goodwill would be far more advantageous to him than applause. He did not offer advice unless he had been very much pressed to do so, and then he studied the inclinations, not the Interest or the duty, of the person asking advice.

In short, he found the secret of pleasing everybody, while he had so unshakable a contempt for the human race (for the Cheating, the Weakness and the Injustice which he had observed in all nations) that he judged nobody worthy of his Confidence, and measured his esteem for human beings as one does for dogs and horses, not for the services which they have performed but for those which they are capable of performing.

He had never allowed himself to be dazzled by a Reputation for learning or for wit. He saw such reputation as useless financially, and very often damaging, through the envy which it never fails to excite. He carefully concealed his Taste for Reading,[1] although he had always retained it, but he did not take his maxims from his Books,[2] well persuaded that the Authors were not saying what they believed but what they wished others to believe. He never permitted himself the lightest mockery, although he was naturally inclined to it. He seldom blamed anyone, and never praised the absent. Having no sincere attachment, he made no Enemies in attempting to Defend his

---

[1] As MWM advised that her granddaughters should do (*CL* iii. 22–3), and as Lord Chesterfield advised his son (22 Feb. 1748).

[2] As Docile does.

friends. If he flattered someone (whose protection seemed necessary to him) it was always for Qualities which they affected and not for those which they possessed. He spoke to Beauties of the Vivacity of their wit, and to wits of the Graces of their Person, knowing that Praises make hardly any impression if one is accustomed to them, and that one is charmed to be told one possesses advantages which appear doubtful even to self-love. He attracted the Minister's notice by remarking to everybody that he had a perfectly well-turned Leg. Up till then, he had never heard Flattery about anything except his amazing Genius, and this Encomium had the merit of novelty. This conduct procured universal goodwill towards Fortunate. He left the petty gains of his place to his underlings; they were too little to add to his Fortune, but enough to acquire him the Reputation of the most disinterested man in being, and he knew how necessary that is for anyone who seeks to become solidly established.

It will perhaps be surprising to see such refined Politics at such a very young age. It is necessary to remember that he had always seen himself as in a situation where he believed he might need something from anybody at all. His natural good sense had never been corrupted by Flatterers and, born tough, bold, and self-interested, he found it easy to appear tender, modest, and Generous, without however pretending to any of these Virtues to the extent of doing the least damage to his Fortune, which he never lost sight of. He had already been named for a more considerable position when his old Patron died and left him a hundred thousand Louis in cash and in various Funds, and holdings to the same value in the American Colonies. He was as surprised as anybody by this prodigious Opulence. He had always flattered himself that he would be heir to the Bourgeois, who seemed to have no favourite and no relative, but he was very far from believing him to possess these immense Riches. The town had always been divided in its Sentiments about him. Some said he was a Scurvy old fellow who had buried his Money, and others that he had no doubt suffered a secret bankruptcy which had forced him to withdraw from Commerce, at which he had excelled, to reduce himself to the bare necessities of one male and one female servant. Sir Fortunate, who saw him at closer range, had always seen a comfortable air which persuaded him that his frugality was the result of Preference and not of necessity. But he did not expect to discover a sum of this magnitude. Self-love would have whispered to him that this was the deposit which some illustrious Father had entrusted to the Citizen for his own use; but having no proof of it, he rejected this flattering Idea.

His prudence had not abandoned him, though it was a little shaken by this sudden good Fortune. He Reflected that he was now in a position to excite envy, and that all the riches in the world could not conceal his equivocal Birth. He felt his Heart too puffed up to endure a Country where this was known. He Resolved to make the tour of Europe and at the same time to change his Name, and decided to settle in that Kingdom where he should find most to please him. He left the Court with an Air of modesty and Gratitude, assembled himself a Decent[1] Equipage, and began his Travels despite the regrets of a crowd of friends of every station, who seemed despairing over his departure, and the tears of the Maids of honour, each of whom wished to convince him that he had long been her secret choice. He had made some stay in all the great cities, and after several Years of travel, was returning to that of Good Children, with the Design of Settling there for life. He had increased his train to give himself an air of Greatness, and called himself Count Goodhope.

He was then nearly thirty Years old, his Physiognomy noble and cheerful, his air Gallant though a trifle serious, his Stature just right. It would have been flattering him to call him Handsome, but impossible not to find him infinitely amiable. He presented himself to Docile with as much respect as if her rank had been known to him. She was so made to inspire respect that one could not fail to feel it in approaching her. This noble and modest Beauty, rendered still more touching[2] by the Languour which accompanied it, changed the Ideas which the Count had formed from the Landlord's remarks. He had expected to see a pretty young person to whom his purse could advantageously introduce him. He had no doubt that she would try to soften him by reciting her woes and to inflame him by little affectations. He saw a completely natural Innocence which seemed to know nothing of her charms or of the effect they were capable of producing. Simple truth was depicted on her face and the carelessness of her dress made it clear that she had no designs on his Heart.

'I am deeply obliged to you, Sir (said she naïvely) for your uncommon Generosity. But I shall be unable to accept it unless you will do me the pleasure to keep this Ring. I am every moment expecting

---

[1] Altered from 'noble' (App. II, p. 248).

[2] Cf. the first fairy gift MWM awards herself in 'Carabosse': 'une Beauté noble et touchante' (*E&P* 154).

My Husband, who will not fail to redeem it, and to testify to you his gratitude for your goodness towards an unhappy stranger.'

He tried to protest that he did not know what she was talking about. But she was not deceived, and after a fairly long dispute, he dared not refuse to place the Ring on his finger. He made his visit last as long as good breeding would permit; he tried to amuse her, by speaking to her of different Countries which he had seen. He was surprised to see that she had a perfect grasp of Geography. He understood that she had read a great deal, and slipped some details of History into his stories. He found that she was equally well instructed in ancient and modern history. He could not understand where she had had her Education, very sure that it was not in a Convent, and when he left her it was with feelings of admiration that were quite new to him. He had not risked the least compliment on her appearance; accustomed to studying the Characters of all those he saw, he unravelled hers quite easily. He clearly saw that the only way to continue his Acquaintance with her was to keep far from her Imagination the suspicion of any design, and he was able to give his Conversation an Air so relaxed and ingenuous, that he left her with much esteem for him and without suspecting that he felt anything more for her.

He had asked permission to come again, which she had been pleased to grant him. He did not fail to profit by this: for a week they were together almost every day, he always Skilfully concealing the project which he had formed, and she enchanted to have found a friend of such perfect integrity, who amused her so far that she sometimes forgot her sad situation, to which nevertheless she paid some sighs which did not escape Count Goodhope. But he did not dare display a Curiosity which might perhaps have shocked her, and he waited for her to Confide an Inclination which he flattered himself he was inspiring. He had got some Girls to come to serve her; he forgot none of those attentions which the desire of pleasing can produce. She had little curiosity, but gratitude made her take an Interest in his affairs, and she wished to know to whom she owed such obligations.

As soon as she admitted this he prepared to gratify her, with the air however of a man resolved to refuse her nothing, but to whom this Obedience was costly. Prefacing it with several sighs which he appeared to stifle, he began on the finest Romance in the world: his life. He mingled in it the marvellous, the pathetic, and the amusing, always a Probity equal to every test, a Generosity without parallel, and an infinite tenderness. He passed lightly over the finest parts, but she believed she could see it all through the veil of his Modesty, and he understood so well how to stir the Feelings of the innocent Docile, that she was sometimes seized with Admiration and esteem, and sometimes moved to tears, as it pleased him to vary his recital. He did not speak of his birth but let it be seen that it was of the most illustrious, and that he had Generous reasons for concealing it. She had too much generosity to press him on the subject. He gave her to understand (but with respectful delicacy) that he passionately wished to know something of a person of such singular virtue, and who must have had truly extraordinary adventures to be in circumstances so little in tune with her merit. She hesitated over the reply she would make him. It seemed to her that his confidence, full of Frankness, well deserved the same from her; but she Reflected that it was impossible to relate her Story aright, without giving disadvantageous Impressions of her Mother and her Husband. These two persons were sacred to her.

She replied, letting fall some tears from her beautiful eyes, that it was renewing her sorrows to talk of them, and she begged him as a boon not to insist on this mark of Obligingness from her. He asked a thousand pardons for his Indiscretion, appearing touched to the soul by the Pain he had caused her, and changed the Conversation, proposing a walk to distract her from her sad thoughts. He talked to her of fishing, of hunting, but he saw that only the Amusement of Reading was to her Taste. He had two or three Cases of chosen Books, which he carried on all his Travels.[1] He sent them to the Queen. She threw herself on the Poetry, which was new to her. Her Genius was naturally inclined to it, but the Hermit had always spoken to her of it as the source of impiety, and the Philosopher had treated it as Trifling. Since her accession to the Crown she had been too much occupied to have the leisure to apply herself to it, and she was astonished to find so many charms in it. She passed whole nights in Reading. This new Taste assisted a great deal to soften her Heart, and breathe a certain tenderness through all her Actions, which augured well for the Count.

He assisted her in her studies, and made her distinguish between the good, the excellent, and the mediocre. He forbade her to let herself be seduced by the ear (as most young people do), and he taught her to despise false thinking even if ornamented with a brilliant

---

[1] MWM took three cases of books on her European travels (*CL* ii. 153).

style.[1] But he instructed her with so much Delicacy that she hardly perceived he was giving her Lessons, though she certainly felt that she profited a great deal from his conversation. The day flew very quickly in such agreeable Pastimes, and the evening was ordinarily spent walking. This was often in a little wood, close to the town, where art had not yet laid her hand, but Nature had formed the paths, which were quite convenient. The Count had caused rustic Canopies to be placed there, covered with moss and Foliage. There they listened to the melody of Nightingales,[2] which was sometimes interrupted by an exquisite music Group which he had summoned from the Capital, which the distressed Beauty could not listen to without pleasure in spite of all her Sorrows, which never left her but which were very much softened by the care which the Count took to supply her with amusements for every hour. One evening when she had walked for longer than usual, she was surprised to find on her return her chamber (which was equipped like that of a common Inn) adorned with furniture of infinite taste and convenience. Nothing was lacking to render it worthy of her.

Poor Docile had innocence which functioned for her like stupidity. She saw all these pains, without imagining that they had any other end but that of assuaging her melancholy, and she attributed this design to the Generosity which she believed she saw shining in all the Count's conversation. She understood that he had a great esteem for her, and was far from suspecting him capable of forming a bold design on her. She nevertheless reproached him for a zeal which she called misplaced, but there was such gratitude mingled with her reproaches that he was delighted to have drawn them upon him.

He was as much in love with her as his Character permitted him to be, that is to say he found her necessary to the agreeableness of his life. His Ambition was sated in the matter of Fortune; he wanted to satisfy his Taste for pleasure. Docile's Beauty stirred his desires, and her virtue his Vanity. He promised himself to triumph over it, and was indifferent enough as to the manner, having none of those delicate sentiments which prevent one from enjoying a happiness unshared by the beloved object. He resolved to try every kind of method to make himself loved. If he did not succeed, or if her Virtue, still stronger than her Love, refused to make him happy, he flattered

---

[1] As MWM hoped her daughter would do for her granddaughters (*CL* iii. 68).

[2] Cf. MWM's own 'improvements' in her 100-acre wood near Gottolengo (*CL* ii. 403).

himself he could become so by stratagems, which he believed to be as legitimate in Love, as in War. He sought to get some light cast on her condition. His Landlord could tell him nothing more than he had learned from the postilion: that she came from the Court of King Goodchild.

He dispatched there his favourite Valet de Chambre, bold, secretive, and well informed. They were still talking about the Capricious Beauty who had quitted the Court with such an ill grace. He did not doubt (from their manner of depicting her) that she was the one who was charming his Master. He gathered every detail regarding her. The Count had ordered him to inform himself whether she was married, and what her Husband was like, and he obeyed him so well that he informed himself of everything down to the Colour of his hair and the dress that he wore. He came back in a few days to relate to his Master the success of his mission. It was not complete enough for the Count's curiosity: he still did not know her Name, her Country, or her rank. But he hoped to be able to turn to advantage the little that he knew.

It was already nearly two months, that he had been languishing at the feet of his Unknown beauty. The time seemed very long to his Impatience, accustomed to making love in short order. He determined upon a Treachery which he believed (perhaps) necessary to their mutual happiness, for he saw clearly that he had inspired in her an esteem so tender that it lacked but little to be love itself. She never knew at what hour he would be in her Company. The Women whom he had placed about her informed him that everything disgusted her in his Absence, and that she often spoke of him in fulsome terms of Praise.

The poor Queen did not herself notice any of these symptoms of a dawning tenderness. She attributed the ennui she felt when alone to her sad situation; it was natural that a conversation as delightful as that of the Count should give some relief to her sufferings, and she threw herself into Praising him as the single sign of gratitude that she was in a position to give him. She performed this duty with so much pleasure, that there was no grace of his person that she overlooked. He was charmed with the progress he was making in her Heart, but he understood her enough to know that this same Heart (full of heroic sentiments) was capable of making a long resistance as soon as she noticed that he was passing the bounds which her virtue had laid down for him.

The Count was attentive to the very slightest things that could amuse Docile. She found the newspapers of the day on her Dressing-table every morning. She was struck to see in one of these Broad-sheets, that a dead Body had been found by peasants in the Forest, which had so many Wounds as to make people judge it had been assassinated, that it had long brown hair, and a coat of crimson velvet, but that its face was very much disfigured because of the time it had remained exposed to the air, and that it had been carried to the town to see whether anyone could identify it. She was seized with trembling all over as she read this article. Her Husband was wearing a Coat like that the day she left him; he had brown hair. Could it be possible? What a terrible fate! of which she could accuse herself of being the cause. But no: why might it not be some other? must she terrify herself on such slender hints?

In this confusion of thoughts, she sent to seek the Count, who behaved like one astonished when he saw her pale, trembling, and agitated by so many different emotions that one could not distinguish whether it was fear or grief which was affecting her so violently. She did not give him time to enquire. She cried out, 'Ah Monsieur, have pity on me. Explain to me what this news-item is saying' (and she showed him the paper). He pretended not to have heard tell of it, and ran to inform himself about it with the haste of a Man who shares someone's feelings too completely to examine their motives. He came back in a short time to assure her that it was true, that the corpse of this unfortunate man had been brought to the town the day before yesterday, and that it was still exposed on the Quayside where the whole population were resorting to look at it, but that so far nobody had identified it.

'I want to go myself too' (she said with a distracted Air). He sought to oppose this Resolution. She did not listen to him at all. She went down the staircase at such speed that he could hardly follow her to offer his hand. She did not stop till she was ten paces from the dead Body: she believed she perfectly recognized her Husband. Horror, mingled with a thousand conflicting emotions, seized her, and she fell fainting into the Count's Arms. He had her placed in a chaise, he threw fresh water in her face, poured English drops[1] into her mouth, and she gave a few sighs by which it was understood that she had not

---

[1] Not the familiar hartshorn, but a compound dating from the Restoration, which according to Voltaire would recall the dead to life. It contained aloes, and a high proportion of alcohol (Voltaire, *L'Ingénu*, x; Larousse).

yet departed from this world, although she seemed to hate its Light, never opening her eyes until she was in her Apartments.

There the Count left her, while her Women undressed her, and returned to her Bedside as soon as she was laid there. He found her melted in tears. He threw himself on his Knees by her pillow. 'In God's name Madam (said he in a tenderly sorrowful tone) do not persist in locking up in your bosom those griefs which you deny.[1] Perhaps it is possible to lighten them, at least to share them. Look upon me as a man who is devoted to you. If you knew the strong interest I take in everything that concerns you, and how much I am wounded by your Mistrust, I am convinced that—'

'Alas Sir (said she, interrupting him), do not do me such wrong as to suspect that I could have the least distrust of a Friend to whom I owe everything. But—' she paused for several moments, still uncertain whether she ought to give him her entire Confidence, although she certainly felt herself besieged by an excessive abundance of Ideas, which is at least as much a threat to the Reason as an excessive abundance of blood is to the health. She could no longer deny herself the consolation of relating her sorrows to the only Friend she had. She did not forget or disguise any detail of her past life. Her illustrious Birth gave the Count great pleasure, and where is the Man who would not be gratified at finding the object of his Love to be a great princess? The adventure of the Prince of Venus gave him little pain; he believed it rather an Inclination than a Passion. He was delighted that she had had reasons to complain of her Husband; he saw that her affliction was only an Effect of her duty, and that by a Refinement of Delicacy she was moved to accuse herself of his Death, to punish herself for not having loved him during his life. At the end of her recital she began to weep, and the Count to dream.

Her Quality came very close to changing all his plans. He considered whether they were not too dangerous to pursue. One does not trifle with persons of that Rank without repenting it, and up to now he had done without any pleasures that were liable to bring repentance upon him. Since the spirit of Self-interest which had always governed him was directed by good sense, few men in the world had done so little harm as he had. He knew that all vices bring troubles, at least by the ill name they acquire, and that the Reputation of Probity is absolutely necessary to those who intend to sacrifice it: this sacrifice should always be reserved for great occasions.

[1] Apparently MWM's French is mistaken here (below, p. 252).

The trick which he had played on Docile, the news which he had had printed, the Corpse which he had bought in a neighbouring Village, were a scheme to quiet this Beauty's scruples and to prepare her to receive him as Husband, if she wanted no Lover. He had believed her to be of a middling rank, that if her Husband should return he could calm him down with his money, or if he was not of an accommodating humour could make him believe that he had made a mistake in believing her to be a widow on her own genuine belief, which was not impossible. Prince Sombre (whose Character he knew) seemed to him dangerous in every respect, incapable of forgiving and difficult to deceive. He would be a great King one day, and the most reasonable Course that the Count could take would be to abandon poor Docile there the very next Morning, so as not to expose himself to her Strange Husband's Vengeance. But no one so easily abandons a Scheme which has already cost plenty in pains and Assiduities, and which is progressing so fortunately; for he did not at all doubt his success with an Innocence which suspected nothing. He flattered himself that the same reasons (whatever they might be) which had delayed the arrival of the Prince for two months, might continue in force for two more. That was more than he would need to win, to wear, and to grow tired of his Mistress. While waiting he decided to employ so many spies that he would have warning before any stranger entered the town, and he would have time to retreat, in case an inconvenient Husband came to interrupt his pleasures.

Let us leave him shaping his plots, and the unhappy Queen weeping her misfortunes, to see what is going on in her Kingdom. King Wildman had had the Generosity to accept it on the terms offered him by the parliament, and had given the Viceroy's position to the High Priest. The Queen Mother had returned to the Palace, where she promised herself to rule more absolutely than ever before, just as that saintly man swore to her a thousand times that she would be enabled to, if he should ever attain to a Dignity to which he aspired for no other reason but to have the honour of executing her commands. She was much surprised a few days later, when he presented himself to give her (he said) some advice for the good of her Honour, her Repose, and her Safety. These were three things which she had never taken care of, but Curiosity made her attend to the opening of his Speech, and later Rage and astonishment produced a silence which allowed him to continue it. He represented to her very movingly that retirement was the only fitting position for a Queen dowager, and advised her to retire herself among the vestal Virgins, with an air of Authority which was as good as a positive command. She made to burst into tears, complaints, and threats; he listened neither to the one nor to the others, and quitted her chamber with the same respectable Tranquillity with which he had entered it.

It was with difficulty that she obtained a second visit, being warned next Day that her Retinue was ready according to the orders given by H[er?] M[ajesty].[1] She dared not refuse to go, but she begged as a boon to speak once more with the High Priest. He came, with all the Pride of a Viceroy, sharpened with a Priestly insolence, which disconcerted the Queen to such a degree that it was only with trembling that she dared demand of him the Treasures which she had entrusted to him. 'I perceive, Madam (he replied with a disdainful half-smile), that King Wildman was well informed. The Death of the King your Husband, worthy Object of your tenderness, the Flight of the Queen your Daughter, who has so ill repaid your Care, and the Revolution in the state, have shaken your Reason. If that were unscathed, you would know that the Treasure of the late King could not possibly belong to you, that a great Princess like yourself could not commit a Theft, and a man like myself could not be a Receiver of stolen goods. If I followed the rigour of my King's orders, you would be imprisoned in a place proper to make you come to terms. But I flatter myself that the Gods (whom up to now I have never besought in vain) will grant my fervent prayers for the return of your Health. I see nothing that might be able to contribute more efficaciously to that than the sanctified repose which you will find in the House where I shall have the honour of conducting you.'

With these words he offered her his hand. She had not the Courage to refuse it, and let herself be led two leagues from the town, where she was received with Transports of joy from a Decrepit Superior and superannuated Virgins which did not moderate her grief in the least. She shut herself up in the black-hung room which was allotted to her, where she abandoned herself wholly to her rage: after having thoroughly wept, sworn, and torn out a few grey hairs, she remembered the Fairy, and decided to implore her protection, despite the prohibition which she had laid on her. She wrote her a Letter full of Abasement and Submission; touches of gross Flattery

---

[1] This is probably the correct (bitterly ironic) expansion of the initials, which *could* stand for 'Her' or 'His'.

were not spared, and great promises of eternal Devotion, if she would deliver her from her Prison. Her Letter was returned to her still sealed, but she was not discouraged by the ill success of her first attempt, having nothing else to do but to compose Letters.

The Fairy was persecuted by them. She found them on her Dressing-table, in her Closet, among her books; her Palace was strewn with them, and as this Queen had acquired her Friendship by her Negligence, her importunities drew upon her all her hatred. To escape finally from her, she turned her into Brie Cheese.[1] She is still preserved in the Contrary Museum, where she stands among fossilized plants and rare Shells, very near an Image of Vishnu which pissed miraculously at the time of a great Fire, five hundred years previously.[2] Mr Patin[3] writes of it in the same letter where he gives his description of that Foetus which was perfectly Elephant-shaped, and which he judiciously supposes to be the result of a more eccentric love than that of Pasiphae.[4]

The Destiny of Prince Sombre was quite different. He had wandered eight hours on end in the Forest, sometimes loitering and wrapped in his thoughts, sometimes giving Cuts of the spurs to his horse when his Rage seized him. The poor Beast, too sensible to nourish itself with fantasies like its Master, was ready to sink with Hunger and Exhaustion. Its Weakness made the Prince remember that it was necessary to find a Lodging, and he spurred towards a little Cabin where an old Peasant gave up his bed to him. He laid himself there without the least thought of Sleeping, but in order to give himself up to his Reflections. He was the man of all men who deduced Consequences most accurately, and the one who was most often mistaken as to principles. He believed he had entirely lost that Reputation for Austere Wisdom which had distinguished him from the Crowd of Princes; he had even lost it with himself. He could not

---

[1] Lady Mary wrote 'Fromage', then added 'de Brie'.

[2] Perhaps alluding to the Great Fire of London (1666); perhaps to Gulliver's extinguishing the palace fire with his urine (*Gulliver's Travels* (1726), book 1, ch. 5); perhaps to the Hindu belief that Vishnu in one of his forms put out with rain the Cosmic Fire which his breath (in another form) had fanned (*Mythologies*, compiled by Yves Bonnefoy (1981), trans. Gerald Honigsblum (1991), ii. 821, 823). The British Museum was set up in 1753, and opened to the public (as MWM noted) in 1759 (*CL* iii. 210).

[3] Perhaps an allusion to medical writer Charles Patin (1633–93).

[4] A human foetus is meant. Pasiphae mated with a bull and produced the Minotaur. It was also held that foetuses could be shaped by things their mothers saw close to the time of conception (e.g. William Gregory in *Philosophical Transactions of the Royal Society*, 41 (1739–40), 764–7, on a monkey-like child).

forgive himself the Follies he had performed, for a light and ungrateful Woman, and this dishonour rankled with him as deeply as Docile's infidelity. He replayed in his Imagination all her words, her gestures, even her Glances. He found in everything manifest proofs of her Perfidy.

'At least (said he in his reveries) if she had been Candid, I would have forgiven her Gallantry. Women are accustomed to believe that that is permitted; her youth, a Mother she could neither respect nor be counselled by, a neglected Education, all these excuse her. But when I asked her, in a Friendly manner, for the history of what had set her at odds with her parents, when I let her perceive that I was intending to overlook everything in favour of her sincerity, she related to me (unmoved) the least likely Story that was ever invented. It must have been that she had as much Contempt for my Wit as for my person. When she would have persuaded me that she had been the Dupe of My Lady Artifice, a Woman so well known to be deceitful that she can no longer deceive anybody, it was then that I ought to have renounced her for ever. Blind that I was! But no: I saw her bad Character. It was her Beauty which obscured her faults, that fatal Beauty. What God, what enemy to mankind, gave that Ray of his Divinity to cover a Soul so black, and so unworthy?'

It was true that two days after his Marriage he had had the harshness to demand of his innocent Bride in what manner she had lost her jewels, which he had heard about (he said) only confusedly. She had related the story naïvely, and he had replied in a tone of displeasure (which he believed to be very moderate) that he advised her never to repeat this story, which would meet with very little Belief in the world. She did not understand at all what he meant to insinuate, and he remembered that Innocence which was not abashed, as the Boldness of someone hardened in crime. He examined into all of her conduct in the same manner. Her favourites, he told himself, had always been contemptible Women, so far her inferiors as regards Wit that they could only please her by a Congeniality of morals. That Emily who had been so dear to her, a despised Coquette! (At the same time, however, that he was making this Reflection he combined with it a blind Faith in all her Calumnies against her Mistress.)

At length he no longer doubted that she was the most abominable of her Sex, and formed the Resolution of no longer honouring her with his Remembrance. He turned all his thoughts to his affairs. He decided to return to that Island of which he was legitimate Sovereign.

He knew that there was there a fairly large number of partisans, and that his Father's Government was not designed to make itself beloved. He hoped to be well received by a few principal men of the Country who were attached to him, and that moving in disguise among them he could form an Alliance strong enough to overthrow a Government founded on injustice, and exercised by Tyranny. He would already have chosen this path, if his Passion for Docile had not made him imagine greater happiness in living privately with her than in reigning. His Ambition re-awoke, and gave some respite from his Torments. He pursued this design with ardour. He made a fortunate arrival and found lodging with a Great Lord who adored the memory of the Queen his Mother, and who would have sacrificed his life to put him in possession of the Throne which belonged to him.

While they worked to establish him there, the unhappy Docile was in the hands of a Lover of a very different Character. Alas! why did not some benevolent Deity give the Prince the Understanding of the Count, or the Count the integrity of the Prince? But the Gods in this century left the trouble of the Earth to the Fairies, and no longer concerned themselves with the affairs of Mortals. Count Goodhope let his beautiful Widow weep for several days, without trying to console her otherwise than by sharing her affliction. When its excess had a little diminished, he proposed to her that she should leave this place where she had the sad Spectacle of her Murdered Husband always present to her Imagination, and retire to a Castle which he had just bought a dozen leagues away. He had had the solicitude to give a magnificent Funeral to the Corpse which she believed to be that of the Prince, and this Generosity had made such an impression on Docile, that she believed herself authorized by Virtue itself to comply with his pressing solicitations to spend some time at his house.

It was truly an enchanted spot. Good Taste and Magnificence reigned everywhere; all the brilliance that Architecture, Painting, and Sculpture could supply was to be seen there. Its walls were covered in the latest mode by the leading Parisian decorators; its situation was favoured, on a Hill covered in Woods, at the foot of which could be seen one of the most beautiful streams in the World, watering the Meadows through which it wound, whose dazzling green was enamelled with flowers. A Garden had been added, and nothing spared to render it worthy of the Palace. It was the work of one of those favourites of Fortune whom she raises suddenly by the help of Faro.[1] He had caused the greatest Geniuses of Italy and France to work there, and they had acquitted themselves perfectly. But hardly was it complete when its Unhappy Master saw himself in disgrace with the capricious Goddess who had favoured him. He lost considerable sums, and found himself obliged to sell his House to pay his Workmen.

Count Goodhope profited by his Misfortune and enjoyed the fruits of his labours, for a quarter of what he had expended. The Beautiful Docile (to whom he presented the keys of his Castle on her arrival) was confirmed in the Idea she had of his Quality, by seeing Magnificence so well understood; but she was even more touched by his modest and respectful manners. He continued for nearly a month the same manner of living; at the end he hazarded a few sighs, and played the role of timid lover. She took note of this change with real distress: she found herself reduced to the choice of listening to him or of leaving him. Ought she resolve, out of a (perhaps) ill-grounded delicacy, to render Unhappy a man who had heaped her with obligations? Had Prince Sombre treated her in such a manner as to merit being eternally wept for? Were there no examples of Queens who had married twice? Would it not be very sweet to make the happiness of a Knight whom merit alone rendered worthy to reign over the whole world?

These Reflections occupied her night and day. The Count understood the reason for her reveries, and chose the most favourable moment to make her decide. He represented his sufferings, claimed some merit for the Respect which up to now had constrained him to silence, and finished by offering to withdraw himself the next day, if she was untouched by his Passion, although he was certain that he would not survive a separation a thousand times more cruel than death. He accompanied these words with tender looks, stifled sighs, and tears half suppressed, in short, with all the artifices which a pitiless Heart sets at work to take innocence by surprise. That of Docile succumbed. After some objections, faintly pronounced, which he demolished with ease, she confessed to him blushing that she could not refuse him her hand, if his happiness was bound up in it.

It will perhaps cause surprise that, with the Character he possessed, he did not attempt to seduce her in another manner. He had

---

[1] A card game, banned by English law in 1739.

not neglected any of the advantages which his situation offered him,
but he always saw in her so great a horror of any Gallantry, that he
dared not expose himself to her hatred, which would not have failed
to fall on him from the first moment she had suspected such a design.[1] He perceived that it was his Respect, and the Idea she had of
his Virtue, which gave Birth to the favourable Sentiments she had
for him, and that it was not possible to deceive her except by a Show
of honour and Generosity. One may be sure that he received with
transport the obliging assurance that she made him; he testified to
this by expressions of submissiveness and of ardour, and appeared so
much affected by Gratitude and pleasure, that she was enchanted at
having bestowed happiness on a lover so worthy of it. There is nothing so gratifying for a Heart like hers, as to make the happiness of
those whom one esteems. He had received her whole heart,[2] and she
took it upon herself as a duty to devote the rest of her life to pleasing
him. But she did not wish to jettison the scruple which bound her to
proper behaviour. She insisted on the rule which obliges Widows to
a year of Mourning,[3] and neither his whole Eloquence nor his tears
could reduce this period by more than two months. He would have
been in despair, if he had not flattered himself that she would find it
possible to reduce it by as much again every day, and that he would
soon see an end to his Martyrdom.

He was mistaken, however, although he attempted to profit by all
the advantages given him by the Right of the Future. He hardly ever
left her any more, he sometimes spent half the night in her chamber.
He gave entertainments for her, wrote songs for her, which she found
the prettiest in the world, and insinuated himself so well into her
Soul, that she forgot all her past sorrows, and gave herself up entirely
to the pleasure of loving and of being loved. She was no longer the
sad Beauty he had seen buried in a melancholy so habitual that it
seemed natural; she became gay, and gave free rein to all the charms
of her wit. She was lively and merry at table, serious and reasonable
in passing judgement on the Authors he put into her hand. He had a
Gallery where she found a large and well-chosen Library. He caused
her to read those dangerous books which, in destroying prejudices,

---

[1] In this Docile would behave unlike Richardson's Pamela.

[2] This seems to be the meaning, despite a lapse in gender in the French (p. 258 below).

[3] MWM's widowed Indamora 'staid my year' before marrying her first true love (above,
p. 15); a suitor misses his chance by thinking it 'Indecent to ask' her professional widow 'till
my Year was out' (*E&P* 71).

obliquely attack morals. He sometimes commented on them in such a fashion as to have offended the scrupulous Queen, if she had understood his Aim. Far from that, she imagined that he wished to mould her mind, while he was trying to corrupt her Heart, of which she let him see every emotion, with a Candour never seen in anyone but her.

He led her to agree that all Ceremonies had their origin in the Political, that they were neither founded on Nature nor essential to Virtue. He meant to conclude that sensible People would ignore them whenever they incommoded them. She did not accept this Reasoning. She spoke of honour as of a Divinity, to whom one must sacrifice everything except Virtue.[1] She admitted that if through some extraordinary Circumstance one found oneself compelled to abandon the one or the other, then one must suffer infamy rather than commit the least Crime; but that no pleasure, no advantage, and even no Passion could dispense with the laws of proper behaviour; that one was accountable to one's Ancestors, to one's Posterity, and to all those who might be led by one's example, for every step one took, and that after Virtue itself, nothing ought to be so dear as one's reputation, even though the world has very often thrown a ridiculous enough light upon it.

This was to explain herself in such a manner as to alter the tendency of the Conversation. The Count veered towards her reasoning, which (said he) he found admirable, adding that he had known certain Philosophers who maintained that one might dispense with too rigid rules, provided that secrecy insured one against scandal.[2] 'That is to sin against truth (she cried), which is the most heinous of all crimes. Truth is the sole, the visible Divinity,[3] who gives to all men some ray of her brightness, who rewards her faithful worshippers with that inner Peace which is never abashed. Those who dare offend her are punished by remorse, which tears them eternally. Abandoned to themselves, they become a shame to humans, and a thousand times more contemptible than the foulest of Beasts.' The Count interrupted to swear that he had always been of this opinion, and that he had cited the other only to show how far wit was capable

---

[1] Unlike Pope's Thalestris: '*Honour* forbid! at whose unrival'd shrine | Ease, Pleasure, Virtue, All, our Sex resign' (*The Rape of the Lock* (1714), iv. 105–6).

[2] MWM approved when her first Islamic contact argued that the élite may behave more laxly than the 'common people' so long as they avoid scandal (*CL* i. 318).

[3] One of the earliest of her writings which MWM thought worth saving was 'Irregular Verses to Truth' (*E&P* 178).

of misleading itself. She took him at his Word, and the only reflection she made on this conversation, and several others of the same kind, was to admire the good faith of the Count, who was so well persuaded of her Virtue as to risk acquainting her with maxims which the majority of men conceal from Women, fearing lest they make a bad use of them.

Such obliging Confidence increased her esteem by half as much again. Such esteem increased her tenderness, and the time devoted to her Widowhood began to weigh heavily upon her. She was young, in flourishing Health; she had at her side an amiable lover, submissive but pressing, and one who let no moment escape which might prove favourable to him. She sustained with difficulty the resolution which she had taken of a ten-month mourning. The Count found the secret of reducing these to six, of which two were already past, but it was impossible to obtain any other reduction, and he was forced to be content with that.

At length that final, so much longed-for month arrived. The Count left her for three days, to take a Look at a Coach he had ordered in the Capital.[1] Although the absence would be short, it was very much felt by the tender lovers. Docile let a few tears fall, and he sighed as he kissed her hand, as if he had been able to see into the future. She withdrew into her Closet as soon as he was gone, and throwing herself on her Sofa abandoned herself to emotion which the Count would have turned to great advantage, had he been present. She enumerated to herself all his noble behaviour since she had known him; his attractions were not forgotten. She wondered at her good fortune in having found a Heart worthy of her own, and longed to see that moment when she would no longer be obliged to pain his tenderness. These Reveries were too agreeable not to continue; she pursued them until the hour for walking. She plunged deep into the wood that touched her garden, and was entertaining herself with loving dreams beside a Spring, when she saw arriving at a Gallop a young Knight, who looked at her fixedly, then came and threw himself at her feet. She recognized him as being the one who had been the most favoured among Prince Sombre's Officers. He had been brought up as a Page to him, and by his Fidelity and his diligence had obtained as much of his Trust as can be Met with from a Master so

---

[1] Choice of a coach was an important element in the courtship correspondence of MWM's friend Philippa Mundy (Mundy-Massingberd MSS, Lincoln Record Office, 2MM b/18/37, 31 May 1714).

severe. He presented her, on his knees, with a Letter, which she received tremblingly and opened impatiently. As I believe that such another letter has never been seen, I shall reproduce the complete text.

Madam,

Public reports have no doubt informed you of the Death of the King my Father, though it was only a few days since. I am in peaceable possession of my dominions, and I hasten to restore your own to yourself. If your subjects are unwilling to accept you, I offer you my Troops and my Treasure to reduce them to their Duty. May it please the Gods that your future behaviour may cause them to forget the misconduct of the past. Our Marriage had so few witnesses that if you wish to conceal it, I shall not publish it; if you find it convenient to own it, I shall not contradict you. Whichever decision you take, in renouncing you I renounce all the advantages which I might draw from alliance with you. I neither offer you advice, nor any prohibition. Follow your inclinations, whatever they may be, and never enquire for news of

King Sombre.

It would be beneath me to dispatch an Ambassador to demand you back from King Goodchild. I have sent this Gentleman in haste, counting on his discretion. Take his advice on the matter of your repossession of your throne, and do not reveal to anyone that he has to do with me.

Docile's first thought on seeing her Husband's Handwriting was that he had written before he was assassinated. But to know him to be living, and more unjust than ever, overwhelmed her with so many conflicting Ideas that she had not the strength to unravel a single one, and she remained in a seizure which verged on stupefaction.

Her silence allowed the Knight to follow the orders he had received to instruct her as to the state of her affairs. He related to her that the Prince had found a strong party in his interest on the Island whither he had retired; that he had taken infallible measures to put himself in possession of his rights, and that he was on the point of bringing them to fruition when news of his Father's death arrived; that he chose this moment to show himself to the people, who received him with the liveliest demonstrations of joy; that the Ambassadors from the Kingdoms of Wildman and Contrary had come to pay him Homage; that he had sent away the latter, telling them that he would devote his best efforts to seeking out their Queen. 'The same evening (continued the Knight) H[is] M[ajesty] did me the honour to call me to his Closet. He entrusted me with his

Letter, and directed me to the Kingdom of Good Children, to present it to Y[our] M[ajesty] with positive orders to obey her in everything,[1] and I beg her most humbly to believe that she has no subject who will serve her with greater Zeal and attachment than myself.'

The Queen was not sufficiently herself to reply to his speech. She left him complete freedom to prolong it, and he continued: 'I have been at the Court where I believed I should find her. I tried in vain to discover the place of her retirement, although I made all the enquiries possible without revealing my commission (which I dared not do without [?his] orders). I was returning sadly on my tracks. My good fortune decreed that I stopped at a little Inn where I heard talk about an unknown Lady, of a kind to make me hope for the honour which I now enjoy in presenting myself at her feet. I was told that this Lady had retired to this Castle, and the Gods have been so propitious to my prayers as to give me the glorious honour of being the first of her subjects to pledge my Duty to her.'

He ceased speaking, but Docile had neither voice nor will to answer him. Her Blood, half frozen, denied her the strength to open her mouth. She did not weep, she barely breathed. She had remained a full quarter of an hour in this state, with him still on his Knees, believing he ought not to stand up again without her permission, when she noticed through the trees, the Maiden whom she most favoured among those in attendance on her, who was bringing her her Lute, which she had asked for as she went out. This sight revived her sufficiently to give her strength to say to the Knight, 'Come back here at the same hour tomorrow.' He left; but the Maiden had already seen him, and could not think what speculations to make about having surprised her beautiful Mistress giving audience to a young, handsome stranger, who was entertaining her, no doubt, with something deeply interesting, since he was speaking on his Knees, and she was listening attentively. She dared not ask for any explanation from the Queen, who called her in a feeble voice. 'Give me your arm Julie, she said, I am very ill.' Indeed, her extreme pallor perfectly bore out her words, and the frightened Girl called her companions. It was all they could do to drag the languishing Queen as far as her Apartments, where she read and re-read the Letter she had just received. She did not fail to perceive her Husband's Generosity of sentiments, even though wrapped up in his usual Harshness. She was touched by

---

[1] The original French makes this awkward switch from the second person to the more formal third (p. 261 below).

it, but even if she had not been, she was too much the slave of her Duty to hesitate over the course of action which she ought to pursue. She meant to throw herself at his feet, submit herself to whatever punishment he ordained, and cede her Kingdom to him, only too content if he would permit her to finish her sad life among the Vestals.

'Poor Count, what will become of you? (she said to herself) Is this the reward of your generous care? Have you known me only that I should be the sorrow of your life? You must forget a miserable heart which can never forget you.' This softening Idea made her dissolve in tears. She felt her Heart a little comforted after having wept a great deal, and she took up her meditations again. She represented to herself the Count's despair; she did not flatter herself that she had the strength to be able to resist it. She feared that when she saw him she would not be able to sustain her Resolution of leaving him. This was, nevertheless, necessary for her honour. Virtue demanded it, but love is able to conquer every other feeling, and she dared not promise herself she could refuse anything to the Entreaties and the tears of him whom she loved. She had no doubt that he would press her to run away with him to some corner of the world to spend their days together. She would have found a charm in the most frightful desert if her Duty had permitted it, but Reason opposed it as strongly as Virtue. Even her tenderness for him made her consider that the King her Husband would pursue him to the ends of the Earth to sacrifice him to his Vengeance, and she would expose the worthiest of all men to be slain (perhaps) before her eyes. This final consideration decided her more than all the others, that she must flee before his Return. She dared not confide in any of her Women, knowing that they were wholly devoted to him. She imagined that his passion was violent enough to make him follow her traces with no thought for the Consequences, and she foresaw with horror all the Results that must be expected from that. But by going without leaving him a letter, she would expose herself to the most shocking suspicions. He would accuse her of ingratitude, of lightness, and of Perfidy; could she resolve to lose the esteem of him whom she adored? There is no sacrifice so costly as that. She reproached herself, nevertheless, with hesitating when it concerned the happiness and safety of her dear Count. 'Let him despise me (she said), let him detest me, if that is necessary for his Tranquillity. But let him live, and let him live happy! It is Weakness, it is self-love, it is myself I weep for. If I cannot find contentment in sacrificing myself to procure him this Tranquillity, I am only too much changed.'

This Resolution appeared to her so fine that it began to console her. She wrapped herself in her Virtue, and this gave her Strength enough to present herself punctually at the time she had indicated to the officer of King Sombre. He arrived a moment later, and she made haste to tell him that she wished to return with him to her Husband's side. She commanded him to bring a horse and a set of men's clothing to her at the edge of the Wood, at midnight, and that she would come and join him to begin their journey.[1] This command appeared to him so extravagant that, although he had been ordered by the King his Master to obey her unreservedly, he doubted whether he ought to do so. 'I have my reasons (she said as she noticed his astonishment) for acting in this fashion. They are indispensable. No objections: obey.' She left him with these Words. He went away, not knowing whether he ought to suppose her insane, or whether she was following Bizarre orders from the King. He resolved, however, blindly to obey. He brought her his finest Suit of clothes, presented her with his horse, and followed her on another which he had bought. She had put on her disguise in the depths of a dark Thicket, and had taken the precaution of filling her woman's costume with Stones and throwing it into the River, and rode away at a rapid pace from the only Object of her love, by whom she believed herself tenderly loved, to seek him whom she feared to see, and by whom she was certain to find herself abused.

Her Damsels did not become aware of her flight until the next morning. She had supped at her usual time; she had been seen to go to bed, and she had got up and descended to the garden, escaping from there without anyone's suspecting it. One can imagine the huge surprise among her Domestics. There was none but Julie who believed she held the key to the mystery. She had always regarded Docile as kept Mistress to the Count. She knew nothing of her rank, or her design of Marriage. It seemed very clear to her that she had acquired another lover. She would have given the same Idea to everyone if she had related the adventure of the Wood, but, more discreet than most of those of her station, she kept this secret for her Master,

---

[1] A 'prodigious number of heroines' of French 17th-century romance don men's clothes for heroic ends (Ian MacLean, *Woman Triumphant: Feminism in French Literature, 1610–1652*, 1977, 206); Villedieu's heroine in *Les Mémoires de la vie de Henriette-Sylvie de Molière* (1672–4) (which MWM owned in a Paris edn., 1717) does so in order to make love to women.

while promising herself, however, to recompense herself for this restraint by telling it to the whole world the moment she had informed the Count.

He arrived before nightfall, with all the eagerness of a man who expected the reward of so many cares and sighs. What became of him as he learned of the Queen's flight? He had difficulty in believing it, even though he could see it, and was revolving a thousand imaginings in his Head when the assiduous Julie communicated to him the scene which she had seen in the Wood, which brought his astonishment to its height. In all his life he had never esteemed anyone but Docile alone. He had always regarded Virtue as a chimerical Idea which had no more real existence than the Phoenix.[1] He had altered this opinion on account of her, and now she herself, none but she, was deceiving him in the cruellest manner, and one as mortifying to his Vanity as to his affection. He, who prided himself on knowing the world so well, to find himself the Dupe of a young person who had covered her hand with an Innocence which appeared so natural as to have inspired pity. In his Imagination he ran through all her manners, her words, down to her least looks, without being able to discover any trace of that artifice which formed the basis of her Character, since she was capable of so black a Treachery, at the moment when she seemed to live only for him. He sent away all her women, and returned to the Court of Good Children, where he met with much Courtesy on the part of the King, a thousand embraces from the Courtiers, and little coquetries from the Ladies, which made him forget the faithless woman—who, however, occupied her mind with him alone during the fatigues of her sad journey.

Her Guide was not without his anxieties. He had never seen the Queen but with eyes that looked upon his Sovereign. He used to say, like everybody, that she was a perfect Beauty, without daring to give himself up to Gazing at her. Now he was seeing her alone, and in a condition which, stripped of the splendour of her rank, revealed all her charms. It is common knowledge how much male dress is becoming to Beauties. Being unaccustomed to dressing herself, she had so badly fastened her hair-net[2] that it fell down at the horse's first

---

[1] Hobbes writes that the names of virtues and vices are problematic: what is desired is good, and what is abhorred is bad (*Leviathan* (1651), i. 4, 6). Mandeville writes that 'Honour in its Figurative Sense is a Chimera without Truth or Being' (*The Fable of the Bees* (1714), ed. Phillip Harth (1970, 1989), 212).

[2] 'Bourse', generally a purse, also means a net to contain a chignon.

step, and she had her shoulders covered with fine, fair, naturally waving locks. The air and exercise had given her that vivid colour that goes with the flower of youth. Judge then how dazzling she appeared to the Knight.

When the Rising Sun allowed him to look at her, his admiration mixed itself with confusion which left him no Freedom for thinking. He abandoned himself to the Pleasure his eyes were receiving without noticing that his Heart was concerned in it. She was too much buried in her Thoughts to pay him the least attention. In spite of the firmness upon which she prided herself, every step which carried her further from the Count made him more dear to her Imagination. She pictured to herself his Despair, his Fury, his hatred, and at last his Contempt for a Woman so ungrateful and so perfidious as she must appear to him. 'If at least (she thought) I durst inform him that it is for him that I sacrifice myself? But no, my sacrifice would be rendered useless. He would expose himself to the Vengeance of My Husband, and I should have to reproach myself with the death of a man worthy to have been immortal. I must submit to the rigours of my fate, and rest content that I have no other witness but my Heart to the sincerity of my motives. True Virtue is independent of Applause,[1] and I offend her if I seek in her for anything but herself.' By Reflections like these she was enabled to keep to her Resolution.

People today are quite ready to mock the old maxim that Virtue is its own reward.[2] It is nevertheless very true. Properly considered, self-love is the most perfect pleasure, the only one that is pure, and which never grows stale, and I am convinced that those who are lucky enough to be truly intoxicated with this Enthusiasm, find a greater pleasure in conquering their passions than the liveliest man has ever experienced in satisfying them. Docile proved the truth of this; she arrived at the seaport in a state of Tranquillity which increased her Beauty.

She found there a merchant Vessel ready to make sail for the island where his officer had left King Sombre. She embarked, refusing to listen to this faithful Squire, who would have persuaded her to take a day for repose. She had cause to repent this haste two days later. A Corsair of Tunis, which was preying in these seas, attacked their Ship, which was in poor case to defend herself. But the fear of slavery

---

[1] MWM urged this maxim on James Stuart Mackenzie in 1742 (*CL* ii. 282–3).

[2] This maxim, from Ovid's 'Pretium sibi virtus' (*Tristia*, 5. 14, line 31), was about to make a strong comeback as moral to innumerable novels, many of them by women.

worked miracles on the whole Crew.[1] The Knight, who gave out that he was Docile's Brother, outdid and inspired all the others. He was fighting under the eyes and for the Freedom of his adorable Queen. Nevertheless he had to yield to Force; he had the Glory of dying at her feet, pierced by a thousand wounds. She gave a cry, which was followed by a swoon so deep that she appeared dead, and would have been thrown into the sea among those who had been killed, if her great Beauty had not attracted the notice of the Captain of Corsairs. He had remarked her when the boarding began, and promised himself great profit from his prize. The Bey[2] of Tunis had a Taste for keeping Pretty Pages always around him, and he did not doubt of making his fortune by offering him such a fine present. With this in mind he had Docile lifted up, and seeing that her clothes were not bloodied, he thought that fear alone had made her faint. He had her carried to his Cabin. She came to herself (by the help of water which they dashed in her face) to find herself in the midst of Barbarians from whom she must expect all kinds of insults. She decided to throw herself into the sea at the first attempt which might wound her modesty. She counted it nothing to be a slave. In truth she had always been one, she only lacked the name; and she resolved to Support this misfortune as she had so many others. She remembered how Télémaque had been a slave,[3] and of all the consolations which wisdom had given him through the medium of Mentor.

The Captain so acutely feared to tarnish the splendour of her Beauty by giving her any Displeasure, that he served her with as much Respect as if she had been at her own Court. Nobody presented themselves before her except to bring her food, and that was the best of everything they had, always casting down their eyes in the manner of Turkish politeness.[4] This conduct relieved her of her principal fear. She turned her thoughts on the sad events of her life, and tenderly wept the cruel fate of her faithful Servant. She remembered that he had been sole witness to the purity of her intentions, and did not doubt that this last effort of her Virtue, which had cost her so dear, would pass in the World for an act of Folly. King Sombre was not exactly disposed to do justice to her. Count Goodhope,

---

[1] The city of Tunis was controlled, 1574–1881, by the Ottoman Empire. Islamic law forbids enslaving its own subjects, so slaves (captured or bought) had to come from outside the empire (Bernard Lewis, *The Muslim Discovery of Europe* (1982), 187).

[2] Ruler of a province subject to the Sultan at Constantinople (Istanbul).

[3] See above, p. 114, n. 2.

[4] This MWM had experienced for herself in 1717–18.

embittered by resentment, would easily believe the appearances which were all against her, and she would die (perhaps) in chains,[1] detested by those very people for whom she had sacrificed herself. She had no consolation except in that unconquerable Virtue which had always Sustained her, and which gave her a kind of Tranquillity despite all the persecutions of Fortune.

The Ship was making sail for Tunis slowly enough, having been badly damaged in the battle, but towing her prize behind her. The third day of sail, they met a Maltese Galley, which seeing her almost beyond defending herself did not hesitate to attack her, and very soon obtained the Victory. The Corsairs were put in irons, and their slaves at Liberty. In command was a young Knight of Malta, lively, bold, and amiable, in short a younger son of a great French Family.[2] He was struck with Docile's Appearance, and examined her more carefully than the Turkish Captain had done. He began to suspect her sex; his looks embarrassed her, and her blushes confirmed him in the Idea that she was a girl in men's clothes. He learned from the sailors that she had been voyaging with a Brother who had been killed fighting like a true Hero. He approached her with that air of courteous temerity which is the Frenchman's birthright.

'Fear nothing Mademoiselle (he said to her very softly, observing that she trembled), your sex and your Beauty are made to rule, not to be afraid. It is I who am your slave; rely on my discretion if you do not want to be recognized, but permit me to pay you the respects that I owe you. I flatter myself that my assiduities will win your confidence, and as soon as I have given some necessary orders I will return to learn, at your feet, if you have anything to command me.' This compliment completed the Unfortunate beauty's discomposure; she did not know what course of action to follow. She feared that if she persisted in concealing her sex she would be exposing herself to a humiliating examination, and resolved to admit it on his return, hoping to find safety in the chevalier's Generosity. She could not adopt this resolution without doing extreme violence to her feelings, and he found her in tears when he arrived. He appeared softened by this. 'How worthy you are to be loved, said he, watching her tenderly,

---

[1] This reflects her Western misapprehension of Turkish slavery.

[2] Members of the Roman Catholic religious-military order of Knights Hospitallers were called Knights of Malta, from their island headquarters (ceded to them in 1530). They comprised only the highest nobility (cf. *CL* i. 372, 404). In 18th-century fiction they became 'des personnages presque indispensibles' (Claire-Eliane Engel, *L'Ordre de Malte en Mediteranée*, 1957, 303).

since you know so well how to love! For I do not doubt that it is your dear Brother for whom you weep, and that he belonged to you by a tie stronger than that of blood.'

'No Sir (she replied, recovering herself), I regret him only as a Servant who was very attached to me. But I find in my situation reasons enough to afflict myself; I am not surprised that it gives you prejudices against me. But I am an Unhappy Woman, who was travelling to seek her Husband when—'

The Chevalier did not permit her to continue; he interrupted her by throwing himself at her feet and kissing her hands with Transport. 'So you are Married (cried he). Ah, from what great disquiet you deliver me! I simply hate all dealings with Girls. It takes a century to conquer them and two more centuries to get rid of them. It seems to me that you are ten times more beautiful since I know that you have a Husband. I even flatter myself that he is infinitely amiable; I love disputing a Heart with a Rival, and I am willing either to die or to supplant him in yours.'

All this spoken with a half-jesting manner was proper enough to dispel any other melancholy than that of Docile, but she replied seriously, 'I ought to be the object of your Compassion, and not that of your raillery. I am not accustomed to listen to such jokes, and if your offers of service are real the only service you can render me is to put me ashore at the first port from which I can write to my Husband. He will find (perhaps) means to reward your Generosity. I have nothing to offer you but my tears—'

'You believe you are still in the power of Corsairs, Madam (replied he). Do you fear that I wish to extort a ransom, or make a bad use of my victory? We Frenchmen ask for nothing from Ladies but what their Goodness bestows on us, but we must be permitted by the way of Gentleness to attain to the good gifts of Fortune. Mine seems to me so brilliant, I could not lightly abandon the Glorious enterprise which I have conceived of becoming pleasing to you. It is true that I am perhaps anticipating things, and that I ought, out of respect, to conceal my design from you for two or three days more; but alas! we are no longer in the century of Amadises, and yet more distant from that of the Patriarchs.[1] How can I tell? I might die in twenty-four

---

[1] In the 15th-century chivalric romance *Amadis de Gaul* (based on even earlier materials), Amadis enters Oriana's service at the outset, aged 12; each is pursued by innumerable other suitors before they are united at the very end. In Genesis 29 the future patriarch Jacob serves fourteen years for Rachel.

hours, and I should have the grief of dying without having told you that I adored you. No, no, one must not run the risk of such a terrible misfortune—I am in haste to Live.'[1] He ended with this snatch of Song, in an agreeable voice which seemed to Docile so far from serious that she began to be reassured.

She believed that the most reasonable course of action with a character like his would be to leave him to enjoy his Visions (the tempting fruit of his Vanity) and to get herself out of his hands with all possible promptitude. She flattered herself that he would very soon grow tired of fruitless efforts, and that she would be able to count on his courtesy to restore her Freedom when once he had seen the failure of the attractions which he believed so irresistible; and she feared that if she shocked him by a severity inducing despair, he might be piqued enough to stoop to Insolences of which just the thought made her tremble. These hastily adopted reasonings decided her to pretend some degree of complaisance, and she replied with a half-playful air that he sang nicely, without appearing to have listened to his libertine speeches. 'You love music? (said he) You enrapture me; it is my Passion. I would put my hand in the fire to wager that you sing like an Angel; your voice has a ravishing timbre. Let us sing the Duet in the second act of the latest Opera, the one which is so much admired at Court. Were you not at Paris at the time it was presented?'

'I have never been to Paris, Sir,' she replied.

'Is it possible? (cried he) There is nothing foreign about you. That Figure so delicate and so easy, that angle of the Head, can they be learned elsewhere? We must go there; a three Months' stay would put the final brush-stroke to your Graces. Your Beauty will be the ornament of the Tuileries,[2] and five or 6 evenings promenading will add that certain *je ne sais quoi* so necessary to beauties. But I see you are tired; no one could escape that; a naval Battle is not a spectacle to see unmoved. No doubt you were transfixed with fear, and you must need rest. I have with me a Boy who is the World's greatest genius in bouillons and consommés.[3] He will bring you something made to his recipe; sleep well on it. Remember that I love you madly; we shall see one another again tomorrow Morning.'

---

[1] Hildebrand Jacob, 'The Alarm', concludes ''Tis time to be in haste, to live!' The speaker is a 35-year-old man of pleasure alarmed by his first grey hairs (*Works* (1735): quoted in Roger Lonsdale, *The New Oxford Book of Eighteenth-Century Verse* (1984), 228).

[2] MWM had written of the Tuileries in her first version of 'Indamora'; visiting them in 1718, she reported them 'much finer than our Mall' (above, p. 10, n. 2; *CL* i. 442).

[3] MWM had in her library in 1739 a *Cuisinier françois* (Wh MS 135).

He departed with a light step, singing, and left Docile feeling an astonishment which displaced her sorrow. She did not know what consequences to expect from his behaviour. This kind of Gallantry was entirely new to her, and she was lost in reflection. She took care to fasten the door of her cabin tightly before going to bed, a precaution by no means necessary. He was a great deal more tired than she was, and fell asleep much more quickly. He was not fundamentally at all dangerous for Ladies like her, but much to be feared by those who were Gallant, that is to say, formed to arouse desire in them, and much given to offering them those affronts of omission which are never forgiven. In the height of fashion from his Childhood, he had spent himself in the service of the sex. He retained nothing but the appearance and the language of a man of good estate. More ardent than ever in his pursuits, he had been seeking for two years that divine Beauty who would rekindle his appetite. He remembered Docile's beauty as he awoke, and believed he had found his destiny. Her Novice-like manner and her Modesty were at least as surprising to him as his Boldness and his mannered behaviour had been to her. He concluded that she had had few adventures as yet, and that she was charming enough to make an untried Heart desirable. He had never encountered one of these, and resolved to omit nothing to effect the Conquest of it, and afterwards to take her to Paris. She was beautiful enough (he told himself) to please all the greatest people. 'Should I be the first who has made his Fortune by means of a pretty Mistress? I shall say she is a Sultana;[1] the novelty of that alone will have a great Effect.'

Flattered by these Ideas, he made haste to have his hair curled in the latest taste, and carried her Coffee to her with his own hands in a magnificent service. She had been up for a long time, and received him politely, although a little embarrassed to notice that he was earnestly gazing at her legs, which were perfectly well formed. A blush showed on her face. 'I am so unhappy, Madam (said he) as to be always causing you Confusion. For God's sake, compose yourself. I see nothing but what is admirable; let those blush who dare not show themselves till they have exhausted the mysteries of the Toilette. It is true that in letting certain things of great beauty be seen, you are hiding others; I am sure that in your woman's garb you would show an incomparable Bosom. I shall make sail towards

---

[1] MWM herself had made a social impression by popularizing Turkish costume.

Naxos. We will find some costumes for Greek ladies, which are not ugly,[1] if what you are wearing causes you pain.'

'I should prefer to remain in my disguise, she said, until an opportunity occurs of returning to my Husband.'

'You are very cruel, replied the chevalier smiling, to parade before my face the haste you are in to rejoin him. Dare I ask you how long ago you left him?'

'Almost a year ago,' said she.

'And you have not yet forgotten him? interrupted the chevalier: that is a Constancy that has never been seen since Penelope.[2] Your eyes are too bright for you to give yourself up to those whims of Antiquity. I rather suspect that little brother, or faithful Servant (if you prefer) sticks at your Heart. They say he was handsome, but by god he is in the wrong in being dead as much as the other in being Absent. It is best to forget those who leave us; let us enjoy the present moment, and regret nothing but lost time. I am entirely yours: I would exchange a little present tenderness towards my sufferings, for all the grief which you would pay my ashes, from which assuredly I shall get no good. Can one ask more from the most virtuous woman in the world, than Fidelity while you are together? There are few who carry it as far as that. A Parisian Lady usually has a Lover in her Closet[3] while another is in her chamber. The number of her conquests does honour to a Beauty as much as to a Hero,[4] and I heard a very witty woman say that a wise Beauty always has reinforcements, like a skilful General. Who can tell what may happen? There are strange misfortunes in the world, and I have known more than one who have found it very lucky they had a Lover in Reserve. Do not be offended, my lovely Queen (he continued, seeing that she blushed with anger at hearing this libertine discourse), I believe you are too delicate for that. But to carry Fidelity as far as the Absent, and as far as Corpses, has been out of fashion for a hundred years. You know the candour of my Nation; I have more of it than others. Permit me to tell you my thoughts frankly. I believe that a gentle knight carried

[1] MWM had described the dress of Greek peasant women: 'short petticoats fastend by straps round their shoulders and large Smock sleeves of white Linnen, with neat shoes and stockings, and on their heads a large piece of Muslin which falls in broad folds on their shoulders' (*CL* i. 419).

[2] Penelope waited twenty years (repelling suitors by stratagem) for her husband, Odysseus, to fight in the Trojan War and return home.

[3] Small private room.

[4] MWM repeated in two separate poems the line 'Monarchs and Beauties rule with equal sway' (*E&P* 203, 241).

you off from a Husband whom you no longer love, or whom you have never loved. I cannot imagine there is a Husband in the world who would permit a person of your Age to travel alone with a handsome Boy. Confess your Adventure to me. I am discreet to a fault. I am going to give you a fine proof of this: for nearly 24 hours I have known your sex without having spoken of it to anyone. I should be well teased if this were known at Paris; Discretion is as much discredited there as Fidelity. One durst not take one's stand on old-fashioned ideas there; but you are beautiful enough to perform miracles. I am ready to do and to believe everything you wish, even if you tell me that you put out to sea equipped with a great Train of Servants, and that those Rascals of Turks ate up your Footmen and your Chambermaids.'

This raillery opened Docile's eyes. She saw in full clarity the extravagance of her enterprise, and understood that she could not show herself to King Sombre again unless she were prepared to expose herself to the most humiliating Treatment, which would be justified by appearances, which were all against her. After a moment of silence she said, sighing, 'I recognize, Sir, that you see me in a condition which must give you a very disadvantageous opinion of me. I am not able to explain my reasons to you, and even if I could resolve to do so you are not obliged to believe me. It is quite unnecessary for me to enter into detail about my Misfortunes. I have only one boon to implore you: put me into some convent (whether on the Isle of Naxos or elsewhere). I shall be one of the sister-servitors of the Enclosed Nuns, only too happy to live and to die unknown.'

Although she spoke these words with a most touching sadness, he could not prevent himself from giving vent to a burst of laughter. 'A fine decision to make, Madame! (he replied) Then you sentence those delicate white hands to ironing Wimples, and those little tapering fingers to making Knick-knacks for adorning images. If Piety appeals to you, choose a kind which is more reasonable. Look on your Beauties as precious gifts of Heaven; employ them for the ends to which they were created,[1] and do not believe it is permitted you to deface or to entomb them. That is theft from the universe. You were born to spread pleasure; follow the sweet promptings of

---

[1] Libertines commonly put a sexual slant on the orthodox doctrine that woman was created to minister to the needs of man; MWM had already made fun of this idea (*CL* ii. 59). Christian feminists like Astell applied the same argument to women's intellectual capacities which the Knight applies to their bodies.

Nature, and believe it is the Divine voice which speaks. I have never thought to play the part of Missionary, but I discover in myself a Zeal for your service which is as good as being inspired. I must teach you your Duty.—'

'It is not out of Piety (she interrupted) that I choose retirement. My Honour obliges me to it, and the necessity of my situation.'

'Now there is something else! (cried he) I am delighted that you are not a dupe of the Priests; let us examine a little what this Honour is which oppresses you so cruelly. This is the first time in my life that I have amused myself in working at definitions. I was not brought up in the greasy dust of Books, thank God. I understand music, I dance pretty well, I have mastered my academic exercises, and I have enough Mathematics to understand Navigation and fortification. It seems to me that this is all a man of Quality needs. However, one enjoys a certain natural enlightenment which makes visible many kinds of abuses. By that honour of which you speak so respectfully you no doubt signify a general esteem, the applause of society, and the approbation of men of good will. You are right: these are good things which one ought ardently to pursue. Do you know that they depend on the Fashion, no less than Coiffures do? That which looks well in one century is ridiculous in another.[1] Our Ancestors are all dead; there are no more Romans in the world. I have heard tell a thousand times of the merit of Mademoiselle de L'Enclos, and Lucretia is mentioned only to be mocked.[2] If a Princess had made a vow, during the time of the Crusades, to walk barefoot to Jerusalem, she would have enjoyed the Glory of a place in the Legend,[3] and we should be celebrating her feast to this day. If another were to make the same pilgrimage today, malicious people would say she was a loose woman using pilgrimage as cloak to conceal her debaucheries, and the more moderate would speak of her as a Madwoman who ought to be locked up. The world has grown more enlightened, and in truth I find antique Honour in just as bad taste as Antique Cuisine. Those fine sentiments which are expatiated on by the ancient Romans, are good for nothing but to render you the plaything of

---

[1] MWM had voiced this fairly new sense of historical relativity in addressing the 17th-century Anna Maria van Schurman (*E&P* 165–6).

[2] Ninon de Lenclos (1620–1705) was a beauty, wit, and *salonnière*; rumours abounded of her love affairs in advanced age. Lucretia, in 510 BC, was raped by Tarquin and killed herself to avenge her husband's honour.

[3] The legend (meaning something to be read) was a term for the saints' lives appointed to be read at church services and convent meal-times.

those who do not share them. Believe me, my Beauty, the great secret
of life is never to be bored. To speak in sailors' language, one must
sometimes go with the current, or be shipwrecked. The Glory of
modern Women is intertwined with their pleasures. They become
illustrious by a generous distribution of their charms, and I maintain
that that celebrated pedant Lucretia, if she were living here and now,
would be the greatest Coquette of Paris, by the same principles
which led her to take her own life. Do you suppose she would have
done that violence to herself, if she had imagined she would be
judged ripe for bedlam? The good Lady wanted to shine in her
generation;[1] we shine at less cost nowadays, and much more agree-
ably. The gentle sex has repossessed all its rights; they are no longer
the dupes of Jealous men, who invented that Phantom Honour
which you make such a noise about. It is true that we have as many
Nuns as ever, but their motive is different. They are unhappy Victims of their parents' avarice or ambition. The poor Creatures do
everything they can to rid themselves of the suspicion of having retired voluntarily, and by libertine Speeches, bawdy songs, and
heartily cursing those that have enclosed them, they give us to understand that it is by compulsion and not by Trickery that they have
taken the veil.

> 'Give way to gentle tenderness,
> 'Love while time is young,
> 'Give ear to lovers as they press,
> 'Let reason hold its tongue.

'It is Rhyme that forces that last Line from me. After all it is very
badly turned, and true Reason counsels following the dictates of
one's Heart.—What do you say to this, my Goddess? It seems to me
that your silence reproaches me for having thrown away precious
moments in frigid reasoning.'[2]

She hastened to turn him from this Opinion, by telling him: 'I am
not acquainted with the manners of your Country, but it seems to me
that your Actions do not accord with your Words. You despise Honour as a Phantom, and I see you risking your life to obtain it.'

---

[1] Mandeville observes that Lucretia resisted against threats to kill her, but 'when he threat-
en'd her Reputation with eternal Infamy, she fairly surrender'd, and then slew herself; a certain sign that she valued her Virtue less than her Glory' (*Fable of the Bees*, 223).

[2] When Pope transcribed MWM's eclogues, he gave these sentiments to a married woman
addressing a suitor, in a revision which MWM rejected (*E&P* 192).

'Did I not tell you, Madam, he replied, that I regulate my life according to fashion? One must admit that our Women have more spirit than we have; they have thrown off their chains, and we are still groaning under ours. I do not despair of seeing, one day, the stupidity of exposing oneself to danger as much ridiculed by men as Prudery is already ridiculed by the Ladies. If the human spirit progresses during my lifetime to the point of making mock of this prejudice, you will see me a notable Coward.[1] Is there indeed any common sense in risking one's life or in renouncing one's pleasure? It would only take half a dozen eminent Cowards to fix Glory in avoiding Danger. Unfortunately the Eminences have decided long ago that they are privileged by their situation to take good care of their persons, and it is for us miserable fellows to face dangers. Here is serious stuff indeed! One must love you as much as I do, to plunge oneself like this in Reflections, to rescue you from error. You are still stuffed with the Lessons of some stupid mother, or some idiot Governess. A fortnight at Paris will change your whole way of thinking.—'

'I have no desire to go to Paris, Sir (replied she) and—'

'I guess your thought (he interrupted with Vigour), you will find a thousand resources there. Your Beauty is as good as a note of exchange for a hundred thousand ecus.[2] I foresee that you will have adventures brilliant enough to make you forget all your Sorrows, whatever those may be. I will try meanwhile to amuse you, and I flatter myself that you will feel some gratitude for such disinterested behaviour as mine. I should wish to persuade you to love yourself; love me also, even if only to keep yourself from being bored during the voyage. Have no fears of any compulsion on my part. Frenchmen are not made to wreak violence on Ladies; we never violate anyone unless we have been given to understand that that is what they want.'

This assurance won him a smile from Docile; he began once more to beg her to sing with him. She thought she ought not to refuse him this slight Compliance, and the rest of the day was spent in Music and raillery (which he knew the secret of introducing everywhere). He feared, almost as much as she did, the consequences of too tender a conversation. Although he perfectly understood the technique

---

[1] An idea voiced by Rochester as 'all Men would be Cowards if they durst' (*A Satyr against Mankind*, line 158) and approved by Mandeville as true of most men (*Fable of the Bees*, the Remark or section already quoted twice: 231).

[2] Three livres or francs made one ecu.

of making fun of ladies' objections to this kind of thing, Docile had inspired him with a real Inclination for her. He did not choose that she should despise him, and he did not dare to risk taking a step which he knew would be very slippery for him.

They sailed[1] towards the Island of Naxos to take on water, while King Sombre was cudgelling his brains to guess the reason why he received no news of his Officer. He finished by imagining that he had been assassinated by King Goodchild's orders; he blamed the evil disposition of Docile, and felt no doubt that she had made a sacrifice of his Letter to her Lover. He was more enraged at this than all the other causes he believed he had to complain of her. He wanted, in full sight of the world, to help her to ascend her Throne, but he wanted to be seen to be doing it out of Generosity and Justice, without anyone accusing him of having an interest in her person, and he could not imagine without Fury this sign of his weakness having come to King Goodchild's hands. He dispatched the Lord who he thought the most devoted of his Court, as Envoy Extraordinary to King Goodchild, to carry the news of his accession to the crown and to renew an ancient Commercial treaty, with secret orders to inform himself skilfully of all the news of the Court, quite resolved that if Docile had settled there as his declared wife, he would avenge this insult in fire and blood.

Far from finding her, his Minister would not even have heard her Name, if there had not been a powerful party in Docile's Kingdom who, tired of being oppressed by a foreign power, longed passionately for her return, and, making use of King Sombre's declaration to the Parliament that he wished to re-establish her, were having her sought for throughout the world. The High Priest had been Stoned to death by the people, who had long groaned under his Insolence and his exactions. When the News of King Wildman's death first broke, everyone was disposed to receive Docile as their Rightful Queen. Many Knights undertook to seek her out; each set out for a different Court, carrying her portrait. One of them arrived at the Court of Good Children, a little before the envoy of King Sombre.

Docile had a face too charming to be forgotten. The first people to whom he showed her Portrait recognized her as the same Beauty whose Bizarre behaviour had caused such a stir. King Goodchild, who was the best-natured man in the world, had her sought for with

---

[1] These words in the original form a link with the discarded Fragment II (below, p. 189), which was presumably replaced by the preceding discussion of fashions in honour.

all possible care. It was discovered that she had been for some time at the Sea port, and afterwards with Count Goodhope. The Count had often been teased about this Adventure before anyone suspected his Fair one's Rank. Julie had not failed to recount her flight with the young Officer. People had made fun of the Count's despair. He had carried off the affair with spirit, and been the first to laugh about it, but when he saw that her Rank was known, he hastened to assure the envoy of King Sombre that he had lived with her as respectfully as if he had known it himself. This last claim was so little credible that nobody took any notice of it beyond praising his Discretion.

Heaven knows how the Unhappy Docile was torn to pieces. People were equally astonished at her Artifice and her Wantonness, which masked so corrupt a Heart with an appearance of such great Modesty. They credited her Mind with a tactical astuteness of which she was incapable, and pitilessly stripped her of all the virtues on which in fact her Nature was grounded. The envoy sent a courier post-haste with Letters to his Master, where he omitted nothing of what he had heard. King Sombre, still convinced that she had been kept by King Goodchild, imagined that her innate Inconstancy had prompted her to leave him and give herself to the Count, and that in consequence of this same flighty humour she had had herself carried off by a new Favourite. He found some consolation in flattering himself that his Marriage was not publicly known.[1]

In fact it was spoken of as doubtful. There was only Emily to testify to it, and she was a witness whose veracity could not but be suspected. When she saw that her story was being taken this way, she did not persist in it, and was willing to hint that it had been her good Nature trying to cloak her Mistress's vice. Docile's subjects, Ashamed of their search for so unworthy a Queen, submitted themselves again to King Sombre. Pamphlets about the imaginary Adventures of Docile were published in several countries, while she spent her life in Penances harsher than those of a Carmelite, but her Reputation was that of a Messalina.[2]

---

[1] Not, that is, in his own kingdom; even about this he is deluded.

[2] The mendicant order of Carmelites, founded in 1451, was made yet more rigorous by St Teresa in the 16th century; Messalina, wife of the Emperor Claudius, was a byword for debauchery. In *La Princesse de Clèves* the heroine is left dividing her time between a convent and home life 'in holier occupations than those of the strictest religious order'; but unlike Docile she is admired for this conduct (trans. Robin Buss (1992), 175–6).

Princess Docile: Fragment I

Textual note. These two paragraphs, in a scribal hand, with corrections by MWM, H MS 80, fo. 294, seem to be an alternative opening to 'Docile II' (p. 145 above).

The Unhappy Docile Walked on, given up to Reflections from which she could find no escape. At eight in the morning she arrived at the Sea port which the prince her Husband had appointed. She was not surprised not to find him there, being well aware that he could not arrive until five hours later: she went to bed exhausted by her thoughts and by the speed with which she had travelled. She tried to Sleep, but sleep pitilessly shunned her. After having rested for half the day, she became very much surprised not to hear any news of the prince.

We must now see what prevented him from appearing at her side. After getting leave from the King to pursue her, he pressed his horse in the direction of where she was awaiting him. As chance would have it he met with some of the King's troops who were going to change their quarters, taking the road to the sea port. His imagination, which always produced the wildest ideas in order to torment him, made him suppose, against all appearances, that he was going to be ambushed there. He no longer had any doubt that they had orders to arrest him. He no longer felt astonished by the calm manner which had surprised him at his recent audience with the King. He believed that Docile had schemed with the latter to have herself carried off, in order to conceal from the public a step which must cover her with infamy. His unbridled imagination suggested to him that she was already, perhaps, in the King's hands, and he suddenly decided to avoid an encounter with these troops, whom he clearly saw he could not resist, and took a route quite opposite from that which he had to follow in order to find poor Docile, who was in the most embarrassing situation. She had not taken the precaution of supplying herself with the necessary money. She had entrusted the care of everything to her husband, who was fleeing from her at the very time that she had abandoned everything that could be most tempting in order to comply with his caprices.

Princess Docile: Fragment II

Textual note. Most of this passage, in MWM's hand, occupies both sides of H MS 80, fo. 322 (now bound between her pages 7 and 8 of the 'Docile' MS); the conclusion occupies fo. 368. Two cancelled concluding words link it to the main text at p. 186 above. But it throws a different light on the Knight of Malta, gives Docile a force and dignity at odds with her imminent final suppression, and allots to gender reversal and scientific discourse an importance they do not have in 'Docile' as it stands. The way the science comes filtered through the prism of Algarotti might connect the fragment with summer 1738, when MWM first read his adaptation of Newton, but more probably with her resumption of her friendship with him in late 1756 (*CL*, ii. 117, iii. 117).

He found her one evening on Deck leaning on her Hand, gazing at the Heaven with such great concentration that he was right beside her before she noticed him. It was one of those fine summer nights when the stars show themselves in all their Beauty, and the wind breathed gently, refreshing the air without disturbing it. 'Is it permitted, Madam, he said, to interrupt your reveries? It seems to me that they please you well; you have a peaceful, languorous air, which allows one to guess at many things.'

'Perhaps you guess wrongly, Sir (she replied, smiling a little). I was admiring the order of those stars, that force of Gravity and attraction which directs their movements, and I was amusing myself by imagining the different beings who people them.'

'Then you do not doubt they are inhabited,' he resumed.

'I have no doubts at all about it, she continued.[1] In vain would anyone object to me that there are some so close to the Sun that the excessive heat would in one instant destroy all the inhabitants of that Earth. Why should there not be Creatures to whom fire is as natural as water is to fish? I am certain that if there existed an Island where the rivers and the surrounding sea were devoid of fish, you would not be able to make those Islanders accept that water was populated with an Infinite number of species. They would tell you that any animal

---

[1] Her silence as to the Prince of Venus can be variously interpreted. Her belief would be warranted by Fontenelle's *Entretiens sur la pluralité des mondes* (1686).

would be drowned in it, that they could not breathe in it for half an hour, and that life cannot subsist without breathing. Never could human imagination conceive how animals could be made which can survive in an element which destroys all other animals. Human vanity is always ready to find anything impossible which goes beyond common Knowledge. Nevertheless, the surprising discoveries of this century ought to persuade us that there are many more truths which are as much hidden from us as the dissection (if I may use that term for it) of the Sun's rays, and the cause of the Rainbow, were from our Ancestors. Gravitation, which is so clearly demonstrated by Geometrical proofs—'[1]

The Knight interrupted her again by laughing with all his might. 'Is it possible, Madam, that you have wasted so many hours of Youth, which is designed for sweeter amusements, making the calculations which are necessary for the demonstrations you speak of so learnedly? Those fine eyes, from which a single tender glance would have crowned a Lover's happiness, have been employed in poring through Telescopes.'[2]

'Do you account that time lost, Sir (she replied), that one gives to research into such important truths?'

'A fine importance, indeed! he cried, beginning to laugh again, I know more about that than you suspect, I, who have never read anything but pamphlets. I was in love for a whole week with the Marquise of Caprice. Frankly, I was not displeasing to her. She got it into her head to form my mind; she did me the honour of inviting me to one of her philosophical suppers, where I listened for two mortal hours to an obstinate Cartesian disputing with a fanatical Newtonian. I was born curious, and in spite of the tedium gnawing at me, I listened attentively to their debate. It had to do with the issue of whether there is a void in nature, or a plenitude.[3] In truth the

---

[1] Sir Isaac Newton published his much earlier findings about the prismatic splitting of white light into the spectrum in his *Optics* (1704) (adapted and popularized by MWM's lover Francesco Algarotti in 1739), and about universal gravitation in *Philosophiae naturalis principia mathematica* (1687). MWM wrote to her daughter of discoveries yet to be made (*CL* iii. 17).

[2] Fontenelle's letter 11 in *Lettres . . . de M. le Chevalier d'Her**** (1683) (which Montagu owned) reproves a young man for loving a woman of intellect and science, in terms not unlike the Knight's.

[3] René Descartes (1596–1650) posited, to explain the planets' elliptical courses, an all-pervading ether through which they are whirled by vortices. According to Newton refracted through Algarotti, the Atomists pictured atoms moving in a cosmic vacuum, which Descartes saw as filled by infinitesimal matter ground from the atoms' edges (*Sir Isaac Newton's Theory of Light and Colours* (1742), i. 37–50). Algerotti's *Newtonianismo* uses the vacuum–plenitude

Question did not appear to me of much interest. Nevertheless they argued as fierily as if the salvation of the human Race depended on it. They became heated to such a degree that at one moment I thought they would come to blows. For myself, I confess I perceived no great difference between the subtle matter of Descartes and the subtle ether of Newton, which he claims to be the cause of attraction, refraction, and movement in general.[1] I agree that Vortices, which our Fathers were so charmed with, are exploded by Newton's reasoning, and that his System appears to me much more solidly grounded than his Predecessor's.[2] But all these dazzling truths serve only more clearly to prove our invincible Ignorance about the most essential matters, and I do not see that any of the researches which established that great Mathematician's Fame have contributed the least bit in the world to human happiness. The Longitude (the knowledge of which would be so useful to us navigators) remains as impenetrable as ever,[3] and I feel a greater gratitude to Guido Reni and Correggio,[4] who have presented to our eyes, by their admixture of Colours, and disposition of Lights and Shades, objects which clearly convey to me the infinitesimal gradations which make up a ray of light, and the analogy between sounds and colours. I have a greater esteem for the first pastry-maker, who invented an art which gives so much pleasure, and that great man who found out the secret of smoking Hams and composing Sausages, which bring delight to so many worthy People. But those were such modest Philosophers

debate to stand for all warfare of opposing hypotheses (ii. 4). (I have cited the 1742 translation because, unlike Elizabeth Carter's *Sir Isaac Newton's Philosophy Explain'd*, 1739, it is available on microfilm.)

[1] In Descartes the 'most subtle and volatile Substance of all . . . the *Subtile Matter*' forms the sun and stars revolving at the centre of vortices: 'the Vortices are as useful to *Des Cartes*, as the Cacao-tree to the *Indians*, which supplies them with all they want' (ibid. i. 51, 63). The end of Newton's argument, as rendered by Algarotti, tentatively suggests that perhaps variations in transmission and refraction of light are caused by its passage through 'an exceedingly subtile Fluid' (ii. 216).

[2] Algarotti describes Newton and Malebranche as exploding the vortex theory (ibid. i. 171, 191, ii. 2). See *Principia*, end of book 2, where Newton denies that vortices affect planetary movement; but (always hating controversy) adds that he can tolerate other thinkers' belief in cosmic 'subtle matter'. The cause of gravity remained for Newton 'an open question', with ether as a strong possibility (Arthur Koestler, *The Sleepwalkers* (1959, 1964), 511; I. Bernard Cohen, *The Newtonian Revolution* (1980), 114–15, 306 n. 1).

[3] In 1714 the British Parliament, after a committee of inquiry before which Newton gave evidence, offered a large cash prize for the discovery of how to measure longitude at sea; it remained unawarded until 1765.

[4] Guido Reni (1575–1642) and Antonio Allegri, called Correggio (1494–1534), were MWM's 'particular favourites' in 1718 (*CL* i. 431).

that we don't even know their names, although we benefit from their labours every day. They contented themselves with being useful to us, without affecting that Fame which is the chief aim of the midnight studies of these celebrated astronomers.[1] You laugh to hear me give the title of Philosophers to those who apply themselves to perfecting the art of cookery. Know that I have my reasons for that. I asked the gentlemen who award themselves this fine title what it means. They answered me that it was a compound Word which signified Lover of Wisdom. Since I have known that, I call Philosophers all those Generous Sages who devote their minds to refining our pleasures, but Philonugae, lovers of trifles, those who neglect the earth (for which they are made) to study the movements of the Planets, to which they will never reach.[2]

'I see you are shocked at the contempt I evince for Philosophy. It is true I have a grudge against it since that supper with the Marquise, who was very appealing to me (in spite of the leanness which her profound learning had given her). She had set aside that night to reward my cares; those cursed Philosophers had so chilled my blood by their demonstrations that after they left, despite the attraction of her beauty I remained in a state of Gravitation towards the centre of the earth, which was as much a matter of grief to her as to me. I believe she had already experienced troubles of the same kind, for without showing much astonishment, she had the cruel Generosity to propose to me a return meeting for Next day. I could not honourably refuse the engagement, although I felt strongly that I could never in my life see her without the same ideas reawakening, and that I should always remain in relation to her like the Moon in its Course around the Sun, always attracted but never able to alight upon it.[3] She would not accept this excuse. I was Dismissed. I took up my pleasures again with a little dancer who did not know how to read, and ever since that unhappy adventure I fly from demonstrations and calculations like the plague.'

Docile's Modesty was pained by the libertine manner of his narration, but he was not in other respects bold enough to offend her.

---

[1] In *Candide*, ch. 25, Pococurante ranks the inventor of the art of making pins above the whole Academy of Science; MWM twice joked about the immortal fame she expected for teaching the Italians to improve their cookery (*CL* ii. 447, 485).

[2] The Knight concurs with Milton's Raphael (*Paradise Lost*, viii. 172–6). Algarotti calls philosophers 'a Set of People whose Looks are always directed to Heaven, and have very little regard for our Earth' (*Sir Isaac Newton's Theory*, ii. 113).

[3] The confusion about the moon's course must be the Knight's.

APPENDIX I
Memorie Italiano

Mi riusciva molto noiosa la dimora in Avignone, e bramavo molto di ritornare in Italia, senza però aver l'ardire d'intraprendere un tale viaggio, essendo allora l'Italia il Teatro della Guerra. Il Conte Palazzi era digià arivato in Avignone, quale m'era stato presentato a Venezia dalla Signora Pisani Mocenigo, come un Giovane, che ella proteggeva, e che ella aveva racomandata per essere amesso al Serviggio del Prencipe di Sassonia, e perciò era partito da Venezia pochi giorni dopo; ciò fu nell'anno *1740* e d'allora in poi io non ho sentito a parlare di lui sino al suo arivo in Avignone, che fu nell'anno *1746*.

Venne, adonque a farmi visita; ed io fui molto contenta di parlare con lui de miei Amici di Venezia, e li dissi in conversazione, che sarei ben stata felice se avessi potuto ritornarvi. Egli mi rispose, che andava a Brescia a ritrovar sua Madre e mi pregò di permetterli di servirmi di scorta almeno sino a Brescia, e che sua Madre sicuramente non avrebbe sofferto che io dormissi in un Albergo, ma che si sarebbe stimata molto onorata se io avessi voluto alloggiare in Casa sua. Li risposi che non bisognava pensare a questo, mentre io non sarei andata mai in Casa d'una Dama, senza esserne stata invitata. Riguardo a ciò, che concerne al viaggio ho capito che egli voleva risparmiarne la spesa, e cosi andavo bilanciando se dovevo caricarmene.

Dopo alquanti giorni egli venne a portarmi una lettera di sua Madre, che pareva la risposta d'un'altra che egli li avesse scritto, nella quale lettera gli diceva, che era consolata che egli fosse divenuto bastevolmente discreto per essere amesso alla compagnia d'una Dama si rispettevole qual'io fossi. Mi faceva mille complimentosi ringraziamenti, e mi pregava di passare in casa sua come se fosse stato il più grande onore che io li avessi potuto fare.

Alla fine essendo molto bramosa di uscire d'Avignone io presi questo incontro come l'unico, che da longo tempo si era presentato. Io mi preparai a partire, feci le doute visite agli Amici, ed avendo ordinate le sedie di posta, la sera avanti la mia partenza il Conte mi disse che egli era veramente mortificato, ma che siccome tutti li suoi beni erano in mano di sua Madre e che avendo scarse rimesse era stato sforzato a far debiti, e che egli non poteva partire d'Avignone senza trecento zecchini de'quali egli mi averebbe fatto un biglietto e che sua Madre non averebbe potuto rifiutare di pagarli al nostro arivo. Io dubitai un poco a fare tale imprestanza, e viddi che egli metteva troppo alto il prezzo della scorta che mi voleva fare; nonostante avendo molte forti ragioni di lasciare Avignone li contai li *300* zecchini, e presi il suo biglietto. Confesso il vero che la sua scorta mi fu molto necessaria; noi siam stati obbligati di passare l'armata spagnola, ed è infallibile che se non fossi passata come Dama Veneziana col favore di sua Compagnia sarei stata certamente in grande pericolo.

Fui riceuta dalla Contessa Palazzi con tutta l'imaginabile politezza, ella mi parlò con confidenza e mi disse: che suo Figluolo aveva rovinato la sua Casa per le stravaganze fatte in Sassonia, e da ciò compresi, che non era d'umore di pagare li suo debiti, e così credei inutile di presentargli il biglietto d'Avignone. Ero sul dissegno di continuare il viaggio sino a Venezia quando mi sopragionse la febre maligna, quale mi aresto. Restai due Mesi nel letto dopo di che mi rimase una debbolezza, ed una depressione che credetti vero ciò, che li Medici mi dissero cione che l'aria della Campagna era assolutate necessaria per lo ristabilimento della mia sanità. Il Conte mi propose una sua Casa di Campagna; io consenti d'andarvi, benchè tanto debbole che convenne che fossi portata in un Branca; la Contessa Palazzi mi acompagnò. Ritrovai la Casa tanto mal concia, e rovinata, che se avessi saputo lo stato nello quale era, non vi sarei entrata giammai, ma non vi era più tempo di esitare. Mi misi a letto, e la febre mi riprese; mi fù dato la quinquina, e la mattina la febre mi lasciò, e così fui in stato di levarmi. La Contessa Palazzi mi fece mille scuse per la necessità ove ella si ritrovava di dovere ritornare a Brescia per certi affari importanti. Ella parti con suo Figluolo e pochi giorni doppo egli rivenne, e mi disse che sua Madre non poteva ritornare che dopo qualche tempo, ma che io ero padrona della sua Casa, e di tutto ciò che dipendeva da lui. La febre trattanto era divenuta intermittente: io dissi al Conte che io ero mortificata che madama Palazzi si fosse tanto incommodata per me, e che rimanevo confusa pensando all'imbarazzo ed alla spesa che ella aveva fatto per mia cagione, e lo pregai di dirmi naturalmente qual regallo li averei potuto fare che li fosse grato. Egli esitò qualche tempo e dopo molte cerimonie mi disse: che sua Madre era la Donna del Mondo la più interessata, abenchè molto ambiziosa e che se ella avesse riceuto qualche regalo da me si sarebbe creduta in dovere di farmene un'altro, e che sarebbe rimasta molto mortificata, ma che se mi fossi ostinata a fargli un pagamento ella non si sarebbe fatto scrupolo di ricevere danari contanti, qualora gleli avessi pagati secretamente, e che lui s'impegnava di fargleli ricevere. Gli diedi adonque duecento zecchini per questo effetto, ed egli parti la mattina (com'egli diceva) per portargleli.

Ricevevo trattanto molte visite di Dame delle vicinanze, la più parte delle quali eran parenti della Famiglia Palazzi. Venne la Contessa di Cigole, e mi fece mille cortesie. Ritrovavo trattanto che l'aria della campagna mi riusciva molto salutifero e speravo di perfettamente risanarmi in breve, benche non fossi ancora in istato di poter uscire della stanza. Il Conte Palazzi ritornò mi fece novi complimenti da parte di sua Madre, novelle scuse per non poter lasciar Brescia per venire a tenermi compagnia; era allora il Mese di

Novembre. Egli m'invitò a nome della Contessa di Cigole per mangiar l'oca di San Martino in Casa sua, ove sarebbe stato radunnato tutto il suo Parentado, e gll'Amici. Mi ripresentò, che questa buona Dama sarebbe restata molto mortificata se io non li avessi voluto far questo onore; che ella si sarebbe fatto il più grande piacere di ricevermi in Casa sua e che averei ritrovato le Persone più qualificate del Paese, che molto bramavano di vedermi. Io li risposi: che sarei stata molto consolata di far piacere alla Contessa di Cigole sua Zia, ma che temevo di arischiare la mia sanità, mentre la febre mi ritornava frequentemente. Egli mi rapr[es]entò che non era che due miglia lontana, che io avevo una Carossa ben chiusa, e che potevo andarvi vestita come volevo, che il giorno era bellissimo, e cosi aven-dovi consentito, ed essendomi involta in una Pelissa credetti potermi azardare d'espormi all'aria. Diedi ordine alla mia Camariera di non uscire dal mio Apartamento, e mi preparavo a sortire. Il Conte mi disse: che voleva la Moda del Paese che si conducessero le Donzelle per servire le Dame, e che se a Caso mi fossi ritrovata amalata, la mia mi sarebbe stata necessaria, e che il mio camariere mi doveva servire a tavola. Queste due sole Persone erano al mio servizio; e fù con mio grande spiacere che io lasciai la guardia della mia Camera a Persone, che io non conosceva; abenche egli mi dicesse che rispondeva della fedelta del suo camariere che sarebbe stato incaricato di custodirla, mentre non v'erano ne chiavi, ne sarature in Casa. Ritrovai a Cigole molte Personne di qualita ed un magnifico pranzo. Ora si pranzava in un Salone l'aria mi offese, mi venne freddo, e cosi fui obbligata di levarmi di tavola, e dimandai la Carossa per ritornare. Madama di Cigole usci con me, ne volle mai permettere che io ritornassi. Vi si ritrovò un medico, che avendomi toccato il polso, asseri che io avevo un gagliardo accesso, e mi con-segliò di mettermi a letto, quale mi fece riscaldare la Contessa con tutta l'imaginabile attenzione. Il Conte Palazzi parti con l'Abate suo Fratello, io restai a letto sino a due ore avanti il mezzo giorno, e dormi tranquillamente sul mattino, e quando mi risvegliai, il Medico mi ritrovò senza febre.

Volevo partire per non portare incomodo alla Contessa; il Conte Palazzi era venuto per ricondurmi ed io ritornai a Gottolengo. Restai sorpresa nel entrare nella Camera, vedendo molte cose mosse dal loro sito, ed intend-endo che il Camariere, che aveva auto la custodia era andato alla Caccia. Ricercai le casse delle mie gioie delle quali avevo le chiavi in scarsella, ed avevo messo le sudette casse in un sacco di velluto sotto il mio letto. Non ritrovai nè il sacco, ne il contenuto; feci avertire il Conte della perdita che avevo fatto, fingeva d'aver pena a crederlo, ma quando fu persuaso venne a gettarsi a miei piedi dileguandosi in lagrime non potendosi consolare, come diceva, del disonore arrivato alla sua Casa: io li risposi solamente, che bisog-nava procurare di ritrovarle, e la febre mi riprese, e mi rimisi al letto. La mattina seguente ritornò dicendomi: che aveva ricercato tutto il Castello in-utilmente, e che egli averebbe fatto delle perquisizioni all'intorno, ma che si richiedeva qualche danaro. Io li contai quaranta zecchini per fare queste pretese ricerche, e cosi egli usci a cavallo per ricercare li Ladri. Restò fuori tre' giorni dopi li quali mi racontò con lagrime e singhiozzi, che egli non aveva trovato alcuna traccia, e che se io non avevo pietà di lui, egli era un Uomo perduto; che egli sarebbe diventato l'obbrobrio di sua Famiglia; che sua Madre, essendo digià mal contenta di lui, si sarebbe servita di questo pretesto per disevedarlo; che egli aveva de'sospetti sopra l'Abate suo Fratello, che essendo un Uomo molto cattivo, avesse fatto questo colpo. Io li chiusi la bocca allora, e li dissi, che non doveva nutrire questi sospetti, e che senza prove dimostrative, doveva sepelirli in fondo del suo cuore, e conciderare: che egli poteva far torto ad un Ecclesiastico suo proprio Fratello. Oh Dio! rispose, piangendo amaramente, io sono matto, non sò ciò, che dico: abbiate pietà d'un miserabile, che si conosce disonorato per questo crudele accidente. Nonostante tutte queste sue dimostrazioni di dispiacere, non mi si levava un segreto sospetto, che egli medesimo fosse stato il Ladro, di che però io mi facevo un scrupolo di mostrarne la menoma idea, senza averne prima valide ragioni per confirmarlo, che io credevo che non averebbero potuto mancare in poco tempo, se egli era il colpevole: io mi imaginai, che egli averebbe prese le sue misure, e che egli sarebbe ritornato in Polonia, ove con le mie gioie si sarebbe fatto un Equipiaggio. All contrario lo vedevo andare sempre e ritornare disperandosi, e volendo far dare la corda a'Domestici, se io l'avessi permesso.

Madama Roncadelli sorella di Suo Padre venne a visitarmi; questa è una vecchia Dama rispettabile che era vissuta con onore, ed era in stima di santità: ella pianse al mio letto, e m'obbligo di darli una lista delle mie gioie, che ella volle inviare a tutti li Gioillieri d'Italia. Io lo credetti inutilissimo, mi lasciai però vincere dalle sue importunità, e gle ne dettai una, non essendo in istato di scrivere, avendo attualmente la febre, e per questo ragione una tale lista fù imperfetta, benche vi fossero notati li capi principali. Madama Roncadelli la fece stampare, e l'inviò in tutte le più grandi Città. Io hò conosciuto tanto candor e buon procedere nella sua condotta, che io ho preso una vera stima per lei, ed ella mi ha dimostrato sempre grande amicizia. La quinquina mi levò la febre, ma l'Inverno era tanto avanzato, e la mi sanita tanto debbole, che mi viddi sforzata a restare a Gottolengo sino la Primavera con mio grande spiacere. Comperai un antica poltrona molto cattiva che mi fu fatta pagar ben cara; il conte mi asseri che era unica in tutto il vilaggio, e che non v'erano che careghe di Legno in casa. Feci mettere delle serature alle porte, e vetri alle finestre; mi lamentai dell'umidità de muri. Il Conte mi disse, che un certo Conte Martinengo voleva vendere le sue vecchie tapizzerie, ma non voleva dividerle. Mi rincresceva di caricarmi di si grande quantità, ma li miei mobili erano ancora in Avignone, ed ero molto incomodata dal freddo. Feci adonque una tale spesa, e feci coprire tutta la casa, e vi soggiornai comodamente.

La mia sanità si andava giornalmente rinvigorendo; tutti vantavano la buontà e veramente credevo doverne essere contenta, nonostante risolsi di partire il mese d'Aprile, non volendo far racomodare una Casa, che mi sarebbe costata come una nova fabrica. Trattanto tutti li Parenti del Conte venivano a ritrovarmi, ed egli si serviva de miei Cavalli, ed andava, e veniva, lo che io permettevo come un piciolo vantaggio, che non valeva la pena di rifiutare. Quando li dichiarai il dissegno di partire egli riprese a fare il disperato, dicendomi che io lo perdevo d'onore, e lasciavo una macchia eterna alla sua Famiglia. La sua condotta mi pareva cosi pazza in tutte le cose, che io perdetti il sospeto della sua furberia, e lo concideravo come degno di pietà. Mi credetti ancora obbligata in qualche maniera a riparare una disgrazia che gli era succeduta per mia cagione, benche fosse per sua propria imprudenza. Si faceva vedere la grande spesa che si richiedeva per rendere abitabile la sua casa, e che non vi era giardino, quale è necessario ed agradevole per una Casa di Campagna.

Poche sere dopo questa conversazione venne a dirmi: che egli aveva fatto un ritrovamento, che poteva in qualche maniera riparare il danno arivato, che un vecchio Prete moribondo voleva vendere una sua picciola serra per pagare li suoi debiti, che io l'averei auta bon mercato, col permettergli d'occupare la casa sua vita durante, che eravi un grande Giardino, che poteva essere abellito secondo il mio gusto, che era assai vicino al Castello per servire a tutti li bisogni, e che in ogni caso lo potevo vendere con vantaggio ogni qual volta avessi voluto. Io feci esaminare queste cose da persone abili, andai io stessa e trovai il luogo assai bello, e lo comperai per ottocento zecchini in contanti. Mi divertii a piantarlo, ed avrò speso per un tal luogo duecento altri zecchini: ciò fù nell'anno *1747*. Lo che feci, benche non fossi determinata di fissare il mio soggiorno in Gottolengo. Avevo lasciato il mio grosso bagalio in Avignone in casa del Vice Legato, credevo molto difficile il farlo venire in tempo della Guerra, ed aspettavo la pace per farlo trasferire, incerta ancora dove dovessi restare. Io mi acostumai insensibilmente alla solitudine di Gottolengo, mi divertivano le passeggiate, l'aria m'era giovevole, e mi lasciai indurre ad agiustare la vecchia casa. Il Conte ritornò da Brescia ove aveva veduto, come diceva, il Signor Bettoni grande mercante, che andava in Avignone; diceva che il Signor Bettoni aveva grandi obbligazioni alla sua casa e per questo si comprometteva di far venire il mio Bagaglio. Io conoscevo la riputazione del Signor Bettoni, e non dubitai del suo credito, e venendo molto pregata dal Conte, li permisi d'incaricare il Signor Bettoni di tale comissione. Arivò il mio Bagaglio in pessimo stato; mancavano molti pezzi de miei mobili, de miei vascellami, e quattro belle tabacchiere, delle quali una era incrostata di diamanti, e di rubini. Ero molto mal contenta di questo, ed il Conte rassembrava arrabiato; malediva tutti li mercanti come Ladri, e si oferse con ogni onestà di far dare un archibuggiata al Signor Bettoni. Risi di questa sua esagerazione, e lo pregai di non attaccare il credito d'un Negoziante cosi acreditato, e che senza fallo ciò era succeduto per colpa, o per negligenza di qualcuno de suoi Agenti.

Io credetti così, ed andavo divertendomi co miei Libri, quali trovai tutti sani, e salvi, e pagai 200 zecchini che il Conte mi richiese a nome del Signor Bettoni per le spese del trasporto. Il Conte mi assegnò la sua Casa di Gottolengo con scrittura in presenza de Testimoni, ed io la feci riparare, ed acrescere, e feci mobigliarla co' miei Mobili. Due mesi dopo venne da Brescia con la gioia dipinta sul viso. Dio sia lodato, mi disse, io ho ritrovato l'occasione di riparare, almeno in parte, la perdita, che voi avete fatta in Casa mia, che si rapresenta sempre al mio spirito accompagnata d'orrore. Vi è un Vecchio Caducco a Trenzano, poche miglia lontano da Brescia, quale non ha' Figliuoli; egli mi ha' offerto di vendere li suoi Beni per un vitalizio di mille, e seicento zecchini per anno. Egli ha nonant'anni. Lo che sarà verificato dal registro del suo Battesimo di cui vi portevà l'attestato; le sue terre vagliono almeno settantamilla ducati; io le ho' fatte esaminare, ed estimare da genti perite in questa professione. Le ho' vedute, e ne sono inamorato. Questo povero decrepito non potrà vivere che sei mesi, e il soprapiù sarà per voi. Io li risposi che non ero una Persona avida de Beni, e che non volevo imbarazzarmi di terre in un Paese straniero. Allora egli grido: che volevo levargli il solo mezzo di redintegrare le mie gioie, e che in facendomi questo servizio, averebbe fatto vedere, che egli non era capace di farmi torto; che egli s'adulava che averei auto questa Carità per un Miserabile che bramava morire per riparare il suo onore, e che egli aveva assicurato il Signor Castelli, che io averei accettato questo mercato, che egli sarebbe venuto a Gottolengo la mattina dopo con l'istrumento solo da sottoscrivere, e che se io l'avessi fatto mancar di parola, io averei dimostrato un sospetto tanto ingiurioso per lui, che sarebbe divenuto la favola di tutto il Paese, e principalmente di sua Madre che si era vantata di avere ritrovato il mezzo di riparare la perdita delle mie gioie.

Castelli (ò pur qualch'altro che si chiamava tale) arrivò. Quest'era un Vecchio tutto bianco, curvo e tramante; portò con lui la stima de'suoi Beni segnata da'Stimatori publici, e l'istromento col quale li vendeva alle sudette condizioni. Io lo segnai in presenza del Nodaro di Gottolengo, e di due testimoni, e pagai la prima ratta anticipata. Lo che fù nell'anno 1749.

Continuai nella solitudine a trattenermi co' miei Libri, e col Giardino. Il Conte veniva rare volte del che ero molto contenta, perche egli rovinava li miei Cavalli, e rompeva le mie sedie. Nel Mese di Marzo 1750 presi uno sfredimento al passeggio, la febre mi sopravenne con accidenti molto fastidiosi. Feci venire de Medici da Brescia, e da Cremona, e mi ricuperai con grande pena molto lentamente. Il Conte venne a ritrovarmi, e mi portò mille complimenti da parte di sua Madre, assicurandomi che sarebbe venuta ella stessa a servirmi, se non averse auto la sanità molto cagionevole, e se le strade non fossero state rotte da piogge eccessive, onde non ardiva azardare.

Due giorni dopo egli richiese d'entrare in mia Camera. Con un'aria di spavento, mi disse: che egli aveva riceuto un espresso inviato da sua Madre, per informarlo, che era stato representato al Podestà di Brescia, Angelo Contarini, che egli mi riteneva Prigioniera nel suo Castello, che ciò veniva senza alcun fallo da Rodenghi, antichi Nemici di sua Casa, e che si trattava della perdita di tutta la sua Famiglia, e mi suplicò con le lagrime agl'occhi di salvarlo. Io li risposi, che non vi era cosa più giusto, ne douta, e che io ero pronta a disponere che io restavo volontariamente, e che egli non mi aveva giammai mancato di rispetto. In fatti due ore doppo arivò un Officiale del Podestà, che aveva ordine di parlarmi a solo.

Mi ritrovò sopra la mia Carega, ancora debbole per la passata malattia; io l'assicurai, com'era vero, che io non avevo riceuto che politezze dalla Casa Palazzi, ed io stessa scrissi al Signor Contarini per ringraziarlo della sua attenzione, e nel medesimo tempo, per ripettergli le medesime testimonianze. Il Conte andò a Brescia, e ritornò due giorni dopo con una Letica che sua Madre mi mandava, pregandomi di grazia di andare in Casa sua, per aquiettare tutti li falsi strepiti che correvano ancora, e che la mia sola presenza poteva soprimere. Il medico m'assicurò, che io potevo fare il viaggio senza pericolo, ed io lo feci in tanta debbolezza, che la mia Donzella mi sosteneva nella Letica; ed il Conte e l'Abate suo Fratello mi condussero con pena nell' Apartamento, che mi era destinato. Ritrovai in Casa Loro la Signora Roncadelli loro Zia, loro Madre, e loro Sorella, che di presente è Monaca. Mi fecero ogni possible onore e politezza, dormi bene, e la mattina fui in istato di ricevere visite. Fui adonque visitata da grande numero di Dame e Cavalieri; ridevo sopra l'idea d'essere ritenuta in Gottolengo per violenza, e mi rassembrava molto naturale, che una Donna della mia età ricercasse il ritiro, e cosi lo dicevo a tutti coloro, che vedevo.

Tutta la Famiglia mi pregò di restare a Brescia sino all'arivo del novo Podestà, che si aspettava di giorno in giorno, acciò ripettessi a lui la stessa cosa.

Consenti tanto più volentieri a questo, quantoche la Signora Gradenigo era la Podestaressa; io bramavo molta di rivedere una Dama a cui ero doverosa di molte cortesie riceute in Venezia. Mi ritornarono le force; ma il Dottore Guadagni, vecchio Medico, mi consigliò di prendere l'aque calibeate; mi fù detto che ven erano a Lovere, ed io mi preparai per andarvi dopo aver fatto li miei complimenti alla Signora Giustiniana Gradenigo. Il Conte faceva le su passeggiate secondo il suo solito; venne, e mi disse che eravi un Palaggio bellissimo, ed un Giardino d'un perfettissimo gusto, che averei potuto aquistare con poco. Mi pregava di andare almeno a vederlo. Non ho voluto sentir parlare di questo, e facevo tutta la premura per andare a Lovere.

La Sera avanti la mia partenza il Conte mi averti, che io dovevo passare un Bosco molto pericoloso, e che se io avevo del danaro averei fatto bene a lasciarlo nelle mani d'un Banchiere; mi racomandò molto il Signor Francesco Ballini; diceva che suo Padre aveva fatto la sua richezza e che riguardava loro come suoi Padroni: per altro era un Uomo d'una conosciuta probità, e d'una grande richezza. Io chiesi di vederlo, egli mi rispose che aveva la gotta; ma che egli li averebbe portato il dannaro, e mi averebbe consegnato il biglietto. Veramente mi sono scordata precisamente della somma consegnatoli, ma mi pare fossero duecento zecchini. Io parti; il Conte volle venire ad acompagnarmi. Le Dame mi fecero visite di partenza, e di desiderio per lo ristabilimento di mia salute, quali infatti intieramente fù ristabilita per favore dell'aqua, e della bon'aria di Lovere.

Vi ritrovai un luogo molto gradevole abitato da Genti onorate, e vi averei fatto più longo soggiorno se avessi potuto ritrovare una Casa più commoda, ma io ero tanto male alloggiata che mi lamentai col mio Medico il Dottor Baglioni, e gli dissi: che io non averei mai potuto risolvermi a ritornarvi la Primavera se egli non poteva ritrovarmi qualche Casa; egli la ricercò longo tempo inutilmente. Alla fine poco avanti la mia partenza mi disse che ve'n era una da vendere picciola, e mal in ordine, e che per questo sarebbe stata venduta per trecento scudi, ma che io averei potuto aumentarla, ed acomodarla; era posta sopra il lago, ed aveva una bella prospettiva. Diedi al Dottor Baglioni un biglietto nel Ballini per questo danaro con ordine di comperarla.

Trattanto il Conte venne da Brescia, e ciò fù nel tempo che io volevo partire da Lovere. Io credetti dover passar per Brescia non sapendo che vi fossero altre strade per ritornare a Gottolengo, ma egli mi fece passare per altro cantone per evitare, come egli diceva, certi cattivi passi. Egli mi condusse a vedere il Palazzo di cui mi aveva parlato quale era a Solferino, quale ritrovai tanto bello come lo aveva dipinto. Confesso che ne fui sorpresa, e mi informo, che era stato confiscato dall'imperatrice Regina, e che se io avessi scritto al Generale Stampa, sarei stata senza fallo favorita della vendita. Lo che feci, e dipoi passa a Gottolengo, avendo passato tra Gottolengo, e Solferino sino al Mese di Maggio 1754.

Avevo sovente desiderato di fare un viaggio a Venezia per vedere gli Amici, che vi avevo. Feci venire Cavalli di Posta da Brescia per tre volte a questo dissegno, e ne fui ditornata per diversi motivi: che talora le strade erano incommodate da truppe di Banditi, che v'erano de torrenti impassabili, e qualche volta col pretesto di malattie contaggiose nelli Alberghi. Se il Conte mi avesse fatti questi raconti io gli forsi stimati falsi, vedendo chiaramente l'avantaggio che egli aveva del ritenermi a Gottolengo; ma egli non vi era, era il Medico, il Parroco, e tutti coloro a quali io parlavo, quali tutti m'assicuravano della medesima cosa. Mi furono contate parimenti mille istorie di Casa sorprese, e de Padroni, che erano stati amazzati, e mi si fece tanta paura, che io fui determinata a non tenere nient'altro apresso di me, che il dannaro necessario per la spesa corrente della Casa.

Il Conte mi conseglió di rimettere tutto ciò che mi veniva d'Inghilterra tra' le mani del Signor Ballini, quale averebbe auto attenzione per le mie lettere di cambio, e mi averebbe reso un conto esato, e fedele. Lo che feci, ed egli mi mandò la sua riceputa di duemilla, e quattrocento lire sterline. Ero sempre determinata d'andare a Venezia; feci impachettare li miei Bauli, e non attendevo che la bella staggione. Il Conte venne per racolgere le sue entrate, egli aveva auto una grande malattia come diceva, ed in effetto v'era l'aparenza, mentre era stroppiato de piedi, e delle mani. Fu portato in un picciolo Apartamento lontano dal mio, ove egli rimase nel letto. Due mesi doppo quando io pensavo di venire a Venezia, essendomi ritrovata tardi al passeggio, fui sorpresa da una flussione sopra la guancia, quale divenuta molto infiata m'impediva di dormire, accompagnata essendo da un poco di febre. Il Conte mi mandò il suo Medico, quale mi assicurò che io ero pericolosamente amalata; io mi feci beffe di lui, e non volli prendere alcuno rimedio; abenche il mio male continuasse, e mi facesse molto soffrire. Io viddi due giorni doppo arivare in Posta il Dottore Baglioni di Lovere. Il Conte mi mandò a dire per la mia Donzella che mi dimandava perdono della libertà, che si era presa, ma che il suo Medico l'aveva assicurato che io ero malissimo, e che io non avevo alcuna confidenza in lui, e che perciò aveva fatto venire il Dottore Baglioni, di cui io avevo altre volte sembrata contenta.

Ella si servi di questo per esaggerare l'attenzione, che il Conte aveva di mia salute, del che non dubitai, sapendo che la mia vita gli era molto profittevole. Il Dottore Baglioni mi giurò che io ero in grande pericolo, che se la flussione fosse caduta sopra il petto sarei morta in due giorni, e che dovevo incominciar a guarire col cangiar aria, che quello di Venezia mi sarebbe stato tutt' afato contrario, che io avevo la mia picciola Casa di Lovere in ordine per entrarvi, che io avevo digià provata la buontà dell'aria, e che egli m'averebbe acompagnata. Alla fine egli mi persuase di partire con lui la mattina seguente. Io ritrovai la Casa apena abitabile ma la mia flussione fù risanata in poche giorni.

Egli mi persuase a prendere le aque, e li bagni; me ne trovai molto bene, e veggendo che bisognava restarvi qualche Mese, io mi divertii ad agiustare la Casa, ed avevo formato dissegno d'agrandirla, perche ero allora obbligata di far alloggia fuori li miei Domestici. Misi il dissegno in mano d'un Uomo molto onorato, pratico di fabriche, e mi facevo un piacere di vederlo ad eseguire. Passeggiavo spesso in barca sopra il Lago, e godevo d'una sanità perfetta. Baglioni ne parlava come d'un Miracolo, e diceva sovente, che se il Conte avesse voluto venire, e confidarsi in lui, abandonando gl'Ignoranti che egli praticavà egli averebbe ricuperato la sanità. Il Conte venne il Mese d'Agosto, ed entrò in una Casa vicina alla mia, ove il Baglioni li aveva trovato un Apartamento. Andava apena sopra li bastoni, e veggendolo in questo stato mi faceva pietà. Mi disse aver riceuto una lettera dal Signor Hermann, Banchiere della Duchessa di Guastalla, scritta per ordine suo, per dirgli, che ella aveva ordinato alcuni mobili, e vascellami in Inghilterra, e che se lui avesse potuto ottenere da me qualche biglietto di cambio per quel Paese li sarebbe stato di grande piacere. Egli m'aveva frequentemente parlato di questa Principessa della quale egli pretendeva esserne il Favorito, e mi diceva, che egli passava la più parte del suo tempo alla sua Corte; egli mi aveva invitato più volte in suo nome. Io dubitai del grand favore di cui si vantava, ma non averei mai creduto che egli avesse auto l'ardire di servirsi del suo nome senza fondamento, ed ero molto contenta di fare a questa Principessa un cosi piciolo serviggio. Li diedi biglietti di cambio per il valore di duemilla zecchini, che promise di farmi pagare a Venezia, o pure ove avessi voluto passare l'inverno. Il Dottore Baglioni insisteva sopra la necessità di prender il latte d'Asina per due Mesi; e vennero grandi pioggie sul finire dell'autunno, e la staggione si fece si rigida che mi fù persuaso facilmente il periglio d'intraprendere un viaggio, e cosi non sapendo far meglio io restai a Lovere. Avevo fatto mettere un forno nella mia Camera, avo fatto portar Libri, e mi contentavo della Conversazione di quelle Poche Persone che venivano a ritrovarmi. Il Conte diveniva ogni giorno più amalato. Era sempre circondato da Medici, e da Chirurghi.

Al cominciare dell' anno 1755 mi mandò a dire tal Dottor Baglioni, che egli aveva preso un secretario, quale aveva la riputtazione d'un grande sapere, e di molta probità, che egli si lusingava che mi sarebbe stata gradevole la sua conversazione; il Dottore aggionse che egli lo aveva racomandato sul riflesso che era veramente un amazzare se stessa lo continuo studiare, che io facevo. Io gli risposi, ridendo, che io non ero mai meglio, che quando ero sola, che io non studiavo, ma mi divertivo, che ero nonostante consolata, che egli avesse ritrovato un uomo onesto, non avendo giammai veduto che meschini al suo serviggio.

Era il Dottor Bartolomeo Mora quegli di cui mi parlava, quale arrivò il giorno doppo. Ritrovai in questo Uomo, spirito, ed erudizione, e conobbi in lui un carattere dolce, e sincero. Avevo cessato da qualche tempo di pagare la rendita vitalizia al Castelli, temendo di pagare di più di quello valeva il suo terreno; avertii il Conte del mio scrupolo, quale mi confessò con un aria di franchezza, che poteva essere benissimo, che fosse stato ingannato, e che conveniva che questo vecchio Ruffiano (questo era il suo stile) morisse presto, e che a tutto peggio, io averei auto li miei dannari, come un credito. Non mi fidai al suo parere, ma feci vedere il contratto al Dottor Mora, quale l'esaminò, e mi disse, come era in effetto, che era troppo apparente, che ero stata ingannata e non dubitava che io potessi legitimamente ridimandare il mio dannaro.

Il Conte intanto menava la vita la più ridicola del mondo. Il Dottor

Baglioni mi racontava cento belle istorie, e mi averti seriosamente, che egli temeva, che diventasse matto. Teneva academia di gioco in Casa sua; m'invitò di venire alla sua Bassetta, ma non vi andai.

Il mese di febraro mi preparai per la partenza. La mia prima Camariera che avevo condotto da Francia divenne amalata gravemente, come mi veniva asserito. Ella mi era necessaria per il viaggio, ed io volevo aspettare il suo risanamento, quale fù ben lento; ella non si risannò che dopo un Mese. Il Mese di Marzo è tanto rigido in quel Paese di Montagne che io ascoltai il consiglio del Dottor Baglioni che mi vietava sotto pena della vita di mettermi in viaggio, e quando io pensai di partire il Mese d'Aprile, mi sopravenne un'indisposizione, che me lo rese impossibile. Mi continuò la diarea senza intiera continuazione, sei settimane. Il Conte mi fece intendere che andava all'aque di Bormio per ordine de Medici, e mi pregò umilmente di ricevere il suo Addio su' la riva. Lo viddi andar in Barca, e gli desiderai il buon viaggio, e lo ristabillimento di sua salute. Quando la mia fù ristabilita pensai dal mio canto a partire. Il Dottore Baglioni mi disse che li scoli delle nevi avevano rotto le strade a un ponto tale, che averei ritrovato de precipizi impraticabili in sedia, ma che egli s'impegnava di ritrovarmi una Letica, che averebbe fatto venire da Bergamo. Questa Letica era venuta con un grande Signore in Milano, e si aspettava di giorno in giorno il suo ritorno in Bergamo. Alla fine di scusa in scusa, al dispetto di tutti gli miei sforzi per uscire, v'ero ancora quando il Conte ritornò, come egli diceva, da Bormio. Rassembrò sorpreso di ritrovarmi, e ciò era nel mese di settembre; io m'ostinavo a partire per Venezia, ed egli mi pregò d'una maniera somessa di passare per Gottolengo per prendere la consegna de mobili, che vi avevo lasciati quasi in abandono per la mia improvisa partenza. La mia camariera mi ripresentò che era necessario, che ella impachettasse le biancarie. Il giro non era molto longo, e mi fù persuaso di farlo. Il Conte volle venire al mio dispetto ad acompagnarmi; mi disse che le strade erano mal sicure per li Ladri, e benche la sua scorta personale non valesse niente, essendo portato in un Brancard, l'aparenza però d'un grande seguito averebbe impedito d'essere attacati, che altresi richiedevano li suoi affari che egli rivedesse le sue terre. Partissimo adonque, ed io volevo passare per Brescia per abocarmi col mio Banchiere Ballini, che non avevo per anche veduto. Quando fossimo ad Iseo, il Conte rassembrava malinconico, perche diceva essersi rotto un Ponte, e che eravamo obbligati a passare per Delo, ove noi restassimo dieci giorni per la grande pioggia, quale aveva inondata la Campagna. Arivassimo sul finire d'Ottobre in Gottolengo. Io pensai di restarvi che due giorni, e proseguire il mio viaggio, ma la pioggia continuvò, e questo Paese, che è paludoso era si fangoso, che mi lasciai persuadere, che non si poteva uscire. Rimandai li Postiglioni co' loro Cavalli di Posta, pagando ancora quelli del Conte, ed altresi la polizza delle spese del viaggio, che era molto stravagante. Li passai questa scroccheria, come avevo fatto molte altre; lo credetti provero, e lo vedevo stolto, e credevo che anch'egli venisse ingannato, quando anch'egli m'ingannava. Egli diventò più amalato che mai, e si ritenne in letto quasi due Mesi. Facevo chiedere qualche volta come stava, e l'ordinaria risposta era: che la porta era chiusa. Mi mandò a dire, che un Negoziante suo Amico, di cui egli rispondeva, sen andava in Inghilterra, che se io avessi auto qualche cosa a spedire, l'averebbe consegnato in mano propria della Persona a cui io l'avessi adirizzata. Mi sovenne d'un anello, che era il solo che mi restava delle mie gioie, avendolo auto nel ditto, quando mi furono rubbate le altre; lo sugellai in una scatola, e l'inviai a mia Figliuolina, quale fù renduto fedelmente per mano del Signor Prescot.

Pochi giorni dopo una lettera del Duca di Portland mi significò la Morte di Madama Madre di sua Moglie, mia vicina Parente, e cara Amica. Ella mi aveva fatto un Legato per ricordanza di quattrocento zecchini. La sua morte mi aflisse si sensibilmente, che io parlavo della mia aflizzione a tutti coloro, che vedevo. Il Conte m'inviò per sua parte complimento di condoglienza.

Un Mese dopo egli si fece portare nella mia Anticamera per dirmi che quel medesimo Negoziante, che mi aveva si fedelmente servita suo Amico, e servitore, aveva bisogno di certa somma de danari in Londra che egli mi averebbe rimesso in Gottolengo. Resi[s]tei alle sue importunità, ma avendo per un Mese di seguito continuato, scrissi un biglietto al Duca di Portland per pregarlo di contare li quattrocento zecchini a chi averebbe presentato il biglietto per mio uso.

La Primavera era avanzata, ed io mi preparavo per fare il viaggio di Venezia, e fù allora che io conobbi che ero Prigioniera. Si servi di tutta sorte d'invenzioni per farmi restare: le mie sedie erano rotte, li miei Cavalli stroppiati, la mia Camariera amalata, li fiumi esalveanti. Nel tempo che si facevano questi raconti ebbi la fortuna di ricevere la visita del Generale Grem, Parente di mio Genero, quale era stato pregato da mia Figlia a ricercarmi, non avendo auto nove di me, abenche io scrivessi quasi tutte le settimane. Mi lamentavo anch'io del suo silenzio ed erano molti mesi che non avevo lettere d'Inghilterra, ed incominciai a sospettare, che venissero intercette.

Il Conte si era fatto portare a Cremona e mi ritrova imobile a tutte le machine che egli aveva adoperato per farmi restare a Gottolengo, e che mi beffavo del medico, che mi minacciava di morire per strada. Egli si propose un altro stratagema. Mi fece pregare per un certo Prete suo favorito, chiamato Don Geronimo Zarza, d'entrare per un Momento nella sua Camera, che egli mi chiedeva perdono di questa libertà, ma che non era in istato di levarsi. Aggiunse il Prete che era stato travagliato per tutta la notte da'dolori violenti, e che egli credeva, che forse vicino il suo finimento. Io ritrovai nel suo Letto sostenuto da Cucini con un volto pallido, e sfigurato. Fece segno a Don Geronimo di restare alla Porta, e mi disse con voce bassa, che si richiedeva un grande secreto in tali affari, che egli credeva di poter ritrovare le mie Gioie, quali erano state impegnate ad un grande Ecclesiastico Parente del Papa, e che bisognavano dodecimila zecchini per riscuoterle. Questo raconto mi pareva si ridicolo, che mi fece ridere; gli risposi che non avevo auto mai gioie di tale prezzo, e che forse gli averebbe cavato qualche zecchino sotto questo pretesto, e che era longo tempo, che avevo abandonnate queste ricerche, e che non averei dato un soldo per tali informazioni. Sortii ridendo, credendo che il pover'uomo si fosse sognato, oppure che avesse ritrovato questa bella invenzione per ritardare il mio viaggio, col pretesto di aspettare nove da Bologna.

Il doppo pranzo si fece portare nella mia Anticamera, e mi ripresentò piangendo il poco riguardo, che avevo al suo onore mille volte più caro, che la sua vita, che averebbe datti tutti li suoi beni, presenti, e futturi per levare questa macchia dalla sua Famiglia; che le mie gioie erano impegnate ad una Marchesa di Bologna grande Dama, e Parente del Papa, che essendo stato moribondo il Ladro, l'aveva rivelato in Confessione, e che il Monaco, che era stato incaricato di fare la restituzione era attuale in Casa, ma non voleva essere nommato. Mi pregò in grazia di vederlo; vi consenti tutta stordita da questa istoria. Il Conte si fece portare nella sua Camera, non potendo più sostenersi (come diceva). Mi mandò il Frate, quale io viddi con grande mio stupore avendo una valise, quale avevo veduto essere del Conte; egli l'aperse, e cavò fuori una bella Coperta ricamata venuta dall'India, e poscia cavò fuori molti altri capi, che credevo essermi stati rubbati dall'Agente de Signori Bettoni, una parte di fornimenti, la tabacchiera di diamanti e di rubini perduta nel tempo stesso, e poscia molte delle mie gioie rubbate due anni prima, che li miei mobili venissero d'Avignone, ma queste rotte, e nello stato in cui sono ancora. Viddi allora ciò, che dovevo credere e conobbi altresi il mio pericolo essendo in cosi cattive mani. Ocultai il mio pensiere al Frate, galantuomo, che dava la mano ad una tale furberia. Finsi d'essere contenta d'aver trovato le mie gioie, almeno in parte, ed esaminandole, vi ritrovai una grande Croce di Smeraldi intornata di piccioli diamanti, ed un anello di detta pietra che sembrommi ornamento di Vescovo. Io dissi: queste cose non sono mie; ma le voglio custodire sin tanto che veranno reclamate, essendo state rubbate.

Il Frate, che sempre tenne il suo viso coperto sotto il suo Capuccio, aveva molta difficoltà nel lasciarmi le mie gioie, ma gli parlai d'un tono, che non ardi di replicare, e retirossi mormorando. Un'ora dopo, il Conte mi mandò a dire che la Croce, e l'anello erano suoi; me li chiese, ed io li rendetti senza esitanza. Sulla sera mi mandò Don Geronimo Zarza per dirmi: che egli aveva impegnato tutti li suoi beni presenti, e futuri a questa Marchesa di Bologna per riavere le mie gioie, che egli temeva che ella ne prendesse il posesso, e che io ero obbligata sul punto d'onore di cavarlo da questo si difficoltoso passo, ove egli si era messo per zelo di servirmi. Io li risposi: che una tal Lite sarebbe stata si male fondata che non era da temersi, che sin'adesso nessuno aveva scapitato per farmi piacere, e che certamente egli non sarebbe stato il primo. Mandai a ricercare li Cavalli di posta, che arivarono molto tardi su la sera; proposi di partire la matina.

Il Conte mi fece dire, che gli Rodenghi, suoi Nemici, avevano sparso nel volgo che egli mi aveva trattenuta per forza e per minaccia in Gottolengo. Mi pregò di farli una lettera, per significare che io ero contenta del suo procedere verso di me. Compresi ciò, che bramava, e cosi glene scrissi una, che contenendo alcune verità, non soddisfaceva però tutte le sue brame; era, però, cosi polita, che egli non ardi di chiederne un'altra.

Allorche io l'ebbi scritta, Don Geronimo Zarza venne a dirmi (sembrando offeso di tale insolenza) che il Postiglione era annoiato di attendere alla mia Porta, e che egli era partito. Li feci correr dietro il Dottore Bartolomeo Mora, che ebbe bastevole spirito per comprendere il mio pericolo, e bastevole premura per procurare di salvarmi. Egli arrivò il Postiglione, e lo sforzò di aspettare gli miei ordini. Furono ventitrè ore avanti che potessi uscire della Casa.

Ritrovai il Conte nella Corte su la sua Carega quale vi si era fatto portare per dirmi L'Addio, lo che fece nella maniera la più rispettosa, benche egli procurasse di mettermi in timore per gli Banditti. Vedendo che nulla guadagnava, mi richiese per ultimo favore che pasassi per la Casa di Campagna della Signora Roncadelli, che m'invitava (come egli mi diceva) con grande premura, e che sarebbe restata molto mortificata, se io avessi lasciato il Paese senza vederla: che ella era tutt'afatto vicina di Pontevico, e mi fece ricordare dell'obbligazione che li avevo d'aver fatto stampare il Biglietto per la perdita delle mie gioie, e fatto spargare per tutta l'Italia, senza il quale sarebbero andate perdute per sempre. Li risposi che ne ero molto persuasa, e promisi volontieri di fargli visita.

Continuava Ballini a servirmi di Banchiere; avevo tenuto un conto esato con lui, ed egli aveva nelle sue mani più di quattromila zecchina. Il Conte mi chiedeva dove volessi che fossero pagati, ed io gli risposi: che avevo dissegno di passare per Brescia e che li averei lasciato li miei ordini. In questo ponto (egli soggiunse) mi scrive per informarmi: che essendo obbligato a pagare una considerabile somma in Londra, li farete un grande piacere di spedirgli un biglietto di cambio per quella Città. Io li risposi che gli averei parlato. Oh, gridò, mia Zia vi ama troppo per non permetteresi di partire che doppo qualche giorno, ed il bon uomo è molto pressato, e mi pare: che un poco di dannaro di più non vi sarà di peso in Venezia. Li feci un biglietto di quattrocento zecchini.

Partii adonque acompagnata dalla mia Damigella in Carossa, dal Dottor Mora, dal mio vecchio Camariere a Cavallo, dal mio Lacchè, a quali il Conte volle aggiongere alcuni Paesani armati, e dal suo fedele Don Geronimo Zarza a Cavallo per mia sicurezza. Il Postiglione mi condusse cosi male, e ritrovò, o finsè di ritrovare, le strade cosi cattive, che fù notte quando arivassimo alla villa di Fianello. Confessò il Postiglione, che non aveva mai fatto una tal strada, e mi disse che era peggiore andar avanti, e che egli mal volontieri si arischiava a condurmi. Don Geronimo mi disse: che io potevo dormire in Casa d'un Mercante d'Alfianello, e che era stato digià avertito in caso che io ne avessi auto bisogno, ed esaggerò molto questa attenzione.

Mi fermai, avendo perduto per strada il mio Camariere Svizzero, quale facilmente si era lasciato sedurre all'Osteria. La Casa mi parve onesta; ma entrandovi, la mia Damigella fu sopresa da vomiti si violenti, che ella non fù più in caso di servirmi. Fui sforzata di spogliarmi da me stessa; e Don Geronimo mi disse, che era obbligato di partir la mattina per andare alla Fiera di Brescia; mi chiese se avevo qualche cosa a comandarli. Li augurai il buon viaggio, ma lo pregai di portare una mia lettera a Ballini e che se egli avesse voluto partire avanti giorno averei scritto quella sera; egli mi suplicò di non affaticare gli miei occhi con candele, che egli sarebbe venuto alla mia colazzione e che poche ore bastavano per un cosi picciolo viaggio. La mia Donzella non potè dormire in mia Camera per cagione del suo male; il mio Camariere, che ritornò ubbriacco due ore doppo, si collocò nell'Anti-camera; li Preti dormirono assieme in basso. Avevo fatto fare due grandi scarselle di pelle: in una tenevo le cassette delle mie gioie, nell'altra un sac-chetto legato, ove avevo riposto le ricevute de Banchieri, quelle del Castelli, il suo Contratto, ed in somma tutte le mie carte di conseguenza.

L'agitazione del corpo, e dello spirito, per cui ero stata tanto travagliata, mi fece dormire profondamente. Avevo riposte le mie scarselle sopra una tavola, ove le ritrovai la mattina. Ero tanto contenta d'essere uscita di Gottolengo, che mi pareva d'essere in perfetta salute. Mi svegliai avanti tutti li miei Domestici, mi vestii, e feci svegliare li altri. Restai sorpresa quando il Dottor Mora m'averti, che Don Geronimo era partito due ore avanti giorno dopo avermi pormesso d'aspettare la mia lettera. Biasimai la sua rusticità, ed ordinai che fosero ataccati li Cavalli.

Il Dottor Mora ritrovò una rota rotta, allora conobbi essersi formato il dissegno di farmi restare; egli ebbe lo stesso sospetto. Fece venire un Maestro di legname, e fece fare un altra rota, e la fece mettere al dispetto del Postiglione, che parve mal contento di quest'opera, e ciò fu la sera avanti che io potessi partire, che partirono li Paesani, che mi erano stati dati per iscorta dal Conte. Lontano un miglio da Pontevico, mandai il mio Lacchè ad avertire Madama Roncadelli della mia venuta; apena egli fù partito che viddi venire di tutta forza un Sbirro, giovane Uomo con un grande Archibuggio, quale spavento il Dottore Mora, che era pochi passi avanti la mia Carossa. Venne alla finestra della mia Carossa con li occhi intorbidati, con li capelli radrizzati, e mi confessò dopo che egli aveva creduto d'essere al ultimo ponto del suo vivere. Mi presentò una lettera del Conte diretta a lui, nella quale vi era un mandato col sigillo della Republica, per il quale la

Marchesa Bolognese prendeva il posesso de tutti li suoi beni, e li scriveva, che per conservarli era stato sforzato di riscuotere il mio dannaro. Pregava il Dottor Mora d'ottenere il suo perdono, senza il quale sarebbe stato disonorato lui, e tutta la sua Casa, e che egli si sarebbe dato un colpo di pistolla. Quest'articolo era tanto sciocco, che doppo avere veduto tali carte, le gettai al Dottor Mora, gridando al Postiglione di andare avanti.

Pochi momenti doppo viddi arivare il bell'equipaggio della Marchesa Roncadelli con molti de suoi Domestici. Fui pregata per suo ordine di servirmene, facendomi scusa se non veniva ella stessa ad incontrarmi essendo indisposta. Nonostante la ritrovai sù la porta per ricevermi; ella m'abracciò con cordialità, e mi conduce in un Salone ove eravi un Cavaliere suo Amico Cremonèse.

Avevo la testa tutta ripiena dell'accidente del Sbirro e glela racontai naturalmente, dicendogli che non sapevo comprendere qual danaro il Conte poteva aver preso, non avendone io in sua mano; che li biglietti de miei Banchieri non erano pagabili che a me stessa, ed a mio ordine. Per mostrargleli, tirai dalla mia scarsella il sacchetto, ove li avevo riposti, con gli scritti de contratti delle terre, che avevo comperate e li ritrovai cangiati in carte bianche fatte sù la medesima figura di grandezza.

Madama Roncadella parve tanto offesa che me stessa; ella mi promise di far fare la restituzione, e mi chiese in grazia di restare in Casa sino all'arivo del suo infame Nipote. Egli arivò il giorno doppo su la sera, in tale abattimento, o vero, o finto, che si distese sul letto.

Madama Roncadelli mi pregò di ascoltarlo, ciò, che io rifiutai di fare che in sua presenza. Ella piangeva, e mi prese la mano, me la bacciò, e mi condusse nella Camera, ove egli era. Egli voleva fare un longo discorso con singhiozzi. Io gli tagliai tal sermone, e gli dissi: che io non ero venuta per ascoltar le sue scuse, ma che li dimandavo la restituzione delle mie carte. Sono brucciate (rispose piangendo) e quando non lo fossero, non vi sarebbero per questo più avantaggiose, mentre erano tutte false. Sua Zia sembrava di andare in svenimento, ed io sortii dalla Camera dicendo: Voi siete un Ladro indegno.

Mi richiusi in mia Camera, ove feci riflesso sopra il stato ove mi ritrovavo. La mia situazione mi pareva molto pericolosa; avevo buona opinione di Madama Roncadelli, che era una Dama universalmente stimata, mi credetti sicura in Casa sua. Ma bisognava far viaggio, e vedevo un Uomo disperato, capace d'ogni Crime, che teneva al suo servizio de scelerati d'ogni specie, e non dubitai che egli mi averebbe fatto amazzare su la strada se avesse creduto che lo avessi voluto perseguita per Giustizia. Presi la risoluzione di nascondere il mio resentimento in parte.

Ricevetti la Mattina, Madama Roncadelli con un volto tranquillo. Ella pianse amaramente; avevo una vera pietà della sua canizie. Mi protestò che non aveva chiusi gli occhi di tutta la notte, e mi scongiuro di ascoltare qualche accomodamento per salvare l'onore di sua Famiglia: che era impossibile che mi restituisse tutto il mio dannaro, quale lo aveva speso a Turino, a Milano, ed in molti altri Luoghi; e che ella non era bastevolmente ricca per redintegrarmi. Quando lo foste, Madama (l'interuppi) non sarebbe giusto che voi pagaste per le sue ribalderie. Io non vi dimando niente, e non prenderò niente da voi. Ella diede mille lodi alla mia generosità, e mi propose di fare novi istromenti per le terre della Fornace, e di Solferino. Riguardo alla Casa di Gottolengo, ella era fideicomesso. Io ero la Padrona di restarvi, ma se avessi voluto abbandonarla, era meglio permettergli d'occuparla per ascondere la sua vergogna in un Paese, ove li suoi Antenati erano vissuti con onore: che mi sarebbe s[t]ato reso il biglietto de quattrocento zecchini, che gli avevo dato avanti partire. Io li rimisi tutti gli miei interessi, e feci tutto ciò, che ella stimava a proposito. Io non uscivo dalla mia Camera, ove mangiavo sola un piatto. Vi erano grandi andate e ritorni di genti del parentado, ove non volevo essere a parte. Alla fine Madama Roncadelli mi averti: che il Conte, benche amalato, aveva fatto formare una scrittura che mi pregava di sottoscrivere, ed aveva preparato il dannaro del ultimo biglietto quale mi sarebbe stato contato con gli istromenti delle terre. Ella mi fece entrare il Nodaro che mi presentò la scrittura in presenza del sudetto Cavalier Cremonese, due altri de quali mi sono scordata il nome, ed il Dottor Mora.

Quando io l'ebbi letta vi ritrovai: che in termini oscuri mi confessavo d'aver vissuto dieci anni a sue spese. Io ruppi la carta in mille pezzi, dicendo altamente che mi volevano tradire villanamente. Il Dottor Mora mi si avicinnò tutto tremante, e mi disse con voce bassa: Madama siate meno focosa, e pensate al vostro pericolo. Li risposi alzando la voce: voglio piuttosto morire, che sottoscrivere una mensogna tanto infame, che mi disonora. La Dama e tutti gli asistenti sortirono confusi, ed io andai a letto.

La mattina ritornò chiedendomi perdono d'avermi fatto presentare una scrittura, che ella non aveva veduta, che ella ne avrebbe fatto fare un'altra, nella quale io permettessi di contentarmi della restituzione delle mie terre, e de quattrocento zecchini; che ella mi diede parola d'onore che avrebbe custodita, e che non sarebbe giammai stata remessa a suo Nipote, sinche non avessi la posessione delle terre. Fui contenta di sottoscrivere a queste condizioni, pensando che senza questo non averei giammai potuto uscire.

Finsi di scordarmi del passato, senza però vedere il Conte, quale mi fece dimandare per alcuna grazia di lasciarmi acompagnare sino a Mantova, ove egli aveva de Parenti. Gle lo permisi. Il Conte Ignazio suo Fratello m'acompagnò a Cavallo. Diedi un Addio eterno a Madama Roncadelli, che mi disse cento cose obbliganti, e tenere. Lasciai il Conte a Mantova in Letto, e seguitai il mio viaggio.

Fui sorpresa a Vicenza nel intendere che egli aveva occupata una Camera nell'Albergo, ove dovevo restare. Non mi giudicai in diritto di chiedergli ragione di questo, ed andai a Padova senza vederlo. Lo rincontrai un miglio lontano da questa Città, e mi fece dire, che mi aveva preparato un Aparta-mento. Io compresi che voleva ocultare al Publico li suoi cattivi procedi-menti, ed entrai nel medesimo Apartamento. Vi restai due, o trè giorni, ne quali io presi una Casa in Padova, e dopo andai a Venezia. Il Conte mi aveva ancora preparato un Apartamento; io vi restai tre giorni, e ritornai a Padova. Ove ritrovai il Conte che si era alloggiato in Casa mia nella Camera del Svizzero vicina alla Porta. Lo feci avertire che io non tenevo locanda, e lo pregai di partire. Gli dimandai che mi facesse dare li scritti delle mie terre, e mi dicesse il nome del Mercante, che aveva riscosso il Legato della Contessa di Oxford. Mi rifiutò l'uno, e l'altro, e partì per Gottolengo. Ritornò alcune settimane dopo, ma non mi ha' reso ne gli istromenti, ne mi ha' voluto dire chi abbia riscosso il dannaro dal Duca di Portland.

APPENDIX II

La Princesse Docile I

Textual note. MWM's French spelling and grammar do not match her remarkable fluency and wide vocabulary; but even Voltaire's letters show instances of, for instance, feminine adjectives qualifying masculine nouns. While obvious slips have been corrected, disagreements of gender or number are not usually marked with 'sic'.

Il y avoit une Reine de je ne scai quel Royaume très favorisée d'une vielle fée, sans trop de raison, car C'etoit peutêtre la personne du mond qui la meritoit le moins: mais il est assez ordinaire de voir le caprice ou le hazard decider de la faveur de Grands. La Nourice de la Reine etoit devenûe femme de chambre de la Fée. C'étoit un bon Coeur de Paysanne qui parloit eternellement de son éleve, sans autre raison que par le plaisir qu'elle trouvoit a rappeller les années de sa jeunesse, et par la vanité qu'elle sentoit d'avoir allaitée une Reine. Ses discours naifs avoient fait une si grande impression sur la Fée, qu'elle avoit accordé les grands entrées a la Reine qui étoit souvent au chevet de son lit, quand sa porte estoit refusée a tout ce qu'il y avoit de respectable, ou d'aimable sur la terre. Effectivement cette bonne femme avoit pris l'ascendant sur sa Maitresse, sans que l'une ni l'autre s'en aperçût. La Fee la grondoit toujours, et ne parloit jamais d'elle sans la qualifier de, cette pauvre radotteuse, pourtant comme c'étoit elle qui la veilloit quand elle étoit malade ou croyoit l'etre, et qui lui donnoit ses remedes, elle s'étoit insensiblement acquise le droit de dire tout ce qu'elle voulût, et ses jaseries continuelles faisoient plus d'effet sur l'esprit de la Fée, que la plus grande Eloquence n'auroit <pû> faire. Tout cela tournoit au profit de la Reine. La pauvre Nourice ignoroit son credit qu'elle auroit peut estre Employée a toute autre chose si elle l'avoit voulûe.

La conduite de la Reyne de Travers (c'estoit son nom) fortifiait beaucoup l'Idée que la Fee avoit pris de son Merite, elle y alloit tres rarement et disoit peu de chose. La fée accoutumée a voir que des gens qui lui demandoit [*sic*] des graces ou du secours et qui étois accablée tous les jours de dix mille placets, respiroit quand elle voyoit une personne qui ne lui demandoit jamais rien. Elle ne douttois pas que ce ne fut l'effet d'une grande modestie, ou d'un grand desinteressement. Il y avoit même des moments ou elle se flattoit de plaire a la Reine au point, de lui faire tout oublier par le charme de sa conversation; cette imagination l'avoit attendrie jusqu'a lui faire dire un soir qu'elle l'avoit aupres d'elle, Mon dieu madame que vous ettes differente de tous ceux que je voy. Vous ne pourez pas ignorer ma Puisance prèsque sans bornes. Au lieu de m'importuner comme mille autres, qui n'ont nulle raison de compter sur moi, vous ne m'avez jamais demandée la plus legere grace, malgre toutes les preuves de bien veillance que je vous ai donnée. Aussi suisje resolüe, pour la recompense de votre retenüe, de vous accorder la premiere chose que vous me demanderai.

Eh que voulez vous que je demande, repliqua La Reine d'un air visant sur l'impertinance? Je suis en habitude de faire des graces et non pas a en demander. Ne suis je pas la plus grande Reine du monde? (Elle ne l'etoit pourtant que d'une petite isle assez mal située.) Mon mari, qui est harangué tous les quinze jours, par des subjets pénétréz de sa sagesse (c'étoit le Roi Imbecile), a pour mes conseils toute la defference qu'il me doit. Je n'ai pas à me plaindre de la nature, ni pour la figure, ni pour l'esprit. (Elle étoit louche et bossue.) Je serois faschée d'avoir la taille droite et pincée d'une Bourgoise, et un regard equivoque convien a une Reine qui ne doit honorer personne d'un regard decidé. Joze dire que je suis encore plus distinguée par ma vertu, que par mon rang ou mes talents: ma severité ne s'est jamais demonti un seul moment de ma vie. (Il estois vrai que née sans gout, avec une imagination froide et un coeur dur, elle n'avoit jamais senti ni tendresse, ni Inclination.) La Fée qui commençoit d'ouvrir les yeux [sur] son Caractere, lui repondit d'un ton sec, Je vois bien que je puis peu de chose pour vostre service; il ne m'est pas permis de me dedire, ainsi je vous accorde telle demande que vous voudrez, mais je vous jure, foi de Fee, de ne vous en accorder jamais une seconde, quand même vous ne serai si contente de vous ou de vostre situation que vous ne parroisez a present. Vous ettes gross; n'aurièz vous rien a souhaitter pour vostre Enfant?

Je ne demande que la Docilité, repliqua la Reine. Quoy que les bien seances me permettent pas, de me fatiguer en l'instruisant moi mesme, je sçaurai lui choisir des gens de merite qui ne manqueront pas de le perfec-tioner, pourvû qu'il soit soumis a leurs leçons.

Allez, lui dit la Fee, je vous reponds d'une Docilité parfaitte; vous accoucherai d'une fille, et vous pouvez la nommer Hardiment, la Princesse Docile.

La Reine se retira fort contente d'avoir soutenüe son Rang, avec un hauteur convenable. La Fée se coucha en pestant contre sa sotte Femme de Chambre de lui avoir donnée une Connoisance si ridicule, et trois jours apres elle prit une autre Favorite de sa main, qui fût assez habile pour profiter de sa faveur et joüer un tres grand Role dans le Monde, quoy que son merite unique, estoit d'avoir un Laquais a son service qui plaisoit beau-coup a la bonne Femme de Chambre.

Mais laissons la Cour de la Fée, et retournons a celle de la Reine de Travers; qui accoucha d'une Fille extremement jolie. Toute sa Cour se tuoit a lui dire, qu'elle la ressembloit comme deux gouttes d'eau; elle en étoit si bien persuadée qu'elle resolût de ne rien negliger pour la rendre la

Princesse la plus accomplie de la Terre. A peine commençoit elle a parler, qu'elle lui fit aprendre 5 ou 6 Langues differentes. La pauvre enfant tachoit de les retenir touttes, et a sept anns elle ne sçavoit s'exprimer en aucune. Elle avoit naturellement l'oreille juste, et le son de la voix charmante. Cétoit un beau canevas pour la Reine; elle vouloit qu'elle aprit a la fois, a chanter dans le goût de toutes les nations, et a jouer de touttes sortes d'instruments. Elle lui donna une vieille fille pour Gouvernante; c'étoit une personne sans reproche, ayant été toute sa vie, d'une laideur respectable, Prude, devote, et sotte, à toute outrance. Elle avoit pour Coadjuteur un Hermite a barbe blanche, qu'on avoit arraché de son desert, ou (dans la meilleure foi du monde) il avoit passé trente anns a manger de Racines, et a estre mangé des Poux, en honneur de Dieux. Il avoit perdu un Bras, pour l'avoir eû etendu sur sa Tête dix anns de suitte, pour faire sa Cour a Brama dont il se croyoit Favori, en consideration de ce qu'il s'étoit fouetté regulierment deux fois par semaine, depuis d'age virile. C'étoit justement des personnes belles qu'on devoit les choisir pour instruire une Princesse destinée a regner.

Elle étoit née tres vive, elle avoit la memoire la plus heureuse, le Coeur parfaittement bien fait, et un grand fond de tendresse. On ne doit pas s'ettoner qu'etant douée de cette Docilité extreme, elle se donnât entierment aux sentiments de ses precepteurs. Obeir en tout, et ne raisonner sur rien, estoient les maximes fondamentales de son Education. Le bon Hermite pleuroit dix fois par jour, de voir l'heureux progress de ses preceptes; peu s'en manquoit qu'il ne la crût inspirée. Elle le devançoit dans les actes de Devotion, et d'austerité qu'il lui recommandoit, elle rencherissoit même sur ses Leçons. A l'age d'onze anns, elle se devoua a rester sept anns assise les jambes croisez en honneur de la Deëse Vichnou. Sa Governante effrayée de cette Resolution a la quelle elle ne s'attendoit pas, en avertit la Reine, qui étoit alors si occupée a élever des Sereins, qu'elle n'avoit pas vû sa fille depuis six mois. Elle entra dans son Apartement, et fût plus choquee encore de voir qu'elle ne se levoit pas pour lui rendre les respects qu'elle lui devoit, que de l'extravagance de sa Devotion. Elle commençoit par la traitter de Desobeissante, et ensuitte de Folle, et de Rebelle. La Princesse, deja pale et maigrie, par ses jeunes, faisoit une vraie figure de Pagode, ses cheveux épars, et mal peignée, sa Coiffure de travers, ses yeux baissez. Elle repondit d'un ton modeste, qu'elle estoit instruitte, que le premier Devoir éstoit envers les Dieux, que si elle plaisoit a Vichnou il lui importoit fort peu, de plaire aux autres, qu'elle voyait tres bien, que son Voeu étoit accepté, puis que la Deëse la jugeoit digne de souffrir des Persecutions, qu'elle regardoit comme de marques de la bonté de la Divinité touttes les Duretez dont il plaisoit a S. M. de l'accabler, qu'elle avoit toujours craint un chemin semé de Roses, qui ne mene qu'a une perte certaine, et que c'étoit par des épines qu'il falloit parvenir au vrai bonheur.

Elle étoit en train de nous donner un fort beau Discours sur la Mortification, si la Reine, qui étoit devenûe furieuse de voir qu'elle faisoit si peu de cas de son resentiment, ne lui eût ordonnée de se taire, et cela d'un ton absolu.[1] Elle se tourna vers l'hermite qui étoit la en extase des belles choses que disoit son Disciple. Voila vos raissonnemens de chien, s'écria t'elle, écoutez, si vous n'otez pas cette Folie a ma Fille en 24 heures, vous serez pendu mardi prochain; travaillez y, et si vous reussissez, je vous recompenserai par la permission de retourner dans vostre desert, ou vous mourez de faim si vous le trouvez bon.

Le pauvre homme étoit naturellement le plus grand Poltron du monde, et qu'oy qu'il eût dit souvent, qu'il étoit assuré de sa place au dessous le petit doigt du pied gauche de Brama, il n'étoit point de tout pressé de la prendre. Cet perspective de potence le fit trembler. La même poltronerie qui l'avoit rendu Saint, l'éloignoit extremement d'estre Martyr. Il se prosterna devant la Reine, en lui jurant que sa Religion exigeoit une Obeissance sans reserve, a tous ses ordres, et qu'il ne douttoit pas de convaincre la Princesse qu'elle ne pouvoit rien faire de [si a]greable aux dieux que d'obeïr [ave]uglement a une Reine parfaite, qui estoit [l'image] vivante de la Deëse. Il tourna si bien l'esprit de son éleve, qu'elle alloit le Lendemain de grand Matin se jetter aux Pieds de sa mere, pleurant amerement du chagrin qu'elle lui avoit causée. Elle n'osa demander le rappel de son cher precepteur; il n'en avoit pas trop d'envie lui même. L'Idée de Bourreau etoit encore dans sa Tête et il se crût plus en seurete parmi les Ours et les Loups qu'aupres d'une reine capricieuse et absolüe.

Il falut luy choisir un successeur, et la Reine déttera au fonds d'un College un Philosophe, bon Geometre, grand Mathematicien, soupsçonné d'etre peu orthodoxe, et même quelque chose de pis. Il avoit raillée sur plusieurs sujets de veneration, il parroisoit douter que le Grand Brama, tout grand qu'il étoit, pût plaire a la fois a soixante mille deesses, et il avoit écrit un Livre pour prouver que Vichnou ne s'étoit jamais metamorphosé en Poisson. Il est vrai qu'il avoit retracté ce livre et l'avoit laissé bruler avec un grand sang froid, mais on croyoit que c'étoit de Crainte d'estre brulé lui même, et on n'etoit pas bien persuadé qu'il fût sincerement penitent d'avoir donné naissance [a] la secte des [douteurs], qui menaceoit un schisme horrible qui faisoit trembler tous les vrais croyans. D'ailleurs, d'une grande Probité, d'une Morale austere, [on ne pouvoit lui reprocher que le manie de vouloir estre honnête homme sans que les dieux s'en mellassent], nouveauté que le Clergé estoit fort empressé de supprimer. La Reine lui recommenda de nettoyer la Cervelle de sa fille, et il trouva le tâche beaucoup plus facile qu'il n'esperoit. Elle aimoit a raisonner; c'estoit sa pente naturelle, elle ne l'avoit étouffée que par sa Docilité extreme. La Vertu telle

---

[1] The rest of this and the next three paragraphs have two slightly differing versions: words in square brackets are supplied from the probably earlier version.

que le Philosophe la representoit lui parroisoit plus pure et plus noble, que sous le fatras dont l'hermite l'avoit bercée. Elle étoit passionée pour la Lecture, et[1] devient infatigable pour l'étude.

Son Maitre charmé de ses dispositions pour les sciences, faisoit Compliment a la Reine sur le Genie surprenant de la Princesse. Elle en étoit peu flattée, n'ayant jamais fait grand cas du bel esprit; elle repondit sechement au Philosophe, qu'elle craignoit que ces Histoires, cette Geographie, et cette Philosophie, dont il parloit, ne la rendissent trop serieuse, et puis qu'elle vouloit lire il la devoit choisir de Livres divertissants. Elle a ses heures de recreations, repliqua t'il, ou elle aprends par Coeur le Telemaque. C'est encore de l'histoire, disoit la Reine d'un air fasché que ne permettoit point de reponse, je veux lui envoyer la Princesse de Cleves pour luy égayer l'esprit. Sa Gouvernante l'avoit deja donnée Pamela, pour lui former le Coeur. Bien tost la pauvre Princesse devient toute paitrie de Sentiments. Elle prenoit avec ardeur les Impressions du Heroisme, elle étoit enchantée de Telemaque surtout quand il voulût perir luy et tous ses amis, plustost que de desavouer son Nom, (sans faire refflection qu'une Page apres, il laissoit mourir un Innocent a sa place, sans faire le moindre pas pour le sauver) et elle se promettoit d'avoir toutte sa vie, la Modestie Silentieuse d'Antiope, la Sincerité de la Princesse de Cleves, et le disinterresment de Pamela, sans sçavoir que c'etoit renoncer a plaire, a estre respectée, ou a s'agrandir. Elle n'avoit nulle Idee d'aucune de ces pretentions. Sa Gouvernante l'avoit accoutumée a negliger sa figure comme une chose indigne de son attention, et lui avoit toujours assuré qu'il ny avoit que des Coquettes ou des Petits Maitres qui songassent aux leurs, ou a celles des autres, et qu'on ne brilloit jamais aupres de Gens sensé que par les Graces de l'ame et de l'esprit.

Elle lui persuadoit plus facilement parce qu'elle se l'etoit fortment persuadée a elle même, et c'étoit l'unique consolation de sa Laideur. L'Hermite et le Philosophe lui avoient tous deux inspiré le mepris des Vaines Grandeurs, sans s'apperçevoir que ce mepris qui étoit tres necessaire pour leur faire supporter l'obscurité de leur état, estoit bien triste pour une grande Princesse a qui il ostoit la douce Jouissance de l'éclat dont elle étoit environnée. Elle estoit parvenue a ce point de perfection de ne pas gouter les plus precieux dons que les Dieux peuvent faire, elle estoit inutilement une de plus belles personnes du monde, et Heritiere d'un Trône, en regrettant l'état de Bergere ou de Vestale. Helas elle ne sçavoit pas que le vraie Sagesse veut extraire du Plaisir de touts les biens qu'on possède, et mepriser seulment ceux qu'on ne peut acquerir.

Cette Beauté pourtant inutile pour elle, devenoit fort a charge a d'autres. La Reine, qui ne la trouvoit jamais assez jolie a quatre ans, la trouvoit beaucoup trop belle a treize. Elle ne pouvoit pas avec justice lui reprocher la

---

[1] End of passage in two drafts.

vivacité de ses yeux; elle faisoit tout ce qu'elle pouvoit pour l'éteindre. Elle travailloit perdre la fleur de son teint par des Lectures qui duroient toute la nuit, et elle tachoit de gater sa taille en écrivant dix heures de suitte, mais la Nature, plus forte qu'elle, avoit rendû toutes ces choses parfaittes, et la Reine ne pouvoit pas la disconvenir interieurement quoy qu'elle disoit tous les jours, qu'elle étoit changée a faire pitée.

Il falût la faire une Maison et sa mere, qui avoit recherché avec tant de Delicatesse des Personnes admirables a qui confier son Enfance, se sentit une tres grand Indifference sur le choix de celles qu'elle mettroit au pres d'elle pour Dames de Compagnie. Elle lui Donna donc sans Refflection ou Distinction, La Comtesse de Bon Sens, et la Marquise de l'Artifice, la premiere uniquement parce qu'elle l'ennuyoit dans son Palais, et l'autre parce qu'elle l'avois beaucoup briguée cette charge.

Le Roi l'avoit envoyé a la Princesse (selon l'etiquette de la Cour) un assortiment de Pierreries magnifiques, et on lui assigna pour sa Residence un Vieux Chateau assez beau, éloigné de 4 lieus de la Capitale, ou elle estoit presque releguée, au grand Plaisir de la Reine, qui ne la voyoit plus qu'a regret, et sans en estre elle meme offensée. Le Philosophe lui fit valoir cette marque de la tendresse de sa Mere, qui aimoit mieux perdre la douçeur de la voir que de hazarder son innocence au milieu du Luxe et du Tumulte. Il étoit lui même charmé de cette retraitte, il avoit assez d'esprit pour s'apercevoir qu'il figuroit tres mal a la Cour. Les Pages lui faisoient de Poliçonneries, les petits maitres, et les Dames aimables (qui sont toujours le parti le plus fort) l'accabloient de complimens en ricanant et se jouoient impitoyablement de sa bonne Foie, et de sa Philosophie. Il estoit tres <?> piqué de ce manege. Malgre tout son mepris pour le public il étoit l'homme du monde le plus sensible au moindre mepris pour sa personne; il s'emport- oit même quelque fois d'une façon a scandaliser les Philosophes et faire rire tous les ignorants. La Gouvernante estoit aussi bien aise d'estre éloignée d'une Cour ou sa Pruderie estoit si peu considerée, de voir souvent des petites Coquettes qui lui faisoit horreur, traittée avec plus de consideration qu'une Chasteté invincible depuis 50 Anns.

Madame Bons Sens etoit peutestre un peu faschée de la Solitude ou elle etoit condamnée, mais elle etoit en habitude de se taire, et elle sçavoit même s'amuser des ridicules qui ennuyoient les autres. La Marquise estoit celle qui regrettoit la Cour la plus, mais elle sçavoit aussi cacher ses sentiments, et se flattoit de se recompenser a merveille de la contrainte qu'elle se don- noit. Elle avoit ses vûes quand elle avoit demandé d'estre placée aupres de la Princesse, et elle ne s'en écartoit pas un moment. Elle tacha de s'en faire aimer, et il etoit tres aisé dÿ reüsir; la pauvre Enfant n'avoit jamais vû aupres d'elle que des personnes qui vouloient l'instruire et qui ne songeoient pas a lui plaire. Elle regardait la defiance comme un sentiment indigne d'une ame Genereuse et se livra toute entiere a la seduction de la Marquise avec une bonne Foy qui auroit donnée des remords a un Coeur capable de les sentir; mais Madame d'Artifice n'estoit pas accoutumée a de pareilles Foiblesses. Elle estoit vive, insinuante, complaisante, badine ou tendre selon l'humeur de la Princesse, et sçut si bien profiter de tous ses mouvements qu'en peu de jours elle ne pouvoit plus se passer d'elle.

Il etoit tres naturel que les manieres douces et prevenantes de la Marquise dussent faire une grande impression sur un Coeur neuf, jusque la tiranisé par des pedagogues. La Reine ne s'etoit jamais relachée de soutenir avec hauteur la Dignité royale et maternelle, l'hermite lui avoit annoncé ses visions avec authorité comme des Inspirations divines, le Philosophe étoit dur et sec dans ses entretiens, et la Gouvernante avoit mille raisons d'estre toujours de mauvaise humeur. La Belle Docile avoit naturellement un si grand penchant vers la tendresse, qu'elle l'auroit donnée (faute d'objet) a une femme de Chambre, si la Gouvernante ne les avoient pas toujours chassées, aussi tost qu'elle les distinguoit, et lui faisoit de reprimandes tres aigre si elle s'abaissoit a leur dire le moindre mot agreable. Elle estoit donc livrée a elle même, et je croi que c'etoit pour s'en distraire qu'elle avoit formée le voeu bizarre qui avoit fait tant de bruit; aimant mieux estre a Vichnou qu'a personne.

Cette fantaisie étant passée, elle se sentoit une vuide qui la desesperoit. Elle n'attendoit que la premiere occasion pour placer les plus beaux sentiments du monde; on lui avoit representé l'amour comme une Passion si honteuse qu'elle n'osoit pas seulment y penser, mais la belle Amitie estoit le comble de la vertu. Telemaque qu'on lui proposoit pour modele, en étoit sensible au point de vouloir se tuer quand on lui ostoit son cher Mentor, et Minerva elle même en faisoit ses delices. C'estoit bien assez pour determiner la Princesse a se jetter dans ces aimables sentiments[1] qui rendent content a la fois, le Coeur et la Raison. La Cour qui lui faisoit Madame de l'Artifice, lui parroisoit l'effet de la Sympathie la plus tendre; elle auroit crû l'outrager en lui refusant son estime entiere; elle estoit touchée de reconnoisance pour ses flatteries, et le Goût qu'elle prit a sa Conversation, acheva de la rendre toute a elle. La Marquise estoit trop connoiseuse pour ne pas voir l'ascendant qu'elle avoit pris sur l'innocente Princesse; elle la tournoit comme elle vouloit. Sa premiere demarche fût de l'eloigner de Madame Bon Sens, qui voyoit toutes ces scenes de sang froid; elle n'estoit pas faite pour la Cour, elle craignoit également d'estre Favourite ou disgraciée, et en faisant simplement les devoirs de sa charge, sans Empressement, ni negligence, elle se garentissoit de l'un et de l'autre.

Pendant quelques mois, la Tranquillité, la Pais, les plaisirs mêmes regnerent dans le Chateau. Le Mystere que ces tendres amies étoient obligées de mettre dans leur commerce pour se sauver de l'envie de la Gouvernante,

---

[1] Altered from 'cette delire Charmante'.

la rendoit encore plus cher. Tout contribuoit a leur bonheur quand celui de la Princesse fût troublé, en voyant un air de Tristesse sur le visage de son aimable Marquise qui sembloit augmenter tous les jours, quoy qu'elle fit son possible pour la cacher. Elle s'efforçoit de paroistre gaye mais il étoit aisé de voir que ces efforts lui coutoint [*sic*] et qu'elle avoit un fonds de Malencholie que ni la presence ni les carresses même de son adorable Princesse ne pouvoit dissiper. Quel chagrin pour cette tendre Amie! Elle mouroit d'envie d'aprendre la cause de ce changment funeste, sans oser la demander pour ne pas l'embarrasser. Elle étoit assez delicate, pour craindre de lui donner a soupsçonner qu'elle presumoit de son rang, pour vouloir exiger son secret, et elle souffrit plusieurs jours tout ce que la Curiosité pouvoit lui faire souffrir sans chercher a s'éclaircir, persuadée que la Marquise ne pouvoit rien refuser a son moindre desir, mais que sans doute elle avoit des raisons tres fortes pour son silence puis qu'elle ne lui confioit pas son inquietude.

Cette Discretion de la Princesse étoit encore plus a charge a Madame de l'Artifice. Elle vouloit estre importunée, elle vouloit même qu'on lui arrachat son secret; elle redoubla la dose de Tristesse qu'elle avoit repandûe sur toute sa figure, et ne faisoit pas une geste qui ne la decoüvrit. Tant tôt elle tomboit dans une reverie si profonde, qu'on lui parloit au moins deux fois, avant qu'elle repondit, tant tôt elle avoit des larmes aux yeux, et quand la Princesse la surprenoit dans cet état, elle tachoit de sourire avec un air de Langueur qui penetroit jusqu'a l'ame de la Douce Docile. Elle pleuroit souvent dans son cabinet des chagrins qu'elle ne comprenoit pas. Que sçai-je pourtant (pensoit-elle un soir que cette chere amie lui avoit paru plus triste qu'a l'ordinaire) si je ne puis pas soulager cette affliction, au moins je puis pleurer avec elle; peutestre que cest uniquement la crainte de m'affliger qui lui fait cacher le malheur dont elle est accablée. Qu'elle connoist mal l'exces de ma tendresse! Je sacrifirai tout pour la tirer du moindre embarras, toute souffrance m'est supportable hors celle de la voir souffrir.

Remplie de ces Idées elle écrivit un billet qu'elle glissa dans sa Main, par lequel, elle la prioit tendrement de se rendre par l'escalier derobé dans sa ruelle quand sa Gouvernante seroit couchée. Quoy qu'il nÿ eût que ces peu de mots dans le billet, c'éstoit assez pour aprendre a la Marquise que son projet alloit avoir le succes qu'elle souhaittoit. Elle ne manqua pas le rendezvous. Le premier quart d'heure se passa en demonstrations de la plus vive reconnoisance pour la Distinction dont elle l'honoroit; elle se jetta a genoux a costé de son lit, elle baisa ses belles mains en les moûillant de larmes qui sembloint partir d'un Coeur penetré de ses bontez. La pauvre Princesse tout enchantée de sa tendresse, y mela les siennes.

Mais ma chere Marquise, disoit elle d'une voix mal asseurée, malgre tous ces preuves de vostre amitie, j'ai a me plaindre de vous—De Moi! s'écria la marquise en l'interompant comme hors d'elle même, suis-je malheureuse au point de vous avoir deplû un seul instant? Que vous faut-il pour vous prouver mon zêle et mon attachment? Trop heureuse si en versant tout mon sang a vos pieds, vous avoüez, que jamais devoûement n'a égalé le mien.

Je veux le croire, repondit la Princesse, mais ne puis-je donc vous rendre contente; vous me cachez quelque chose qui vous touche infiniment, et quand on aime bien on n'a plus de reserve pour l'objet aimé. Je sçai que je me fais un plaisir, de vous developer touttes mes pensées, et je me ferai un Crime de vous cacher aucun de mes sentiments—

Pendant que la Princesse parloit, Madame de l'Artifice prenoit l'air d'une personne qui voit son plus grand secret decouvert. De la surprise elle passa a l'accablement, et en suitte l'interompit par ses sanglots. La Princesse la serra entre ses bras en la conjurant de se confier a elle, et renouvella les protestations d'une amitie éternelle, et a toute épreuve. Enfin la Marquise ceda comme ne pouvant pas resister a ses ordres, et apres la prelude de quelques soupirs qu'elle étouffa, elle commença la triste recit de ses malheurs.

Vous pouvez juger belle Princesse, dit-elle, que je ne puis estre sensible a rien que par rapport a vous, vous ne pouvez pas ignorer avec quel ardeur j'ai sollicité l'honneur de vous servir. Je vous avois vû, et peut-on vous voir sans souhaitter vous voir toujours? Toutes mes demarches auront été inutiles, si je m'etois pas addressée au Valet de Chambre favori de la Reine. Vous ne sçavez pas peutestre que c'est le plus avare, et le plus avide de tous les hommes, toutes les graces passent par ses mains, et il profite de la necessité, ou de l'ambition de tous ceux qui ont affaire a la Cour. La miene se bornoit a m'attacher a vostre altesse, mais il étoit trop vif pour échapper a la penetration d'un homme accoutumé a étudier tout ceux que se presentent a lui. Il me demanda une somme excessive pour sa recommendation, en me faisant entendre une exclusion positive si je ne la donnasses pas. Tout ce que j'avois a vendre ou engager ne montoit pas a la moitie de ce qu'il m'avoit demandé; j'ai pris le parti d'emprunter le reste a des Marchands qui se sont fié a ma Parole. Ma conduitte passée avoit donnée un Idee si avantageux de ma bonne foye, qu'on ne fit aucun scrupule de sÿ livrer. Je devois reçevoir en peu de mois dequoy m'acquitter, mais dans le têmps que je l'atendoit, j'ai appris que mon Mari s'en est saisi pour payer une dette du jeu. Mes Creanciers deviennent importuns, ils se plaindront hautement, je seray regardée comme indigne d'être aupres de vous. Celui qui m'a pris mon Argent est homme a le nier; on m'accusera de disipations honteuses, ma Reputation si entière jusqu'ici sera fletrie, mais le comble de mon Malheur sera d'estre éloignée de vous. Quand j'envisage celui la, je nen sçaurois voir d'autres. Elle finit en fondant en larmes, dont la moitie estoient versées en pure perte; la princesse estoit deja si attendrie qu'elle se seroit arrachée les yeux, si ils avoient été necessaire pour sauver la Marquise des malheurs qui la menacoient.

Elle l'embrassa tendrement. Me croyez vous donc si dure (dit elle) de vous laissez dans cet état affreux? Quand je ne vous aimerai point, puis-je refuser a moi même le plaisir divin, de secourir une personne vertueuse, dont le bon Coeur a causé l'infortune? Il est vrai que je n'ai point d'argent, c'est ma Gouvernante qui a la disposition de ce que m'est assigné, et quelque fois elle m'en refuse, quoy que je n'en demande jamais que pour faire du bien. Je n'ose pas lui en parler dans cet occasion; vous sçavez quelle est jalouse de vos agrements. Elle me refuseroit seurement. Mais voici la Clef de cette cassette que vous voyez sur ma Toilette; mes Pierreries y sont enfermées. Prenez les, vous sçavez que je ne m'en soucie guerre. Je n'ai jamais osé esperer qu'elles me procureroint un plaisir si vif, un joi aucun de comparable[1] a celui d'estre utile a une Amie pour qui je donnerai ma vie si elle pouvoit asseurer son bonheur!

Apres que Madame de l'Artifice eut joué la surprise, de la Generosité inoüie de la Princesse, sans oublier tous les éloges qui devoient naturellement la Confirmer dans ses beaux procedès, elle refusa nettement d'en profiter, en representant que comme les belles ames étoient rares, quand cette Histoire éclateroit, on ne manquerait pas dÿ donner des Couleurs abominables, et qu'elle seroit chassée de la Cour avec ignominie. La Princesse s'offensa presque de voir qu'elle ne la croyoit pas capable d'un secret inviolable. Elle lui jura que nulle extremité ne l'obligeroit de deceler une chose, ou son honneur etoit intteressé. Cela tourna en une belle Scene des Sentiments.[2] La marquise ne pouvoit se resoudre qu'avec la plus grande repugnance a un action qu'on pouvoit soupsçonner d'interêt. Quoy que (dit-elle) il y est de la Douceur a avoir de l'obligation a celle qu'on aime, elle lui fit entendre aussi, par un raffinement de Generosité, qu'entre les amis parfaits, peutestre celui qui reçevoit donnoit la plus grande marque d'amitie; que c'étoit le plus fort sacrifice de l'amour propre, et qu'il nÿ avoit qu'une tendresse sans bornes, qui put faire faire a une personne bien née, une chose si humiliante, que d'accepter un bien fait de cette Nature. Docile étoit toute penetrée de ces raisonnements, qui lui parroisoient les plus justes du Monde, et elle ne se lassoit pas de remercier son Amie genereuse, de la preuve qu'elle reçevoit de son attachment, quand elle avoit la bonté de vuider sa Cassette. Elle laissa la Princesse dans l'admiration de sa vertu, et tres contente d'elle même, de s'estre saisie aussi promptement de la premiere occasion qui s'etoit presentée de faire un Action Heroique. Elle dormit avec ces Idées agreable, et on ne l'avoit jamais vûe si gaie qu'elle fût plusieurs jours apres. La Marquise avoit repris toute sa vivacité, elle etoit devenue doublement chere a sa jeune Maitresse depuis cet avanture, et les jours passeoient filez d'or et de soie, mais le Bonheur est rarement durable.

---

[1] Next phrase altered from 'que celui que je resens dans cet moment, que je me flatte'.
[2] Last two words altered from 'et ne s'estoit aucune dispute que sur les beaux Sentiments'.

Le jour du Naissance du Roi approchoit, toute la Cour devoit paroistre en grand Galla. La Princesse ne pouvoit pas se dispenser dÿ aller, et on fut bien surpris de la voir sans Pierreries quand toutes les Dames en etoient parée a l'envie. Les jugements furent diferents dans cette occasion: les uns crurent que c'étoit un reste de Devotion, d'autres l'attribuerent aux conseils du Philosophe, et il y en avoit qui imaginoint que c'etoit un commencement de Coquetterie, que la princesse ne voulat rien cacher de la plus belle Gorge qu'on eut jamais vû, ni charger des petites oreilles bien tournez de Pendants qui les auroient defigurez. Le Roi Imbecile s'en formalisa d'une étrange façon, et la Reine, qui avoit trouvé sa fille tres grandise et d'une Beauté a faire enrager la meilleure Mere de l'univers, ne manqua pas d'inspirer a son Mari, que c'etoit lui manquer de respect et qu'elle meritoit au moins un exil de quelques années pour lui aprendre a vivre, et puis qu'elle faisoit si peu d'usage de ses presents, il falloit les reprendre. Elle les demanda de sa part avec beaucoup de Dureté. La Princesse repondit en rougissant qu'elle ne les avoit pas.

Eh qu'en avez vous fait insensée? dit la Reine. Vous ne repondez point, vous palissez, vous baissez les yeux—seroit-il possible? Mais non; mon sang ne peut s'oublier jusque la, vous avez été volée sans doute, et je ferai mettre tous vos gens a la Question.

Helas Madame, dit la Princesse en tombant a ses pieds et fondant en larmes, n'en accusez pas des innocents, j'en ai disposée,—Vous! vous! interompit la Reine en fureur, a Qui? en quelle occasion? quel service pouvoit meriter une recompense de cette force?

Il ne m'est pas permis de m'expliquer, repondit Docile, mais je suis seure que vous auriez faite vous même ce que j'ay fait si—

Moi! s'écria la Reine avec un redoublement de Colere, Vous me croyez donc aussi Bête que vous, capable de derangements infames, car je ne suis pas la dupe de vostre air modeste. Il ny a qu'une Passion dereglée qui peut faire commettre une Folie pareille; et j'ai le malheur d'avoir mis au monde une Fille degenerée, indigne de mon avoeu puis qu'elle a manqué a sa Vertu. Ce reproche perçoit le Coeur de la pauvre princesse, qui s'evanouit, sans faire la moindre Pitie a sa mere, qui ne pouvoit lui pardonner de l'avoir crüe capable d'aimer chose au monde mieux que ses pierreries. Elle fût portée a demie morte, dans une Tour destinée aux Criminels destat, accompagnée seulement de son affreuse Gouvernante, qui avoit ordre de se servir de toutes sortes de moiens, pour l'obliger a confesser le detail de sa mauvaise conduitte. Cette violence allarmait la Cour et fit beaucoup de Bruit par tout le Roiaume. Mille contes extravagants furent debittés. On disoit que la Princesse avoit conspiré de detroner son pere, d'autres ajouterent qu'elle avoit tiree un poignard contre la Reine, quelqu'uns asseurent qu'elle étoit grosse de 7 mois. Les Femmes qui craignaient une Beauté qui les effacoit, et une Vertu qui étoit de mauvaise example, se dechainairent contre elle, mais en General, on convenoit que comme Heritiere presomptive de la Couronne, son Crime, quel qu'il fût, meritoit explication, et qu'elle ne devoit pas estre prisoniere sans une convention des états generaux.

Les provinces envoyerent des Deputez, et les magistrats firent des remonstrances au Roi, qui n'écouta ni les uns, ni les autres. La Reine lui fit entendre qu'il étoit obligé de soutenir l'autorité Roiale, et elle traita avec tant de mepris et de Hauteur, tout ceux qui osoient lui demander ses raisons, qu'on commençoit a respecter sa fermeté et sa Politique. Son extravagance triompha, dans le temps quelle etoit le plus marquée, et elle retint tout le monde en respect et en silence.

Ce n'est pas la premiere fois que le Vertu outrée et credule s'est attirée l'infamie, et il est assez ordinaire de voir la folie hardie et audacieuse arracher l'aprobation du Public. C'est ici un beau Champs pour deployer mon erudition, je pourrois citer quatre cents cinquante et huit passages de l'histoire ancienne et moderne, pour prouver cette verité, mais je veux menager l'impatience du Lecteur,[1] il est sans doute tres inquiet sur le sort de la Princesse.

Apres que sa premiere surprise fût passée, elle s'arma de Philosophie, s'envelopa dans sa Vertu, et trouva même de la douceur a souffrir pour une Cause si glorieuse, et une Amie si parfaitte. Son seul chagrin étoit celui qu'elle crôioit causer a la Marquise, elle l'imagina abismée dans les plus vives douleurs, et son plus grand soin étoit de les soulager, en lui donnant de ses nouvelles. Un de ses Gardes touché de sa Beauté et de sa douceur, au hazard de sa vie lui fournit de quoy écrire, et entreprit de rendre sa Lettre. Elle passa le moitie de la nuit a étaler sa tendresse a ce cher Objet, se gardant bien pourtant de lui rien toucher de la part qu'elle avoit a sa disgrace. Elle lui dit plus d'une fois que le bonheur de l'aimer lui tenoit lieu du tout, et finissoit en l'asseurant que comme la plus cruelle Tyrannie ne pouvoit pas lui oster son Image, elle avoit toujours dequoy se consoler, parmi les plus vives persecutions.

Madame de l'Artifice fut fort allarmée en reçevant cette Lettre, on pouvoit peutestre decouvrir qu'elle l'avoit receû. C'en étoit assez pour l'exposer aux Fureurs de la Reine, et peutestre la faire soupsçonner d'un commerce criminel avec la Princesse, qu'on regarda comme Prisoniere d'état. Elle prit son parti en Femme habile, elle porta la Lettre a sa Majesté, qui tres contente de ce sacrifice, fit pendre le Garde qui s'en étoit chargé, et envoya la lettre a la tendre Docile en l'accablant de tous les reproches qu'elle crût que son obstination, et la peu de respect qu'elle avoit pour son resentiment meritoit. La Princesse ne douta pas que son Malheureux messager n'eût été surpris, et étoit fort éloignée d'imaginer, la Trahison de la

---

[1] Altered from 'de mon cher Lecteur'.

Marquise. Mais sa Gouvernante avoit ordre de l'instruire, et ajouta qu'elle estoit nomée Intendante de la Maison de la Reine pour recompense de cette belle Action.

On demandera peutestre, que devient Madame Bon Sens pendant tout ceci? elle si retira de la Cour, ou elle n'a jamais reparû depuis.

Je laisse des imaginations vives et tendres, a se figurer l'affliction de la Princesse en cette occasion; la mienne n'est pas assez forte, pour lui en fournir les expressions. Mais apres avoir pleuré, gemi, soupiré, et parlé fort longtemps aux murailles de son Chateau, elle se soûvint d'une maxime de son Philosophe, qu'il vaût mieux estre trompé par mille Fourbes que de refuser son secours a un seul vraiment digne de pitié. Elle se sentit tres consolée par cette Refflection, et en suitte fit voeu d'estre dupe toute sa vie. Toute autre qu'elle, auroit écrit a la Reine l'histoire veritable de cette affaire, et par la justifié son innocence, et se seroit vengée de la perfidie de la Marquise, mais elle étoit liée par son serment, et nulle consideration ne la pouvoit tenter de le violer.

Sa prison dura six mois, et auroit duré beaucoup plus longtemps, si le Roi ne se fût pas crevé des champignons, et de Punch fait avec de l'eau des Barbades. La Reine s'étoit fait generalement hair de tous ses sujets, et peut estre que le grand desir qu'on avoit de se voir vengé des impôts dont elle les avoient accablez avoit beaucoup de part a l'empressement qu'eurent les états, de retirer la Princesse de son triste chateau, en la proclamant Reine.[1] On ne douta pas, qu'elle ne commençat son regne par le procez de sa Mere, et on s'attendoit a la voir condamnée au moins a un exil ou a une Prison perpetuelle. Elle craignoit quelque chose de pis. A peine le Roi fut il mort, qu'elle se refugia dans un temple, n'oubliant pas dÿ porter toutes les pierreries de la Couronne, et la cassette roiale. C'étoit de quoy mettre le Grand Prètre dans ses Interèts, Precaution que ne lui estoit pas necessaire. La Nouvelle Reine lui écrivit une Lettre respectueuse et affectionée, et la solicitoit de retourner au Palais et d'occuper le mesme apartement qu'elle avoit quitté. Enfin elle lui temoignoit plus de soûmission qu'elle n'avoit fait de sa vie, mais tout cela ne pouvoit pas attirer sa Confiance, elle crût que n'osant violer le sanctuaire, elle vouloit l'en retirer par rûses. Elle s'obstina a y rester, et ne voulût pas même voir sa fille, quoy qu'elle vint en personne avec peu de suitte, pour luy rendre ses devoirs. Madame de l'Artifice qui avoit beaucoup plus de raison de craindre son resentiment avoit mieux étudiée son caractere, elle ne songa ni a füir, ni a se cacher, elle poussa l'effronterie jusqu'a venir parmi les autres Dames la feliciter sur son avenement au Trone. Docile se contenta de la regarder avec mepris, et ne daigna pas lui faire des reproches. Par cette conduitte elle donna beau jeu a la Marquise, qui ne manqua pas de faire remarquer a tout le monde, le peu de

---

[1] Altered from 'Reine absolue'.

fonds qu'on pouvoit faire sur sa faveur, puis qu'elle étoit capable d'oublier si tôst une personne qui lui avoit ete si attachée.

Ce Peuple qui avoit esperé voir un lit de Justice, (Spectacle qui fait toujours grand plaisir dans son commencement) estoit choqué de cette clemence Philosophique, qui ne sçavoit pas faire respecter son autorité. Les Prêtres gagné par les tresors de la Reine Doüariere, n'oublierent pas de semer mille Calomnies contre la Regnante, l'histoire de sa Galanterie pretendûe fut renouvellée. Elle en fût informée, mais au lieu d'en punir les auteurs, elle defendit de les rechercher, disant tout haut, qu'il ne faut jamais venger les injures personelles. Cette maxime repandue ostoit entierment la Crainte de l'offenser. Elle brusquoit les Flatteurs, ce que degouta fort ceux qui lui faisoit le Cour. Elle declara que trouvant le Tresor vuide, elle vouloit retranchir toute les depenses superflues, pour épargner ses Sujets, qu'elle ne vouloit pas charger d'impôts. Il n'y avoit evidemment point de Fortune a faire aupres d'elle, les recompenses etoient destinées a la vertu, ou aux grandes actions. On n'etoit pas disposé a passer par ces voyes penibles, on estoit trop accoutumé a s'enrichir d'une façon plus commode, mais ce que la perdit totalement dans l'esprit du Peuple, étoit l'air negligent avec lequel elle assistoit aux sacrifices. La Reine de Travers avoit paru toujours tres devote, et peutestre l'étoit de bonne foy, au milieu des vices. Sa fille detestoit l'Hipocrisie, et depuis qu'elle avoit perdu son enthusiasme, elle ne voulût pas paroistre en avoir, ce qui revolta contre elle, la Noblesse, le Clergé, et generalment tous ses sujets, qui n'attendoit que le moment pour changer la Face du Gouvernement.

On traitoit avec le Roi Farouche pour lui livrer leur Isle, cetoit le plus puissant de leurs voisins, Ambitieux et par consequent point de tout scrupuleux. Il n'hesita pas de conspirer avec des sujets mal intentionez contre une Reine Legitime qui n'avoit nul defaut que sa Vertu. Il envoya son Fils le Prince Sombre, pour se mettre a la tête de la conspiration quand il seroit temps de le faire éclatter. Il couvrit le veritable motif de son voyage, par les prepositions d'un Mariage entre le Prince et le jeune Reine qui touchoit a sa seizieme année. Il imagina qu'on pouroit lui persuader facilement, que le Prince deja frappé de la Reputation de sa Beauté, vouloit lui faire la Cour en personne, etant impatient de voir des charmes qui faisoit tant de bruit dans le Monde. Il fût reçeu avec toute la politesse qu'on devoit a son rang, et la Reine lui fit un accueil tres obligeant, dans le temps qu'il travailloit a sa perte. Son Innocence, sa douceur, et cet air de bonté qui accompagnoit toutes ses actions, le toucha pourtant de Compassion. Il n'avoit pas le Coeur mauvais, malgre les moeurs feroces de son Païs, il avoit de l'honneur et de la Probité, et detestoit la Bassesse, et n'avoit accepté cette commission qu'avec grande repugnance, et seulment pour obeïr a un Pere violent et absolu. Quoy qu'il crût la plus part de tout ce qu'on lui avoit dit au desavantage de la Reine, sa vûe faisoit quasi sa justification. Au moins c'étoit une monstre bien aimable, et il forma la Resolution, dez leur premiere conversation, de la servir au lieu de lui nuire. Il falaît cacher ce dessein pour le faire reüssir et il le fit avec tout l'art possible.

Il avoit toutes les Qualitez de l'honnete homme et pas une seule de l'aimable, une Raison droite mais dure, un secret impenetrable, inaccessible a la flatterie, d'une fermeté inébranlable, mais d'une Jalousie qui alloit jusqu'a une defiance perpetuelle, juste a sa parole, peu gracieux dans ses procedez, grand et bienfait mais l'air fier et sans graces. Dans ses Conversations même avec la Reine, il songoit moins a lui plaire qu'a l'étudier, aussi ne lui plaisoit-il nullement, et il ne s'en aperçevoit que trop pour son repos. Il étoit peu accoutumé a frequenter de Dames. Des Caracteres comme le sien sont fort éloignez de la Galanterie, son Rang le dispensoit de certains devoirs envers elles, et il les avoit toujours traitée avec un froideur approchant du Mepris. Il ne craignoit pas leur charmes et s'exposoit tous les jours a ceux de la Reine, qui lui avoit fait une grande impression sans qu'il s'en doutât. Il nommoit Generosité l'interêt qu'il prenoit a elle, et auroit peutestre ignoré longtemps sa passion, malgre ses refflections, s'il ne s'etoit pas senti piqué jusqu'au vif d'une louange assez legere qu'elle avoit donnée a un jeune étranger qui parroisoit depuis quelques jours a sa Cour. Il étoit dificile de le voir sans le louer, c'éstoit un cavalier d'environ vingt anns, dont la taille estoit façonnée par les mains des graces, et les traits parroissoient formés par l'amour même: un air modeste et naiff, qui sembloit ignorer les charmes qu'il possedoit, un maintien noble et naturel, une Politesse melée de Dignité relevoit ses attraits, il parloit peu, mais toujours juste, et ne decidoit jamais, il évitoit la louange, sans choquer ceux qui lui en donnoient. Les Coquettes les plus determinées devenoient timide dans sa compagnie et n'osoit entreprendre de le seduire, elles respectoient malgre elles une Sagesse modeste qui sans affectation, ne se dementit jamais. Ses yeux pourtant assuroient que son Coeur n'étoit pas fait pour estre insensible, ils estoient rempli d'une douce langueur qui en inspiroit à toutes celles qui les voyoient, il n'en distinguoit aucune, et cette retenue avoit donné occasion a la Louange qui faisoit tant de peine au Prince Sombre.

Il s'apperçût de son amour en sentant sa Jalousie. Une Prude devote devenûe amoureuse de son Palfrenier ne pouvoit pas estre plus outrée contre sa passion. Il l'étoit au point de presque haîr la personne qu'il aimoit, il ne pouvoit pas lui pardonner sa Conquête, aussi fit-il tout son possible pour rompre ses chaines. Il se souvenit de tous les Contes qu'on lui avoit fait de sa mauvaise Conduitte, il tachait de se persuader de leur verité, il se reprochoit comme la derniere des lachetées le moindre sentiment en sa faveur. Il parvint a se flatter qu'il la meprisoit, et avec cette belle Idée, il alla a la Cour dans l'intention de lui dire des brusqueries pour s'en attirer de lui arracher d'autres qui pourroient achever un goût qu'il regardoit comme une fletrissure a son honneur. Il tourna le discours sur le Cavalier étranger, en regardant la Reine avec une malice qu'elle ne comprenoit pas. Elle repondit a ses propres impertinens avec tant de douceur, et un Innocence si ingenüe, qu'il la trouva plus aimable qu'elle n'avoit jamais été, et il sortit d'aupres d'elle avec un redoublement d'Amour et de Fureur.[1]

Cet Amour loin d'estre accompagné des jeux et des ris, n'avoit a sa suitte, que le depit et la tristesse. Il sentit comme une Humiliation, qu'elle étoit necessaire a son bonheur, et son Orgueil aura voulû se suffire a soy mesme, mais cette passion est accoutumée de triompher de la Fierté et de la Sagesse. Il etoit deja son esclave, et elle ne perdit aucune de ses droits. Livré a des pensées nouvelles, et occupé d'une Guerre interieure, il parroisoit froid et reveur parmi les conjurez. Ils s'assembloient tant tôt chez lui et tant tôt chez le Grand Pretre, Viellard consommé dans la Politique, et qui avoit ses vûes a part. Quand il avoit commencé a traitter avec le Roi Farouche, ce n'étoit ni le zele pour les Autels, ni la Crainte des innovations, qu'il disoit aprehender, qui le faisoit agir. Il visoit au moins au Ministere, il ne pouvoit pas l'esperer par la Reine.

Elle l'avoit offerte a son Philosophe, qui fût assez sensé pour refuser une charge qu'il se sentit incapable d'exercer avec honneur, et il fût assez foû de demander pour recompense de ses services, la permission d'aller en Laponie faire des experiences sur l'air. Il y fut gelé l'ann 1709.

Dans le desespoir où étoit le Grand Pretre de satisfaire son ambition aupres de Docile, il avoit pris le Dessein temeraire de la detroner, et il lui coutoit peu de sacrifier sa patrie a son Ambition. Il s'étoit si bien insinué aupres de la Reine Mere, qu'elle donnoit la main a tout ce qu'il vouloit, et il s'en servoit pour noircir sa Fille dans l'esprit du peuple. Tout tendoit a une revolution prochaine, et tout s'arretoit par les Bizarreries du Prince Sombre. Il faisoit naitre de Difficultez, il retardoit les enterprises, et on comprit aisement qu'il ne souhaittoit pas la reüiste, sans deviner ses motifs. Effectivement il étoit si peu d'accord avec lui même, qu'on ne pouvoit pas penetrer des Desseins, qui netoient pas encore decidez. Il voyoit trop de froideur dans la Reine pour pouvoir se flatter de lui plaire, il craignoit qu'elle n'eût une Inclination secrete pour un Objet fait pour l'inspirer. Avec ces sentimens, il ne vouloit pas l'épouser, mais il vouloit encore moins la voir enfermée parmi les Vestales, comme il etoit resolu dans le Plan de la conjuration.

L'air fier et mécontent, qu'il gardoit dans leur assemblées, et la façon brusque avec la quelle il contrarioit souvent le Grand Prêtre, lui avoit inspiré une Crainte, qui termina par la Haine la plus vive, qu'il cachoit sous les plus profonds soûmissions, mais il envoya un courier de Confiance au Roi Farouche, pour l'informer de la conduitte extrodinaire du Prince son fils. Il l'accusoit du Dessein de s'emparer du Roiaume pour lui même, et

---

[1] A sentence struck out, which began 'Des Caracteres comme le sien ne peutestre guerre sentir . . .'

pretendoit le prouver par mille circonstances, vraies ou suposées. Le Roi violent, et naturellement cruel, sans trop examiner les faits, lui envoya une commission d'arreter le Prince dans le mesme jour qu'il enfermit la Reine, et de le tenir prisonier jusqu'a nouvel ordre, nommant le Grand Prêtre son Vice Roy, le quel ne songea plus qu'a avancer le moment qui devoit combler son Ambition.

La belle Docile ne soupsçonnoit nullement ce qui se trainoit contre elle, mais elle avoit des inquietudes d'une autre espece, qui lui donnoient des agitations beaucoup plus vives que celles que l'interët pouvoient lui causer. Un Coeur aussi tendre que le sien ne pouvoit pas rester entierement vuide. La perfidie de Madame de l'Artifice ne l'avoit pas detrompée sur la belle Amitie, elle n'acusoit que son mauvais caractere et ne sçavoit pas qu'en cherchant une amie fidelle elle cherchoit la pierre Philosophale en morale. Elle crût l'avoir trouvée dans la personne d'une de ses filles d'honneur a peu pres de son age, qui avoit un air d'innocence et de modestie qui en auroit imposé a une personne d'une plus grand experience que la jeune Reine. Sa complaisance et son attention acheverent de gagner sa confiance et elle la donna toute entiere a l'aimable Emilie, qui sous le dehors d'une timidité naive soutenue par les graces de la jeunesse etoit la plus dangereuse coquette de la Cour. La Reine se debarrassoit aussi souvent qu'elle pouvoit, et plus qu'elle ne devoit, de la foule qui l'Obsedoit, pour joüir du plaisir de lui developer ses pensées.

Un soir en se promenant dans la Labyrinthe par un beau clair de lune, en s'appuyant sur son bras, Avez vous remarque ma chere Emilie, lui dit elle, cet étranger qui se nomme Philocles? Emilie auroit crû que la Reine alloit lui reprocher les agaceries qu'elle lui avoit fait, et qu'elle ne lui pardonnoit pas d'avoir neglidez, si elle n'avoit pas remarqué un ton de tendresse dans la voix de la Reine qui lui donna des Idees, qui en la raisseurant lui inspiroient cette reponse flatteuse.

Oui Madame, repliqua telle finement, on ne remarque que lui depuis qu'il est arrivé, et il ne voit que V[otre] Majesté. La Reine rougit et changea le discours avec un promptitude qui expliqua mieux ses sentiments, que n'auroit fait la Confession la plus detaillée, mais Emilie avoit trop d'esprit pour faire semblant de s'en apercevoir. La conversation dura peu, la Reine devint reveuse, et se retira bien tôst, pour se livrer aux monologues qu'elle vouloit faire dans son lit.

Toute Prude qui lira cette histoire, se trouvera scandalisée que cette Docile d'une vertu si rigide soit capable de rever (car on se doute bien du sujet de sa reverie) a un jeune homme qu'elle connoisoit a peine, et qui parroisoit d'un rang bien inferieur au sien. Mais souvenez vous, sil vous plaist Mesdames, de la sympathie; vous en avez presqu'toutes eprouvé sa force dans de certaines occasions. C'est assez pour la vertu de la Reine, qu'elle ignorat ses propres sentiments, et qu'elle les combattit a proportion qu'ils se developoient a elle même. La reponse de sa Confidente, lui avoit fait sentir un plaisir melé d'une honte qu'elle n'avoit jamais eprouvée. Apres avoir passée une Nuit tres inquiette, elle se leva fortement resolûe de ne plus faire attention a ce Cavalier, dont la figure alteroit son repos. Elle alla au temple dans cette disposition. Le premier object qui frappa sa vûe fut just-ment lui. Elle se detourna dans un embarras, qui l'auroit beaucoup flaté s'il avoit eû de l'experience ou de la Fatuité. Modeste, timide, et sincerement Amoureux, il éstoit craintif et tremblant dans sa presence, il l'observoit avec trop d'attention pour qu'aucun de ses mouvements lui échappassent, mais il crût voir du deplaisir, et peut estre de la Colere, dans le soin qu'elle se don-noit d'eviter ses yeux. Il imagina qu'elle avoit reçeu quelque impression a son desavantage, et il en souffrit si cruellement, qu'il s'en trouva mal, il voulût se retirer.

La Foule étoit grande, la Reine tourna la tête en entendant le bruit qu'on faisoit, en lui faisant place, elle le vit Pale et defuit, elle devint rouge, et con-fuse. Le Prince Sombre étoit aupres d'elle, qui expliqua ses regards d'une façon bien differente que n'avoit fait Philocles. Ses soupsçons se changer-ent en certitude et il meditoit des projets de vengeance qui s'evanouirent en retour a son Palais. Il y trouva un espion, Habille, qu'il avoit gagné, entre les confidents du Grand Prêtre, dont le vrai Caractere ne lui étoit pas inconû. Cet homme avoit eû l'address d'enlever la Cassette de son maitre et lavoit porté chez le Prince, qui l'ouvrit avec Impressement. Il y trouve <?la lettre> foudroyant du Roi son Pere et par la Copie de sa reponse il vit que la nuit proch<aine> étoit destinée a un soûlevement general et l'execu-tion de la plus noire Trahison qui eût jamais été projettée. Il nÿ avoit pas du temps a Perdre. Il demanda une Audience a la Reine qui lui l'accorda avec son bonté ordinaire. La Pitié, et l'amour s'empara de son ame en la voyant, et se joignant a sa Generosité naturelle sans detruire sa Jalousie, changerent tous ses desseins. Il prit tout d'un coup, celui de tout sacrifier pour la sauver. Il exposa l'affreuse situation ou elle se trouvoit, en lui montrant les preuves.

Il seroit inutile, Madame, ajouta t'il, de faire arreter les Coupables. Ils sont trop nombreux, et trop puissant, peutestre ne souhaittent t'ils rien de mieux, qu'un pretexte de defense pour colorer leur revolte. Vous n'avez qu'un parti a prendre, sauvez vous. Je m'offre de vous conduire en lieu de seureté. Je vous menerai dans un Isle dont je suis souverain; elle a été le dot de feû ma mere, on ne peut pas me la disputer sans un Injustice qui revolt-eroit toute la Terre.

Mais seigneur, interrompit la Reine toute surprise des nouvelles si extro-dinaires et si accablantes, quel que soit mon Danger, dois-je l'eviter en abandonnant ma Gloire? ne sera t'elle pas ternie a jamais, en me livrant a la Conduitte d'un Prince qui. . . .

Dites Madame, s'écria't'il, d'un Prince a qui vous auroi donné vostre main, et qui vous rendra souveraine de ses états,— La Generosité de cet offre dans la circonstance presente, frappa la Reine d'une vive reconnois-ance. Elle resta dans la Silence, les yeux baissez, quelques moments, puis elle les leva en soupirant. Helas seigneur, dit elle, je suis trop touchée de vos procedez pour ne pas souhaitter d'estre digne de vostre attachment. Je voudrois pouvoir faire vostre bonheur, mais si ce sont mes sentiments qui doivent le faire, j'avoûe que je suis incapable d'en avoir d'autres que ceux de l'estime et de la reconnoisance. Je ne puis forcer mon Coeur, qui repugne a une tendresse que je ne doute pas que vous n'inspirerais a quelque Princesse plus juste que moi.

Je vous entends Madame, repliqua t'il, ce n'est pas de ce moment que je sçai que je suis l'objet de vostre Aversion. Je sçai encore plus, un autre. . . . n'importe; vous estes perdue si vous me refusez, et peut estre me sçaurez vous grê un jour, de vous avoir arrachée a un peuple qui vous outrage, et a une Inclination qui vous deshonore.

Ces paroles prononcée d'un air qui auroit determiné toute autre que l'innocente Docile, a ne se mettre jamais sous la puissance d'un Amant si peu respectueux pour ne pas dire Brutal, firent un impression toute differ-ente sur son esprit. C'éstoit la premiere fois de sa vie, qu'elle s'étoit fait un reproche. Elle sentit au fonds du Coeur la justice de celui du Prince, elle se trouva si coupable, et si humiliée, qu'elle crû devoir a la fois, se punir de sa Foiblesse, et recompenser la tendresse du plus genereux de tous les hommes. Elle lui tendoit la main, les larmes aux yeux. Puis que vous voulez, dit elle, vous charger d'une miserable qui n'a rien a vous offrir que la recon-noisance, je me mêts sous vostre protection. Je vous donne ma foy, et vous n'avez qu'a ordonner de quel façon vous voulez que je me conduisse.

On s'attend peutestre a voir des transports de joie au Prince de ce succes presqu'inattendu, mais il estoit accoutumé a tout critiquer, et a trouver tou-jours du chagrin. Sa Jalousie augmenta de la moitie, peu s'en falût qu'il ne se repentit de la preposition, qu'il venoit de faire. Il la baisa la main assez froidement, et sans s'amuser a la remercier de la Grace qu'elle lui faisoit, lui indiqua seulment qu'elle devoit se trouver a l'entrée de la nuit au jardin accompagnée d'une seule femme, qu'il y meneroit un Flamin a sa devotion; que la Ceremonie de leur mariage faite, une chaise de poste les conduiroit au premier Port de Mer, ou il auroit une Challoupe prête a faire voile; la revolte ne devait éclater qu'apres minuit, qu'ils seroient deja a l'abri de toute poursuite. Il sortit sans attendre sa reponse, et je croi qu'il l'auroit at-tendue longtemps, s'il avoit resté. Elle estoit devenûe mûette de Confusion et toute remplie d'Idées qu'elle ne pouvoit debrôüiller. Elle fût tirée de sa reverie par l'arrivée d'Emilie qui lui aprit que Philocles estoit dans l'anti-chambre, et qu'il lui demandoit audience avec tant d'empressement, et d'un air si embarrassé, qu'elle ne doutôit pas, qu'il ne vint chercher son protection, ou l'informer de quelque incident bien extrodinaire.

Son Nom fit tressaillir la Reine. Son premier mouvement fût de refuser de le voir, mais pourquoy aussi refuser de voir un étranger qui paroissoit d'un rang distingué, qui ne lui avoit jamais manqué du respect, qui venoit implorer son Secours, ou peutestre lui donner quelques avis important? Ces refflections faites a la hâte la determina de lui accorder l'entrée. Il parût et Emilie se retira dans l'embrazure d'une fenestre eloignée, d'ou elle étudioit jusqu'au moindre de leur regards. Il se jetta aux pieds de la Reine, et la conjura de l'écouter d'un ton qui exiga toute son attention. Je n'oserois me presenter devant vous, Madame, dit-il d'une voix tremblante, apres avoir remarqué que ma vûe vous est desagreable, s'il ne s'agissoit pas de vos interêts qui me sont mille fois plus cher que ma vie. Je viens de reçevoir un avis du Genie mon Pere, qui est l'intteligence qui preside sur l'etoile de Venus. Il est vertueux, et protege hautement la Vertu. La vostre ne lui est pas inconûe. Sa science est sans bornes, mais sa puissance a des limites. Il ne peut rien pour la service des habitants de la Terre, mais il se flatte de vous en retirer. Il y a longtemps qu'il est touché de vostre situation, et qu'il admire vostre personne. Ne vous etonnez pas qu'il vous connoisse, il a de Telescopes de son invention infiniment plus parfait que ceux des plus celebre opticiens de ce Globe. Vous avez fixé son attention, il m'a souhaité la Gloire de vous plaire. Je suis son fils unique. Il m'a envoyé ici, incognito, a ce dessein. La tendresse paternelle lui a donné une esperance, dont je sens toute la temerité, et je n'oserois vous en parler, s'il ne m'avoit pas écrit, qu'il a decouvert par ses Telescopes une defection universelle parmi vos sujets. Vostre vie même est en danger. Sauver cette vie precieuse, et sauvez le plus passioné et le plus respectueux de tous les Amants d'une douleur eternelle, puis que mon Essence ne me permet pas de mourir, Parlez divine Princesse, mais souvenez vous que vous aller decider sur vostre Destin et le mien. Consentez a mon bonheur, et vous joÿeras avec moi de l'imortalité. Une Nüage peut nous transporter dans un instant dans le Palais de mon Pere, et vous regnerez sur une Planette qui n'est pas le moins agreable dans le systeme de l'univers.

Le Lecteur judicieux a sans doute preveû la naissance plus qu'illustre de mon Heros.[1] Jeune et beau sans vanité, de l'esprit sans envie de le montrer, joignant a toutes les graces de la nature, une modestie que ne lui permettoit pas d'aperçevoir qu'il plaisoit. Jamais on <n'a?> vû un mortel de cet espece. Mais la Reine avoit peu d'experience pour faire cett refflection.

Elle fut si étonnée qu'elle perdit la Parole pendant quelque temps. Elle ne revint de cet étonnement que pour sentir toutes les Douleurs dont une Ame peut estre dechirée. Il nÿ avoit pas une heure qu'elle avoit donnée sa foy a un petit Prince de toute façon indigne d'elle; on lui presentoit le sort le plus brillant avec un qu'elle adoroit. La raison, l'ambition, et l'amour qui immagoit un Coeur nouvellement soumis a ses lois, soliciterent pour lui.

---

[1] This sentence added in margin to replace: '<?> mon Lecteur a compris del commencement que Philocles tel que je l'ai depeint n'etoit pas de cet monde.'

Mais cette Foy solennellement donnée estoit une Barriere qui resistoit a tout. Elle resolût d'imoler a sa vertu, son bonheur et celui de son aimable Amant, mais ou trouver des expressions pour adoucir cet arret cruel? Elle n'avoit pas la force de le prononcer, et elle fondoit en larmes, dans un silence, que le malheureux Philocles interpretoit en Aversion marqué pour sa personne. Un desespoir parfoit donne de la hardiesse. Elle avoit une main languissantment penchée sur le bras de son Fauteuil, pendant que l'autre tenoit son mouchoir devant ses yeux. Il osa prendre cette belle main et y imprimer mille baisers.

Il se seroit bien gardé d'une action si temeraire, s'il s'etoit crû aimé; il auroit craint d'offenser la pudeur delicate de la Reine, et lui donner a croire qu'il se prevaloit de son Inclination pour lui. Mais en s'imaginant detesté, il se crût au comble du Malheur, et peutestre que sa bonté pardonneroit les derniers Adieux d'un Amant miserable qui l'adoroit toujours; s'il y a au Monde une fille de dix sept anns, naturellement tendre, a qui jamais homme n'a approché que de deux cent pas, et qui sent les premiers ardeurs d'une passion naissante, c'est a elle seule de juger de l'emotion qu'éprouva Docile quand elle sentit sur sa main l'impression des lêvres tremblantes de Philocles. Elle ne pensa pas a la retirer, en pouvoit-elle penser dans cet <instant> delicieux? un yvresse de Plaisir suspendit tout autre mouvement. Sa Vertu la reveilla, elle s'efforca d'appeler Emilie, et lui dit d'une voix Foible, Conduissez ce Cavalier—

Elle passa dans son Cabinet et se jetta plus morte que vive sur son Canapé; Emilie ne comprenoit rien a cet Scene ou elle n'avoit rien entendu. Elle voyoit que la Reine aimoit passionement, qu'elle etoit aimée, mais pourquoy ces Pleurs et ce desespoir? Elle imagina cétoit sa fiereté qui resistoit a son Amour, et crût qu'elle ne resisteroit pas long<temps>. Deja outrée contre Philocles, de sa froideur pour les avances qu'elle lui avoit faites, elle jura de se venger a la premiere occasion. Elle retourna aupres de la Reine pour tacher de penetrer son secret, mais elle n'avoit pas la force de parler. Ce ne fut que larmes, sanglots, et assoupissement, jusqu'a l'heure marquée pour son rendezvous fatal avec le Prince Sombre.

Elle descendit dans le jardin suivie d'Emilie. Le marriage se fit dans un Pavillon, et tout de suite elles monterent dans une chaise de poste que le Prince et six de ses officiers escortoit. Tout ceci se passa dans un silence profond. Le Prince, qui la vit arriver toute defigurée de ses pleurs, se soutenant a peine par l'aide de sa fille d'honneur, auguroit fort mal de son Mariage, et en prononca les paroles mysterieuses presque a regret, sans lui en dire une seule d'obligeante. Elle étoit trop accablée pour articuler même durant la Ceremonie, et Emilie etonnée de ces procedez pensa qu'elle avoit pris la resolution de se donner un Mari pour se garantir de poursuite d'un Amant trop aimable. Cette precaution lui parût peu seure, et elle envisageoit deja une Intrigue formée entre la Reine et Philocles, elle <?> crût destinée a en estre la Confidante, <?>olût de n'omettre rien pour s'epargner <?> Role insupportable.[1] Elle roula divers projets <da>ns sa tête pendant trois heures qu'elles se cheminerent vers la mer. Quand elle vît qu'il estoit question de s'embarquer, elle se determina a planter la sa Maitresse; elle imagina qu'elle alloit a la Cour du Roi farouche, dont elle avoit un Idée fort triste, et elle ne voulût pas partager le malheureux sort de la Reine; encore moins voulût elle souffrir qu'elle l'adoucir par la Presence de son Amant. Elle ne douta pas qu'il ne fût assez amoureux pour la suivre, et elle voulût en avertir le Prince Sombre. Elle le pria de l'écouter a part, ce qu'il accorda tres volontiers. Il avoit deja formé le dessein de la corrompre, pour aprendre jusqu'aux pensées de la Reine.

Elle commença son discours par le supplier de permettre qu'elle se retirât en lui faisant entendre qu'elle avoit des raisons tres Essentielles pour quitter le service de Docile. Elle se fit beaucoup prier pour les conter, il falût même un Diamant d'un grand prix pour la determiner. Enfin elle l'informa de l'entrevûe de la Reine et du bel étranger. Ses larmes, son Desespoir, la main baissée, nulle circonstance ne fût oublié et le tout enpoisoné. Jugez Seigneur (disoit-elle en soupirant et en essuiant des yeux qui étoit bien sec) si une Fille de ma Naissance peut rester aupres d'une Princesse qui s'oublie au point de permettre des Libertez parreilles. Je la croi pourtant (ajout telle d'un air de bonté) fonçierement tres vertueuse, mais les imprudences nuisent a la Reputation autant que le vice. La mienne m'est tres precieuse, et elle m'oblige de retourner chez mon Pere; je ne serai pas capable de le faire, si je n'avois pas la Consolation de la laisser heureuse, étant unie avec un Prince qui ne manquera pas de faire son bonheur, quand elle aura perdue le souvenir de ce petit Monsieur dont elle s'est engoués. Le Prince étoit trop frappé de ce quil entendoit pour y repondre. Il se contenta de donner des ordres pour qu'elle retournat dans la Chaise, en même temps qu'il entra dans la Chaloupe avec la Reine, qui lui dit seulement, vous me quittez Emilie! et tombe évanoüie entre les bras des officiers du Prince. Il estoit trop outré contre elle, pour offrir de la secourir dans un état si touchant.

Ils mirent a la voile, quoy que le temps s'obscurcit, et Emilie s'en retourna a la Cour, ou elle publia en recommandant le secret a tout le monde, que l'inclination excessive que Docile avoit pour la Galanterie l'avoit choquée depuis longtemps, qu'elle avoit tenté toute sorte de moyens pour lui oster ce penchant honteux, qu'enfin cet Enlevement projetté a son insçu, et executé avec un hardiesse non pareille, l'avoit degouttée a un point qu'elle avoit refusé les offres les plus brillants, et aimoit mieux rester dans une mediocrité qui ne coûtoit rien a son Innocence.

Ce discours lui reüsit a merveille. De six marriages qu'elle se menagoit elle parvint au plus avantageux qui ne lui seroit jamais tombé en partage,

---

[1] MS partly illegible.

sans cet avanture. La delicatesse qu'elle avoit montrée en meprisant la fortune pour conserver son honneur, effacoit toutes les impressions que sa Coquettrie passée avoit donné. On y ajouta plus de foy parce que la Conspiration n'avoit parû qu'apres la disparade de la Reine. Le Grand Prêtre, qui en étoit l'ame, n'etoit pas si peu habile que d'estre sans espions; un Page l'avertissoit de tous les pas de Docile. Il sçavoit les deux Audiences qu'elle avoit accordées. Il ne douta pas, qu'elles n'eussent quelque suitte extrodinaire, et il esperoit un pretexte pour donner a sa Rebellion l'air d'une revolte genereuse contre une Princesse indigne de regner. Il retarda son entreprise, et elle n'éclatta qu'apres que toute la ville fût en Tumulte par l'absence de Docile. Toutes sortes de contes se debiterent, quand le retour d'Emilie aprit qu'elle s'étoit enfui avec le Prince Sombre.

Le pauvre Philocles devint si eperdu de cet Bizarre incident que je ne doute pas qu'il n'en fût devenu foû, si heureusement pour lui, l'Intelligence son Pere n'avoit pas eû dans ce moment l'Oeil au Telescope. Il vit son cher Fils qui s'arrachoit ses beaux cheveux de Desespoir. Il le transporta dans l'instant aupres de lui. Ses sages Leçons, les Brillantes Beautez de sa Cour, le temps et l'éloignment contribuerent a guerrir le Prince de sa malheureuse passion. Il oublia Docile, et fit voeû de ne jamais revoir cette planete, ou un honnête homme est toute sa vie exposé a une Guerre aussi inegale que celle des Americains nûs contre les Espagnols armé d'épées et de Fusées.

Le Grand Prêtre parût a la tête du Clergé et de la Noblesse. Il convoqua les états; il fit une Harangue patetique; en gardant toujours le respect pour l'autorité royale, il ne laissa pas de dechirer la Reine par les Calomnies les plus attroces. Pourtant, dans les termes managez, des yeux levez souvent au Ciel faisoient admirer sa Moderation. Il s'etendit sur la Sagesse, du feu Roi, la Pieté etc., de la Reine Mere, l'education raisonable qu'elle avoit donnée a sa fille dont elle n'avoit jamais pû corriger les égaremens, que finissoient par un abdication de ses états pour aller courir le monde avec l'objet d'une folle Passion. On sçait assez (continua til) jusqu'ou nous avons porté la soumission a nos Maistres, toujours plus ardent a la temoigner qu'a conserver nos droits les plus legitimes. Je serois encore zelé a vous retenir dans la Fidelité dûe a nostre souveraine, mais c'est elle qui nous abandonne. Le Roi Farouche redoutable par ses armes, et respectable par sa Prudence, saisira sans doute cette occasion pour faire une Descente. Sommes nous en état de lui resister? Un tresor vuide, des Finances mal reglées, un petit nombre de Troupes mal payez! Pouvons nous nous flatter de n'estre pas obligez de ceder a ses Forces, et ne seroit-ce pas attirer sa Vengeance a juste titre, que de lui montrer une resistance que nous ne pouvons pas soutenir? Implorons sa Protection, je ne doute pas qu'il ne nous l'accorde; sa Generosité sera intteressée a nous conserver nos Privileges. Je croy que nos Dieux tutelaires m'ont inspiré cette Idée, comme la seule voye de detourner nostre perte totale; puisse leur bonté ouvrir vos yeux sur vostre situation, et vous donner le courage de former une Resolution salutaire pour l'état, et necessaire pour épargner le sang du peuple.

Ce discours (comme tous les discours du monde) fit des effets differents sur les esprits, mais le plurarité [*sic*] des voix l'emporte, et elles furent conformes aux sentiments du Grand Prêtre, qui depecha des Deputez au nom de l'assemblée au Roi Farouche pour le supplier de venir prendre possession de leur Isle, abandonné de leur Reine, et exposée aux insultes de leur voisins.

La triste Docile durant cette negotiation, voguoit vers la petite Isle, qui appartenoit a son nouveau Seigneur. Jamais voyage n'eût si peu d'agrements. Quand elle sétoit assez calmé l'esprit pour arranger ses pensées, elle les donnoit entierement a plaire au Prince Sombre, et même a l'aimer. Elle se representoit sans cesse l'obligation qu'elle croyoit lui avoir de ses procedez disinterressez; elle tachoit d'embellir toutes ses bonnes Qualitez, et de s'aveugler sur ses defauts. Ne pouvant pas parvenir a forcer son Inclination, elle s'efforcoit de donner au moins les apparences d'une tendresse dont il devoit estre content. Ce n'etoit pas dans le desein de paroistre ce qu'elle n'étoit pas, mais pour tacher a devenir, ce qu'elle voulût estre. Cette Intention, qui auroit charmé un homme raisonnable, acheva d'outrer le Prince. Il étoit trop penetrant, et elle dissimulût trop mal, pour qu'il ne s'aperçût pas de la contrainte qu'elle se faisoit pour cacher une tristesse qui la devoroit. Il deployoit sa mauvaise humeur sans menagement, c'étoit tant tôt des reproches, quelques fois des railleries picquantes, et jamais un seul moment de Confiance, d'estime ou de tendresse. Sa Dureté ne lui donnoit nulle compassion pour une Jeune Princesse elevée dans la Delicatesse d'une Cour magnifique qui souffroit toutes les fatigues et les incommoditez de la mer, sans murmurer. Sa douceur, sa patience etoient perdues pour lui, il ne s'en apperçevoit pas, uniquement occupé a considerer les mouvemens de son Coeur et trouvant toujours des sujets de s'en plaindre. Si, lassée d'une contrainte continuelle, et excedée de ses propos outrageants, elle laissoit paroistre sa melancholie, il lui reprochoit le souvenir d'un Amant cheri en lui faisant entendre brutalement qu'il croyoit qu'elle l'avoit favourisé; si elle s'efforcoit devant son Monde de masquer sa Tristesse sous le dehors d'une Gaïté enpruntée, il étoit si persuadé de sa Galanterie, qu'il cherchoit lequel de ses officiers avoit l'honneur de lui plaire. Enfin a voir sa conduitte, on auroit crû par le soin qu'il se donnoit a deplaire, que son bonheur dependoit de se faire haïr d'une epouse qu'il adoroit.

Il eut un chagrin d'un autre espece en arrivant près de l'Isle ou il pretendoit regner. Il vit le Port occupé par la Flotte de son Pere. Les vents contraires avoit assez retardé son voyage pour avoir donné le temps au Roi Farouche (qui se doutoit de sa retraitte), de s'en saisir, et il nÿ avoit pas de seureté a l'aborder. Il falût chercher une autre azyle, mais ou la trouver? Les états du Roi de Bons Enfants n'etoient pas loin, il etoit ennemi du Roi

Farouche, et auroit receû avec plaisir son Fils disgracée [*sic*] s'il avoit voulû demander sa protection, mais il l'auroit regardé comme une flettrissure a son honneur et peutestre craignit-il de montrer la Belle Docile a une Cour aussi aimable et aussi galante que celle la.

Il prit le parti de descendre a un port peu frequenté, sous le titre de particulier d'une Condition mediocre. Il congedia la plus part de ses gens, et leur distribua la moitie de ses pierreries pour recompenser leur Fidelité. Il vendit le reste dans une ville prochaine, et acheta une maisonette qui étoit assez propre en dedans quoyque le dehors eût l'air d'une chaumiere. La situation etoit charmante, a l'entrée d'une Forêt, pres d'un ruisseau qui couloit d'une source de la plus bel eau. Une Colline couverte de Bois la garentissoit des Vents. La vûe etoit etendûe et diversifiée par une Campagne bien cultivée sous un beau ciel, la maison environnée d'une petite terre qui fournissoit abondamment a tous les besoins de la vie. Tout leur train étoit reduit a deux Valets, et deux femmes.[1] Cette solitude estoit faite pour inspirer la Tranquillité, et tout autre que le Prince Sombre l'auroit trouvée dans la conversation de l'aimable Docile, toujours complaisante et obligeante, mais il n'etoit pas fait pour en joüir. La continuation de ses Caprices lui rendoit ce sejour aussi inquiet que la Cour la plus tumulteuse sans la resource de la Dissipation qui sÿ trouve. Les seuls moments de relache pour la malheureuse Reine étoient ceux quil passait a la chasse, qui etoient assez frequents.

Elle se promenoit un de ces jours dans la Forêt suivie d'une de ses femmes a qui elle ne parloit jamais. Cette reserve n'étoit pas une suitte de la triste experience du malheur que ses Confidences lui avoient attiré, mais elle ne se seroit jamais pardonnée, si elle avoit proferée la moindre plainte contre un Mari qu'elle regardit toujours comme l'objet a qui elle devoit le plus inviolable attachment. Sa distraction l'avoit menée assez loin de sa maison, quand le son bruiant des Cors de chasse, les cris des piqueurs, et le bruit d'une meûte lui annoncerent l'aproche d'une chasse magnifique. Elle tache de gagner sa retraitte, mais le Cerf passa la traverse et immediatement apres les chiens qui le poursuivoit. Elle vît un Cavalier de bonne mine, galamment vêtu, monté sur un beau cheval, et a la tête d'une suitte nombreuse et brillante, qui arrette ses pas.

Un Chapeau de paille, un corset du fin lin, et une petite robe d'un taffeta leger, composoient tout son ajustement. Cette simplicité est faite pour relever les charmes d'une jeune personne dont la fraicheur n'a pas encore besoin du secours de la Toilette. Docile parroisoit infiniment plus belle que sous les a<b?>rs[2] de sa Roiauté. Le Roi de Bons Enfants (car vous croyez bien que c'étoit lui), ebloüi d'une figure si peu ordinaire, oublia l'ardeur de la Chasse, pour l'entretenir. Sa cour n'auroit pas été surprise si sa Beauté

[1] Substituted for the more particular 'une femme de chambre, et une servante'.
[2] Illegible: see above, p. 138, n. 2.

avoit été moins touchante, c'éstoit le Roi du monde le plus familier, jamais gené par son Rang. Les vieux Courtisans l'accusoit de l'oublier trop souvent. Il se moquoit de leur Formalitez, il n'étoit jamais si content qu'a Table ou l'esprit seul distinguit les convives, et il courtissoit indifferemment toutes les Belles sans s'embarrasser de leur Genealogie: d'ailleurs le meilleur coeur du monde aimant mieux inspirer la joye que le respect.

Il voulût absolument conduire Docile chez elle. Elle n'osa dire qu'elle craignit la Jalousie de son Mari, et toute autre raison fût inutile pour l'en detourner. Il l'accompagna suivi d'une trentaine des seigneurs jusqu'a cent pas de sa Maison, ou ils rencontrent le Prince Sombre. Son air noble quoyque fier changa le compliment que le Roi lui avoit destiné. Je suis persuadé (lui dit il) que vous n'estes pas né pour habiter la chaumiere que je vois. Les charmes de Madame vostre femme, m'avoit deja apris ce que j'en devois penser. Je ne veux pas demander vostre secret, mais je ne souffriroy pas que des personnes comme vous restent dans un état si indigne d'eux. Vous ettes étrangers; si je ne puis pas corriger vostre destin, au moins vous serriez plus convenablement a la Cour que dans l'obscurité de cette Forêt, dont je veux que vous sortiez a l'heure même. Il ordonne sans attendre sa reponse un char pour les conduire, et marcha lui même a Côté, entretenant Docile avec une Politesse galante qui desesperoit le Prince. Il resta dans un morne silence, que les Courtisans intterpreterent comme un exces de joye pour le bonheur inesperé qui lui arrivoit.

Le Roi nÿ fit pas attention, il estoit trop occupé du soin d'amuser la Belle étrangere. Il reçevoit avec facilité toutes les impressions agreable, et il n'en avoit jamais éprouvé de plus forte qu'aupres d'elle. Né pour la joye, liberal, gaÿe et (ce qui paroistra incroyable a plusieurs personnes) dans sa premiere vigueur quoy que 25 anns: tout respiroit le plaisir a sa Cour. Il donna un apartement aux Etrangers, assez magnifique pour leur convenir quand il auroit connu leur rang; ils mangerent des ce soir même a sa table. Il proposa le jeu apres souper et les retint assez longtemps pour donner le temps de preparer l'apartement de Docile selon ses ordres. Elle y trouva une Toilette superbe decorée d'un écrain de Diamants, des Garderobes remplies de plus belles étoffes et des dentelles de la derniere mode, des Filles aimable destinées a la servir. Rien ne fût oublié pour marquer l'intention qu'il avoit de rendre son Palais agreable.

On peut imaginer de quel façon le Prince Sombre goûtoit cette magnificence. Il commenca par quereller Docile sur sa promenade qui leur avoit attiré cette avanture; il poussa l'injustice jusqu'a dire, que c'étoit sans doute l'effet d'un dessein premedité, qu'elle avoit écrit au Roi, pour sÿ trouver, et qu'elle étoit deja convenüe du prix de ces honneurs dont il les combloient. Elle éstoit assez accoutumée aux injures pour n'éstre pas surprise de celle ci, et y repondit avec une soumission qui auroit changé tout autre Coeur que le sien. Quand je vous ai donné la main, Seigneur, dit-elle, je me suis soumise sans reserve a vostre volonte. Vous n'avez qu'a ordonner, vous me verrez toujours obeïr.

Je ne vous contraindrai pas Madame, (repondit-il d'un ton sec) si le Roi vous plaist, vous n'avez qu'a rester. Pour moi, je me retireray quand la mort la plus cruelle en seroit la Consequence. Si vous voulez que je vous croye innocente, contre toute apparence, demandez vostre retraitte d'une façon a l'obtenir sans que je m'en mêle. Je rougiray de disputer une Femme assez legere pour balancer entre un Amant et son Mari. Elle promit d'agir selon ses desirs, et convint avec lui de hazarder une Fuitte, s'il étoit impossible d'avoir leur congé.

Tout ce qu'il y avoit de Grand ou d'aimable de deux Sexes, se presenter-ent le Lendemain a sa Toilette, et mit en oeuvre tout ce que l'esprit et l'envie de plaire pouvoient fournir pour se rendre agreable. Les hommes encenso-ient sa beauté, les Femmes l'accabloint des carresses, et d'Offres d'amitie qui n'étoit pas si peu sincere qu'on pourroit douter. C'est l'ordinaire des Courtisans de se former sur le Modele de leur Roi. La Franchise étoit sa vertu favorite, l'envie et la tracaserie lui deplaisoient si fort que la mode en étoit passée. Une femme même auroit été si ridicule en dechirant une autre, qu'aucune n'osoit l'entreprendre. Les prudes et les Hipocrites avoient été obligées de se retirer en province, et la Galanterie étoit si bien établie a la Cour, qu'il nÿ avoit ni Mere, ni Mari, assez hardi pour y trouver a redire. Il est vrai que ce n'estoit pas le Païs des Sentiments; ils ne cherchoient que des plaisirs sans peines. Les goûts et les convenances formoient tous leur arrangements; ils se moquoient des langueurs et ne respectoient guerre les soupirs. On ne voyoit aucun de ses Romans qui preche la delicatesse; des Contes Libres, des Operas Comiques, et des Comoedies enjoüées faisoient toute l'occupation des <?Poetes, qui> ne manquoient jamais d'etre recom-pensez s'ils avoient reüsis a divertir.

Le Roi avouoit hautement qu'il faisoit plus de cas d'une chanson a boire galamment tournée, que d'un volume de Metaphysique. Les panegyristes en General furent exilez, comme pertubateurs du Plaisir publique par l'ennui qu'ils inspiroient. Les Philosophes et les Astronomes etoient libre d'etudier dans leur chambres, avec defense expresse de publier aucune ouvrage, ou on ne trouvoit ou de l'utilité, ou de l'amusement. Tout Theo-logien, Casuiste, ou Controversiste, auroit été envoyes aux Galeres s'ils avoient osé se declarer; il nÿ avoit de Prêtres que pour le service des Autels, et comme le culte de la Religion (a ce qu'ils disoient) demandoit une grande simplicité, il leur etoient defendûs d'aprendre a lire ou a écrire. Une Musique excellente estoit l'unique Office de Temples, et c'étoit pour varier ses plaisirs que le Roi y alloit souvent. On presentoit des Victimes ornées de Guirlandes, qu'on immoloit point; on brûloit les parfums le plus exquis. La belle Jeunesse dançoit en honneur de Dieux, une Volupté sacrée se repan-doit dans tous les Coeurs, et quand on s'étoit bien rejoui, on croyoit avoir rendu un homage agreable a la Divinité, qui se plaisoit (selon leur systeme) a voir des heureux, et detournoit les yeux avec horreur de ces Monstres ingrats qui refusoient de joüir de ses bien faits. Ils eviteroient les exces pour conserver la Santé comme la base du Plaisir, mais ils ne la cherchoient que par l'exercice du Corps et la Gaïté de l'esprit. Ils ne se servoient quasi jamais de remedes; de tout l'art de la Medicine, la seule étude de simples étoit permise.[1] Les Loix etoient en petit nombre, exprimée avec netteté, et n'avoient jamais été commentées.

Tels estoient les moeurs de ce peuple singulier, qui étoient plus envié que redouté par leur voisin. Ils ne projettoint jamais de Conquetes et se contentoint de se tenir sur la defensive, uni entre eux. Le Roi Farouche quoy que beaucoup plus fort, avoit toujours échoué dans ses entreprises contre leur nation. Leur Roi n'etoit pas honteux de plaisanter sur tous les Conquerants passés, present et a venir. La vie est trop courte, disoit-il, pour de vastes projets; joüissons mes Amis de Biens qui sont a nostre portée, et laissons joüir aux autres de ceux que les Dieux bien faisants leur ont donnés en partage. Ces maximes ne font pas un Heros. Elles font mieux, elles font un toute honnête Homme et un roiaume il se picquoit florissant de toutes les Vertûs de l'humanité.

Sa Cour étoit le refuge de tous les gens de bien persecutez de la Fortune. Les Talents, et la figure passoient aupres de lui pour des titres de noblesse. Aussi avoit-il fondé un ordre, dont les preuves requise pour y estre admis, etoient celles du desinterresment, de la Generosité, et de l'amitié; sa politesse et ses attentions pour les Etrangers qui parroissoient les meriter passoient tout ce qu'on pourroit imaginer. Jugez comme il s'en acquitta pour la Belle Docile. Il vint en personne la prier d'honorer sa Cour de sa presence. Il disoit des choses gracieuses au Prince Sombre quoy qu'il y repondit assez mal, et d'un air mécontent se retira de quelques pas, pendant que le Roi s'avançoit vers Docile, qui saisit cette occasion de lui demander la permission de retourner a sa retraitte, en lui marquant pourtant toute la reconnoisance qu'elle devoit a ses bontez. Il parroisoit bien étonné d'une demande si capricieuse, est vous si tost lasse Madame, disoit-il, de faire l'ornement de ma Cour? vous a t'on manquée? ou craignez vous (ajouta til en baissant la voix) de me trouver trop sensible a des charmes qui effacent tout ce qu'il y a de plus aimable? Je vous avoûe ma defaitte, mais en perdant ma Liberté, je ne perdray pas mon respect; vous n'avez qu'un esclave de plus, depuis que je vous ai vû; je ne vous parlerai jamais sur un autre ton. Vous me rendrez heureux, si vous me jugez digne de l'estre. Si vous trouvez un autre plus capable de vous plaire, je tacherai de trouver mon Bonheur, dans la vostre, et ne le traverserai jamais—ne seroit ce pas Monsieur vostre Mari qui vous oblige de vous retirer? Il n'est pas naturel qu'a vostre Age vous souhaittez de vous enseveler dans un Bois, et de cacher une Beauté

---

[1] Sentence struck out: 'on voyoit des herbistes mais point d'Apothécaire'.

faite pour triompher de tous les Coeurs. Les Maris sont souvent incommodes—il faut le gagner.

Il la quitta sans attendre sa reponse, et avança vers le Prince Sombre, avec cet air ouvert qui sied si bien et qu'on voit si rarement aux princes. Il lui fit tous les offres le plus magnifiques et le plus attrayantes, pour lui persuader de se fixer aupres de lui. Le Prince Sombre, qui vouloit mettre Docile a la derniere épreuve, repondit, en s'efforçant de paroistre respectueux, qu'il sentoit tout le prix de l'honneur qu'il lui faisoit, qu'il passeroit sa vie avec plaisir a son service, qu'il seroit bien aise de renoncer a une retraitte, dont l'indolence lui étoit desagreable, et qu'il n'avoit choisi que par Complaisance pour sa femme, que si sa Majeste pouvoit changer son humeur insociable, il en seroit enchanté. S'il osoit, même il prendra la liberté de l'en prier.

Le Roi tout etonné, se tourna vers elle en lui disant, Est-il possible Madame que ce soit vous, qui vouliez vous obstiner, de nous abandonner? quelle Raison peut-on trouver pour une disposition si sauvage dans une jeunesse si brillante? est ce Mepris? nous tacherons d'acquerir vostre estime. Est ce tristesse? il faut le guerrir en vous livrant aux amusements convenable a vostre age. Par Consideration même pour vostre époux vous devez rendre au monde un merite qu'il a enterré trop longtemps. Je ne suis pas surpris que vous puissiez lui tenir lieu de tout, mais soyez genereuse a vostre tour, cedez a son desir, et quittez cette solitude, qui rende inutile des personnes que les Dieux ont destinez pour faire le bonheur de Mortels.

La malheureuse Docile tendit les yeux baissez pendant ce discours, et quand elle les levoit elle voyoit ceux du Prince Sombre attachez sur elle, ce que ne lui apprenoit que trop, ce qu'il voulût qu'elle repondât. Elle insista sur sa demande, sans entrer en aucun raisonnement la dessus, et cela avec une melancholie si profonde, que le Roi ne douta pas un moment de son Humeur extrodinaire. Son amour en diminuât de la moitie. Il sortit en disant qu'il falloit attendre du temps, qu'elle prit une resolution plus favorable, et laissa ces deux personnes dans un état dificile a décrire.

Le Prince Sombre rompit le silence le premier. Je vois bien (dit il) que le Roi veut nous retenir ici, malgre cette feinte Douceur dont je ne suis pas le dupe. Il se flatte aparement que cette violence vous seroit agreable. Des solicitations ne serviront de rien aupres de lui, il faut prendre une Resolution hardie, et l'executer avec fermeté. On ne m'espione pas, je gagnerai une chaise de poste qui serait prête a deux heures apres minuit. Si vous voulez vous conserver pour moi, vous monterois dedans, et prendrais le chemin de la mer; je vous suivrai de le Lendemain. Si je vâs avec vous, on m'accusera de vous avoir enlevée; nous serons poursuivie, peutestre pris; je serois exposé au Resentiment d'un Monarque absolu et irrité. L'interet de son Amour demande ma perte et la pretexte serait assez plausible pour le justifier. Parroisez au Cercle se soir, pour detourner les soupsçons de vostre dessein; mettez les pierreries qu'il vous a envoyé. Je serois charmé, qu'un esperance detrompé mette le comble a sa mortification quand il vous voit perdue a jamais. Elle repondit simplement qu'il sera obeïé, et entra dans son cabinet pour donner cours a des larmes, qu'elle avoit retenûe avec peine pendant qu'il parloit.

Le Caractere de Docile occupoit toute la Cour: on louoit sa Beauté en blamant son Coeur. Les Dames qui lui avoint fait des avances d'amitié se plaignoient de sa froideur, et les hommes ne cessoient pas d'admirer l'air distrait et insensible avec lequel elle avoit reçeu les Galanteries du Roi. On conclût en general qu'elle avoit l'ame dure, et lon plaignit son Mari d'avoir a souffrir des caprices, qui nuisoient si visiblement a sa Fortune. Elle parût, et sa presence detruisit toute Critique. On ne songea qu'a sa Beauté, relevée par sa Parure et encore plus par les Graces naturelles de sa personne. Le Roi en parroisoit enchanté; il oublia qu'elle avoit souhaittée de lui quitter, et se flatta qu'elle l'avoit oubliée aussi. Elle soupa en Public avec lui, et affecta un Air de satisfaction qui persuada tout le monde qu'elle s'etoit determinée avec plaisir de rester dans une Cour ou elle étoit adorée.

On [ne] s'aperçût de sa fuitte, que 4 heures apres son depart. Le Prince Sombre fut le premier qui l'annonça, et en parru desesperé. Il assura le Roi qu'il ne falût pas douter qu'elle avoit pris le chemin de sa Solitude, que sil estoit possible de la faire revenir, elle cederait a ses prieres plus tost qu'a la violence. Il demandoit permission de la suivre seul, ce que le Roi lui accordat assez Volontiers, en lui recommandant de ne la point contraindre. Asseurez la de ma part (dit-il) qu'elle aura toujours ma Protection, et si elle se plaist dans sa Forêt je ne l'obligerai jamais d'en sortir.

Le Prince ne sçavoit que croire de la froideur que le Roi temoignoit dans un Occasion, ou il s'attendoit de le voir au desespoir. Il soupsçonnoit a son ordinaire quelque commerce secret entre lui et Docile. S'il ne l'avoit pas toujours gardé a vûe, il n'auroit pas douté qu'un Amour satisfait, produisoit le calme ou il voyoit le Roi de Bons Enfants. Il etoit pourtant tout simple. Le Roi n'etoit pas d'humeur a languir aux pieds d'une cruelle. Il ne courroit jamais apres les plaisirs, au travers des Obstacles. Il disoit que le vrai Sage les attendoit dans le bras de l'indolence et quils ne manquoient jamais de se presenter a ceux qui les vouloient attendre, que la delicatesse étoit le poison de la Felicité, et la Constance mal recompensée une Platitude indigne de l'humanité, inventée peutestre par quelque vieux decrepit, qui vouloit finir ses jours en adorant une Insensible, pour voiler sa Caducité qui ne pouvoit plus rendre homage a une Beauté tendre et favorable.

Le Cour s'epuisoit en raisonnements sur l'extravagance de la belle étrangere. On trouva même de la perfidie dans ses procedez, et ceux qui en parloient le plus favorablement la traittoit de Folle et d'insensée, pendant qu'elle sacrifioit a sa Vertu, son repos, son bonheur, et son honneur, car elle sentoit bien, le tort que cette inegalité de Conduitte lui faisoit. Mais elle obeïssoit, et elle se fit un devoir indispensible d'obeïr.

La Princesse Docile II

Le Prince Sombre tourna ses pas, vers le Port ou il avoit donné rezdevous [*sic*] a sa Docile, par des chemins écartez qui allongeoient son voiage de plusieurs leius, et il n'arrivoit en vûe de la ville qu'au jour. Il aperçût d'assez loin un Corps de troupes qui en sortoit. Il les regardoit avec la plus grand attention, et son Imagination, qui étoit d'une fertilité singuliere a lui fournir des tourments, lui fit voir qu'ils entouroint une Chaise. Il ne douta pas un moment qu'ils ne ramenerent Docile a la Cour. Il crût voir l'explication de l'indifference que le Roi avoit fait paroistre, quand il lui avoit annonçé son depart. Il se souvenoit de la soûmission avec laquelle elle avoit suivie ses ordres, et conclût qu'elle avoit fait ses Conventions avec le Roi, qui devoit l'enlever pour sauver son Honneur; il regardoit son Obeissance comme le dernier des outrages. Tres resolu de n'etre pas le dupe de son Hypocrisie, et craignant encore qu'on avoit ordre de l'arreter, il se plongea dans une Forêt voisine, avec des sentiments si vif et si confûs qu'il ne sçavoit pas ou il alloit, et point de tout ou il vouloit aller. Les troupes qui lui avoient tant allarmé, n'étoit pourtant autre chose, que le Garnison qui changoit de Quartier.

Laissons le promener par le Demon de la Jalousie, qui le rendoit furieux, et retournons a Docile, qui étoit si accablée de Fatigue et des refflections, qu'elle se mit au lit en arrivant a la poste, ou son epoux lui avoit asseuré qu'il la joindroit le même soir. Elle étoit bien ettonnée de ne pas entendre parler de lui ni ce soir ni tout le lendemain. Elle n'avoit jamais soupçonnée quil etoit capable de lui manquer de parole, et n'avoit que tres peu d'argent, qui fût dissipé en deux jours. Elle l'attendoit a tous moments, mais l'Hotesse n'etoit pas d'humeur a attendre son argent; elle le demandoit avec Vivacité, n'ayant pas trop bonne Opinion d'une jeune femme qui voiagoit ainsi toute seule.

La pauvre Princesse se trouvoit dans létat le plus embarrassant. Elle n'avoit d'aut[r]e resource que de mettre entre les mains de l'Hôte une belle Bague que le Prince Sombre l'avoit donné quand il l'epousa etc, en lui priant de l'engager, disant que son Mari ne manquera pas de venir la degager. Il n'en crût rien, il trouva même le Diamant trop gros pour estre fin; il le prit pourtant, determiné de la souffrir encore quelques jours chez lui. La Beauté a toujours des droits sur les Coeurs le plus rustre, et ce n'etoit pas un effet mediocre de celle de Docile, d'attendrir une Ame comme celle de son Hôte.

A minuit ce même soir, un Vaisseau arrivoit au Port, et debarqua un Cavalier avec tout l'equipage d'un grand Seigneur. Il vint demander a loger a cette auberge, suivi de tout son train des pages, des Gentilhommes et des laquais. L'Hotesse se dese[s]paroit que Docile occupoit sa plus belle

Chambre, et étoit couchée depuis longtemps. Elle auroit eûe la Brutalité de l'eveillir pour la faire sortir, si son Mari l'auroit permis, mais il se contenta de faire ses excuses au nouveau venu, de ce qu'il ne pouvoit lui donner son meilleur lit pour cette nuit, en ajoutant que s'il vouloit s'accomoder ce soir d'un moins bon, qu'il chasseroit demain la personne qui y dormoit et qui n'avoit pas asseurement dequoy le payer.

C'est peutestre quelque pouilloux que vous y avez mis, disoit le cavalier en riant, et je me garderoi bien de prendre sa place. L'Hôte se piqua d'honneur, d'estre accusé de loger des pareils gens. Il faisoit le portrait de Docile avec toute l'eloquence dont il étoit capable, et finissoit en montrant la Bague qu'elle lui avoit remise, disant qu'il voyoit tres bien qu'elle étoit Stras, qu'en tout cas elle pourroit valoir un ou deux Loüis, mais n'ayant point de Jouallier dans cette ville il ne sçavoit pas son prix au juste. Le Cavalier que étoit tres fin connoisseur jugea bien autrement, il lui ordonna de la faire mettre sur la Toilette de la Dame avant son levée accompagnée d'une Bourse qu'il tira de sa poche, ou il y avoit plus de cent louis. L'Hôte la prit en disant d'un ton goguenard, Ah monseigneur, je voye bien que c'est n'est [*sic*] pas la Bague que vous voulez acheter. Ecoutez Mon Ami, repondit le Cavalier d'un air severe, apprenez a parler avec respect des personnes que vous ne connoissez pas. C'est peutestre une Femme de Qualité que le Malheur a reduite a un état indigne d'elle, suivez mes ordres avec Fidelité et vous en trouverez la recompense; si vous osez me tromper—L'Hôte l'interrompit pour lui jurer une obeissance parfait, et pour lui prouver qu'il pouvoit s'y fier, commença une Kyrielle des histoires qui auroient durée toute la nuit, si le Cavalier aura eû la patience de les entendre. Il se coucha aussi tost que ses gens lui avoient dressé un lit de camp Magnifique qu'il avoit porté avec lui.

Docile étoit bien eloignée de passer la nuit aussi tranquillement. Ses malheurs passez et ceux qu'elle devoit craindre, occupoint trop son esprit pour lui permettre le sommeil. Elle tachoit d'esperer de revoir son Epoux; elle se souvenoit (malgre elle) de toutes les duretez qu'elle avoit essuiée de sa part, et craignoit d'en estre abandonnée, quoy qu'elle rejettoit cette pensée comme trop injurieuse pour lui, et contre la confiance qu'elle croyait lui devoir. Abimée dans ses refflections, elle s'assoupit vers le matin; elle n'avoit pas joüi de cet repos une heure quand elle entendit quelqu'un ouvrir la porte de sa chambre, et en regardant a travers ses rideaux, elle vit l'hotesse qui posa doucement sur sa Table, la Bague et la Bourse. Elle l'appella, pour la demander l'explication de cet action, dont elle etoit toute étourdie. L'Hôtesse qui n'étoit pas faschée d'estre surprise sur le fait pour avoir une pretexte de parler du Cavalier dont la bonne mine, et la magnificence lui avoint fournie un tas des conjectures qu'elle bruloit de communiquer.

Ah Madame, s'ecria t-elle d'un ton beaucoup plus respectueux qu'aparavant, nous avons eû un bonheur inoüie hier au soir; il est arrivé a nostre maison indigne, le Seigneur du monde le mieux fait, un train de prince, un Equipage superbe. Et quel rapport a tout ceci a ma bague? intterompit la Reine infortunée. Oh, beaucoup, Madame, continua la jaseuse. Mon Mari lui a parlé de vous (j'ose vous asseurer que vous lui avez cet obligation); il ne se fit pas prier pour vous servir. Il ordonna avec empressement qu'on met la Bague sur vostre Table, avec cette belle bourse, qui est bien garnie, je vous en reponds, en nous defandant pourtant de vous fair sçavoir d'ou elle venit; mais je vous aime trop pour vous rien cacher, d'ailleurs il me semble que quand on fait un action genereux on doit estre bien aise que tout le monde le sache et je ne comprends pas par quelle Bizarrerie il veut celer une chose qui lui fait honneur.

Je la comprend moi, disoit la Reine. Allez mon Enfant, je veux rever a ce que j'ai a faire. L'hotesse qui vouloit lui faire sa Cour, obeit.

Docile admira la Generosité de l'inconnu, mais elle se sentit si capable d'en faire, qu'elle ne la regardoit pas comme un avanture aussi merveilleux qu'aura faite une personne de plus d'experience, elle ne laissa pas de sentir la reconnoisance la plus vive, melée de cette honte qui a toute Ame genere-euse qui est reduitte a reçevoir un Obligation. Elle condamna ce sentiment comme un effet d'amour propre, et prit la Resolution de voir l'étranger, determinée de lui faire garder la Bague, au moins jusqu'elle pouvoit lui rendre son Argent. Dans cette vûe elle envoyoit lui prier de l'honneur de sa Compagnie. Il comprit par son message qu'elle sçavoit de quel part étoit venu ce secours inattendu. Il avoit deja pris soin de s'habiller d'une pro-preté galante ornée d'un Air de negligence, et hâtoit de satisfaire sa curi-osité en voyant cette Beauté dont il avoit entendu tant des merveilles.

Mais il me semble que jai trop tardé de contenter celle de mes Lecteurs, qui sont sans doute en peine de sçavoir qui étoit ce Cavalier si extrodinaire. Je ne sçaurois le dire au juste, puis qu'il l'ignorât lui même. On lui avoit jamais parlé de sa Naissance: un Bourgois retiré lui avoit elevé; a l'age de six anns, il l'avoit mis a une école celebre, ou il avoit si bien profité, qu'a Douze il étoit dans le premier Classe. C'estoit alors que son Protecteur l'en retira, malgre les asseurances que le maitre du college lui donnoit, qu'avec la memoire heureuse, l'esprit juste, et l'inclination que cet Enfant avoit pour les Lettres, il ne pouvoit pas manquer de faire l'ornement de l'université sil vouloit lui permettre de continuer ses études.

Le Bourgois écouta son Discours eloquent avec un Sang froid qu'on ne trouve que dans son Païs, et sans rendre aucune raison de sa conduitte, mis le Garçon chez un procureur fort renommé pour sa Science dans les misteres de la Chicane. Malgre sa grande jeunesse, il ne laissa pas de trouver extrodinare le soin que son Bienfaiteur avoit eû, de lui paitrir des Auteurs Classiques, qui lui parroissoient assez inutile dans la proffession a la quelle il lui destinoit. Mais il avoit assez d'esprit pour comprendre que son role étoit d'obeïr, et non de raissonner. Il ne connoisoit aucun Ami que le vieux Bourgois, il ne se pouvoit dire d'aucune famille, n'ayant jamais entendu aucun nom quil avoit, excepté celui de Janot. Le bon homme ne lui traita jamais avec la tendresse d'un Pere, ni avec le mepris d'un superieur. Il lui avoit peu parlé dans toute sa vie; c'étoit toujours avec un grand serieux, qui defendit a l'enfant d'oser lui questioner sur rien.

Il comprit que son unique Interêt present étoit de lui plaire, et une soûmission entiere lui parroisoit le seul moyen dÿ parvenir. Il entra sans murmurer dans la maison du Procureur, qui s'aperçût bien tost qu'il avoit un Genie a faire fortune, subtil, complaisant, et capable d'une grande aplication. Il resolût de cultiver ces rares Talents, qui pouvoient lui servir quelque jour, et l'instruisit avec plus de Soin, qu'il ne donnoit a ses autres eleves. Il avoit resté aupres de lui deux anns et avoit fait un progress etton-ant dans son metier, quand son Patron lui osta de la, pour l'envoyer aux Indes avec un Negotiant de ses amis, qui y avoit fait une fortune immense par son habilité dans le negoce, qu'il s'engagea d'aprendre au jeun homme, moyenant une Somme considerable que le Bourgois lui donna. Il fit un sejour de deux anns a la Chine, et revint heureusement avec un Vaisseau chargé de riches merchandises. Il ramena Janot chez son Protecteur, (un peu halé, beaucoup grandi et d'une figure aimable) en lui asseurant qu'il n'avoit jamais été si content d'aucun Garçon de sa vie. Il ne se lassoit pas, de louer sa prudence, sa Modestie et son Industrie.

Le Vieillard l'écouta sans dementir son sang froid, reprit son éleve chez lui, et peu apres, lui acheta une leiutenance dans un Regiment qui partoit pour la Guerre, en lui donnant le Nomme de Fortuné. Il étoit naturelle-ment brave, et quand il ne l'auroit pas été, il s'étoit fait une si grande habit-ude de regler ses actions selon l'interet present, que sa raison aurez surmonté une timidité naturelle. Il se trouva a deux battailles, et un Siege cette campagne, ou sa bravoure et sa conduitte lui fit distinguer. Il avoit sçû gagner la bienveillance de tout son Regiment: le Soldat n'avoit jamais vû d'officier si compatisant, attentif a tous leur besoins et leur soulagant en tout ce lui étoit possible; ses Camarades etoient charmé de sa Complais-ance; et les Officiers du plus haut rang, parlerent avantageusement d'un Jeune homme qui leur faisoient la Cour sans bassesse. La Paix se fit peu de mois apres, et le Chevalier Fortuné avoit la permission de retourner chez ses parents, c'est a dire, chez le bon homme qu'il n'osa appeller tel. Il le reçût comme a son Ordinaire, sans le blamer ni le louer, malgre le bien que tout le monde lui en disoit. Il lui laissa encore un Ann dans l'armée.

C'estoit alors pour le premier fois de sa vie qu'il osoit songer a se divertir, mais c'éstoit sans exces, dont il voyoit les tristes effets dans le plus part de ses Compagnons. Ils le menerent quelque fois dans des Leiux de Debauche, mais il n'alla que par Complaisance, et sans jamais se commettre. Il se sentit un inclination assez vif pour le plaisir, mais il le vouloit avec plus de Goût, et moins de Danger. Il tachoit de s'introduire dans de Compagnies honnètes; ses Amis furent ravi de lui presenter a leur Femmes et leur Soeurs, et il profita de la bonne volonté de toutes celles qui vouloient de lui. Il avoit pris a l'armée cet air aisé qu'on acquit rarement ailleurs, sans quitter une Modestie insinuante, qui paroit tous ses Agrements, et le rendît d'une Commerce dangereuse pour les Coeurs du beau Sexe. Il n'en trouva guere qui lui resisterent, mais loin de semer le Division dans les Familles, il y mettoit toujours la Païx. Sa premiere Leçon aux Belles (a qui il étoit en droit d'en donner) étoit, de se mettre parfaittement bien avec leur Maris, et il lui arriva souvent d'établir l'harmonie dans des menages, ou on avoit desesperé de le voir. Les epoux et les epouses furent egalement content de lui. Il n'étoit pas pourtant scrupuleux sur la fideleté ou la Constance ni amoureux d'aucune au point de lui en inspirer. Il regardoit la femme comme une espece de Gibier fait pour l'amusement de l'homme, et s'en divertît sans s'engager. Il n'avoit garde de debiter ces maximes, même parmi ses Camerades, au contraire il ne parloit jamais de la Galanterie que sur un ton serieux qui lui attiroit quelque fois les railleries de jeunes gens, mais que lui preparoit la Confiance des Dames.

Effectivement elles n'avoient aucune raison de s'en plaindre. Il étoit d'une Discretion parfaite, et avoit autant de menagement pour celles qu'il quittoit que pour celles qu'il poursuivoit. Il tachoit de leur remplacer un Amant perdû par un ami utile. Quand elles ne voulurent pas prendre le change, il se retira, en disant toujours de bien d'elles, avec des procedez si doux et si honêttes qu'elles avoient honte d'estre de ses Ennemis. Quand il étoit quitté (ce que lui arrivoit rarement) il ne faisoit ni reproche ni menace, et resta Ami de la personne qui l'avoit une fois favorisée. Il avoit assez d'esprit de faire une Refflection que n'est pas de la portée de tout le monde, que c'est la Vanité qui est la source de presque tous nos chagrins. Il sçavoit étouffer ses premiers mouvements, jamais il n'en tirât de distinctions que les Belles avoient pour lui, il ne visoit jamais qu'aux faveurs que leur Coeurs lui voulûrent accorder, et ne chercha pas celles de la Bourse comme font tant d'autres.

Aimé de Dames et recherché des Hommes, il étoit en possession de l'estime generale quand son Patron trouvoit a propos de le retirer des Troupes, ayant acheté pour lui une de ces petites charges a la Cour qui sont sans éclat, mais dans laquelle on voit beaucoup mieux l'interieure que dans celles qui sont plus élevés. Cette nouvelle Caprice du Bourgois lui coûtoit beaucoup d'obeïr. Il balança meme s'il devoit le faire: il esperoit de s'avancer par la faveur de son colonel, et quittoit avec regret les plaisirs auxquelles il s'étoit livré. Mais le Vieilard étoit fort cassé, il ne voulût pas renoncer a l'esperance d'une succession que quoy qu'incertaine, lui parroisoit aussi bien fondée qu'aucune que sa situation lui permettoit; et comme jusque la il avoit suivi son Interêt sans se detourner de cette vûe, qui

étoit l'unique a la quelle il étoit attachée, il resolût de se conformer aux ordres du Bourgois, avec son Submission ordinaire, et il entra en garde peu
des jours apres.

Il fit son devoir avec une assiduité que le Roi même remarqua; on ne
pouvoit jamais lui accuser ni de Tracasserie ni de redittes; il observa tout,
sans paroistre rien voir, d'un air si simple et si naturel que les plus vieux
Courtisans se trompoient dans son Caractere. Il rendoit a toutes les Dames,
le Respect qu'il leur devoit, sans distinguer aucune. Il voyoit parmi elles,
une Politique, un esprit de Parti, et un ambition qui abimoint toutes leur
passions. Il evitoit leur Confiance comme la chose la plus Dangereuse qui
pouvoit lui arriver. Ses observations lui faisoit voir les premiers lueurs de la
Faveur ou de la disgrace, et il faisoit sa cour de si bonne heure a ceux qui
commencerent de jouïr de bonnes graces du Ministre, qu'il n'étoint pas
possible de demêler si cestoit une suitte de leur Fortune, ou une Inclination
pour leur service. Il n'étoit pas moins diligent a se retirer d'aupres de ceux
qui etoient sur le declin de leur credit; il leur laissoit toujours une Foule
des Courtisans moins éclairez, et il étoit souvent le seul dont ils ne croyoint
pas avoir raison de se plaindre, qu'il les l'abandonnoit dans le même temps
que la Fortune. Il n'avoit fait dans toute sa vie, ni Ami, ni Maitresse du
Coeur; il ne se laissoit pas entrainer par son Goût, et n'examinoit jamais
personne par rapport a leur merite, mais par l'utilité qu'il pouvoit tirer de
leur commerce. Il decidoit rarement, et ne contrarioit jamais. Il chercha de
plaire et non de briller dans la Conversation, croyant que la bienveillance
lui seroit beaucoup plus avantageuse que l'applaudissement. Il ne donnoit
des conseils que quand il étoit fort pressé de la faire, et alors il étudioit l'inclination de celui qui en demandoit, et point du tout son Interêt, ni son
devoir.

Enfin il trouva le secret de plaire a tout le monde, pendant qu'il avoit un
mepris si solide pour le genre humain, (par la Fourberie, la Foiblesse, et l'injustice qu'il avoit remarqué dans tous les états) qu'il ne jugea aucun digne
de sa Confiance; et reglait son estime pour les hommes comme on fait pour
les chiens et les chevaux, non sur les service qu'ils ont rendu mais par ceux
qu'ils sont capable de rendre. Il ne s'etoit jamais laissé eblouïr par la
Reputation du sçavant ou de bel esprit; il la regardoit comme inutile a la fortune, et tres souvent nuisible, par l'envie qu'elle ne manque jamais d'attirer.
Il cacha soigneusement son Goût pour la Lecture quoy qu'il l'avoit toujours
conservé, mais il ne puisa pas ses maximes dans ses Livres, bien persuadé
que les Auteurs ne disoient pas ce qu'ils pensoient mais ce qu'ils souhait-
tassent que les autres pensassent. Il ne se permettoit pas la raillerie la plus
legere, quoy qu'il y etoit naturellement porté. Il blama peu, et ne loua point
les absents. N'ayant aucune attachment sincere, il ne se faisoit pas des
Ennemis, en tachant de Justifier ses amis. S'il flattoit quelqu'un (dont la
protection lui sembloit necessaire) c'étoit toujours sur les Qualitez qu'il

affectoit et pas sur celles qu'il possedoit: il parloit aux Belles de la Vivacité de leur esprit, et aux beaux esprits de Graces de leur Figure, sachant que les Louanges auxquelles on est accoutumé ne font guere d'impression, et qu'on est charmé de s'entendre dire en possession des agrements, qui paroissoint douteux même a l'amour propre. Il s'attira les regards du Ministre en faisant remarquer a tout le monde qu'il avoit la Jambe parfaitment bien fait; jusqu'a la, il navoit jamais entendu que des Flatteries sur son Genie surprenant, et cette Louange avoit le merite de la nouveauté. Cette conduitte lui valût une bienveillance universel, il laissoit les petits avantages de sa charge a des subalterns, c'estoit trop peu pour ajouter a sa Fortune, mais assez pour lui acquerir la Reputation de l'homme du monde le plus desintteressé, et il sçavoit a quel point elle est necessaire pour celui qui cherche un établissement solide.

On sera peutestre surpris de voir une Politique si raffinée, dans une si grande jeunesse. On doit se souvenir qu'il s'etoit toujours vû dans une situation a croire qu'il pouvoit avoir besoin de tout le monde. Son bon sens naturel n'avoit jamais été corrompu par les Flateurs, et né dur, hardi, et intteressé, il lui étoit aisé de paroistre tendre, modeste, et Genereux sans affecter pourtant aucune de ces Vertûs au point de faire le moindre tort a sa Fortune, qu'il ne perdoit jamais de vûe. Il etoit deja nommé pour un charge plus considerable quand son vieux Protecteur mourût et lui laissa cent mille Louis argent comptant, dans des Fonds differents, et le valeur d'autant dans les Colonies de l'Amerique. Il etoit autant surpris que personne de cette Opulence prodigeuse. Il s'etoit toujours flatté de la succession du Bourgois, a qui il ne voyoit ni favori, ni parent; mais il étoit bien eloigné de lui croire de cette Richesse immense. La ville avoit toujours été divisé dans ses Sentiments sur son sujet: les uns disoint, que c'étoit un vieux Crasseux qui enterroit son Argent, et les autres qu'il avoit sans doute fait quelque banqueroute secrette, qui l'avoit forcé de se retirer du Commerce ou il avoit brillé, pour se reduire au simple necessaire, d'un Valet et d'une Servante. Le Chevalier Fortuné, qui le voyoit de plus pres, l'avoit toujours vû un air d'aisance qui lui persuadoit que sa frugalité étoit l'effet de son Goût et non de la necessité; mais il ne sÿ attendoit pas, a trouver une somme de cette force. L'amour propre voulût lui suggerer que c'étoit un depôt qui avoit été confié au Bourgois par quelque Pere illustre, pour son usage; mais il n'en avoit aucune preuve et il rejetta cet Idée flatteuse.

Sa prudence ne l'avoit pas abandonnée quoy qu'elle fût un peu ébranlée par cette Fortune subite. Il fit Refflection qu'il étoit alors en état d'exciter l'envie, et que toutes les richesses du monde ne pouvoint pas cacher sa Naisance equivoque. Il se sentit le Coeur trop élevé, pour souffrir un Païs ou elle fût connûe: il prit la Resolution de faire le tour de l'Europe, en changeant de Nomme, et determine de se fixer dans le Roiaume, ou il trouvera le plus d'agrement. Il quitta la Cour avec un Air de modestie et de

Reconnoisance, se fit un Equipage Honète,[1] et commença ses Voiages malgre les regrets d'une foule d'amis de tous les états, qui parroisoint deseperez de son Depart, et les larmes de Filles d'honneur qui voulûrent chaqu'une lui persuader qu'il avoit été longtemps leur Inclination secrette. Il avoit fait quelque sejour dans toutes les grandes villes, et apres plusieurs Années de Course, se retournoit a celui de Bons Enfants comme le plus agreable, dans le Dessein dÿ Finir ses jours. Il avoit augmenté son train pour se donner un air de Consideration et s'appella le Comte d'Esperanza.

Il avoit alors pres de trente Anns, la Phisonomie noble et heureuse, l'air Galant quoy q'un peu serieux, la Taille parfaitte; on l'auroit flatté de l'appeller Beau, mais on ne pouvoit pas se dispenser de lui trouver infiniment aimable. Il se presenta a Docile avec autant de respect que si son rang lui fût connû: elle estoit si faitte pour en inspirer qu'il estoit impossible qu'on n'en ressentit en l'approchant. Cette Beauté noble et modeste qui étoit rendûe encore plus touchante par le Langueur dont elle étoit accompagnée, changea les Idées que le Comte avez pris sur le discours de son Hôte. Il s'etoit attendû a voir une belle et jeune personne a qui sa bourse pouvoit lui introduire avec avantage; il ne douta pas qu'elle ne tachoit de lui attendrir par le recit de ses malheurs, et l'enflammer par ses agaceries. Il voyoit une Innocence toute naturelle qui sembloit ignorer ses charmes ou l'effet qu'ils etoient capable de produire; la verité toute simple étoit peint sur son visage, et la negligence de son ajustement faisoit voir clairment qu'elle n'avoit nulle dessein sur son Coeur.

Je vous suis fort obligée Monsieur (disoit elle naïvement) d'une Generosité peu commune, mais je ne sçaurois l'accepter si vous ne voulez pas me faire le plaisir de garder cette Bague. J'attends a tous moments Mon Epoux, qui ne manquera pas de la degager, en vous temoignant sa reconnoisance pour la bonté que vous avez eû pour une malheureuse étrangere.

Il voulût lui protester qu'il ne sçavoit pas de quoi elle parlât, mais elle ne prenoit pas le change, et apres une contestation assez longue, il n'osa pas refuser de mettre la Bague au doigt. Il faisoit durer sa visite aussi longtemps que la bien seance pouvoit la permettre. Il tachoit de l'amuser, en lui parlant de differents Païs qu'il avoit vû. Il estoit surpris de voir qu'elle avoit une connoisance parfaitte de la Geographie. Il comprit qu'elle devoit avoir beaucoup lüe, et glissa quelques traits d'Histoire dans ses recits. Il trouva qu'elle etoit egalement bien instruitte dans l'ancienne et la moderne. Il ne pouvoit pas comprendre ou elle avoit pris son Education, tres seure que ce n'etoit pas dans un Couvent, et quand il la quittoit c'estoit avec des sentiments d'admiration bien nouveaux pour lui. Il n'avoit pas hazardé le moindre compliment sur sa figure. Accoutumé a étudier les Caracteres de

---

[1] Altered from 'noble'.

tous ceux qu'il voyoit, il deméla fort aisement le sien; il voyoit clairment que le seul moyen de continuer son Commerce avec elle, étoit d'eloigner de son Imagination le soupçon d'aucun dessein, et il avoit sçû donner a sa Conversation un Air si degagée et si naïf, qu'il la laissa avec beaucoup d'estime pour lui, sans se douter quil sentit quelque chose de plus pour elle.

Il l'avoit demandé la permission dÿ retourner, qu'elle lui avoit accordée avec plaisir. Il ne manqua pas d'en profiter; pendant huit jours ils étoient presque tous les jours ensemble, lui toujours cachant avec Addresse, l'entreprise qu'il avoit formé, et elle enchantée d'avoir trouvée un ami si parfaittement honnète homme et qui lui amusoit au point d'oublier quelque fois sa triste situation, a la quelle pourtant elle donnoit des soupirs qui n'échapoient pas au Comte d'Esperanza. Mais il n'osa montrer une Curiosité qui l'auroit peutestre choquée, et il attendoit sa Confiance, d'une Inclination qu'il se flattoit d'inspirer. Il lui avoit fait venir des Filles pour la servir; il n'oublia aucune de ces attentions que l'envie de plaire peut donner. Elle estoit peu curieuse, mais la reconnoisance lui fit prendre de l'Interet a ses affaires, et elle souhaittait sçavoir a qui elle avoit tant d'obligation.

Aussi tost qu'elle la temoignoit, il se prepara a la contenter avec l'air pourtant d'un homme qui ne voulût lui rien refuser, mais a qui cette Obeïssance coûtoit. Il preluda par quelques soûpirs qu'il sembloit éttouffer, et debita le plus beau Roman du monde de sa vie. Il y mela le merveilleux, le touchant et l'amusant, toujours une Probité a toute épreuve, une Generosité sans exemple, et une tendresse infinie. Il parcourût legerement sur les plus beaux endroits, mais elle crût voir tout cela a travers sa Modestie, et il sçût si bien remüer les Passions de l'innocente Docile, qu'elle estoit tant tost saisie d'Admiration et d'estime, et tant tôt attendrie jusqu'aux larmes, comme il lui plaisoit de varier son recit. Il ne parla pas de sa naisance mais il laissa entrevoir qu'elle estoit de plus illustre, et qu'il avoit des raisons de Generosité pour le cacher. Elle en avoit trop pour la presser la dessus. Il lui fit entendre (mais avec une delicatesse respectueuse) qu'il desiroit passionement de sçavoir quelque chose d'une personne d'une vertue si singuliere, et qui devoit avoir eûe des avantures bien extrodinaire pour estre dans un état si peu conforme a son merite. Elle hesita sur la reponse qu'elle lui fera. Il lui sembloit que sa confiance plein de Franchise meritoit bien la sienne, mais elle fit Refflection que c'éstoit impossible de raconter son Histoire au vrai, sans donner des Idées desavantageuses de sa Mere et de son Epoux; c'éstoit deux personnes sacrées pour elle.

Elle lui repondit en laissant tomber quelques larmes de ses beaux yeux, que c'etoit renouveller ses malheurs que d'en parler, et elle lui prioit en grace de ne pas exiger cette marque de sa Complaisance. Il lui demanda mille pardons de son Indiscretion, en parroissant touché jusqu'a l'ame du Deplaisir qu'il l'avoit causé, et changea la Conversation, en lui proposant quelque promenade pour la distraire de ses pensées tristes. Il lui parla de la pèche, de la chasse, mais il voyoit que le seul Amusement de la Lecture estoit de son Goût. Il avoit deux ou trois Caisses des Livres choisies, qu'il portoit dans toutes ses Voiages. Il les envoya a la Reine; elle se jetta sur la Poesie, qui estoit nouvelle pour elle. Son Genie y estoit porté naturellement mais l'Hermite lui en avoit toujours parlé comme la source de l'impieté, et le Philosophe l'avoit traité de Bagatelle. Depuis son evenement a la Courronne elle avoit été trop occupée pour avoir eûe le loisir de sÿ appliquer, et elle estoit éttonée dÿ trouver tant des charmes. Elle passa des nuits entieres en la Lecture. Ce Goût nouveau aidoit beaucoup a lui attendrir le Coeur, et repandit une certaine tendresse dans toutes ses Actions, qui estoit de bonne augure pour le Comte.

Il l'assista dans ses études, lui fit distinguer entre le bon, l'excellent et le mediocre. Il ne la permit pas de se laisser seduire par l'oreille (comme font le plus part de jeunes personnes) et il l'aprit a mepriser des pensées fausses, quoy que parez d'un style brillant, mais il l'instruisit avec tant de Delicatesse, qu'elle ne s'apercevoit presque pas qu'il lui donnoit des Leçons, quoy qu'elle sentit bien qu'elle profita beaucoup dans sa conversation. Le jour se coula bien vite dans des Occupations si agreable, et les soirées se passerent ordinairement dans le promenade. C'éstoit souvent dans un petit bois, pres de la ville, ou l'art n'avoit pas encore mis la main, mais la Nature avoit formée des sentiers assez commode. Le Comte y avoit fait placer des Canapés rustiques couverte de la mousse et du Feuilage. Ils écouterent la, la ramage des Rosignols, qui estoit quelque fois intterompû par une Musique exquis, qu'il faisoit venir du Capital, que la Belle desolée ne pouvoit pas entendre sans plaisir malgre tous ses Chagrins, qui ne la quittoient point mais qui estoient extremement adouci par le soin que le Comte avoit de lui fourner des amusements a toute heure. Un soir qu'elle s'etoit promenée plus longtemps qu'a l'ordinaire, elle estoit surprise de trouver a son retour, sa chambre (qui estoit meublée comme celle d'un Auberge commun) ornée des meubles, d'une commodité et d'un goût infini. Rien ne manquoit pour la rendre digne d'elle.

La pauvre Docile avoit une Innocence qui lui tenoit lieu de Sottise. Elle voioit tous ces soins, sans imaginer qu'ils avoient d'autre bût, que celui de soulager sa melancholie, et elle attribua ce dessein a la Generosité qu'elle crû voir briller dans tout les discours du Comte. Elle comprit qu'il avoit beaucoup d'estime pour elle, estant fort eloignée de soupçonner qu'il fut capable de former un projet temeraire. Elle lui fît pourtant des reproches d'une zèle qu'elle appelloit deplacée, mais il y avoit tant de reconnoisance melée dans ses reproches, qu'il estoit ravÿ de les avoir attirées.

Il estoit aussi amoureux d'elle que son Caractere lui permettoit d'estre. C'est a dire il la trouva necessaire a l'agrement de sa vie. Son Ambition étant satisfait du costé de la Fortune; il voulût contenter son Goût pour le plaisir. La Beaute de Docile picqua ses desirs, et sa vertu sa Vanité. Il se promettoit d'en triompher, et estoit assez indifferent de quel maniere, n'ayant point de ces sentiments delicats qui empechent d'avoir du bonheur s'il n'est pas partagé par l'objet aimé. Il resolût de tenter toute sorte de moyens de s'en faire aimer. Si il ne reusissoit pas, ou si sa Vertu encore plus fort que son Amour refusoit de lui rendre heureux, il se flatta de la devenir par des ruses, qu'il crût aussi permise en Amour, qu'en Guerre. Il tacha de s'éclaircir sur son état. Son Hôte ne pouvoit lui dire autre chose qu'il n'aprit du postillon, qu'elle venoit de la Cour du Roi des Bons enfans.

Il y envoya son Valet de Chambre favori, hardi, secret, et intteligent. On parloit encore de cette Belle Capricieuse qui avoit quittée la Cour de si mauvaise grace. Il ne douta pas (de la façon qu'on la depeignit) qu'elle ne fût celle qui charmait son Maitre. Il recueillit toutes les particularitez qui la regardoit. Le Comte l'avoit ordonné de s'informer si elle estoit mariée, et ce qui c'étoit que son Mari, et il l'obeït si bien qu'il s'instruit jusqu'au Couleur de ses cheveux et de l'habit qu'il portoit. Il revint en peu de jours raconter a son Maitre le succes de sa negotiation. Il n'étoit pas assez entier pour la curiosité du Comte: il ignoroit encore son Nom, sa Patrie, et son état. Mais il esperoit mettre au profit le peu qu'il sçavoit. Il y avoit deja pres de deux mois qu'il languissoit aupres de sa belle Inconüe. Le temps sembloit bien longue a son Impatience, accoutumé a faire l'amour en abregé. Il se determina a un Trahison qu'il crût (peutestre) necessaire a leur bonheur reciproque, car il voyoit bien qu'il l'avoit inspiré une estime si tendre, qu'elle ne manquoit que peu de chose d'estre l'amour même. Elle ne sçavoit jamais quel heure il étoit dans sa Compagnie. Les Femmes qu'il avoit mis aupres d'elle, l'informoit que tout l'ennuyoit dans son Absence, et qu'elle en parloit souvent avec des Eloges excessives.

La pauvre Reine ne remarqua pas elle même aucune de ces symptomes d'une tendresse naissante. Elle attribua l'ennui qu'elle sentit etant seule, a sa triste situation. Il étoit naturel qu'une conversation aussi aimable que celle du Comte donnoit quelque relache a ses deplaisirs, et elle s'etendit sur ses Louanges comme l'unique marque de reconnoisance qu'elle estoit en état de donner. Elle remplissoit cet devoir avec tant de plaisir, quil nÿ avoit aucune grace dans sa personne qu'elle oublia. Il estoit charmé du progress qu'il faisoit dans son Coeur, mais il la connoisoit assez pour sçavoir que cet mesme Coeur, (rempli des sentiments heroique) étoit capable d'une longue resistance quand elle s'apercevoit qu'il passoit les bornes que sa vertu lui avoit prescritte.

Le Comte estoit attentif jusqu'aux moindre choses qui pouvoient amuser Docile. Elle trouvoit touts les matins sur sa Toilette, les nouvelles du jour; elle estoit frappée de voir sur une de ces Feuilles volantes, qu'un Corps mort avoit été trouvé par des païsans dans le Forêt, qui avoit assez de Plaies pour faire juger qu'il avoit été assasiné, qu'il avoit des grand cheveux brun et un habit de velours cramoisi, mais que son visage estoit tres defiguré par le temps qu'il avait resté exposé a l'air et qu'on le portoit a cette ville pour voir si quelqu'un pouvoit le reconnoistre. Elle estoit saisie d'un tremblement universel en lisant cet article. Son Mari portoit un tel Habit le jour qu'elle le quitta. Il avoit des cheveux bruns. Seroit-il possible? Quel affreux destin! dont elle pouvoit s'accuser d'estre la cause. Mais non; pourquoy ne seroit-il pas quelque autre? Faute-il s'allarmer sur de si legeres apparences?

Dans cette confusion des pensées, elle envoya chercher le Comte, qui faisoit l'éttoné en la voyant pale, tremblante, et agitée par tant de mouvements differents, qu'on savoit peine a distinguer si c'étoit la frayeur ou la doulour qui la mettoit dans un état si violent. Elle ne lui donna pas le temps de la demander. Elle s'ecria, Ah Monsieur, ayez pitié de moi, expliquez moi ce que c'est que cette nouvelle (en lui montrant le paper). Il feignit de n'en avoir pas entendu parlé, et courût s'en informer avec l'empressement d'un Homme qui partageoit trop ses sentiments pour en examiner le motif. Il revint en peu de temps l'asseurer qu'il etoit vrai, qu'on avoit apporté d'avant hier le corps de cet infortuné a la ville, et qu'il estoit encore exposé sur le Quai ou tout le peuple alloit le regarder, mais que jusqu'alors personne ne l'avoit reconnû.

Je veux aller aussi moi (disoit-elle d'un Air égaré). Il voulût combattre cette Resolution. Elle ne l'écouta point. Elle descendit l'escalier d'une vitesse, qu'il avoit peine a la suivre pour lui donner la main. Elle ne s'arretta qu'a dix pas du Corps mort. Elle crût reconnoistre parfaitement son Epoux. Une Horreur melée de mille sentiments confus la saisit, et elle tomba evanoüie dans le Bras du Comte. Il lui fit mettre dans une chaise, lui jetta de l'eau fraiche au visage, versa les goutes d'Angleterre en sa bouche, et elle fit quelques soupirs par les quels on connoisoit qu'elle n'avoit pas encore quittée cet monde, quoy qu'elle sembloit en detester la Lumiere, n'ouvrant pas ses yeux, jusqu'elle fût dans son Apartement, ou le Comte la laissa pendant que ses Femmes la deshabillerent, et revint aupres de son Lit aussi tost qu'elle y fut placée. Il la trouve fondant en larmes. Il se jette a Genoux a son chevet. Au nom de Dieu Madame (disoit-il d'un ton tendrement douleureux), ne vous obstinez pas a renfirmer dans vostre sein des chagrins qui vous nïent; on pourroit peut estre les adoucir, au moins les partager. Regardez moi comme un homme qui vous êtes devoué. Si vous sçaviez l'interêt vif que je prends en tout ce vous touche, et a quel point je suis blessé de vostre Defiance, je suis persuadé que—

Helas Monsieur (disoit-elle en l'intterompant), ne me faittes pas le tort de soupçonner que je puis avoir le moindre defiance pour un Ami a qui je dois tout. Mais—elle fit une pause de quelques moments, encore incertaine si elle devoit lui faire une Confidence entiere, quoy qu'elle sentit bien qu'elle éstoit pressée d'une plenitude des Idées, qui est pour le moins aussi dangereux pour la Raison, qu'une plentitude de sang est pour la santé. Elle ne pouvoit plus se refuser le soulagement de conter ses malheurs au seul Ami qu'elle avoit. Elle n'oublia ni ne deguisa aucun endroit de sa vie passée. Sa Naisance illustre fit grand plaisir au Comte, et ou est l'Homme qui ne sera pas flatté de trouver l'objet de son Amour grande princesse? L'avanture du Prince de Venus lui fit peu de peine; il le croioit plus tost un Inclination qu'une Passion. Il estoit enchanté qu'elle avoit eûe des raisons de se plaindre de son Epoux. Il voioit que son affliction n'étoit qu'un Effet de son devoir, et que par un Rafinement de Delicatesse, elle voulût s'accuser de sa Mort, pour se punir de ne l'avoir pas aimée durant sa vie. Elle se mit a pleurer sur le fin de son recit, et le Comte a rever.

Sa Qualité estoit bien pres de changer tous ses desseins. Il examina s'ils n'etoient pas trop dangereux a poursuivre. On ne badine pas avec de personnes de cet Rang sans s'en repentir, et jusqu'ici il avoit renoncé a tous les plaisirs capable de lui en donner. L'esprit d'Interêt qui lui avoit toujours gouverné étant dirigé par le bon sens, il y avoit peu d'hommes au monde, qui avoit fait si peu de mal. Il sçavoit que tous les vices attirent les malheurs, au moins par le decri qu'ils donnent, et que la Reputation de Probité est absolument necessaire a ceux qui la veulent sacrifier: ce sacrifice qu'on doit toujours reserver pour les grandes occasions.

La tromperie qu'il avoit fait a Docile, la nouvelle qu'il avoit fait imprimé, le cadavre qu'il avoit acheté dans une Village prochaine, estoient a dessein de calmer les scrupules de cette Belle et la preparer a lui reçevoir comme Mari, si elle ne voulût point d'Amant. Il l'avoit crût d'un rang ordinaire, que si son Epoux revenoit, il pouvoit lui tranquiliser par son argent, ou si il n'etoit pas d'un humeur accomodant, lui faire croire qu'il avoit été trompé, en la croyant veuve sur sa bonne foy, ce que n'etoit pas impossible. Le Prince Sombre (dont il connoisoit le Caractere) lui parroisoit dangereux de toute façon, incapable de pardonner et difficile a tromper. Il devoit estre un jour un grand Roi, et le Parti le plus raisonnable que le Comte pouvoit prendre estoit de planter la, la pauvre Docile de le Lendemain pour ne pas s'exposer a la Vengeance de son Epoux Bizarre. Mais on ne quitte pas si aisement un Dessein qui avoit deja couté beaucoup de soins et des Assiduitez, et qui estoit si heureusement avancé, car il ne douta nullement de son succes aupres d'une Innocence qui ne doutoit de rien. Il se flattoit que les mesmes raisons (quel qu'elles fussent) qui avoit retardée l'arrivée du Prince deux mois, pouvoient subsister encore deux autres. C'estoit plus qu'il n'en fallût pour reussir, joûir, et s'ennuyer de sa Maitresse. En attendant il resolût d'employer tant des espions qu'il seroit averti avant qu'aucun étranger entra dans la ville, et qu'il auroit le temps de se retirer, en cas qu'un Mari incommode venoit intterompre ses plaisirs.

Laissons le former des projets, et la malheureuse Reine pleurer ses infortunes, pour voir ce qu'on fait dans son Roiaume. Le Roi Farouche avoit

eu la Bonté de l'accepter selon l'offre que les états lui avoit fait, et avoit
donné le vice Roiauté au Grand Prêtre. La Reine Mere estoit retournée au
Palais ou elle se promettoit de regner plus absolument que jamais, comme
cet saint homme lui avoit juré mille fois, en cas qu'il parvint a une Dignité
a la quelle il ne visoit, que pour avoir l'honneur d'executer ses ordres. Elle
estoit bien surprise peu de jours apres, quand il se presenta pour lui donner
(disoit-il) un avis salutaire pour son Honneur, son Repos, et son Salût.
C'éstoit trois choses qu'elle n'avoit jamais menagée, mais la Curiosité la fit
donner de l'attention au commencement de son Discours, et en suitte la
Rage et l'ettonnement produissoint une silence qui lui permettoit de le continuer. Il lui representoit fort pathetiquement que la retraitte estoit le seul
état qui convenoit a une Reine doüariere, et il lui conseilloit de se retirer
parmi les Vierges sacrées, d'un air d'Autorité qui valût bien un ordre positif.
Elle voulût éclatter en larmes, plaintes et menaces. Il n'écouta ni les uns, ni
les autres, et sortît de sa chambre, avec la même Tranquillité respectable
qu'il y estoit entré.

C'estoit avec peine qu'elle obtint une seconde visite, étant averti le
Lendemain que son Equipage estoit prest, selon les ordres que S[a]
M[ajesté] avoit donnée. Elle n'osa refuser d'aller, mais elle demandoit en
grace de parler encore un fois au Grand Prêtre. Il vint avec toute la Fierté
d'un Vice Roi, relevée par une insolence Prelatique, qui deconcerta la Reine
a un tel point que ce n'estoit qu'en tremblant qu'elle osa lui demander ses
Tresors qu'elle lui avoit confiée. Je voie bien Madame (repondit-il en souriant a demi, dedaigneusement) que le Roi Farouche a été bien informé. Le
Mort du Roi vostre Epoux, digne Objet de vostre tendresse, la Fuitte de la
Reine vostre Fille, qui a repondue si mal a vos Soins, et la Revolution de
l'état, a troublées vostre Raison. Si elle estoit entiere, vous sçaurez que les
Tresors du feu Roi ne pouvoit pas vous apartenir. Une grande Princesse
comme vous ne pouvoit pas faire un Vol, et un homme comme moi ne
pouvoit pas en estre le Receleur. Si je suivai a la rigeur l'ordre de mon Roy,
vous seriez enfermée dans un endroit propre pour vous faire traitter, mais
je me flatte que les Dieux, (que jusqu'ici je n'ai jamais solicité inutilement)
accorderont a mes ferventes prieres le retour de vostre Santé. Je ne voie rien
qui puisse y contribuer plus efficacement que le saint repos que vous
trouverez dans la Maison ou j'aurois l'honneur de vous conduire.

Il lui presenta la main avec ces paroles. Elle n'avoit pas le Courrage de la
refuser, et se laissa mener a deux lieus de la ville, ou elle fût receûe avec des
Transports de joye par une Superieure Decrepite et des Vierges surannées,
qui ne dimunirent point sa douleur. Elle s'enferma dans un apartement
tendu du noir qui lui éstoit destiné, ou elle s'abandonna a toute sa rage;
apres avoit bien pleurée, pesté, et arraché quelques cheveux gris, elle se
souvint de la Fée, et resolût d'implorer sa protection, malgre la deffense
qu'elle lui avoit faitte. Elle lui écrivit une Lettre remplie d'Humiliation et

de Soûmission; des traits d'une Flatterie grossiere ne furent pas epargnez, et des grandes promesses d'un Devouement eternel, si elle voulut la delivrer de sa Prison. Sa Lettre lui fût renvoyée toute cachtée, mais elle ne se rebuta pas par le mauvais success d'une premiere tentative, n'ayant autre chose a faire qu'a composer des Lettres.

La Fée en étoit assassinée. Elle en trouvoit sur sa Toilette, dans son Cabinet, parmi ses livres. Son Palais en étoit semé, et comme cette Reine avoit acquis son Amitie par son Negligence, ses importunitez lui attira toute sa haine. Elle la changea en Fromage de Brie pour s'en delivrer a jamais. On la conserve encore dans le Musaeum de Travers, ou elle est placée parmi des plantes petrifiées et des Coquilles rares, toute aupres d'une Image de Vichnou qui avoit pissée miraculeusement dans le temps d'une Incendie, il y avoit cinq cents anns. Mr. Patin en parle dans la mesme lettre ou il fait la description de cet Foetus qui estoit Elephant parfait, et qu'il suppose judicieusement étoit l'effet d'un amour plus extravagant que celui de Pasiphae.

Le Prince Sombre eût une Destinée bien differente. Il avoit erré dans la Forêt huit heures de suitte, tant tost a petit pas enseveli dans ses meditations, tant tost donnant de Coups d'eperons a son cheval quand la Rage lui transportoit. La pauvre Bête, trop sensée pour se repaître de chimeres comme son Maitre, étoit prêt a succomber de Faim et de Lassitude. Sa Foiblesse fit souvenir au Prince qu'il étoit necessaire de trouver une Gîte, et il picqua vers une petite Cabanne, ou un vieux Paysan lui ceda son lit. Il s'ÿ mit sans le moindre envie de Dormir, mais pour se livrer a ses Refflections. Il estoit l'homme du monde qui tirât les Consequences les plus justes, et qui se trompoit le plus souvent dans les principes. Il crût avoir perdu entirement cette Reputation de Sagesse Austere, qui l'avoit distingué de la Foule des Princes. Il la perdoit mesme aupres de lui même; il ne pouvoit pas se pardonner les Folies qu'il avoit fait, pour une Femme legere et ingratte, et cet deshonneur lui estoit aussi sensible que l'infidelité de Docile. Il repassoit dans son Imagination toutes ses paroles, ses gestes, et jusqu'aux ses Regards, il trouvoit par tout des preuves evidentes de sa Perfidie.

Au moins (disoit-il dans ses reveries) si elle avoit eûe de la bonne Foi, j'aurois pardonné sa Galanterie. Les Femmes sont en habitude de la croire permise; sa jeunesse, une Mere qu'elle ne pouvoit pas respecter ni capable de lui conseiller, un Education negligé, tout l'excusoit. Mais quand je lui demandois, avec Amitie, l'histoire de ce que l'avoit brouillée avec ses parents, en la faisant entrevoir que j'etois dans le dessein de lui passer tout en faveur de sa sincerité, elle m'a faite (sans s'emouvoir) un Conte le moins vraisemblable qui fût jamais inventé. Il falût qu'elle eût autant de Mepris pour mon Esprit que pour ma personne, quand elle vouloit me persuader qu'elle avoit été la Dupe de Madame de l'Artifice, une Femme si reconnûe pour trompeuse, qu'elle ne peut plus tromper personne. C'estoit alors que je devois l'avoir renoncé a jamais. Aveugle que j'etois! Mais, non; je voyois son mauvais Caractere. C'étoit sa Beauté qui offusquoit ses defauts, cette Beauté fatale. Quel Dieu ennemi de l'homme a donné cet Rayon de sa Divinité, pour couvrir une Ame si noire, et si indigne!

Il estoit vrai que deux jours apres son Mariage il avoit eû le Dureté de demander a son innocente Epouse de quel façon elle avoit perdue ses pierreries, qu'il n'avoit entendu (disoit-il) que confusement. Elle l'avoit conté naivement, et il l'avoit repondu d'un ton chagrin (qu'il crût fort moderé) qu'il lui conseilloit de ne jamais debiter cet conte, qui ne trouveroit que fort peu de Credit dans le monde. Elle ne comprit pas seulment ce qu'il vouloit insinuer, et il se souvenoit de cette Innocence qui ne se deconcerta point, comme l'Hardiesse d'une personne endurcie dans le crime. Il examina toute sa conduitte dans le même gout. Ses favourites avoient toujours été des Femmes meprisables, si fort ses inferieures par rapport a l'Esprit qu'elles ne pouvoient pas lui plaire que par une Simpathie de moeurs. Cette Emilie qui lui estoit si chere, une Coquette decriée! (Dans le même moment, qu'il faisoit cette Refflection il ajouta pourtant une Foi aveugle a tous ses Calumnies contre sa Maitresse.)

Enfin il ne douta plus qu'elle ne fût la plus abominable de son Sexe, et forma la Resolution de ne l'honorer plus de son Souvenir. Il tourna toutes ses pensées sur ses affaires. Il resolût de retourner a cette Isle dont il estoit legitiment Souverain; il sçavoit qu'il y avoit un assez grand nombre de partisans, et que le Gouvernement de son Pere n'etoit pas fait pour se faire aimer. Il esperoit d'estre bien reçeu par quelques qu'uns [*sic*] de principaux du Païs qui lui estoient attachez, et qu'etant deguisé parmi eux, il pouvoit former une Ligue assez forte pour renverser un Gouvernement fondé sur l'injustice, et exercé avec Tyrannie. Il auroit deja pris cet parti, si sa Passion pour Docile, ne l'avoit pas fait imaginer plus de bonheur a vivre en particulier avec elle qu'a regner. Son Ambition se reveilla et donna quelque relache a ses Tourments. Il poursuivit ce dessein avec ardeur. Il arriva heureusement et se logea chez un Grand Seigneur qui adoroit le memoire de la Reine sa mere, et qui lui auroit sacrifié sa vie pour le mettre en possession du Trône qui lui apartenoit.

Pendent qu'ils travaillerent a cet établissement, la malheureuse Docile estoit entre les mains d'un Amant d'un Caractere bien different. Helas! pourquoy quelque Divinité favorable ne donnoit-il pas au Prince les Lumieres du Comte, ou au Comte la probité du Prince? Mais les Dieux dans ce siecle laissaient aux Fées le soin de la Terre et ne s'occupoient plus des affaires de Mortels. Le Comte d'Esperanza laissa pleurer quelques jours sa belle Veuve, sans tacher de la consoler autrement qu'en partageant son affliction. Quand l'exces etoit un peu diminué, il la proposa de quitter cet endroit ou elle avoit toujours present a son Imagination le triste

Spectacle de son Epoux Assasiné, et de se retirer a un Chateau qu'il venoit d'acheter a douze lieus de la. Il avoit eû l'attention de donner des Obseques magnifique au Corps qu'elle croyoit estre celui du Prince, et cette Generosité avoit faite tant d'impression sur Docile, qu'elle se crût autorisée par la Vertu même, de ceder a ses instances pressantes de passer quelque temps chez lui.

C'étoit veritablement un endroit enchanté. Le bon Goût et la Magnificence regnerent par tout; on y voyoit tout ce que l'Architecture, la Peinture, et la Sculpture pouvoient fournir de brillant, meublé a la derniere mode par les premiers Tapissiers de Paris. La Situation estoit heureuse, sur une Colline couverte de Bois, au pied de la quelle on voyoit une de plus belle rivieres du Monde, qui arrosoit en serpentant, des Prairies dont la verdure éclattante estoit emaillée de fleurs. On y avoit ajouté un Jardin, ou rien n'étoit epargné pour le rendre digne du Palais. C'étoit l'ouvrage d'un de favoris de la Fortune, qu'elle éleve subitement par le secours de Pharon. Il avoit fait venir les plus grands Genies de l'Italie, et de la France, pour y travailler, et ils s'étoient acquitez parfaittement. Mais a peine fut-il achevé que le Malheuruex Maitre s'est vû en disgrace aupres de la Deëse capricieuse qui l'avoit favorisée. Il perdit des sommes considerables, et se trouva obligé de vendre sa Maison pour payer ses Ouvriers.

Le Comte d'Esperanza profita de son Malheur, et joüit de ses travaux, pour le quart qu'il y avoit depensé. La Belle Docile, (a qui il presenta les clefs de son Chateau en arrivant) étoit confirmée dans l'Idée qu'elle avoit de sa Qualité, en voyant une Magnificence si bien entendûe; mais elle étoit encore plus touchée de ses manieres modestes et respectueuses. Il continua pres d'un mois la même façon de vivre. A la fin il hazarda quelques soupirs, et joua le role d'amant timide. Elle s'aperçût de ce changement avec un vrai affliction; elle se trouva reduitte au choix de l'écouter, ou de l'abandonner. Devoit-elle se resoudre a rendre Malheureux un homme qui l'avoit comblé d'obligations, pour une delicatesse (peut estre) mal fondé? Esce que le Prince Sombre l'avoit traitté d'une maniere a meriter d'estre pleuré eternellement? Nÿ a t-il point d'exemple des Reines qui sont mariée deux fois? Ne seroit-il pas bien doux de faire le bonheur d'un Cavalier que le merite seule rendoit digne de regner sur toute la terre?

Ces Refflections l'occupoint nuit et jour. Le Comte comprit la Raison de ses reveries, et choisit le moment le plus favorable, pour la faire determiner. Il representa ses souffrances, faisoit valoir le Respect que jusqu'ici l'avoit contraint au silence, et finissoit en offrant de se retirer le lendemain, si elle étoit insensible a sa Passion, quoy qu'il étoit asseuré qu'il ne survivra pas une separation mille fois plus cruelle que la mort. Il accompagnoit ses paroles de regards tendres, de soupirs éttouffez, et de larmes a moitie supprimez, enfin de tous les artifices qu'un Coeur sans pitié mette en oeuvre, pour surprendre l'innocence. Celui de Docile y succomba. Apres des objections froidement prononcé, qu'il detruisoit aisement, elle lui avoua en rougissant, qu'elle ne pouvoit pas lui refuser sa main, si son bonheur y étoit attaché.

On sera peutestre surpris que du Caractere qu'il estoit, il n'a pas taché de la seduire d'une autre façon. Il n'avoit pas negligé aucune des avantages que sa situation lui offroit, mais il lui voioit toujours un si grand horreur pour toute Galanterie, qu'il n'osoit s'exposer a sa haine, qui n'aurois pas manquée de l'accabler du premier moment, qu'elle se seroit doutée d'un tel dessein. Il s'aperçût que c'étoit son Respect, et l'Idée qu'elle avoit de sa Vertu, qui donnoient Naissance aux Sentiments favorables qu'elle avoit pour lui, et qu'on ne pouvoit la tromper que par des Apparences d'honneur et de Generosité. On peut juger qu'il reçût avec transport l'asseurance obligeante qu'elle lui faisoit. Il le temoignoit par des soûmissions, des vivac- itez, et en parroissant si penetré de Reconnoisance et de plaisir, qu'elle étoit enchantée d'avoir rendüe heureux, un amant si digne de l'étre. Il nÿ a rien de si flatteur pour un Coeur comme le sien, que de faire le bonheur de ceux qu'on estime. Il avoit acquis toute la sienne, et elle se faisoit un devoir de devoüer le reste de sa vie a lui plaire. Mais elle ne vouloit pas passer sur le scrupule que l'attachoit a la bien seance. Elle insista sur le regle qui oblige les Veuves a une année de Deüil, et toute son Eloquence, ni ses pleurs, ne pouvoit retrancher que deux mois de cette terme. Il se seroit desesperé, s'il se n'étoit pas flatté qu'elle pourroit retrancher autant tous les jours, et qu'il verroit bien tost le fin de son Martyre.

Il se trompa pourtant, quoy qu'il tachoit de profiter de tous les priveleges que le droit du Futur lui donnoit. Il ne la quittoit presqu'plus, il passoit quelque fois le moitie de la nuit dans sa chambre, il lui donnoit des fetes, faisoit des chansons pour elle, qu'elle trouva les plus jolis du monde, et s'insinue si bien dans son Esprit, qu'elle oublia tous ses malheurs passez, et se livra entierement au plaisir d'aimer et d'estre aimé. Elle n'étoit plus la triste Beauté, qu'il avoit vû ensevlie dans une melancholie si habituelle qu'elle sembloit naturelle. Elle devint gaÿe et deploya toutes les graces de son esprit. Elle étoit legere et badine a table, solide et raisonable quand elle jugoit des Auteurs, qu'il lui mettoit a la main. Il y avoit une Galerie ou elle trouvoit une Bibliotheque nombreuse et bien choisie. Il lui faisoit lire ces livres dangereux, ou en detruisant les prejugez, on attaque obliquement la morale. Il les commentoit quelque fois d'une façon a offenser la Reine scrupuleuse, si elle avoit comprit son But. Loin de cela, elle imagina qu'il vouloit former son esprit, quand il tachoit de corrompre son Coeur, dont elle lui laissa voir tous les mouvemens avec une Sincerité qu'on n'jamais vû qu'en elle.

Il lui fit convener que toutes les Ceremonies avoient leur origine dans la Politique, qu'ils netoient ni fondez sur la Nature, ni essentielles a la Vertu. Il voulût conclure que les Gens sensez s'en passaient toutes les fois qu'elles

les incommodient. Elle n'adoptoit pas cet Raisonnement. Elle parloit de l'honneur comme d'une Divinité, a la quelle on estoit obligé de tout sacri-fier, hors la Vertu. Elle avouoit que si par des Circonstances extrodinaire, on se trouvoit forcé d'abandonner l'un ou l'autre, qu'il faloit souffrir l'infamie, plus tost que de commettre le moindre Crime, mais que nul plaisir, nul avantage, ni mesme nulle Passion pouvoit dispenser de Loix de la bien seance, qu'on avoit a repondre, a ses Ancestres, a sa Posterité, et a tous ceux qui pourit estre entrainez par l'exemple, de chaque pas qu'on faisoit, et qu'apres la Vertu mesme, rien de devoit étoit [*sic*] si cher, que ses appar-ences, quoi que le monde les avoit tres souvent placez assez ridiculement.

C'étoit s'expliquer d'une maniere a faire changer de tournure a la Conversation. Le Comte se rendit a ses raisons, qu'il trouvoit admirable (disoit-il) en ajoutant, qu'il avoit connu des certains Philosophes qui soutenoient qu'on pouvoit se dispenser de regles trop rigide, pourvû que le secret garentissoit du scandale. C'est pècher contre la verité (s'écria t-elle), qui est le plus enorme de tous les crimes, la Verité! qui est la seule Divinité visible, qui donne a tous les hommes un rayon de sa lumiere, qui recom-pense ses fidelles sectateurs de cette Paix interieure qui ne se deconcerte jamais. Ceux qui osent l'offenser sont punis par de remors qui les dechirent éternellement. Abandonné a eux mesme, ils deviennent l'oprobre des humains, et mille fois plus meprisable que les Bêtes le plus immonde. Le Comte l'intterompit pour jurer qu'il avoit toujours été de cet sentiment, et qu'il n'avoit cité cet opinion que pour montrer jusq'ou l'esprit estoit cap-able de s'egarer. Elle lui crût sur sa Parole, et le seule refflection qu'elle fit sur cette conversation, et plusieurs autres de la même espece, estoit d'ad-mirer la bonne foi du Comte, qui estoit si persuadé de sa Vertu qu'il hazard-oit de lui aprendre des maximes que le plus part des hommes cachent aux Femmes, cragnant qu'elles n'en fassent une mauvaise usage.

Cette Confiance obligeante augmenta son estime de la moitie, cette estime augmentoit sa tendresse, et le temps destiné a son Veuvage com-mencoit lui peser beaucoup. Elle estoit jeune, d'une Santé florissante; elle avoit aupres d'elle un amant aimable, soumis, mais pressant, et qui ne laissoit échapper aucune moment qui pourroit lui estre favorable. Elle soutenoit avec peine la resolution qu'elle avoit formée d'un Deüil de dix mois. Le Comte trouva le secret de les reduire a six, dont deux estoit deja passé, mais c'estoit impossible d'obtenir un autre retranchement, et il falût se contenter, de celui la.

Enfin ce dernier mois si desiré arriva. Le Comte la quitta pour trois jours, pour donner un Coup d'Oeil a un Equipage qu'il avoit commandé au Capital. Quoy que l'absence devoit estre courte, elle estoit tres sensible aux tendres amants. Docile laissa tomber quelques larmes, et il soupira en lui baissant la main comme s'il avoit été instruit de l'avenir. Elle se retira dans son Cabinet aussi tost qu'il fût parti, et se jettant sur son Canapé s'abandonna a un attendrissment dont le Comte auroit tiré des grands avantages, sil avoit été present. Elle se representoit tous ses beaux procedez depuis qu'elle l'avoit connu, ses agremens ne furent pas oubliés, elle admira son bonheur d'avoir trouvée un Coeur digne du sien, et souhaittoit de voir le moment qu'elle ne seroit plus obligée a gener sa tendresse. Ces Reveries étoient trop agreable pour ne pas durer; elle les continua jusqu'a l'heur de la promenade. Elle s'enfonça dans le bois, qui touchoit a son jardin, et s'entretenoit de ses visions amoureux, aupres d'une Fontaine, quand elle vit arriver au Galop un jeun Cavalier, qui apres l'avoir regardé fixement, vint se jetter a ses pieds. Elle le reconnût pour estre celui qui étoit le plus favorisé parmi les Officiers du Prince Sombre. Il avoit été élevé Page aupres de lui, et par sa Fidelité, et sa diligence, avoit acquis autant de Credit qu'on pouvoit Obtenir d'un Maitre si severe. Il la presentoit une Lettre a genoux, qu'elle reçute [*sic*] en tremblant et ouvrit avec precipitation. Comme je croi qu'on n'en a jamais vû un parreille, je veux la copier toute entiere.

Madame,
   Le bruit public vous a apris sans doute le mort du Roi mon Pere, quoy qu'il y a peu de jours. Je suis en possession païsible de mes états, et je m'empresse de vous rendre les vostres. Si vos sujets ne vouillent pas vous reconoitre, je vous offre mes Troupes et mes Tresors pour les ranger a leur Devoir. Plût aux Dieux, que vostre conduitte future peut leur faire oublier le desordre du passez. Nostre Mariage a eu si peu de temoins, s'il vous plaist de la cacher, je ne le publirai point; si vous trouvez a propos de le declarer je ne vous contredirai pas. Quel parti que vous preniez, en renoncant a vous, je renonce a tous les avantages que je pourrois tirer de vostre alliance. Je ne vous conseil, ni vous defends rien; suivez vos goûts tels qu'ils puissent estre, et demandez jamais de nouvelles du

                                                              Roi Sombre.

Il auroit été indigne de moi, d'envoyer un Ambassadeur vous redemander au Roi de bons Enfants. J'ai depèchés cet Gentilhomme, comptant sur sa discretion; écoutez ses conseils pour vostre reétablissement, et ne decouvrez a personne qu'il m'apartient.

La premiere pensée de Docile en voyant le Caractere de son Epoux fût qu'il l'avoit écritte avant son assasinat. Mais de le sçavoir vivant, et plus injuste que jamais, l'accabloit de tant des Idées mixtes, qu'elle n'avoit pas la force d'en demesler aucune, et resta dans un saississement qui tenoit de la stupidité.

   Sa silence permettoit au Cavalier de suivre les ordres qu'il avoit eû de l'instruire de l'état de ses affaires. Il lui racontoit que le Prince avoit trouvé une forte partie pour lui dans l'Isle ou il s'etoit retiré; qu'il avoit pris des mesures immanquables pour entrer en possession de ses droits; et qu'il étoit sur le point de les faire valoir quand le nouvelle arriva de la mort de son Pere; il prit ce moment pour se montrer au peuple qui lui reçut avec les plus vives demonstrations de joie; que les Deputez du Roiaume Farouche et ceux de Travers étoient venu lui rendre Homage; qu'ils avoit renvoyé ces derniers, en leur disant qu'il employeroit tous ses soins a rechercher leur Reine. Le mesme soir (continua le Cavalier) S[a] M[ajesté] m'a fair l'honneur de m'appeller a son Cabinet. Il me chargea de sa Lettre, et m'addressa au Roiaume de Bons Enfants, pour la presenter a V[otre] M[ajesté] avec ordre positif de l'obeïr en tout, et je la suplie, tres humblement, de croire qu'elle n'a point de sujet qui la servirai avec plus de Zèle et d'attachment.

La Reine n'étoit pas assez a elle, pour repondre a son harangue. Elle lui laissa tout le loisir de le continuer, et il poursuivit, J'ai été a la Cour, ou je croiois la trouver; je tachai inutilement de decouvrir le leiu de sa retraitte, quoyque j'ai fait tous les perquisitions possible, sans devoiler ma commission (ce que je n'osois faire, sans ses ordres). Je retournai tristment sur mes pas: mon bonheur a voulû que je m'arrestay a une petite Auberge, ou j'ai entendu parler d'une Dame inconüe, d'une façon a me faire esperer l'honneur dont je joüis en me presentant a ses pieds. On m'a dit que cette Dame s'étoit retiré a ce Chateau, et les Dieux ont été assez propice a mes voeux pour me donner l'avantage glorieux d'estre le premier de ses sujets a lui temoigner mon Devoir.

Il cessa de parler, mais Docile n'avoit ni voix, ni volonté de lui repondre. Son Sang a moitie glacé lui refusa la puissance d'ouvrir la bouche. Elle ne pleura pas, a peine respiroit-elle. Elle restoit une bonne quart d'heure dans cet état, lui toujours a Genoux, ne croyant pas devoir se relever que par sa permission, quand elle aperçut a travers les arbres, la Demoiselle qu'elle distinguoit le plus parmi celles de sa suitte, qui lui portoit sa Luth, qu'elle avoit demandé en sortant. Cette vûe la reveilloit assez pour lui donner la force de dire au Cavalier, Revenez ici a la mesme heure demain. Il partit, mais la Demoiselle l'avoit deja vüe, et ne sçavoit quoy conjecturer d'avoir surprise sa belle Maitresse donnant audience a un jeun étranger bien fait, qui l'entretenoit, sans doute, de quelque chose de bien intteressante, puis qu'il parloit a Genoux, et qu'elle l'écoutoit avec attention. Elle n'osoit demander aucune explication a la Reine, qui l'appella d'une voix foible. Donnez moi le bras, Julie, disoit-elle, je suis tres mal. Effectivement sa paleur extreme secondoit parfaittement ses paroles, et la Fille effrayée appelloit ses compagnes. C'etoit tout ce qu'elles pouvoint faire, que de trainer la Reine languissante jusqu'a son Apartement, ou elle lisoit, et relisoit la Lettre qu'elle venoit de reçevoir. Elle ne manqua pas d'entrevoir la Generosité des sentiments de son Epoux, quoy qu'envelopé dans sa Dureté ordinaire. Elle en étoit touchée, mais quand elle ne l'auroit pas été, elle estoit trop esclave de son Devoir, de hesiter sur le parti qu'elle devoit prendre. Elle voulût se jetter a ses pieds, se soümettre a tel suplice qu'il ordonnoit, et lui abbandonner son Roiaume, trop heureuse si il lui permettroit de finir ses tristes jours parmi les Vestales.

Pauvre Comte que deviendrois tu? (se disoit-elle) Est ce ceci le fruit de vos soins genereux? M'avez vous connu que pour faire le malheur de vostre vie? Oubliez une miserable, qui ne peut jamais vous oublier. Cette Idée attendrissante la fit fondre en larmes. Elle se sentit le Coeur un peu soulagé apres avoir beaucoup pleuré, et reprit ses meditations. Elle se representa le desespoir du Comte. Elle ne se flattoit pas d'avoir la force dÿ pouvoir resister; elle craignoit de ne pouvoir plus soutenir en lui voyant, la Resolution de lui quitter. Elle estoit pourtant necessaire; son honneur, sa Vertu l'exigea, mais l'amour est capable de vaincre tous les autres sentiments, et elle n'osoit se promettre de rien refuser aux Solicitations, et aux larmes, de celui qu'elle aimoit. Elle ne douta pas qu'il ne la presseroit de s'enfuir avec lui, a quelque coin du monde, pour passer leur jours ensemble. Elle auroit trouvée charmant le desert le plus affreux, si son Devoir l'auroit permis, mais la Raison l'opposoit aussi fortement que la Vertu. Sa tendresse mesme pour lui, la representoit que le Roi son Epoux lui poursuivroit jusqu'au bout de la Terre, pour lui sacrifier a sa Vengeance, et elle exposeroit le plus digne de tous les hommes, a estre masacré (peut estre) devant ses yeux. Cette derniere consideration la determinoit plus que toutes les autres, qu'il falût s'enfuir avant son Retour. Elle n'osoit se fier a aucune de ses Femmes, sachant qu'elles lui etoient toutes devouées. Elle s'imagina que sa passion estoit assez violente pour lui faire suivre ses pas, sans songer aux Consequences, et elle prevoioit avec horreur toutes les Suittes qu'elle devoit y attendre. Mais en s'en allant sans lui écrire, elle se livroit a des soupçons les plus outrageants. Il l'accuserai d'ingratitude, de legereté, et de Perfidie. Peut-elle se resoudre à perdre l'estime, de celui qu'elle adoroit? Il ny a point de sacrifice qui coûte tant que celui la; elle se fit des reproches pourtant d'avoir balancé quand il s'agissoit du bonheur et du salût du cher Comte. Qu'il me meprise, (disoit-elle) qu'il me deteste, s'il est necessaire pour son Repos, mais qu'il vive, et qu'il vive heureux! C'est une Foiblesse, c'est l'amour propre, c'est moi mesme que je pleure, si je ne puis pas me contenter de me sacrifier pour lui rendre cette Tranquillité, que je n'ai que trop alterée.

Cette Resolution lui parût si belle, qu'elle lui devint consolante. Elle s'envelopa dans sa Vertu, qui lui donna assez de Force pour se rendre punctuellement a l'heure qu'elle avoit indiquée a l'officier du Roi Sombre. Il vint un moment apres, et elle se hâta de lui dire qu'elle voulût retourner avec lui aupres de son Epoux. Elle lui ordonna de lui mener un cheval et un habit d'homme a l'entrée du Bois, a minuit, et qu'elle viendroit lui joindre, pour commencer leur voiage. Cet ordre lui parroissoit si extravagant, que quoy qu'il avoit été commandé par le Roi son Maitre de l'obeïr sans reserve, il doutoit s'il devoit le faire. J'ai mes raisons (disoit-elle en remarquant son éttonnement) pour agir de cette façon; elles sont indispensible. Point de raissonnement, obeïssez. Elle le quitta avec ces Paroles. Il se retira ne sachant pas si il devoit la croire folle, ou si elle suivoit les ordres Bizarres du Roi. Il resolût pourtant d'obeïr aveuglement. Il lui portoit son plus bel Habit, lui presenta son cheval, et la suivît sur un autre qu'il avoit acheté. Elle s'etoit travestie dans le fonds d'un Bocage obscur, et avoit pris la precaution de jetter son habit de femme remplis de Pierres dans la Riviere, et s'éloignoit a grand pas de l'unique Objet de son amour, dont elle se crût tendrement aimée, pour trouver celui qu'elle craignoit de voir, et dont elle étoit seure de se voir maltraittée.

Ses Demoiselles ne s'aperçurent de sa fuitte que le lendmain matin. Elle avoit soupée a son heure ordinaire, on l'avoit vû couchée, et elle s'etoit relevée, et descendit dans le jardin, par le quel elle avoit echappée sans que personne s'en doutât. On peut imaginer la surprise bien grande parmi sa Domestique. Il nÿ avoit que la seule Julie, qui crût avoir le clef du mystere. Elle avoit toujours regardé Docile comme Maitresse entretenue du Comte; elle ignoroit sa qualité, et son dessein de Mariage; il lui parroissoit tres clair, qu'elle avoit faite un autre amant. Elle auroit donné la mesme Idée a tout, si elle avoit conté l'avanture du Bois, mais, plus discrete que le plûpart de celles de son état, elle gardoit ce secret pour son Maitre, en se promettant pourtant de se dedomager de cette contrainte, en le contant a tout le monde immediatement apres qu'elle auroit instruit le Comte.

Il arriva avant la nuit, avec tout l'empressement d'un homme qui attendoit la recompense de tant des soins, et des soupirs. Que devint-il en aprenant l'evasion de la Reine? Il avoit de la peine a le croire, quoy qu'il le voyoit, et rouloit mille imaginations dans sa Tête, quand l'officieuse Julie lui communiqua la scene qu'elle avoit vue au Bois, qui mettoit le comble a son éttonnement. Dans toute sa vie il n'avoit estimé que la seule Docile, il avoit toujours regardé la Vertu comme une Idée chimerique, qui n'avoit pas plus d'existence réel que le Phoenix. Il avoit changé de sentiment en sa faveur, et c'est justement elle qui lui trompe de la maniere la plus cruelle, et qui est aussi mortifiante pour sa Vanité que pour sa tendresse. Lui, qui se piquoit de connoistre si bien son monde, se trouve le Dupe d'une jeune personne, qui a couvrit son jeu d'une Innocence qui parroisoit si naturelle qu'elle faisoit pitie. Il parcourût dans son Imagination toutes ses demarches, ses paroles, jusqu'a ses moindres regards, sans pouvoir decouvrir aucune trace de cette artifice qui faisoit le fonds de son Caractere, puis qu'elle estoit capable d'un Trahison si noir, dans le moment qu'elle sembloit ne vivre que pour lui. Il renvoya toutes ses femmes, et retourna a la Cour de Bons Enfants, ou il trouva beaucoup de Politesse de la part du Roi, mille embrassades de Courtisans, et des agaceries de Dames, qui lui firent oublier l'infidelle, qui s'occupa pourtant uniquement de lui, pendant les fatigues de son triste voiage.

Son Conducteur n'étoit pas sans ses inquietudes. Il n'avoit jamais vû la Reine qu'avec les yeux qu'on regarde sa Souveraine. Il disoit avec tout le monde, que c'éstoit une Beauté parfaitte, sans oser s'attacher a la Contempler. Il la voyoit a present seule, et dans un état qui, denué de l'éclat de son rang, relevoit toutes ses charmes. On sçait a quel point l'habit d'homme est avantageux aux Belles. N'etant pas accoutumée a s'habiller elle mesme elle avoit si mal nouée sa bourse, qu'elle étoit tombée au premier pas du cheval, et elle avoit ses épaules couvert de beaux cheveux cendré qui estoit bouclez naturellement. L'air et le mouvement lui avoit donnée ces couleurs vifs, qui accompagnent la fleur de la jeunesse. Jugez comme elle parroisoit brillante au Cavalier.

Quand le Lever du Soleil lui permit de la regarder, son admiration estoit meslé d'une confusion, qui ne lui laissoit pas la Liberté de penser. Il s'abandonna au Plaisir que ses yeux recevoient, sans remarquer que son Coeur s'intterressoit. Elle estoit trop ensevlie dans ses Idées pour y faire le moindre attention. Malgre la fermeté dont elle se flattoit, chaque pas qui l'éloignoit du Comte lui rendit plus cher a son Imagination. Elle se representoit son Dese[s]poir, sa Fure[u]r, sa haine, et en suitte son Mepris, pour une Femme si ingratte et si perfide qu'elle devoit lui paroistre. Au moins, (pensoit-elle) si j'osois lui instruire que c'est pour lui, que je me sacrifie? Mais non, mon sacrifice deviendroit inutile, il s'exposera a la Vengeance de mon Epoux, et j'aurois a me reprocher la perte d'un homme digne d'estre immortel. Il faut subïr aux rigeurs de mon sort, et me contenter du seul temoignage de mon Coeur de l'innocence de mes procedez. La vraie vertu est independante des Applaudisements, et je l'offense en cherchant en elle autre chose qu'elle mesme. C'étoit par de telles refflections qu'elle soutenoit sa Resolution.

On se moque aujourdui assez volontiers de la vieille maxime que la Vertu porte sa recompense avec elle. C'est pourtant tres vraie: si on la considere bien, c'est la joüissance la plus parfaitte de l'amour propre, la seule qui est pure, et qui ne degoute jamais, et je suis persuadé que ceux qui sont assez heureux d'estre veritablement ennyvrez de cette Enthusiasme, trouvent plus de plaisir a vaincre leur passions que l'homme le plus vif a jamais senti en les contentant. Docile en fit la preuve, et arriva au port de la mer, avec une Tranquillité qui augmenta sa Beauté.

Elle y trouva un Vaisseau marchand prest a faire voile a l'isle ou son officier avoit laissé le Roi Sombre. Elle s'embarqua sans vouloir écouter cet fidelle Ecuyer, qui vouloit la persuader de prendre un jour de repos. Elle avoit lieu du repentir de cet empressement deux jours apres: un Corsair de Tunis, qui rodoit dans ces mers, attaqua leur Vaisseau, qui étoit peu en état de se deffendre, mais la crainte de l'esclavage faisoit faire des merveilles a tout l'Equipage. Le Cavalier, qui se donnoit pour Frere de Docile, surpassoit et animoit tous les autres. Il combattoit aux yeux et pour la Liberté de sa Reine adorable. Il falût pourtant ceder a la Force. Il eût la Gloire de mourir a ses pieds percé de mille coups; elle fit un cri qui estoit suivi d'un evanoûissement si profond qu'elle parroisoit morte, et auroit été jettée a la mer parmi ceux qui etoient tuez, si sa grande Beauté ne l'avoit pas fait remarquer au Capitaine de Corsairs. Il l'avoit distingué de commencement de l'abordage, et se promettoit des grands avantages de sa prise. Le Bey de Tunis estoit dans le Goût d'avoir toujours aupres de lui de Jolis Pages, et il ne douta pas de faire sa fortune en lui faisant un si beau present. Dans cette vûe, il fit relever Docile, et voyant que ses habits n'etoient pas ensanglantez, il crût que la peur seule l'avoit fait evanoüir. Il la faisoit porter a sa Cabanne. Elle revint, (par le secours de l'eau qu'on lui jetta au visage) pour se voir au milieu des Barbares, de qui elle devoit attendre toute sorte d'insultes. Elle determina de se jetter a la mer, du premier attentât qui pourroit blesser sa pudeur. Elle comptoit pour rien d'estre l'esclave; en effet elle l'avoit toujours été, il ne lui manquoit que le nom; et elle resolût de Supporter ce malheur comme elle avoit fait tant d'autres. Elle se soûvint que Télémaque l'avoit été, et de toutes les consolations que la sagesse lui avoit donnée sous la figure de Mentor.

Le Capitaine craignoit si fort de ternir l'éclat de sa beauté en lui donnant du Chagrin, qu'il la fit servir avec autant de Respect comme si elle avoit été a sa Cour. On ne se presentoit a elle, que pour la porter a manger, et c'étoit tout ce qu'il y avoit du meilleur, toujours en baissant les yeux selon la politesse Turc. Cette conduitte la guerrissoit de sa crainte principale; elle tourna ses pensées sur les tristes évenements de sa vie, et pleura tendrement le destin cruel de son fidelle Domestique. Elle se souvenoit que qu'il [*sic*] étoit seul temoin de la pureté de ses intentions, et ne doutoit pas que cet dernier effort de sa Vertu, qui lui avoit tant coutée, ne passeroit dans le Monde pour un trait de Folie. Le Roi Sombre n'étoit guerre disposé a lui rendre justice, le Comte d'Esperanza aigri par le resentiment croira facilement les apparances qui étoient toutes contre elle, et elle mourira (peutestre) dans les chaines, detestée de ces mesmes personnes pour lesquelles elle s'etoit sacrifiée. Elle n'avoit de consolation que dans cette Vertu invincible qui l'avoit toujours Soutenüe, et qui lui donnoit une espece de Tranquillité, malgre toutes les persecutions de la Fortune.

Le Vaisseau faisoit voile vers Tunis assez lentement, ayant été mis en mauvais état dans le combat, trainant pourtant sa prise apres lui. Le troisieme jour de navigation, il rencontra une Galere de Malte, qui la voiant presque hors d'état de se defendre, ne hesita pas de l'attaquer, et la Victoire estoit bien tost remportée. Les Corsairs furent mis aux fers, et leur esclaves en Liberté. C'estoit un jeun chevalier de Malte qui commandoit, vif, hardi, aimable, bref un cadet d'une grande Maison de France. Il étoit frappé de la Figure de Docile, et l'examinant avec plus d'attention que n'avoit fait le Capitaine Turc, il commença de soupçonner son sexe. Ses regards l'embarrassoit, et sa rougeur le confirmât dans l'Idée qu'elle étoit une fille travestie. Il aprit des matelôts qu'elle etoit passager avec un Frere qui avoit été tué en combattant en vrai Heros. Il approcha d'elle avec cet air de politesse audacieuse qui est la partage de François. Ne craignez rien Mademoiselle (lui disoit-il tout bas en remarquant qu'elle trembloit) vostre sexe et vostre Beauté sont faites pour regner, non pour craindre. C'est moi qui suis vostre esclave. Comptez sur ma discretion, si vous ne voulez pas estre connüe, mais permettez moi de vous rendre les respects que je vous dois. Je me flatte que mes assiduitez attireront vostre confiance, et aussi tost que j'aurois donné quelques ordres necessaire, je reviendrai a vos pieds sçavoir si vous avez quelque chose a me commander. Cet compliment acheva de deconcerter la belle Infortunée, qui ne sçavoit quelle conduitte tenir. Elle craignit qu'en s'obstinant a cacher son sexe, elle s'exposoit a un examen humiliant, et resolût de l'avoüer a son retour, esperant de trouver sa seureté dans la Generosité du chevalier. Elle ne pouvoit pas former cette resolution sans se faire une violence extreme, et il lui trouvoit toute en pleurs quand il arrivoit. Il en parroisoit attendri. Que vous ettes digne d'estre aimée, disoit-il en la regardant tendrement, puis que vous savez si bien aimer! car je ne doute pas que c'est vostre cher Frere, que vous pleurez, et qu'il ne vous apartenoit par quelque lien plus fort que celui du sang.

Non Monsieur (lui repliqua t-elle en se remettant) je ne le regrette que comme un Domestique qui m'etoit tres attachée, mais je trouve dans ma situation assez des raisons pour m'affliger. Je ne m'ettonne pas, qu'elle vous donne des prejugez contre moi, mais je suis une Femme Malheureuse, qui alloit trouver son Mari quand—

Le Chevalier ne la permettoit pas de continuer; il l'intterompit en se jettant a ses pieds, et baissant ses mains, avec Transport. Vous ettes donc Mariée (s'écria t il). Ah que vous me delivré [*sic*] d'une grande inquietude! Je hai beaucoup tout commerce avec des Filles: il faut un siecle pour les vaincre, et deux autres pour s'en defaire. Il me semble qui vous ettes dix fois plus belle, depuis que je sçai que vous avez un Mari. Je me flatte même qu'il est infiniment aimable. J'aime a disputer un Coeur contre un Rival, et je veux mourir ou le supplanter dans le vostre.

Tout ceci prononcé d'un air a demi badin, étoit assez propre pour dissiper toute autre melancholie que celle de Docile, mais elle lui repondoit serieusement. Je dois estre l'objet de vostre Compassion, et non celle de vos railleries. Je ne suis pas accoutumée a entendre des parreilles, et si vos offres de services sont réel, le seul que vous pouvez me rendre c'est de me mettre au premier port d'ou je puis écrire a mon Epoux. Il trouvera (peutestre) le moyen de reconnoistre vostre Generosité; je n'ai rien a vous offrir que mes larmes.

—Vous croyez estre encore au pouvoir des Corsaires, Madame (repliqua til). Est-ce que vous craignez que je veux exiger un rançon, ou mal user de ma victoire? Nous autres François ne voulons rien des Dames que ce que leur Bonté nous accorde, mais il faut nous permettre par la voye de la

Douceur de profiter des bienfait de la Fortune. La mienne me paroist si brillante, je ne sçaurois quitter si legerement l'entreprise Glorieuse, que j'ai formé de vous plaire. Il est vrai que j'anticipe peut estre les choses, et que je devois par respect vous cacher mon dessein encore deux ou trois jours, mais helas! nous ne sommes plus au siecle des Amadis, et encore plus éloigné de celui des Patriarches. Que sçai-je? je puis mourir en vingt quatre heures, et j'aurois le deplaisir de mourir sans vous avoir apris, que je vous adorai. Non, non, il ne faut pas hazarder un malheur si terrible—je suis pressé de Vivre. Il finissoit par ce trait de Chanson, d'un ton agreable qui parroisoit si peu serieux a Docile qu'elle commença de se rassurer.

Elle crût que le parti le plus raisonnable, avec un caractere comme le sien, étoit celui de lui laisser la joüissance de ses Visions (doux fruit de sa Vanité) et se tirer de ses mains avec toute la promptitude possible. Elle se flattoit qu'il s'ennuira bien tost de soins inutiles, et qu'elle pourroit attendre sa Liberté de sa politesse quand il auroit vû échouer ses agrements qu'il croyoit si irresistable; et craignit qu'en le choquant par une séverité desesperante, qu'il pouvoit estre assez piqué pour se porter a des Insolences dont la seule Idée lui faisoit fremir. Ces raissonnements faites a la hate, la determinoient a feïndre un peu de complaisance, et elle lui repondit d'un air a moitie enjoüé, qu'il chantoit joliment, sans faire semblant d'avoir écouté ses discours libre. Vous aimez la musique (disoit-il); vous m'enlevez, c'est ma Fureur. Je mettrai les mains au feu, que vous chantez comme un Ange. Vous avez un son de voix ravissant; chantons le Duo dans le seconde acte du dernier Opera, celui qui estoit si goûté de la Cour. N'etiez vous pas a Paris dans le temps qu'il fût represente?

Je n'ai jamais été a Paris Monsieur, repondit-elle. Est-il possible (s'écria t'il)? Vous n'avez pourtant rien d'étranger. Cette Taille si fine et si degagée, cet air de Tête, peut-on les prendre ailleurs? Il faut y aller, trois Mois de sejour, mettra le dernier coup de pinçeau a vos Graces. Vostre Beauté sera l'ornement de Thuilleries, et cinq ou 6 soirs de promenade ajouteront ce certain je ne sçai quoy, si necessaire aux belles. Mais je voye que vous ettes fatiguée. On le seroit a moins; un Combat navale n'est pas un spectacle indifferent; vous avez été sans doute transie de peur, et devez avoir besoin de repos. J'ai aupres de moi un Garçon qui est le premier Genie du monde pour les boüillons et les consommez. Il vous aportera un de sa façon. Dormez y bien, souvenez vous que je vous aime éperdument, nous nous reverrons demain Matin.

Il sortit d'un pas leger, en chantant, et laissa Docile dans une surprise qui suspendit son affliction. Elle sçavoit quel consequence tirer de ses procedez. Cette maniere de Galanterie estoit toute nouvelle pour elle, et elle se perdit dans ses refflections. Elle avoit soin de bien fermer la porte de sa cabane avant de se coucher, precaution nullement necessaire; il étoit beaucoup plus fatigué qu'elle, et s'endormit beaucoup plus tost. Au fonds il n'étoit point du tout dangereux pour des Dames comme elle, mais fort a craindre pour celles qui étoient Galantes: c'est a dire, fait pour leur inspirer des desirs, et tres sujet a leur faire de ces affronts d'omission qu'on ne pardonne jamais. Fort a la mode de [?] dè son Enfance, il s'etoit perdu dans le service du sexe. Il ne lui restoit que la figure et le jargon d'un homme a bonne fortune. Plus ardent que jamais dans ses poursuittes, il cherchoit depuis deux anns la Beaute divine qui pourroit lui ragouter. Il se souvenoit de celle de Docile en s'éveillant, et crût avoir trouvé son fait. Son air de Novice et sa Modestie estoint pour le moins aussi surprenant a lui, que son Hardiesse et ses mannieres deliberez avoient été a elle. Il concluoit qu'elle n'avoit eû encore que peu d'avantures, et qu'elle estoit assez charmante pour valoir un Coeur neuf. Il n'avoit jamais rencontré de cette espece, et resolût de ne rien oublier pour en faire la Conquete, et en suitte de l'emmener a Paris. Elle est assez belle (se disoit il) pour plaire a tout ce qu'il y a de plus grand. Serois-je le premier qui a poussé sa Fortune par le moyen d'une jolie Maitresse? Je la donnerai comme une Sultane. La nouveauté seule peut faire un grand Effet—

Flattée de ces Idées, il s'empressa de se friser dans le dernier goût et lui porta lui mesme son Caffé sur un cabaret magnifique. Elle étoit levée depuis longtemps, et lui recûte poliment, quoy qu'un peu embarrassée en remarquant qu'il s'attachoit a contempler ses jambes, qu'elle avoient parfaitement bien fait. La rougeur lui montoit au visage. Je suis bien malheureux Madame (disoit-il) de vous donner toujours de la Confusion. Pour Dieu, composez vous, je ne voye rien que d'admirable, laissez rougir celles qui n'osent se montrer qu'apres avoir épuisée la science de la Toilette. Il est vrai qu'en laissant voir de tres belles choses, vous cachez d'autres. Je suis seure que dans vostre habit de femme on vous voye une Gorge incomparable. Je ferai voile vers Naxis; nous trouverons des habits Grecs, qui ne sont pas laids, si celui que vous portez vous fait de la peine.

Je voudrois rester sous mon deguisement, disoit-elle, jusqu'a l'occasion se presente de retourner aupres de mon Mari. C'est une grande cruauté, repondit le chevalier en souriant, de me faire sauter aux yeux l'empressement que vous avez de le rejoindre. Oserois je vous demander depuis quand vous l'avez quittée? Depuis pres d'un ann, disoit-elle. Et vous ne l'avez pas encore oubliée? interrompit le chevalier. Voila une Constance qu'on n'a jamais vû depuis Penelope. Vous avez trop de vivacité dans les yeux pour estre capable de donner dans ces fadaisses d'Antiquité. Je soupçon plus tost ce petit frere, ou fidelle Domestique (si vous voulez), de vous tenir au Coeur. On dit qu'il estoit joli, mais par dieu il a autant de tort d'estre mort, que l'autre a d'estre Absent. Il faut oublier ceux qui nous quitte, joüissons des moments present, et gardons les regrets pour les heures perdûes. Je vous suis toute acquise. Un peu de bonté pour mes souffrances, et je vous quitte de toute la tristesse que vous donnerai a mes cendres, dont asseurement je ne profiterai guerre. Peut-on exiger davantage de la plus vertueuse femme du monde, que de la Fidelité quand on est ensemble? Il y en a peu qui la pousse aussi loin que cela. Une Dame de Paris a ordinairement un Amant dans le Cabinet, pendant qu'un autre est dans sa chambre. Le nombre des Conquests fait honneur aux Belles, aussi bien qu'aux Heros, et j'ai entendu dire a une femme de beaucoup d'esprit, qu'une Beauté sensé a toujours un corps de reserve comme un General habile. Sçait-on ce que peut arriver? Il y a d'étranges malheurs dans le monde, et j'en connois plus qu'une qui se sont tres bien trouvez d'avoir un Amant de Relai. Ne vous offensez pas, ma belle Reine (continua t il, voyant qu'elle rougissoit de depit d'entendre ce discours libertin), je vous croi trop delicate pour cela. Mais de pousser la Fidelité jusqu'aux Absents, et aux Cadavres, c'est de rebût depuis cent anns. Vous connoisez la franchise de ma Nation; j'en ai plus qu'un autre. Permettez moi de vous dire ma pensée naturellement. Je croi qu'un aimable cavalier vous a enlevée d'un Epoux que vous n'aimez plus, ou que vous n'avez jamais aimée. Je ne sçaurois me figurer qu'il y a Mari au monde, qui auroit permis a une personne de vostre Age de voiager seule avec un joli Garçon. Avouez moi vostre Avanture; je suis discret a toute outrance. Je va vous en donner une belle preuve. Il y a presque 24 heures que je sçai vostre sexe sans en avoir parlé a personne. On se moqueroit bien de moi si on sçavoit cela a Paris. La Discretion y est aussi decriée que la Fidelité; on n'ose pas se vanter de ses vieileries la, mais vous ettes assez belle pour faire des miracles. Je suis prest a faire, et a croire tout ce que vous voulez, quand mesme vous me direz que vous vous ettes mise sur mer suivie d'un grand Train de Domestiques et que ces Coquins de Turcs ont mangé vos Laquais et vos femmes de chambre.

Cette raillerie ouvrit les yeux a Docile. Elle voyoit dans tout son jour l'extravagance de son enterprise, et comprit qu'elle ne pouvoit plus se montrer au Roi Sombre, si elle ne vouloit pas s'exposer aux Traittements le plus indignes, qui seront justifiez par les apparences qui étoient tout contre elle. Apres un moment de silence elle dit en soupirant, J'en conviens Monsieur que vous me voiez dans un état qui doit vous porter a des jugements peu avantageux pour moi. Je ne sçaurois vous expliquer mes raisons, et quand je pourrois mÿ resoudre vous n'ettes pas obligée de me croire. Il ne m'est nullement necessaire d'entrer dans le detail de mes Malheurs. Je n'ai qu'une seule grace a vous demander: mettez moi dans quelque couvent (soit a l'Isle de Naxis ou ailleurs); je serois une de soeurs servans au pres des Filles Sequestrez, trop heureuse de vivre et de mourir inconnüe.

Quoy qu'elle prononcassez ces paroles avec une tristesse attendrissante, il ne pouvoit pas s'empecher de faire un éclat de rire. Le joli parti que vous prenez la Madame! (repliqua t-il) Vous destinez donc ces mains blanches et delicates a repasser de Guimpes, et ces petits doigts si bien tournez a faire de Colifichets pour orner les images. Si vous voulez de la Devotion, prenez en une qui soit plus raisonable. Regardez vos Beautez comme des dons precieux du Ciel; employes les a l'usage pour le quel elles ont été faites, et ne croyez pas qu'il vous est permise de les defacer, ou enterrer. C'est un vol que vous faittes a l'univers. Vous ettes née pour distribuer des plaisirs; suivez le doux penchant de la Nature, et croyez que c'est la Divinité qui vous parle. Je n'ai jamais crû faire le personage de Missionaire, mais je me trouve une Zèle pour vostre service, qui vaut un inspiration. Il faut que je vous apprend vostre Devoir,—Ce n'est pas [*sic*] par Devotion (intterompit-elle) que je choisi la retraitte. Mon Honneur mÿ oblige, et la necessité de mes affaires.

En voici d'autres! (s'écria t il). Je suis ravÿ que vous n'ettes pas dupe de Prêtres. Voions un peu ce que c'est que cet Honneur qui vous tyranise si fort. C'est le premier fois de ma vie, que je me suis amusé a faire de definitions. Je n'ai pas été élevé dans la crasse de Livres, Dieu merci; je sçai la musique, je ne danse pas mal, j'ai appris bien les exercises de l'accademie, et je possede assez de Mathematique pour entendre la Navigation et la fortification. Il me semble que c'est tout ce qu'il faut pour un homme de Condition. Pourtant on a des certains lumieres naturelles, qui font voir l'abus de bien des choses. Vous entendez sans doute par cet honneur, dont vous parlez si respectueusement, l'estime generale, l'aplaudissement du monde, et l'approbation des honnètes gens. Vous avez raison; ce sont des biens qu'on doit rechercher avec ardeur. Sçavez vous qu'ils dependent de la mode, autant que les Coiffures? Ce qui est de bon air dans un siecle est ridicule dans un autre. Nos Ancestres sont tout morts, il nÿ a plus de Romains au monde. J'ai entendu parler mille fois du merite de Mlle L'Enclos, et on ne nomme Lucrece que pour s'en moquer. Si une Princesse avoit faite voeu d'aller a pied nûd jusqu'a Jerusalem dans le temps des Croisades, elle aura eûe la Gloire d'estre mise dans le Legende, et nous celeberons sa fête encore au temps ou nous sommes. Si une autre fera la mesme pelerinage aujourdui, les malins diront que c'est une devergondée qui se sert de cette pretexte pour couvrir ses debauches, et les plus moderez en parleront comme d'une Folle qu'on devroit enfermer. Le monde est devenu plus éclairé, et au vrai je trouve le vieux Honneur d'aussi mauvais goût que la Vieille Cuisine. Ces beaux sentimens qui sont étalez dans les anciens Romans, ne sont bon que pour vous rendre le joüet de ceux qui n'en ont point. Croyez moi, ma Belle, le grand secret de la vie, c'est de s'ennuyer jamais. Pour vous parler en termes marin, il faut suivre le courant quelques fois, ou faire nauvrage. La Gloire des Femmes d'aujourdui est entrelacée dans leurs plaisirs. Elles deviennent illustre par une genereuse distribution de leur charmes, et je soutien que cette celebre pedante de Lucrece, si elle vivoit a l'heure qu'il est, sera la plus grande Coquette de Paris, par les mesmes principes qui l'ont poussée a s'oster la vie. Croyez vous qu'elle se seroit faite cette violence, si elle s'etoit imaginée qu'on l'auroit jugé digne de petites maisons? La bonne Dame vouloit briller dans son siecle; on brille a moins de frais a present, et beaucoup plus agreablement. Le beau sexe est rentré dans tous ses droits, et ne sont plus les dupes de Jaloux, qui ont inventé cet Honneur Chimerique dont vous faites tant de cas. Il est vrai que nous avons autant des Religieuses que jamais, mais le motif est different. Ce sont des malheureuses Victimes de l'avarice ou de l'ambition de leurs parents. Les pauvres Creatures font tout ce qu'elles peuvent pour se laver du soupçon de s'etre retirées volontairement, et par de Discours libres, des chansons badins, et en maudissant de tout leur coeur ceux qui l'ont enfermées, elles nous font comprendre que c'est par contrainte, non par Duperie, qu'elles sont coffrez.

> Cedez a la douce tendresse,
> Aimez dans la jeune saison,
> Écoutez l'amour qui vous presse,
> Laissez murmurer la raison.

C'est la Rime qui me force a dire cette derniere Parole; au fonds, elle est fort mal placée, et la vraie Raison conduit a suivre les mouvements du Coeur— Qu'en dit vous ma Deëse? Il me semble que vostre silence me reproche d'avoir perdu des moments precieux dans un froid raisonnement.

Elle s'empressa de lui oster cette Idée, en lui disant, J'ignore les mannieres de vostre Païs, mais il me semble que vos Actions ne s'accordent pas avec vos Maximes. Vous meprisez l'honneur comme une Fantome et je voie que vous hazardez vostre vie pour l'obtenir.

Ne vous ai je pas dit Madame, repondit-il, que je me regle selon la mode? Il faut avouer que nos Femmes ont plus d'esprit que nous; elles ont secouées leurs chaisnes, et nous gemissons encore sous les nostres. Je ne desespere pas que nous verrons quelque jour la sottise de s'exposer aux dangers, aussi ridicule parmi les hommes que la Pruderie est aujourdui parmi les Dames. Si l'esprit humain se develope de mon temps au point de se moquer de cet prejugé, vous me verrez Poltron distingué. Effectivement y a til du sens commun a risquer sa vie, ou resister a son plaisir? Il ne faut qu'une demie douzaine des Poltrons illustres, pour placer la Gloire a éviter le Danger. Malheureusement ces Messieurs la ont decidez depuis longtemps, qu'il sont privelegiez par leur état a bien conserver leur personnes, et c'est a nous autres miserables d'affronter les perils. Voila du grand serieux! Il faut vous aimer autant que je fais, pour m'abismer ainsi dans les Refflections, pour vous tirer de l'erreur; vous ettes encore farcie de Leçons de quelque sotte mere, ou quelque radoteuse de Gouvernante. Quinze jours a Paris changeront toutes vos Idées.—

Je n'ai nulle dessein d'aller a Paris, Monsieur (repliqua t-elle), et—Je conçois vostre pensée (intterompit il avec Vivacité); vous y trouverez mille resources, vostre Beauté vaut un billet de change de cent mille écûs. Je prevoie des avantures assez brillantes pour vous faire oublier tous vos

Malheurs, tel quils puissent estre. En attendant je tacherai de vous amuser, et je veux me flatter que vous aurez quelque reconnoisance pour un procedé aussi desintterresé que le mien. Je voudrois vous persuader a aimer vous mesme; aimez moi aussi, quand ce ne seroit que pour vous desenuyer durant le voiage, ne craignez aucune contrainte de ma part. Les François ne sont pas faits pour violenter les Dames, nous ne violons jamais qu'apres qu'on nous a fait entendre, qu'on le veut bien.

Cette asseurance lui valût un soürire de Docile. Il recommença ses solicitations de chanter avec lui. Elle crût ne devoir pas lui refuser cette legere Complaisance, et le reste de la journée se passa en Musique et en badinage, qu'il trouva le secret de placer par tout.[1] Il craignoit presque autant qu'elle, les consequences d'une conversation trop tendre, quoy qu'il scavoit parfaitement la routine de se mocquer du resentiment des dames en pareil occasion, mais Docile lui avoit inspiré beaucoup de Goût pour elle. Il ne vouloit pas en estre meprissé, et il n'osoit hazarder un pas, qu'il sçavoit estre fort glissant pour lui.

Ils voguerent vers l'Isle de Naxis pour prendre de l'eau, pendant que le Roi Sombre desechoit sa cervelle a conjecturer la raison qu'il ne reçevoit aucune nouvelle de son Officier. Il s'arreta a imaginer qu'il avoit été assassiné par ordre du Roi de Bons Enfants. Il en accusa le mauvais coeur de Docile, et ne douta point qu'elle n'avoit sacrifiée sa Lettre a son Amant, et en étoit plus outré que des toutes les autres raisons qu'il croioit avoir de se plaindre d'elle. Il voulût a la vûe de l'univers l'aider a monter sur son Trone, mais il souhaitât qu'on le regardâtes comme un effet de sa Generosité et de sa Justice, sans qu'on l'accusâtes de s'intterresser a sa personne, et il ne pouvoit s'imaginer sans Fureur que cette marque de sa Foiblesse étoit entre les mains du Roi de Bons Enfants. Il envoia le Seigneur de sa Cour qu'il crût lui estre le plus attaché, en qualité d'envoyé extrodinaire pour donner part de son avenement a la Courronne au Roi de Bons Enfants et pour renouveller un ancien traitté de Commerce, avec ordre secret de s'in[s]truire adroitement de toutes les nouvelles de la Cour, tres resolu s'il estoit vrai que Docile y restoit, s'etant declarée son Epouse, de se venger de cet affront par la feu et le sang.

Bien loin de la trouver, son Ministre n'auroit pas seulment entendu son Nom, s'il y n'ÿ avoit pas eu dans le Roiaume de Docile un fort parti, qui las d'estre dominé par une puissance étrangere, souhaitant passionement son retour, et profitant de la declaration que le Roi Sombre avoit fait aux Deputez qu'il voulût la retablir, la faisoit rechercher par toute la terre. Le Grand Prêtre avoit été Lapidé par le peuple, qui avoit gemi longtemps sous son Insolence et ses exactions. La premiere Nouvelle de la mort du Roi Farouche, et tous estoit disposé a reçevoir Docile comme leur Reine

---

[1] The sentence which follows is altered from: 'Sa modestie n'avoit rien a souffrir, qu'un peu de discours hardi, et elle se rassura assez pour reprendre une partie de sa Tranquillité.'

Legitime. Plusieurs Cavaliers entreprirent de la chercher; chaqu'un portoit son portrait, et partirent pour des Cours differentes. Un d'eux arriva a celle de Bons Enfants, peu avant l'envoyé du Roi Sombre.

Docile avoit une figure trop charmante pour estre oubliée; les premieres personnes, a qui il montroit son Portrait, la reconnurent pour la mesme Beauté qui avoit fait tant de bruit par la Bizzarerie de sa conduitte. Le Roi de Bons Enfants, qui avoit le meilleur coeur du monde, la fit rechercher avec tout le soin possible. On decouvrît qu'elle avoit été quelque temps au port de Mer, et ensuitte chez le Comte d'Esperanza. Il avoit été souvent raillé de cet Avanture avant qu'on soupçonnâtes la Qualité de la Belle. Julie n'avoit pas manquée de conter sa fuitte avec le jeune Officier; on avoit badiné le Comte sur son desespoir. Il s'etoit tiré d'affaire avec esprit, et en rioit le premier, mais quand il voioit qu'on estoit instruitt de son Rang, il s'empressa d'assurer l'envoyé du Roi Sombre, qu'il avoit vecû avec elle aussi respectueusement comme si il l'avoit scût. Cet dernier article estoit si peu vraisemblable que personne nÿ fit attention que pour louer sa Discretion.

Dieu sçait comme la Malheureuse Docile fût dechirée. On admiroit également son Artifice et sa Legereté, qui voiloit avec l'apparence d'une si grande Modestie un Coeur si corrompu; on faisoit honneur a son Esprit d'une politique dont elle estoit incapable, et on lui ostoit impitoiablement toutes les vertûs qui faisoient le fonds de son Caractere. L'envoyé depecha un courier avec des Lettres a son Maitre, ou il n'oublia rien de ce qu'il avoit entendu. Le Roi Sombre, toujours persuadé qu'elle avoit été entre les mains du Roi de Bons Enfants, imagina que son Inconstance naturelle l'avoit portée a lui quitter pour se donner au Comte, et que par une suitte de cet humeur volage elle s'etoit fait enlever par un nouveau Favori. Il s'en consola en se flattant que son Mariage n'estoit pas reçonnue dans le public.

En effet on en parloit douteusement. Il ny avoit que la seule Emilie qui l'avoit declarée, et elle n'estoit pas un temoin dont lon ne pouvoit pas soupçonner la veracité. Quand elle vît qu'on le prenoit sur ce ton, elle ne persistoit plus a le dire, et n'estoit pas faschée d'insinuer que c'étoit son bon Coeur qui avoit tasché de voiler l'impudicité de sa Maitresse. Les sujets de Docile Honteux de rechercher une Reine si indigne, se donnerent encore au Roi Sombre. On fit en plusieurs païs des Brochures des Avantures immaginaires de Docile, qui passa sa vie en des Austeritez plus cruels que ceux d'une Carmelite, avec la Reputation d'une Messaline.

La Princesse Docile: Fragment I

La Triste Docile Marchâ livrée a des Reflexions quelle avoit peine a debrouiller elle même. Elle arriva sur les huit heures du matin au port de Mer que le prince son Mary lui avoit indiqué. Elle n'etoit pas surprise de ne pas le trouver, comptant bien qu'il ne pouvoit arriver que cinq heures après: elle se mit au lit fatiguée de ses pensées et de la vitesse avec laquelle elle avoit courû. Elle chercha le Sommeil, qui la fuÿöit impitoyablement. Aprez avoir resté la moitie de la journée, elle devint fort surprise de ne pas entendre parler du prince.

Il faut voir ce que l'empecha de se rendre auprès d'elle. Après avoir eu permission du Roi de la poursuivre il poussa son cheval du côté ou elle l'attendoit. Le hazard voulut qu'il rencontra des troupes du Roy qui alloient changer de quartier en prenant la route du port de mer. Ses idées, qui lui presentoient les plus grandes extravagances quand il s'agîssoit de le tourmenter, lui firent immaginer contre toute sorte d'apparences qu'il alloit y etre envelloppé. Il n'en douta plus qu'il n'eussent ordre de l'arretter. Il ne fut plus etonné du calme qui l'avoit surpris dans l'audience qu'il venoit d'avoir du Roy. Il croyoit que Docile etoit convenüe avec lui de se faire enlever pour deguiser au public une demarche qui devoit la combler d'infamie. Son imagination dereglée lui rapresenta qu'elle etoit dejà peutetre entre les mains du Roy et il prit subitement la resolution d'eviter la rencontre de ces troupes auxquelles il voÿoit bien qu'il ne pouvoit resister, et prit une route toute opposée a celle qu'il devoit tenir pour trouver la pauvre Docile, qui etoit dans la situation la plus embarrassante. Elle n'avoit pas pris la precaution de se charger de l'argent necessaire. Elle s'etoit confiée du soin de tout a son epoux, qui la fuÿoit dans le tems quelle avoit quitté tout ce qu'il a de plus seduisant pour suivre ses caprices.

La Princesse Docile: Fragment II

Il la trouva un soir sur le Tillac appuyée sur sa Main, en regardant le Ciel avec une aplication si grande qu'il étoit tout aupres d'elle avant qu'elle l'apercevoit. C'estoit une de ces belles nuits d'été, ou les étoiles se montrerent en toute leur Beauté, et le vent qui soufflait doucement refrachisoit l'air sans le troubler. Est-il permis Madame, disoit-il, d'interompre vos reveries? Il me semble qu'elles vous plaisent assez, vous avez un air de tranquillité languissante, qui donne a deviner bien des choses.

Vous devinez peutestre mal, Monsieur (repliqua t-elle en souriant un peu). J'admirai l'ordre de ces astres, la force de cette Gravitation et attraction qui derigent leur mouvements, et je m'amusai a imaginer les differents estres dont elles sont peuplées. Vous ne doutez donc pas qu'elles sont habités, reprit-il. Je n'en doute nullement, continua-telle, c'est en vain qu'on m'objecteroit qu'il y en a de si pres du Soleil, que le chaleur excessive detruira dans un moment tous les habitants de la Terre. Pourquoy n'auroit-il pas de Creatures a qui le feu est aussi naturel que l'eau l'est aux poisons? Je suis persuadée que s'il y avoit un Isle ou les rivieres et la mer qui l'environoit estoit sans poisson, on ne pourroit pas faire comprendre a ces Insulaires, que l'eau estoit peuplée d'une Infinité des especes. Ils vous repondroint que tout animal y seroit noyé, qu'on ne pouvoit pas y respirer une demie heure, et que sans respiration la vie ne pouvoit pas subsister. Jamais l'imagination de l'homme pouvoit se figurer comment devoit estre fait des animaux capable de vivre dans un element qui detruisoit tous les autres. La vanité humaine est toujours prest a trouver impossible tout ce que passe sa Connoisance. Cependant les decouvertes surprenantes de ce siecle doivent nous persuader qu'il a encore beaucoup de veritez qui nous sont cachées comme la dissection (si je puis me servir de cet terme) des raions du Soleil, et la cause de l'arc en Ciel, estoient a nos Ancestres. La Gravitation qui est prouvée si clairment par des demonstrations Geometrique—

Le Chevalier l'interompit en riant de toute sa force. Est-il possible Madame que vous avez perdue tant d'heures d'une Jeunesse destinée a des amusements plus doux, a faire des calculs, qui sont necessaire pour les demonstrations dont vous parlez si savamment? Ces beaux yeux dont un seul regard tendre auroit comblé de bonheur un Amant, se sont employez a mirer des Telescopes.

Comptez vous pour perdu Monsieur (lui repondit-elle) le temps qu'on donne a rechercher des veritez si important?

C'est une belle importance! sécria t'il en recommançant de rire, je sçai plus de cela, que vous ne croyez, moi, qui n'a jamais lû que des brochures. J'étois amoureux huit jours entiers de la Marquise de Caprice. Franchement je ne la deplaisois pas. Elle se mit dans la Tête de me former l'esprit; elle me fit l'honneur de me prier a un de ses repas philosophique, ou j'ai entendu disputer deux mortelles heures, un Cartesian obstiné contre un enthusiast Newtonien. Je suis né curieux, et malgre l'ennui qui me devoroit, j'écoutois leur discours avec attention. Il s'agissoit de sçavoir s'il avoit une vuide ou si tout estoit plein. Au vrai, la Question ne me parroisoit pas fort intteressante. Ils disputerent pourtant avec autant de feu comme si le salût du Genre humain en dependoit. Ils s'echaufferent au point que j'ai vû le moment que j'ai crû qu'ils viendront aux mains. Pour moi, j'avoüe que je ne sentois pas grande difference entre la mattiere subtile de Descartes, et l'ether subtile de Newton, qu'il dit estre cause de l'attraction, reffraction, et du mouvement en generale. Je conviens que les Vortices dont nos Peres étoient si charmez, sont detruit par le raisonnement de Newton et que sa Systeme me paroist beaucoup mieux fondé, que celle de son Predecesseur, mais toutes ces veritez si éclattantes ne servent qu'a mieux prouver nostre Ignorance invincible sur les choses le plus essentielles, et je ne voie pas qu'aucune de ces recherches, qu'ont établies la Reputation de cet grand Mathematicien, a contribuée le moins du monde au bonheur de l'homme.

La Longitude (dont la connoisance pouvoit estre si utile a nous autres Navigators) est aussi incertaine que jamais, et je suis plus obligé a Guido Rheni et Corregio d'avoir presenté a nos yeux par l'assemblage des Couleurs, et la disposition des Ombres et des Lumieres, des objets qui me prouve avec tant d'exactitude les differentes nuances qui formerent un raion, et l'analogie entre les sons et les couleurs. J'estime plus le premier pattisier, qui a inventé un art qui est si agreable, et ce grand homme qui a trouvé le secret de fumer les Jambons et construire des Sauçissons, qui font les delices de tant d'honnêtes Gens. C'estoient pourtant des Philosophes si modestes que nous ignorons jusqu'a leur noms quoy que nous profitons tous les jours de leur travail. Ils se contentoit de nous estre utile, sans affecter la Gloire qui est le bût principal des veilles de ces celebres astronomes.

Vous riez d'entendre nommer Philosophes, ceux qui s'appliquent a perfectioner la cuisine. Sachez, que j'ai mes raisons pour cela. J'a demandois a ces messieurs qui se decorent de ce beau Titre, ce que cela vouloit dire. On me repondit, que cestoit une Parole composite qui signifioit, Amateur de la Sagesse. Depuis que je sçai cela, j'appelle Philosophes tous ces Sages Genereux qui employent leur esprit a raffiner nos plaisirs, et Philonugae ceux qui negligent la terre (pour laquelle ils sont fait) pour rechercher les mouvements des Planettes a laquelles ils ne parviendront jamais. Je voix que vous etes choquez du mepris que je temoigne pour la Philosophie. Il est vrai que je suis piqué contre elle depuis ce souper de la Marquise, qui me plaisoit fort (malgre le maigreur que sa science profonde lui avoit donnée). Elle avoit destinée cette nuit a recompenser mes soins; ces maudits Philosophes m'avoient si fort glacé le sang par leur demonstrations, qu'apres leur depart, malgre l'attraction de ses charmes, j'ai resté dans un état de Gravitation vers le centre de la terre, qui estoit aussi affligeant pour elle que pour moi. Je croi qu'elle avoit deja eprouvée des tels malheurs, car sans s'en ettonner trop, elle a eûe la Generosité cruelle de me proposer ma revanche pour le Lendemain. Je ne pouvois pas honnêtement refuser le partie, quoyque je sentois bien que je ne la verrai de ma vie, sans que les mesmes idées ne me revint et que je resterai toujours aupres delle comme la Lune dans sa Course aupres du Soleil, toujours attrayée mais qui ne peut tomber dessus. Elle ne se paya pas de cette excus. J'eû mon Congé, j'ai retrouvé mes plaisirs aupres d'une petite danseuse qui ne sçavoit pas lire, et depuis cette triste avanture je fuis les demonstrations, et les calculs comme la peste.

La Modestie de Docile en souffroit de la maniere libre qu'il racontoit, mais il n'étoit pas d'ailleurs d'une hardiesse incommode.[1]

---

[1] The words 'Ils voguer' [*sic*] have been struck out.